Series Editors:
Steven J. Taylor, Ph.D.
Julie Ann Racino, M.A., P.A.
Bonnie Shoultz, M.A.

Community
Participation
=====Series

VOLUME 2
HOUSING,
SUPPORT, AND COMMUNITY

EDITORIAL ADVISORY BOARD

The
Community
Participation
Series

VOLUME 2
HOUSING, SUPPORT, AND COMMUNITY

CHOICES AND STRATEGIES

FOR ADULTS WITH DISABILITIES

edited by

Julie Ann Racino, M.A., P.A.
Deputy Director, Research and Training Center on Community Integration
Center on Human Policy
Faculty in Rehabilitation Counseling
Syracuse University
Syracuse, New York

Pamela Walker, M.A.
Research Associate, Research and Training Center on Community Integration
Center on Human Policy
Syracuse University
Syracuse, New York

Susan O'Connor, M.S.
Research Associate, Research and Training Center on Community Integration
Center on Human Policy
Syracuse University
Syracuse, New York

and

Steven J. Taylor, Ph.D.
Director, Research and Training Center on Community Integration
Center on Human Policy
Professor of Special Education and Sociology
Syracuse University
Syracuse, New York

·P A U L·H·
BROOKES
PUBLISHING C?

Baltimore · London · Toronto · Sydney

Paul H. Brookes Publishing Co.
P.O. Box 10624
Baltimore, Maryland 21285-0624

Copyright © 1993 by Paul H. Brookes Publishing Co., Inc.
All rights reserved.

Typeset by The Composing Room of Michigan, Inc., Grand Rapids, Michigan.
Manufactured in the United States of America by
The Maple Press Company, York, Pennsylvania.

This book is printed on recycled paper.

Library of Congress Cataloging-in-Publication Data
Housing, support, and community / edited by Julie Ann Racino . . . [et
  al.]
    p.   cm. — (The Community participation series ; v. 2)
  Includes bibliographical references and index.
  ISBN 1-55766-090-5 :
  1. Handicapped—Deinstitutionalization—United States.
  2. Handicapped—Housing—United States. 3. Social work with the
  handicapped—United States. I. Racino, Julie Ann, 1953–   . II.
  Series.
HV1553.H68   1992
362.4'0485—dc20   92-25579
                                                CIP

British Library Cataloguing-in-Publication data are available from the British
Library.

CONTENTS

CONTRIBUTORS

THE EDITORS

Julie Ann Racino, M.A., P.A., Center on Human Policy, Syracuse University, 200 Huntington Hall, Syracuse, New York 13244-2340

Julie Ann Racino was associate director of the Community Integration Project and is deputy director of the Research and Training Center on Community Integration at the Center on Human Policy. She is a member of the rehabilitation faculty at Syracuse University and has 20 years of experience in the development, provision, and management of community services. Her research interests include social policy and disability, community services and systems change, and the relationship among individuals, communities, and systems.

Pamela Walker, M.A., Center on Human Policy, Syracuse University, 200 Huntington Hall, Syracuse, New York 13244-2340

Pamela Walker is a research associate at the Center on Human Policy, Research and Training Center on Community Integration. She is a doctoral candidate in the Division of Special Education and Rehabilitation at Syracuse University. Her research interests include family supports, residential supports for adults, and social integration into neighborhoods and communities.

Susan O'Connor, M.S., Center on Human Policy, Syracuse University, 200 Huntington Hall, Syracuse, New York 13244-2340

Susan O'Connor is a research associate at the Center on Human Policy, where she is currently a doctoral candidate in the Division of Special Education and Rehabilitation. She has worked both in Morocco and on the West Bank. Her current research interests are in the areas of multiculturalism and family supports.

Steven J. Taylor, Ph.D., Center on Human Policy, Syracuse University, 200 Huntington Hall, Syracuse NY 13244-2340

Steven J. Taylor is director of the Center on Human Policy and the Research and Training Center on Community Integration. He is a professor of special education with an appointment in sociology at Syracuse University. His interests include social policy, qualitative research methods, sociology of disability, advocacy, and community integration.

THE AUTHORS

David Adler, 9-54 Kensington Avenue, Toronto, Ontario, M5T 2K1, CANADA

David Adler is a freelance writer and producer of information for television in Toronto, Canada. He has a B.A. in journalism and a B.Sc. in Chemistry, and has worked as a personal attendant. His interests include the attendant's point of view on attendant care issues.

Judith E. Heumann, M.P.H., World Institute on Disability, 510 16th Street, Suite 100, Oakland, California 94612-1502

Judith E. Heumann is co-founder and vice president of the World Institute on Disability and director of the Research and Training Center on Public Policy in Independent Living. She has been one of the main leaders in the fight to obtain equality for individuals with disabilities for over 20 years and has played a key role in the passage of numerous pieces of civil rights legislation including the Americans with Disabilities Act. In recognition of these activities, she became the winner and first recipient of the Henry B. Betts Award. She has served and currently serves on the boards of national, state, and local organizations, and has consulted internationally, including with the United Nations Office at Vienna, Division for the Advancement of Women, for the first U.N. Seminar on Disabled Women.

Michael J. Kennedy, Center on Human Policy, Syracuse University, 200 Huntington Hall, Syracuse, New York 13244-2340

Michael J. Kennedy is a training associate at the Center on Human Policy at Syracuse University and works on the Center's community integration projects with a particular emphasis on self-advocacy issues. He has lived in several institutions and currently lives in a community setting. He has made numerous presentations on self-advocacy and consumer involvement at professional, parent, and consumer conferences and has presented invited testimony at United States Senate hearings on institutions.

Cory Moore, The Parents' Place of Maryland, Inc., 7257 Parkway Drive, Suite 210, Hanover, Maryland 21076

Cory Moore is co-director of The Parents' Place of Maryland, a federally funded, statewide parent training and information center. Her 17 years of professional involvement include being parent information and education coordinator for the Association for Retarded Citizens/Montgomery County (Maryland) and a community organizer with the Maryland Coalition for Integrated Education. The third edition of her award-winning book, *A Reader's Guide for Parents of Children with Mental, Physical, or Emotional Disabilities,* was published in 1990.

Bonnie Shoultz, M.A., Center on Human Policy, Syracuse University, 200 Huntington Hall, Syracuse, New York 13244-2340

Bonnie Shoultz is associate director for information and training at the Research and Training Center on Community Integration at the Center on Human Policy. She previously worked in a variety of professional and volunteer capacities in the community service system of Nebraska. Her personal and research interests are in the areas of empowerment (parents and people with disabilities) and community regeneration.

SERIES PREFACE

THE COMMUNITY PARTICIPATION SERIES

The **Community Participation Series** is designed to highlight ways in which individuals, families, agencies, groups, or associations promote the full participation of people of all abilities in community and societal life. Whether within the disability field, through community and social movements, or in day-to-day actions, this series describes what we are learning about changing the way we live, work, and play together.

The initial books in the series highlight emerging practices, ideas, and insights shared with us by people around the country who are working diligently to promote community integration. They have helped us to understand both the strengths and limitations of this concept as a future guide. The first books include the perspectives of individuals with disabilities, families, neighbors, friends, and community organizations and focus on the changing roles and perspectives of innovative disability organizations.

As the series progresses, we anticipate presenting a variety of perspectives, such as those of community organizations (which do not have disability issues as their primary mission), and the seldom heard voices of individuals with disabilities, their families, and members of communities. We also expect that our work will lead to future volumes that will provide a clear vision of how the relationship between disability and other social issues can be pursued.

It is our hope that this series will be a useful resource to practitioners, individuals with disabilities, family members, policymakers, advocates, and others interested in the full participation of all people in community and societal life. Although this is not a "how to" series, the community participation books are designed to be of practical use to people who are working today, often from divergent directions, to create better quality lives for all of us.

We invite you to join us as we continue to learn about the changes all of us need to make within ourselves, our organizations, practices, policies, communities, and society to ensure that our homes, schools,

The Center on Human Policy at Syracuse University is a policy, research, training, and advocacy organization involved in the national movement to ensure the rights and inclusion of people with disabilities. Since its founding in 1971 by Burton Blatt, the Center has been involved in the study and promotion of the full participation of people with disabilities in society. Starting in 1985, the Center on Human Policy has operated a national Research and Training Center on Community Integration. From 1985 to 1988, through the Community Integration Project, the Center provided assistance to states and communities on integrating people with the most severe disabilities into community life.

FOREWORD

In this generation, a new way of living with a disability struggles for birth. This movement grows from determined individual, family, and collective resistance to the abusive social forces that push people with disabilities into powerless isolation. Resistance to being an object of discrimination and being oppressed by medical or rehabilitation control of everyday life takes root and flourishes when people find one another, overcome the taboo of silence, share the truth of their experience, and organize to make change.

Passage of the Americans with Disabilities Act (ADA), against substantial and well-organized opposition, signifies the breadth and strength of the movement to bring disability from private trouble to public issue and from individual shame to shared pride. But this victory is only partial. On one hand, people with disabilities and their allies must vigilantly ensure full implementation of ADA against bureaucratic inertia and continuing, widespread prejudice. On the other hand, successfully asserting the civil rights of people with disabilities to equal participation in civic and economic life serves to highlight even more sharply the need for sufficient investment in personal assistance and housing strategies.

Without effective personal assistance, many people with disabilities will lack the means to exercise their rights because they will not be able to get out of bed, get dressed, go to the toilet, understand a lease, or fill out a job application. Without decent housing, people with disabilities will have no safe base for their lives. Without effective personal assistance and effective housing strategies, many people with disabilities will remain trapped and isolated in institutions, nursing homes, and group homes. This book makes important contributions to the search for effective personal assistance and decent housing.

Throughout the book, contributors acknowledge a common point of departure: there is unity and clarity about the validity and the civic importance of the movement of people with disabilities to take their rightful place as full citizens. This book wastes no words debating the merit of policies and practices that isolate or control people with disabilities.

In Parts II and III, the editors bring together accounts from people with diverse experiences and perspectives on the difficult work of developing effective ways to assist people with disabilities. These sections are rich with the lessons of practical, everyday effort to create adequate vehicles for the commitment to offer decent housing, effective personal assistance, and positive support. Taken together, these chapters reflect the hard fact that work for effective personal assistance and decent housing calls for change at many levels: people with disabilities have to learn by making changes and so do their families; support workers have to learn by making changes; agencies have to learn by making changes; policy makers have to learn by making changes; and communities have to learn by making changes. Because these necessary efforts require people to deal creatively with conflicting interests and face deep-seated fears, they require courage, collaboration, risk taking, and coalition.

In a sense, the book itself assembles a coalition. Because the editors value the understandings that arise from differences in point of view on how to make necessary changes, they provide a good model for people who want to work for change. They do not try to homogenize real differences and disagreements or to elevate one perspective over others. As long as people are working to overcome the injustice of isolating and controlling people with disabilities, their perspective matters and offers an important part of the information necessary for effective action. This allows workers for better personal assistance and housing to identify critical areas for discovery and debate, and perhaps to mark points at which people with different perspectives will choose divergent paths. What matters is what we can agree to do and learn from together. The editors' commitment to diversity within unity ensures that every reader is likely to feel the truth of an observation made by African-American civil rights leader Bernice Johnson Reagon: "If you're in a coalition and you're comfortable, you know it's not a broad enough coalition" (Steinem, 1992, p. 180).

Given the variety of sometimes conflicting perspectives, the rapid rate of change in the field, and the very early stage of development of efforts to provide housing and support, the editors have been courageous in authoring the chapters in Section I. These chapters engage the challenge of evolving concepts that will capture what is going on around housing and support in a way that can guide the next steps of discovery. The authors try a number of helpful ways to communicate what is distinctive and valuable about these small, new efforts. Each of their conceptual frameworks illuminates a different aspect of a complex phenomenon: no one framework lights up the whole space. Each attempt represents a search for ways to overcome the inadequacy of a language that reflects mechanistic assumptions about people, human organization, and social action. Each formulation points beyond itself to the simpler but elusive values that underpin human community: deep respect for each person that gives rise to the gift of good relationships and the ongoing struggle for justice.

Ed Roberts   *John O'Brien*
World Institute on Disability   *Responsive Systems Associates*
Oakland, California   *Lithonia, Georgia*

REFERENCE

Steinem, G. (1992). *Revolution from within: A book of self-esteem.* Boston: Little, Brown.

VOLUME PREFACE

In 1987, when we published *The Nonrestrictive Environment: On Community Integration for People with the Most Severe Disabilities,* the typical expectation of life for adults with severe disabilities in the United States was to live in a group home or intermediate care facility (ICF) or to continue living at home with family, usually with minimal, if any, family support services. Today, emerging across North America are new options for adults, whether single or married, to live in their own homes, no matter what their ability level. Termed "supported housing" in the field of mental health, "individualized," "person centered," "supportive living," or "housing and support" in the field of developmental disabilities, and "assisted living" in the field of head injury, this approach starts with the person's choices and preferences in contrast to the dominant practice of placing people in facilities.

As we have traveled to homes and organizations across the United States, we have continued to learn from people with disabilities, parents, and innovators within and outside the disability field. We found people who were working together to create in day-to-day life a vision for and with people with severe disabilities based on the same kinds of hopes and dreams that we all have. These included: a home of their own, a feeling of personal well-being, financial and personal security, friendships and supportive relationships, self-expression, personal development, and contributions to the lives and well-being of others. We also met people outside the disability field who were working to make our neighborhoods, communities, and society inclusive of all.

From early local leaders and innovators of programs such as Options in Community Living in Wisconsin, Centennial Developmental Services in Colorado, and Residential, Inc., in Ohio, we learned about the changing roles of organizations in supporting people with disabilities in the community. On the state level, we found efforts to encourage and support local initiatives, sometimes by dismantling bureaucratic structures to simply allow local practices and innovations to occur to better the lives of people with disabilities.

From people with disabilities, we heard about the critical importance of choice, of their life histories that were often ignored, and the hopes and dreams they held for their futures. Parents who were filled with hope and determination taught us about their new efforts to help create full and meaningful lives for their children, and to play leadership roles in making possible what many told us they always wanted for their children—a regular home, living with people who care about each other.

In the ensuing years, grass-roots efforts have developed in different parts of the United States by parents, community members, service organizations, and, at times, people with disabilities that challenge the standard way of "providing services" in the field of developmental disabilities. As reflected in the 1989 Center on Human Policy statement in support of adults (see Racino & Taylor, chap. 2, this volume), these efforts often involve changes in the way we think about the concepts of home and housing; of supports, personal assistance, and other services and aids; of self-determination, empowerment, and mutual decision making; and of the relationships among individuals, communities, and systems.

Instead of developing residential facilities, personal and local initiatives are becoming more holistic in viewing the lives of people with disabilities. Strategies and tools, such as personal futures planning, support circles, and community building, have helped forge new visions and connections among people. They have moved us from an emphasis on service categories and the compartmentalization of people's lives toward a fuller vision of individual lives and our mutual connections, relationships, and responsibilities in this world.

On the state level, new initiatives, such as the Supported Living Program in Florida, Individualized Supportive Living Arrangements in North Dakota, and the Community Integrated Living Arrangements in Illinois, have offered funding options that previously did not exist in these states for people to live in their own homes. Places like Colorado, Michigan, Wisconsin, and Minnesota provided some of the early experience in state changes that helped others in moving forward. Other states, from Arkansas to South Dakota to Idaho to New York, have modified existing programs, albeit on a small scale, to create some flexibility to allow new options for housing and support to develop. Initiatives by the Developmental Disabilities Councils, such as in Pennsylvania, Minnesota, and Connecticut, have also supported local efforts to help connect people with disabilities with other local citizens.

These changes are also reflected on the federal level, in areas such as the Administration on Developmental Disabilities priority (1991) for "a home of your own," and the new Health Care Financing Administration Community Supported Living Arrangements Services. They are supported by other major initiatives such as the funding of research and training in the area of housing, by the Fair Housing Amendments Act, increased interest in personal assistance services for people with developmental disabilities, and the new civil rights legislation for people with disabilities, the Americans with Disabilities Act.

In practice and research, the issues faced by people with developmental disabilities are basically the same ones facing other disenfranchised individuals and groups, whether older adults, people with physical disabilities, or people of various ethnic and cultural backgrounds. Not only are the concerns and dilemmas similar in nature, but the solutions require a broader framework to move toward the personal and societal changes that are required.

This book is designed to share some stories, experiences, issues, and dilemmas about these changes, particularly on the personal and agency levels, that are occurring primarily throughout the United States. Designed as a resource for parents, people with disabilities, service workers, advocates, planners, and administrators, this book shares practical strategies and information to assist others who are undertaking paths that involve agency or service change.

Moving from a mechanistic view of housing and support, we highlight fundamental values and assumptions that are necessary to move toward fuller quality lives for our citizens who have been excluded from these options. We also hope the book will provide an opportunity for greater bridge building across the fields of developmental disabilities and independent living, and an initial view of the complexity and far-reaching implications of the new paradigms.

Julie Ann Racino, M.A., P.A.
Pamela Walker, M.A.
Susan O'Connor, M.S.
Steven J. Taylor, Ph.D.

Center on Human Policy

ACKNOWLEDGMENTS

We would like to express our gratitude to the more than 15,000 people who shared their insights and experiences with us through our qualitative research studies and technical assistance and training projects conducted between 1985 and 1990 in 35 states in the United States. It is through their vision, determination, and commitment to work toward a better quality of life for all of us that this book was made possible. We were heartened to get to know so many different people in a variety of roles, all working in their own way to make this vision of community life a reality.

As editors, we particularly appreciate the contributions of Bonnie Shoultz and Pat Rogan, who went beyond their series and editorial advisory roles to review book chapters and took time from their busy schedules to share their observations. As always, they could be counted on. They, together with our other colleagues at the Center on Human Policy and the Division of Special Education and Rehabilitation at Syracuse University, especially Michael Kennedy, Bob Bogdan, Rannveig Traustadottir, Carol Berrigan, Doug Biklen, Steve Murphy, Connie Barna, Dianne Apter, Ellen Fisher, Michelle Sures, Nan Songer, and Claudia Stockley, contributed many of the ideas found in this book. Many previous Center colleagues' work is also reflected here, including Jim Knoll, Zana Marie Lutfiyya, and Hank Bersani.

Rachael Zubal, as production administrator, worked closely on all aspects of the book with special attention to the many references involved. Cyndy Colavita, our office manager, contributed in the hundreds of ways that she always does ensuring that the book was completed in a spirit of cooperation. Debbie Simms contributed greatly with the tables and figures, shifting her priorities during fast-paced times. Kathleen Wood also offered her ongoing support. We feel honored to work with such a talented group of people who are committed to better lives for people with disabilities and contribute in their ways to this critical work.

While many people outside the Center contributed directly and indirectly to this book, we particularly express our thanks to John O'Brien, Gunnar Dybwad, Charlie Lakin, and Connie Lyle O'Brien for their ongoing discussion with us of the issues and dilemmas found in this book. They, together with our national advisory board and policy research committee members, continue to share ideas, strategies, and insights along the paths.

We also especially thank the disability agency leaders who created the vision through their daily work—Gail Jacob (Options in Community Living, Wisconsin); Jay Klein (previously of Centennial Developmental Services, Colorado); Jerry Provencal (Macomb-Oakland Regional Center, Michigan); Sandi Landis, John Winnenberg, and Joel Yaeger (Residential, Inc., Ohio); state and national policy analysts who spread the vision through instilling it in their work, including Gary Smith (National Association of State Mental Retardation Program Directors), and Colleen Wieck (Minnesota Developmental Disabilities

Planning Council); the many people with disabilities and their families who led the way, in particular, Leslie Moore and Cory Moore (Maryland) and Nancy Ward (Nebraska); university researchers who also are committed to fuller community lives, especially Ann and Rud Turnbull (Beach Center at University of Kansas), Paul Carling (University of Vermont), Paul Wehman (Virginia Commonwealth University), Phil Ferguson and Diane Ferguson (University of Oregon); and Jan Nisbet (University of New Hampshire); disability activists Judy Heumann, Ed Roberts, Simi Litvak, and Steve Brown (World Institute on Disability), Bob Williams (United Cerebral Palsy Association), George Ebert (The Alliance), and Judith Snow (Frontier College, Toronto); community builders and networkers Kathy Bartholomew-Lorimer (Illinois), Beth Mount (New York), Lou Chapman (Pennsylvania), Frankie Lewis (Georgia), Jerry Kiracofe (Maryland), and Sharon Gretz (Pennsylvania); and housing analysts Bill Mitchell (National Association of Protection and Advocacy Systems) and Elaine Ostroff (Research and Training Center on Adaptive Environments).

We have also learned a tremendous amount from the people in state and regional positions who strive to create changes in their day-to-day work with respect for the people with whom they are working. These include Alex Henry (Minnesota), Dennis Harkins (Wisconsin), Ann Majure (previously of Arkansas), Lyn Rucker (previously of Nebraska and Arizona), Julie Pratt (currently of West Virginia), Dick Lepore (New Hampshire), Mike Hogan, Brian Lensink, and Charlie Galloway (previously of Connecticut, now respectively in Ohio, Colorado, and California), Ginny Harmon and the late Ben Censoni (Michigan), David Merrill (Nebraska), and Nick Arambarri and Reed Mulkey (Idaho).

This book is partially due to the support and encouragement of Melissa Behm, Vice President of Paul H. Brookes Publishing Co. We have come to appreciate her talents even more during this past year, and extend our thanks to her, Roslyn Udris, Production Manager, Tania Bourdon and Sue Vaupel, Production Coordinators, and the production team of the book.

We also express our appreciation to Robert Davila, Assistant Secretary of the Office of Special Education and Rehabilitative Services; William Graves, Director of the National Institute on Disability and Rehabilitation Research (NIDRR); and David Esquith, Roseanne Rafferty, and Deno Reed of NIDRR for their continuing support of our work. Much of the work on which this book is based occurred when Naomi Karp was our project officer. We owe special gratitude to her. We also wish to thank our partners in the Research and Training Center: Alan Abeson and Sharon Davis of ARC-US; Patti Smith of the National Parent Network on Disabilities; Charlie Lakin, Robert Bruininks, Mary Hayden, and Sherri Larson of the University of Minnesota; Liz Lindley and Sheryl Ball of The Association for Persons with Severe Handicaps; and David Braddock, Rick Hemp, and Lynn Bachelder of the University of Illinois–Chicago.

This book was prepared with the support of the U.S. Department of Education, Office of Special Education and Rehabilitative Services, National Institute on Disability and Rehabilitation Research (NIDRR) awarded to the Center on Human Policy, Division of Special Education and Rehabilitation, School of Education, Syracuse University under Cooperative Agreements G0085C03503 and H133B00003-90 for the Research and Training Center on Community Integration and the Community Integration Project (Contract 300-85-0076). Partial support for Chapters 6 and 15 was provided by a contract with the University of Minnesota through their Research and Training Center on Community Living (Cooperative Agreement H133B8048). The opinions expressed herein are those solely of the authors and do not necessarily reflect the position of the U.S. Department of Education and no official endorsement should be inferred.

1

INTRODUCTION

Julie Ann Racino, Steven J. Taylor, Pamela Walker, and Susan O'Connor

The state of the art in community living continues to evolve at a rapid pace. During the late 1960s and early 1970s, residential services or community living arrangements were conceptualized and organized according to a continuum of facilities (Hitzing, 1987; Taylor, 1988). In the mid-to-late 1980s, however, the continuum model began to give way to new, *non–facility-based* approaches (Racino & Knoll, 1986) to supporting people with developmental disabilities in the community.

The residential continuum is commonly represented as a straight line running from the most to the least restrictive placements (see Hitzing, 1980; Schalock, 1983). The most restrictive settings, which are also the most segregated, are seen as providing the most intensive services, and generally have access to the greatest financial resources. The least restrictive settings, which are the most integrated, provide the least intensive services, and generally have access to the least financial resources. The continuum model is the major framework for service design in a range of human services fields, including mental health (Randolph, Laux, & Carling, 1987; Shoultz, 1988), developmental disabilities, and aging (Gelfand, 1988; Hoggs & Moss, 1990).

Whereas specific steps in the continuum vary in different schemes, this conceptual model is based on the following assumptions: 1) community living arrangements are generally agency-owned, operated, and/or licensed facilities; 2) housing and services are linked together (e.g., different types of residential facilities offer varying degrees of services); 3) people with disabilities are expected to make the transition to less restrictive settings as they acquire additional skills or to move to more restrictive settings if "problems" occur; and 4) perceived severity of a disability determines the type of facility in which an individual will be placed.

Both research and practice have been designed around the continuum and facility-based service models. Researchers have asked questions such as, "What is the optimal residential facility for different persons with mental retardation?" (Landesman, 1987). Most research has focused on facilities such as community residences, group homes, community intermediate care facilities (ICFs/MR), and semi-independent apartment living programs. Beginning in the mid-1970s, researchers began to study different kinds of group home facilities (Baker, Seltzer, & Seltzer, 1974; Birenbaum & Seiffer, 1976; O'Connor, 1976).

Presently, group homes have been studied according to almost every conceivable variable; for example, size (Baroff, 1980; Landesman-Dwyer, 1981; Landesman-Dwyer, Berkson, & Romer, 1979); normalization and quality of life factors (Eyman, Demaine, & Lei, 1979; Hill, Rotegard, & Bruininks, 1984); staff attitudes and practices (Lakin, Bruininks, & Hill, 1986); and changes in adaptive and maladaptive behavior after placement from institutions (Conroy & Bradley, 1985; Gollay, Freedman, Wyngaarden, & Kurtz, 1978; Seltzer, 1981). Similarly, a sizeable body of literature has emerged on the financing, administration (Gelman, 1988; Janicki, Mayeda, & Epple, 1983), and staffing (George & Baumeister, 1981; Jacobson & Janicki, 1984; Levy, Levy, Freeman, Feiman, & Samowitz, 1988) of community residential facilities.

Foster and family care and semi-independent living programs followed the topic of group homes as an area requiring serious study. Extensive research has examined the characteristics of foster caregivers, family life in foster care, and the effects of foster family placement as compared to other placements in other types of facilities (Hill, Lakin, Bruininks, Amado, Anderson, & Copher, 1989; Intagliata, Willer, & Wicks, 1981; Sherman & Newman, 1988). More recent research has studied semi-independent living programs for people with mental retardation, especially mild disabilities (Close & Halpern, 1988; Halpern, Close, & Nelson, 1986).

While research to date has yielded a wealth of information about the nature and characteristics of residential facilities on the continuum, it is just starting to keep pace with the state of the art in community living. As we have written elsewhere (Taylor, 1988; Taylor, Racino, Knoll, & Lutfiyya, 1987), the continuum concept is characterized by conceptual and programmatic flaws. Figure 1 depicts a residential continuum and the following list (adapted from Taylor, 1988) summarizes its flaws:

1. Legitimates restrictive environments.
2. Confuses segregation and integration with the intensity of services.
3. Is based on a "readiness model."

4. Supports the primacy of professional decision making.
5. Sanctions infringements on people's rights.
6. Implies that people must move as they develop and change.
7. Directs attention to physical settings rather than to services and supports that people need to be integrated into the community.

MOVING TOWARD MORE FLEXIBLE AND RESPONSIVE APPROACHES

Today, the field is moving away from the notion of a continuum of residential facilities to more flexible and responsive approaches, which we have referred to as a "non–facility-based," "person-centered," or a "housing and support" approach for adults, and as supports for children and their families.

Our conceptualization of these approaches was grounded initially in our study, starting in 1985, of practices in "good" organizations that promoted community integration. Through this study, we identified, documented, and evaluated practices in more than 45 programs nationally (see Racino, 1991; Taylor, Bogdan, & Racino, 1991). For children with mental retardation and developmental disabilities, these approaches centered on supporting children to live with families and to maintain nurturing, stable relationships with adults (see Center on Human Policy, 1987; Taylor, Lakin, & Hill, 1989). For adults with mental retardation and developmental disabilities, we identified agencies that were attempting to support people with a range of disabilities in their own or shared homes as opposed to "homelike" facilities. This included people with severe and multiple disabilities.

We have continued to distinguish between approaches for children and adults for a variety of reasons, including differences in how and by whom decisions are made, issues of children's and parents' rights, and the critical distinction between living with a family of one's own versus living in a shared home with others whom one may or may not view as family. Whereas, theoretically, these distinctions can be contained in one

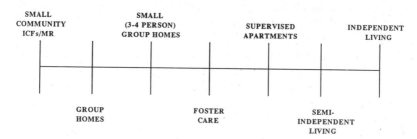

Figure 1.   New community-based residential continuum.

conceptual model, current biases in the developmental disabilities field would tend to result in a family-based model that perpetuates the continued treatment of adults with disabilities as children and would be used as a continued rationale for out-of-home placement of children.

From the late 1980s into the 1990s, new research has been conducted on supports to families and their children, including critical work on empowerment, social relationships, cash subsidies, and/or family support services (e.g., Cohen, Agosta, Cohen, & Warren, 1989; Dunst, Trivette, Gordon, & Pletcher, 1989; Herman, 1991; Singer & Irvin, 1991; Turnbull, Garlow, & Barber, 1991). Although this book does not explicitly discuss children's issues, much of the work in this area is directly applicable to understanding the nature of supports for adults.

Service Characteristics

In the area of housing and support for adults, the late 1980s brought increased interest in the service elements of this approach, which we have identified through our research (Racino, 1988) as separation of housing and support; leasing, home, and cooperative ownership; individualized and flexible supports; close ties among individualized assessment, planning, and funding; and choice and self-determination.

Separation of Housing and Support   In the traditional residential approach, housing and services are packaged together, requiring a person to live in a certain type of facility to obtain a certain level of support. By separating housing and support services, people can obtain supports wherever they may live. This allows, but does not ensure, choice by the person with a disability in a variety of areas, including with whom and where they will live (Johnson, 1985; O'Brien & Lyle, 1986; Taylor et al., 1987).

Leasing, Home, and Cooperative Ownership   In contrast to a situation where a person with a disability is essentially a guest in a facility and is expected to fit in, a housing and support approach extends the roles that people with disabilities may hold to those of tenants, homeowners, and cooperative members. While the American dream of home ownership is not shared by everyone, leasing and ownership challenge what has been the virtual exclusion in many states of people with developmental disabilities from these options. Current prohibitions in social policy extend to other groups such as elders who also may be unable both to maintain a home and obtain the support services they need.

Individualized and Flexible Supports   *Support organizations,* a term we use to describe organizations challenging the traditional approach to residential service provision, respond more individually and flexibly to the needs and interests of people. Support strategies vary for each individual and reflect a unique combination of services, adaptations, goods, and assistance from workers, neighbors, families, and friends to support people to live in their own homes. These strategies also vary for each person as their life circumstances change; the agencies build this flexibility into their service and organizational design.

Individualized Assessment, Planning, and Funding   Support organizations use more community-oriented assessments (see Brost & Johnson, 1982) for the purpose of informed planning *with* people with disabilities. Given that agencies continue to control financing and link this to professional assessments and determinations, more flexibility and choice can theoretically be possible if funding decisions are made closer to the person with a disability. Although there are inherent limitations to personal choice in agency-controlled and -determined situations, which are still typical in the United States, this approach fosters greater choice within these constraints and the possibility for more responsiveness to the unique needs and desires of people.

Choice and Self-Determination   Choice in all aspects of a person's life, including the interaction between the agency and the person in areas of planning, delivery of services, and home and living support arrangements, is central to a housing and support approach. However, in the field of developmental disabilities, these choices remain limited. This approach would be consistent with the use of cash subsidies and with a move toward establishing an entitlement to personal assistance services (see, for example, Heumann, chap. 11, this volume).

Moving Toward a Research Base

Despite the growing interest in innovative housing and support approaches (usually under the rubrics of housing financing and supportive living programs), there has been extremely limited research on these innovative strategies and practices. Both in research and in practice, the field is just beginning to examine these new strategies and practices indepth to see how or if they have an impact on the lives of people with disabilities.

From our initial studies, we have learned that the critical aspects that "good" organizations share are not specific strategies or mechanisms, but the following characteristics (Racino, 1991): 1) clear organization values or philosophy based on some variation of normalization principles; 2) a spirit of self-reflection and learning (O'Brien, 1987a); 3) centrality of people over policies, regulations, financing, and technology; 4) empowering, valuing, and supporting staff; and 5) mutual collaboration and autonomy.

Because organizations learn from each other (Hedberg, Nystrom, & Starbuck, 1976), practices and strategies shared in this book are not provided as models to follow, but as potential opportunities to learn about how others approach issues and dilemmas in moving toward more responsive, person-centered approaches. We have learned that there are many limitations to the roles that disability organizations can and should play in the lives of people with disabilities. Although some of these roles will be discussed in this volume, the next volume in this series will provide a more indepth examination of the roles of community members, the importance of social relationships, and the roles of community places.

FRAMEWORKS FOR UNDERSTANDING THIS BOOK

This book relies on two basic frameworks: the separation of housing from supports and a comparison of three paradigms. The primary framework that we have used in work with agencies and states is the separation of housing from support services. Part I of this volume is based largely on this framework. However, a comparison of the rehabilitation, independent living, and support paradigms or frameworks (see Williams, 1990, for a discussion on whether these are paradigms or world views) reflects a clearer, more long-term vision of alliances and societal change, and examines in more depth the meaning of support as differentiated from support services. These frameworks describe a broader vision for change across community (e.g., relationships, associations), service areas (e.g., employment, housing, recreation), and disability and interest groups. Parts II and III of this book begin to explore aspects of these paradigms. They are written to expand the discussion beyond a narrow view of housing and support to issues that must be addressed in moving toward the goal of inclusive community life. In the conclusion, we will return to a discussion of these three paradigms and their implications.

HOUSING AND SUPPORT

The first framework separates housing from support, which is critical because it allows for the study of support and support strategies distinct from service settings, and expands the ways in which support can be offered. Another outcome of this separation is that options for personal choice related to both housing and support issues are expanded. Finally, a number of clear barriers and issues arise as soon as this separation is considered that can affect the actions of planners, administrators, advocates, people with disabilities, and/or family members.

Table 1 is a preliminary listing developed in 1989 of selected barriers and practices based on our work in states across the country. The barriers include those on the personal, agency, community, system, and federal levels, and are not meant to be comprehensive in nature, but are meant to identify some of the initial areas needing change on the agency or systems levels. Each of these areas requires concerted efforts, although some are in more critical need of change in some states and communities than others.

Housing

As highlighted in Table 1, a range of barriers exists on all levels in the area of housing for people with severe disabilities in the United States. Until recently, in the field of developmental disabilities, housing has been equated with the development of agency-owned, leased, and/or operated facilities. During the 1980s, the primary issues in housing that dominated the disability field included the size of the homes or facilities, the type of housing, funding of facilities, and the reaction of the neighbors to the homes. Once housing is separated from support services, it is clear that many of the housing issues faced by people with severe developmental disabilities are the same ones as those faced by other people in our society. These issues will require efforts outside the narrow specialty field of developmental disabilities, and will need to be resolved in conjunction with housing associations, developers, and realtors.

Housing Principles   The following principles, developed at a national housing symposium and modified by the housing subcommittee of The Association for Persons with Severe Handicaps (TASH), can help guide future directions in housing for people with disabilities (Covert, 1990; Ostroff & Racino, 1991):

Everyone needs and deserves a home.
Housing should be based on an individual's choice and preferences.
The provision of services should be dictated by an individual's needs and circumstances, not by a facility or program. Needed services should be provided regardless of where an individual may live.
Adequate supports should be available to allow individuals to live in integrated, individualized housing situations.

Housing Resources   A range of general housing materials in areas such as trusts (e.g., Center for Community Change, 1989) and cooperatives (e.g., Housing Technical Assistance Project, 1989; Kappel & Wetherow, 1986; Page, n.d.) already exists and is becoming more widely available in the field of developmental disabilities. Many of these materials and related efforts are described in Chapter 5 of this volume. Support organizations can use these materials to change to a facilitative and resource role in relationship to housing organizations.

Research, reviews, and demonstrations within the United States of how these housing efforts actually work and may potentially have an impact on the lives of people with developmental disabilities and their families are still very limited. The case study of the Madison Mutual Housing Association (see Racino, chap. 12, this volume) represents one of the first efforts to study cooperative housing in relationship to people

Table 1. Housing and supports: Practices and strategies

| Housing | | Supports | |
Issues/barriers	Practices/strategies[a]	Issues/barriers	Practices/strategies[a]
Lack of accessible community housing	Funding for home modifications	Legislation, regulations, and policies may prohibit services from being provided in people's own homes.	Changes in state nursing practice acts; modification of (HCBS) waiver to allow supports in people's own homes
Lack of decent, affordable housing	Trusts, cooperatives, subsidies for noncongregate housing entitlements (e.g., SSI); state supplements to entitlements; private sources; tax credits; federal, state, and local funding	Agencies assume both the role of landlord and service provider.	Agencies "invert/convert" to support services role.
Lack of choice in housing	Housing ownership, cooperative housing, shared living arrangements	The types and amounts of available support services may be limited.	Expansion of personal assistance services to people with severe developmental disabilities; funding for emergency devices; broader and more flexible definitions of services categories in HCBS waivers
State barriers to home ownership by parents and people with disabilities	Change in regulations to allow people to own homes and still receive support services paid by the state	Services are designed around supervision needs of people.	Development of individualized and flexible support strategies, including use of unpaid supports
Lack of money for housing expenses or rent deposit	Subsidy covering household expenses, utilities, phone, furniture, miscellaneous household items, and rent deposit	The current design of case management does not adequately address a non-facility-based approach.	Reconceptualization of the role of service coordinator

Barriers	Strategies	Barriers	Strategies
Attitudinal barriers to people with severe disabilities living in typical homes	Demonstrations for people with the most severe disabilities; discussions on issues of risk/liability	Lack of choice and self-determination on supports	Consumer-directed supports; strategies for promoting choice and decision making
Heavy investment by agencies and states in facilities	Strategies such as alternative use plans to divert from current facilities	Deficit-based assessment and program planning	Individual community assessments and services planning
Lack of choice of roommates	Agency support in locating and matching roommates	Ineffectiveness of current monitoring systems for non–facility-based services	Multiple mechanisms for promoting safety and quality of services for non–facility-based services
Lack of experiences or ability to find and maintain home	Support services in home finding, assistance in owning or renting homes, and maintaining households	Isolation of people with disabilities	Community participation strategies
Lack of knowledge by state policy makers and local agencies on community housing	Developing new coalitions with housing/real estate associations	Lack of funding for support services	Cross-disability strategies for increasing funding and creating fiscal incentives for integration
Federal and state disincentives to the use of typical housing	Revisions or alternatives to Housing and Urban Development (HUD) 202	Lack of emergency responsiveness	Individual support plans, including provisions for back-up support
Attitudinal barriers preventing the use of integrated housing options	Training for policy makers on the context of housing in the lives of people with disabilities	Attitudinal barriers	Demonstrations of support services for people with severe disabilities in the community
Lack of knowledge of new roles in a revamped housing/support system	Dissemination and training in emerging research areas	Agencies maintaining traditional roles of evaluator, implementor, and monitor	Agencies change roles, including management and staffing design.
		Lack of trained personnel (e.g., medical, health care) and community resources (e.g., transportation)	Community-wide strategies for improving health care and transportation
		Insufficient opportunities to participate fully in household routines	Personal assistance services

ªThese are illustrative, not exhaustive.

with disabilities from the perspective of a housing organization in the United States.

Housing Financing   Some attention has been devoted to creative financing strategies for people with developmental disabilities and mental health impairments (Randolph et al., 1987), which is an area of great interest to service provider organizations. However, unless these creative financing approaches are used to enable people to improve their quality of life, they may not benefit the vast majority of people with mental retardation and developmental disabilities. For example, we have already seen the development of new group homes, simply under different financing, without any substantial change in other critical aspects of living or any apparent impact on the lives of people with disabilities. We also have learned about people and organizations using high-risk strategies that can jeopardize the future well-being of these arrangements. In addition, service providers are pursuing housing initiatives that may undermine the roles of housing organizations in relationship to people with disabilities by instead subsuming these functions themselves.

Home Ownership and Tenancy   While the options of home ownership and tenancy have potential for increasing control by people with disabilities over their home environments, three major issues are arising in the field and remain largely unexplored. First, the authors have visited sites where legal tenancy appears to have made a difference in people's life quality and sites where it has not made a difference. Some homes are not legally in a person's name, yet appear qualitatively to be in the individual's control. Second, on the state and national level, substantial social policy barriers exist, particularly to home ownership with support services (Racino & Heumann, 1992), for many groups, including people with disabilities and elders. Third, as with other developments in the field, home ownership and tenancy are being approached to some extent as a new "rule" about how people with disabilities should live, as opposed to an option that should be made available. Relatively little thoughtful analysis and experience exists about these new areas and the barriers and dilemmas that will emerge, but the new home ownership projects funded by the Administration on Developmental Disabilities offer an opportunity to further explore these issues.

Distinction Between Housing and Homes   In some ways, the new interest in regular housing has distracted attention from the major issue of housing strategies—the promotion of a comfortable house and home life, and a base from which people can interact with the larger community. One of the critical areas raised in this book is the increasing usage of the words "a home of my own" to refer to a range of situations that vary on a number of different dimensions. Minimally, distinctions need to be made between housing, which includes legal and style dimensions; home as a physical place with its personal, social, control dimensions; and household.

In the literature, home has a variety of meanings, even if primarily viewed as a physical site. These include: a place of housework, leisure, learning, and convalescence and death; a miniature universe of culture and education for the family and visitors; a place of courtship and marriage; a place to raise children and nurture a family, including other adult members of the household; a place to promote health and practice daily routines; and a place to practice religious festivals, rituals, prayers, and customs (see, e.g., Goldin, 1941; Green, 1983).

In contrast, homes of or for people with disabilities are often equated in the literature and in actual life experiences as service settings described by the normalization of routines, styles, and decorations. They are described as places where people physically reside; teaching, controlling, encouraging, and supporting the functioning of the people who live there takes place; rules predominate; issues such as visitation, decisionmaking, and moving into and out of homes are controlled by people outside the home; and strangers determine aspects of housing and home life (e.g., through site selection and housemates).

Given this limited view of homes for and of people with disabilities, it should not be surprising that change in any dimension is experienced by individuals as having a "home of one's own" rather than a "homelike facility." In Chapter 6, this volume, O'Connor and Racino, citing John O'Brien's recent conceptualization, distinguish between the different dimensions of home as a guide to help parents, people with disabilities, and providers think about the various aspects involved in the concept of home.

Support

The word support will be used quite extensively in this book even though there is still little conceptual and practical clarity about this term. Research about support is part of the Center on Human Policy's study of the lives and relationships of people with disabilities and their families. The Center on Human Policy is in the process of analyzing data from this and other qualitative studies as one contribution to the research base for the support "paradigm."

The Meaning of Support   To some extent, support is discussed in this book in contrast to the notion of providing services, with the agency in control and with the primary orientation being to rehabilitate, "fix," or change people. However, for the purposes of this book, the emphasis is still tied more closely with service changes and strategies, which represent one small part of what support may mean.

The meaning of support must be understood from the viewpoints of people with disabilities; yet, their perspectives are just now coming to the forefront. Three of the chapters in Part II of this book bring to life the issues that people with disabilities and their parents believe are ways of understanding housing and support. These include the importance of personal life histories, one's own inner strength and support, and personal support from people who have shared similar life experiences.

Support includes aspects that are not reasonably measurable, but appear essential in the relationship between agencies and people with disabilities: a personal commitment to an individual (e.g., Shoultz, 1991); standing by and with people (Racino, 1991); listening and respecting the person's viewpoints and background, including the person's cultural heritage (discussed in O'Connor, chap. 15, this volume); taking direction from the person with a disability (discussed in Racino, chap. 16, this volume); and recognizing and respecting the person's individuality and humanity (Taylor & Bogdan, 1989).

Relationship of Formal Services and Informal Supports   The nature of the relationship between what have been called formal services and informal supports (e.g., Hagner, 1989; O'Brien & Lyle O'Brien, 1992) remains a major research issue. Without a vision of the lives of people with disabilities based on community presence, participation, competence, and choice (O'Brien, 1987b), well-intentioned efforts at fostering relationships and community involvement through circles of friends (Perske, 1988), support facilitation (Stainback & Stainback, 1988), natural supports in workplaces (Hagner, Rogan, & Murphy, 1992), or bridge-building (Johnson, 1985; Mount, Beeman, & Ducharme, 1988) can actually become ways of encroaching on new domains in people's lives (Bulmer, 1987).

This is not meant to minimize the potential of the efforts by service providers and others to involve family and friends. Such efforts to recognize the roles of communities and relationships in people's lives have made a difference in the quality of lives of many individuals and families (e.g., Klein, 1992; Taylor et al., 1991). As others have expressed (e.g., O'Brien, 1987b), such efforts must be accompanied by careful listening because it is critically important for "people who feel powerless to connect with someone who will listen" (Lord & McKillop Farlow, 1990, p. 4). Often, the voices of people with disabilities are not heard, let alone heeded, even in "good" organizations (Biklen, 1990; Racino, 1990).

Distinction Between Supportive Living Programs and Support
Developing a new program is distinctly different from determining what support means to a person and what role, if any, an organization can and should play. Although new programs may provide opportunities (e.g., for more flexible financing) and the elimination of current barriers (e.g., social policy prohibitions to integration), programs can also undermine existing efforts by rigidifying them and creating new limitations. Even the more flexible, individualized programs coming into existence

may exert forms of social control in the lives of people with disabilities. This is one of the critical issues that must be studied and better understood about efforts such as the federal Community Supportive Living Arrangements (CSLA). Although supportive living programs can be added to agencies and systems as they exist, exploring the concept of support will mean new roles for agencies, communities, and systems.

Personal Assistance Services as a Support   The term *personal assistance* is a long-standing concept in the field of independent living used to describe a range of paid support services, which can be applied across different disability groups. Personal assistance as used in this book includes such diverse tasks as interpreting, homemaking, mobility assistance, social support, medical assistance, transportation, personal hygiene, reading, recreation, and decision-making support (Center on Human Policy, 1989). Personal assistance, if broadly defined, encompasses many of the functions of support workers in the field of developmental disabilities.

Personal assistance is also an internationally recognized concept. In 1989, people with disabilities from 13 countries, including the United States, came together at the European Conference on Personal Assistance and passed a resolution designed to create broad-based support for the financing of personal assistance services. The following principles were included in this resolution:

1. Access to personal assistance services is a human and civil right.
2. Personal assistance users shall be able to choose from a variety of personal assistance modes that offer the choice of various degrees of user control.
3. Services shall enable the user to participate in every aspect of life such as home, work, school, leisure, travel, and political life.

Currently, personal assistance is one of the primary agenda items of the independent living movement on a national level (Litvak, Zukas, & Heumann, 1987; *Resolution on Personal Assistance Services*, 1991). Yet, the inclusion and meaning of such services in the lives of people with mental retardation and mental health labels is just starting to attract the attention it deserves and requires (e.g., Connecticut Developmental Disabilities Planning Council, 1988; Consortium for Citizens with Disabilities Personal Assistance Task Force, 1991; Nosek, 1990; Racino, 1991). Personal assistance, with its strong orientation on self-determination, can have important implications for people with developmental disabilities who often are forced into agency-determined situations where support staff carry out agency programs and have all of the decision-making authority.

Whereas this book will address only a few of the myriad issues involved, it is aimed at encouraging more exchange on the meaning of personal assistance and on critical issues such as the roles of allies and supporters. Chapter 11 by disability rights leader Judy Heumann, Chapter 10 by personal attendant David Adler of Canada, and the case study in Chapter 16 on the Berkeley Center for Independent Living, all provide different perspectives on issues that face people with developmental disabilities.

THE REHABILITATION, INDEPENDENT LIVING, AND SUPPORT/EMPOWERMENT PARADIGMS

The second framework (see Table 2) is based on the comparison of three paradigms or frameworks: rehabilitation, independent living, and the emerging support/empowerment paradigms. These frameworks provide a useful way to start understanding some of the distinctions between the different and converging strategies and perspectives in the disability fields. As illustrated in Table 2, both the support/empowerment and independent living paradigms are based on the assumption that the basic problems facing people with disabilities are within society instead of people, that self-determination and the removal of external societal barriers are critical aspects of problem solving, and that the solutions to all problems are not solely held by professionals. Following are brief comparisons of these paradigms by definition of the problem, locus of the problem, social roles, solutions to the problem, who is in control, and desired outcomes, highlighting emerging critical issues.

Definition of the Problem

Both the independent living and support/empowerment paradigms assume one of the key problems facing people with disabilities is the inadequacy of support services in society (Crewe & Zola, 1983; Smull & Bellamy, 1991). However, services can often be as much of a detriment as a service, and they can create further barriers to integration and participation (Center on Human Policy, 1990; McKnight, 1989). At the same time, not all people with disabilities want to be viewed as a consumer of services (e.g., Clay, 1991). As George Ebert (1990), a powerful spokesperson for the "mental patients' survivor" movement stated, "I am not a consumer of services. I have been consumed by them" (p. 3). Such experiences with the service system, which has been described as functioning as a social control agent (see, for example, Warren, 1981), contribute to the further politicization of the self-help movement (Zola, 1987).

Despite the differences in paradigms, definitions, and practices in the field, many different groups are now facing common issues and problems in community life. For example, a comprehensive review of

Table 2. A comparison of the rehabilitation, independent living, and support/empowerment paradigms

Focus	Rehabilitation paradigm[a]	Independent living paradigm[a]	Support/empowerment paradigm[b]
Definition of problem	Physical impairment, lack of vocational skill, psychological maladjustment, lack of motivation and cooperation	Dependence on professionals, relatives, and others; inadequate support services; architectural barriers; economic barriers	Attitudinal, political, economic, and administrative barriers to societal participation; inadequate supports within society
Locus of problem	In individual	In environment; in rehabilitation process	In society/environment; in rehabilitation process
Social role(s)	Patient–client	Consumer	Coworker, community member, student, neighbor, so forth
Solution to problem	Professional intervention by physician, physical therapist, occupational therapist, vocational counselor, and others	Peer counseling; advocacy; self-help; consumer control; removal of barriers and disincentives	Redesign of schools, homes, work places, health-care systems, transportation, and social environments to include everyone
Who is in control	Professional	Consumer	People in alliance with each other
Desired outcomes	Maximum activities of daily living (ADL), gainful employment, psychological adjustment, improved motivation, completed treatment	Self-direction, least restrictive environment, social and economic productivity	Pluralistic society inclusive of all people; quality lives as defined by people themselves; self-direction embedded in collaborative decision making and problem solving.

[a]Adapted from DeJong, G. (1978). *The movement for independent living: Origins, ideology, and implications for disability research.* Boston: Tufts-New England Medical Center, Medical Rehabilitation Institute; and from DeJong, G. (1983). Defining and implementing the independent living concept. In N. Crewe, & I. Zola (Eds.), *Independent living for physically disabled people.* San Francisco: Jossey-Bass.

[b]From Racino, J. A. (1992). Living in the community: Independence, support, and transition. In F. R. Rusch, L. DeStefano, J. Chadsey-Rusch, L. A. Phelps, & E. Szymanski (Eds.), *Transition from school to adult life: Models, linkages, and policy.* Sycamore, IL: Sycamore Press.

research related to housing and community integration for all disability groups (Carling, Randolph, Blanch, & Ridgway, 1988) concluded that:

1. Housing needs are similar for all groups.
2. Supports are the critical factor that determine if a person can stay in housing of his or her choice.
3. Housing problems are less closely related to disability than they are to economic and social factors, such as poverty.
4. Regardless of disability groups involved, strong differences exist between professionals and people with disabilities about specific needs for housing and support.
5. Choices and control are critical elements.
6. Lack of supports can lead to transience, dislocation, and the risk of reinstitutionalization.

Locus of the Problem

Both the support/empowerment and independent living paradigms define the major problems facing people with disabilities as ones in the society or environment as opposed to problems in the people. Because a strong belief in "fixing" people permeates the disability systems, how an organization views the problems facing people with disabilities is a key factor in deciding whether an approach more nearly resembles the traditional rehabilitation paradigm or a support/empowerment one. In fact, most of the efforts in the United States continue to view people with disabilities as "the problem," and new strategies are aimed at fixing people in new ways (e.g., relationships instead of skills) and developing new continuums (e.g., choice readiness).

Social Roles

Presently, people with disabilities increasingly hold a variety of social roles despite stigma, discrimination, and other stereotypes that continue to permeate our culture and affect people's daily lives (Knight, 1990). Instead of simply being a buyer, consumer, or recipient of services, people with disabilities are participating in valued social roles (e.g., Wolfensberger, 1983) such as community leader, parent, co-worker, classmate, business or home owner, athlete, relative, church member, and musician. The cry of the independent living movement, "abilities not disabilities," has led to changes in society, and highlighted the need to move beyond the disability-based consumer role to a vision of the commonplace, everyday interactions and relationships in home and community life (Ducharme, 1985; McKnight, 1989).

Solutions to the Problems

One key area in understanding the proposed solutions to the problems facing people with disabilities is that of self-help or peer support. As

Bengt Nirje (1985), the Swedish scholar known for his development of the normalization principle, explained, "Integration is based on recognition of a person's integrity, meaning to be yourself among others—to be able and to be allowed to be yourself among others" (p. 67). Self-help and peer support (see Racino, chap. 16, this volume) are strategies that allow people with disabilities to seek strength from each other, share common experiences, and, at times, demand the same rights, respect, and privileges as others in society.

The independent living movement in the United States, although intended to be inclusive of all people with disabilities, has most clearly represented the constituency of people with physical disabilities. Although more public attention is being paid to the involvement of people with cognitive disabilities (see, e.g., Jones & Ulicny, 1986; Nosek, Potter, Quan, & Zhu, 1988; Zirpoli, Hancox, Wieck, & Skarnulis, 1989), people with these labels are just beginning to make connections with the independent living movement. Political connections across disability groups may be essential for further societal change to occur.

Who Is in Control?

The independent living paradigm is based on the belief that people with disabilities should be in control of their own lives. Whereas power is placed in the hands of professionals in the rehabilitation paradigm, people in the support/empowerment paradigm find ways to work in alliance to solve societal problems.

Although there is growing literature on mutuality, reciprocity, and relationships, little attention has been paid to critical issues such as the relationship between self-determination and mutuality. Self-determination, sometimes known as personal control or confused with a "rights" perspective, and mutuality, often used synonymously with interdependence and relationships, are emerging as important areas for both theoretical understanding and practice. While there is ample literature in science, philosophy, and religion (e.g., Colegrave, 1948; Langer, 1967) that discusses the relationship between individuation and mutuality in nature, these concepts in developmental disabilities have often been used exclusive of each other.

People in the field of disabilities tend to "talk past one another" on these issues; for example, one group uses a political perspective (i.e., the relationship of the individual to today's society) and others use a social perspective (i.e., the way we live together as community members). In doing so, many opportunities for potential collaboration—opportunities that are critical for long-term change—are missed.

To some extent, the disability field is just starting to understand, from a research perspective, issues of personal empowerment and its relationship to involvement with others. In his review of the literature,

John Lord (n.d.) notes that the process of participation itself is empowering, and that participation also enhances people's involvement in the process. Yet, one of the outcomes of empowerment seems to be that people become more interested in participating and collaborating with each other. Thus, the nature of the interrelationship of personal empowerment and collaboration with others is becoming increasingly important to understand.

The chapters in this book provide an opportunity to examine these issues from different perspectives. For example, in the study of the Madison Mutual Housing Association (Chapter 12), personal empowerment is viewed as the basis for shared decision making. David Adler speaks eloquently in Chapter 10 about the importance of mutuality between the person with a disability and his or her personal assistant; he believes that mutuality must take precedence over issues of who is in control. In contrast, people with disabilities often stress that the control issue must be addressed first in order for people to come together in mutual relationships.

Desired Outcomes

The support/empowerment and independent living paradigms vary on a number of dimensions including the concepts of least restrictive environment, economic productivity, life quality, and self-direction. As discussed elsewhere (e.g., Ferguson & Ferguson, 1986; Taylor 1988), the concepts of least restrictive environment and economic productivity as desired outcomes are particularly problematic for people with severe disabilities. A goal of an inclusive society also means changing from these concepts to values that can include all people.

Because independence and interdependence are commonly used words in the field of developmental disabilities, in Part I the language of moving from independence (commonly known in the field of developmental and psychiatric disabilities as being on one's own) to one of interdependence (support and reliance on each other) is used. However, the reader should bear in mind the problems with the differences in the use of such terms (see definitions of independence in Racino, chaps. 12 and 16, this volume), which often result in people from different fields talking past one another.

Whereas the support/empowerment paradigm's goal is a society inclusive of all people, the independent living paradigm may or may not have this as a final goal. Objectives and the strategies used to accomplish goals may vary between the paradigms, even when the common goal is for an inclusive society. Further discussion of these issues is contained in the conclusion of this book.

STRUCTURE OF THIS BOOK

This book is divided into three parts, Part I: Housing, Support, and Community; Part II: Perspectives; and Part III: Case Studies of Organizations. Finally, appendices with additional resources are provided to assist the reader in learning more about the issues discussed.

Part I

Part I describes and highlights information on a housing and support approach that was gathered as part of our national study of organizations, technical assistance and training in states, and qualitative research. It is divided into six chapters and is an introduction to the critical aspects of a housing and support approach as well as emerging issues and dilemmas.

Chapter 2, *"People First": Approaches to Housing and Support*, presents the context for a housing and support approach, including a review of residential services in the 1980s, a comparison with facility-based services, the values and assumptions underlying this approach, an overview of what a housing and support approach is and is not, a highlight of critical issues, and suggested avenues for moving toward change.

Chapters 3 through 7 describe some of the different aspects of "housing and support" as understood today, comparing it with the traditional residential services model. Starting with people coming into contact with agencies, the chapters move outward from the individual to choices and decision making, support and support strategies, the roles of staff, the roles of support organizations, housing and homes, and the state role in housing and support.

Chapter 3, *"Whose Life Is it Anyway?": Life Planning, Choices, and Decision Making*, creates a picture of who people with disabilities are, examines how to better understand and listen to their choices, explores critical decisions in planning for housing and support, and discusses emerging issues in life planning and choices.

Chapter 4, *"Being with People": Support and Support Strategies*, provides a brief overview of support, compares the concept of support with that of supervision, introduces the concept of interweaving formal and informal supports, discusses the types of support and support strategies, highlights who should provide support services, and discusses emerging issues in support roles.

Chapter 5, *"There if You Need and Want Them": Changing Roles of Support Organizations*, describes three leading support organizations. The chapter compares these types of organizations with traditional residential service agencies, presents information on the ways in which supports are organized, suggests strategies organizations can pursue for funding and maintaining quality, and discusses the agency change process from a traditional residential service agency.

Chapter 6, *"A Home of My Own": Community Housing Options and Strategies*, highlights a variety of issues on housing, including the distinction between housing and homes, the current national policy, social and legislative context for housing, new directions in housing and home ownership, emerging issues and dilemmas, and strategies for working together toward change.

The last chapter in Part I, Chapter 7, *"Opening the Doors": The State Role in Housing and Support*, presents an overview of state developments and strategies in housing and support. It also discusses current systems issues, such as independent case management, quality assurance, and financing, and it compares different kinds of change and change strategies.

Part II

Part II of this book shares the perspectives of four people, all of whom have been involved in different ways in housing and support efforts. Written as personal essays, each writer, in her or his own way, diverts the reader from the mechanistic aspects of a housing and support approach to a picture of their rich life histories, stories, and personal perspectives.

Echoing the voices of many parents, Cory Moore, in *Letting Go, Moving On: A Parent's Thoughts* (Chapter 8), shares her hopes, dreams, fears, and experiences with her middle child, Leslie. Her message that "feelings and history cannot be discounted" comes to life as she describes Leslie's early years, her move from the family home to a group home, her move to an apartment with a roommate, and then, falling in love.

As a parent who defied the doctors who advised institutionalization, she vividly paints a picture of the family's ever-changing lives, of efforts to maintain a spirit of hope and determination during times of vulnerability, and of the importance of respect, affection, and caring. Within the story, the reader can also find practical suggestions and learn about dilemmas one parent experienced in supporting her daughter to live in her own home with people of her choice.

In Chapter 9, *Turning the Pages of Life*, Michael Kennedy describes his life experiences from living in state institutions and nursing homes to owning a trailer and living with roommates. He discusses how living in his own home differs from living "under an agency," and the lessons he has learned about seeking housing, obtaining services, and feeling supported.

Michael shares his personal philosophy about the importance of believing in oneself. He also describes how his experiences in the institutions continue to affect him today. He concludes by saying that change takes time and that life includes matters that don't work out as well as they may appear.

David Adler's chapter, *Perspectives of a Support Worker* (Chapter 10), is the story of his experiences as a personal attendant in Ontario, Canada. A moving account of his relationship with a man who died during the time he worked for him, David's chapter raises many critical issues on the nature of attendant services. He draws on his experiences both in this situation where he was directly employed by Luke[1] and as an attendant working for an organization.

This chapter provides a unique opportunity to learn about the perspectives of an attendant, and is particularly powerful in its discussion of issues such as relationship, intimacy, mutuality and control, personal valuing, and risks. David also shares his views about why working directly for the person with a disability is important.

The final chapter in Part II, *A Disabled Woman's Reflections: Myths and Realities of Integration* (Chapter 11), is by Judith E. Heumann, one of the leaders of the independent living movement. Sharing her own life experiences and her views on issues affecting people with disabilities today, this chapter offers a range of practical insights in areas relevant to thinking about the notion of support and relationships.

In this chapter, Judith discusses the need for an entitlement program for disabled people of all ages, the importance of flexibility on the part of funders, and a variety of practical issues related to personal attendant services and support. She notes the continued struggles of people against devaluation; yet, she ends with a note of hope that societal prejudices can and will be overcome.

Although each of the chapters in Part II conveys its own story, together they bring forth the core underlying values and assumptions that are implied by a housing and support approach. These might be expressed as moving from a world view that is mechanistic, service, and action-oriented toward an appreciation of:

The ebb and flow of individual lives and the personal meaning of each life

The inner meaning of support and the importance of the personal human qualities of hope, caring, courage, and determination

The weaving together of individual life tapestries of people who come to know and understand each other

---

[1]This name is a pseudonym.

The continued attitudinal barriers that people with disabilities and those sharing lives with them face on a daily basis

Part III

Part III of this book contains five case studies of organizations that have practical, unique illustrations of the concepts and principles discussed in Part I. Each organization has important lessons to share as it continues to grow and change through its experiences. Each of the studies represents a different aspect of housing and support; they include studies of a community housing association (Wisconsin), an organization supporting people with developmental disabilities (Ohio), an organization trying to change (Maryland), an agency finding ways to be sensitive to cultural issues in support (South Dakota), and an independent living center founded and operated by people with disabilities (California).

Approaches that merely shift from one model of service to another, albeit more individualized, are unlikely to create any substantive change in the quality of life experiences of people with disabilities and their families. These chapters, although encouraging a shift in models and approaches, also create a picture of the complexity of human lives and the need to become better at listening to, respecting, and being with each other.

Madison Mutual Housing Association and Cooperative: People and Housing Building Communities (Chapter 12) describes a dynamic community organization dedicated to quality, affordable, resident-controlled housing. Based upon principles of cooperation, the organization provides one example of how people are exploring ways to live and work together to make neighborhoods, communities, and society a better place for all of us.

On a practical basis, this organization has a wealth of experience on housing cooperatives, relationships with support organizations, and the inclusion of people of all abilities in their activities. As an organization whose mission encompasses more than disability issues, this case study offers the reader an opportunity to look at disability issues in a broader context.

Chapter 13, *Regenerating a Community; The Story of Residential, Inc.*, provides a view of a support organization that has strong community ties and is founded on a value base of personal commitment. A small organization in a rural community, Residential, Inc., is a picture of what disability service organizations can become as they move away from traditional residential roles and structures.

The nature of the organization's relationship with the people it supports, its guiding principles, and its mutual problem-solving approach are all worth consideration by other organizations. The Perry Housing Association and its role in the lives of people supported by Residential, Inc., is briefly discussed as well as ideas about how a state might change to better support local efforts for quality living.

"We Don't Put Up the Roadblocks We Used To": *Agency Change Through the Citizenship Project* (Chapter 14) illustrates the dilemmas and issues faced by one agency as it moves from being a residential services provider of small homes and apartments toward a new support role in the lives of the people with disabilities. As an agency that is attempting a guided change process, this case study highlights lessons about the nature of individual and agency change.

The reader is provided with an opportunity to examine some of the differences in the quality of life experiences of people supported by the agency, and to see the many dilemmas in the change process encountered by this organization.

Chapter 15, *"I'm Not Indian Anymore"*: *The Challenge of Providing Culturally Sensitive Services to American Indians,* presents the story of one agency's efforts to understand the lives of Indians (the term preferred by the people interviewed) in South Dakota and to reflect on what their experience means for the organization and its role. As an examination of cultural aspects of support, this case study illustrates how much we need to learn about circumstances and beliefs that may be different from mainstream assumptions.

As a small, rural organization, Southern Hills Developmental Services illustrates the complexity of community integration when viewed from different vantage points. While not providing solutions to the dilemmas, the case study reminds us of the importance of learning to listen and understand the viewpoints of the people involved.

Finally, *Center for Independent Living: Disabled People Take the Lead for Full Community Lives* (Chapter 16), describes the organization that is a visible symbol of the independent living movement and the international civil rights movement of people with disabilities. Founded, designed, and operated by people with disabilities, this center is recognized as an "inspiration and archetype for over 300 independent living centers" internationally.

Because many of the practices identified as part of a housing and support approach within the field of developmental disabilities parallel those in the independent living movement, this study is used to encourage greater sharing of information and exchange between the fields of developmental disabilities and independent living. Holding a strong value stance on choice and decision making, this case study also frames the current housing and support efforts as part of a broader social movement, which is as critical today as it was a decade ago.

CONCLUSION

At this time, many new developments are occurring in the area of housing and support. We hope this book provides an opportunity to reflect on a variety of perspectives that can broaden the way these ideas are understood, and even more importantly, on the way collaboration between people with disabilities, family members, and others takes place.

In most cases, we have included the actual names of the organizations discussed in this volume and in some chapters we have used the real names of people. When pseudonyms for places and people have been used, it is noted in the chapter. Most people were delighted to be included and were eager to share their stories so that others might lead better quality lives in the community. We appreciate their openness and generosity in describing their achievements and the many dilemmas that they all face as individuals and as organizations.

BIBLIOGRAPHY

Baker, B.L., Seltzer, G.B., & Seltzer, M.M. (1974). *As close as possible: Community residences for retarded adults.* Boston: Little, Brown.

Baroff, G.S. (1980). On "size" and the quality of residential care: A second look. *Mental Retardation, 18*(3), 113–117.

Biklen, D. (1990). Communication unbound: Autism and praxis. *Harvard Educational Review, 60*(3), 291–314.

Birenbaum, A., & Seiffer, S. (1976). *Resettling retarded adults in a managed community.* New York: Praeger.

Bogdan, R., & Taylor, S.J. (1990). Looking at the bright side: A positive approach to qualitative research. *Qualitative Sociology, 13*(2), 183–192.

Brost, M.M., & Johnson, T.Z. (1982). *Getting to know you: One approach to service assessment and planning for individuals with disabilities.* Madison, WI: DHSS-DCS.

Bulmer, M. (1987). *The social basis of community care.* London: Allen and Unwin.

Carling, P.J., Randolph, F.L., Blanch, A.K., & Ridgway, P. (1988). A review of the research on housing and community integration for people with psychiatric disabilities. *NARIC Quarterly, 1*(3), 1, 6–18.

Center for Community Change. (1989). *A survey of housing trust funds.* Washington, DC: Author.

Center on Human Policy. (1987). *A statement in support of families and their children.* Syracuse, NY: Author.

Center on Human Policy. (1989, May). *Policy institute 1989: Community living for adults summary.* Proceedings of National Policy Institute on Community Living for Adults, Syracuse, NY.

Center on Human Policy. (1989). *A proposal for a Rehabilitation Research and Training Center on Community Integration for Persons with Mental Retardation by the Center on Human Policy, Syracuse University.* Proposal submitted to the National Institute on Disability and Rehabilitation Research, U. S. Department of Education, Washington, DC.

Center on Human Policy. (1990). [Community study: Confidential research field memos]. Syracuse, NY: Author.

Clay, S. (1991, February). Ballast for bureaucrats. *Empowerment News from the Recipient Empowerment Project, 2*(1), 1–3.

Close, D.W., & Halpern, A.S. (1988). Transitions to supported living. In M.P. Janicki, M.W. Krauss, & M.M. Seltzer (Eds.), *Community residences for persons with developmental disabilities: Here to stay* (pp. 159–171). Baltimore: Paul H. Brookes Publishing Co.

Cohen, S., Agosta, J., Cohen, J., & Warren, R. (1989). Supporting families of children with severe disabilities. *Journal of The Association for Persons with Severe Handicaps, 14*(2), 155–162.

Colegrave, S. (1948). *The spirit of the valley.* Los Angeles: J. P. Tarcher, Inc.

Connecticut Developmental Disabilities Planning Council. (1988, December). *Proposed legislative platform.* Hartford, CT: Author.

Conroy, J., & Bradley, V. (1985). *The Pennhurst longitudinal study: A report of five years of research and analysis.* Philadelphia and Boston: Temple University Developmental Disabilities Center and Human Services Research Institute.

Consortium for Citizens with Disabilities Personal Assistance Task Force. (1991, October). *Draft concept paper on personal assistance.* Washington, DC: Author.

Covert, S. (1990). *A facility is not a home.* Durham: Institute on Disability,University of New Hampshire.

Crewe, N., & Zola, I. (Eds.). (1983). *Independent living for physically disabled people.* San Francisco: Jossey-Bass.

DeJong, G. (1978). *The movement for independent living: Origins, ideology, and implications for disability research.* Boston: Tufts-New England Medical Center, Medical Rehabilitation Institute.

DeJong, G. (1983). Defining and implementing the independent living concept. In N. Crewe & I. Zola (Eds.), *Independent living for physically disabled people.* San Francisco: Jossey-Bass.

Ducharme, G. (1985). On becoming a member of the community. *Canadian Journal of Mental Retardation, 35*(4), 28–30, 40.

Dunst, C.J., Trivette, C.M., Gordon, N.J., & Pletcher, L.L. (1989). Building and mobilizing informal family support networks. In G.H. Singer & L.K. Irvin (Eds.), *Support for caregiving families: Enabling positive adaptation to disability* (pp. 121–141). Baltimore: Paul H. Brookes Publishing Co.

Ebert, G. (1990, September). *Panel presentation on "What are meaning, characteristics, and dimensions of support?"* National Policy Institute on Support sponsored by the Center on Human Policy, Syracuse University, NY.

Eyman, R.K., Demaine, G.C., & Lei, T. (1979). Relationship between community environments and resident changes in adaptive behavior: A path model. *American Journal of Mental Deficiency, 83*(4), 330–338.

Ferguson, D.L., & Ferguson, P.M. (1986). The new Victors: A progressive policy analysis of work reform for people with very severe handicaps. *Mental Retardation, 24*(6), 331–338.

Gelfand, D. (1988). *The aging network: Programs and services* (3rd ed). New York: Springer-Verlag.

Gelman, S.R. (1988). Roles, responsibilities, and liabilities of agency boards. In M.P. Janicki, M.W. Krauss, & M.M. Seltzer (Eds.), *Community residences for persons with developmental disabilities: Here to stay* (pp. 57–68). Baltimore: Paul H. Brookes Publishing Co.

George, M.J., & Baumeister, A.A. (1981). Employee withdrawal and job satisfaction in community residential facilities for mentally retarded persons. *American Journal of Mental Deficiency, 85*(6), 639–647.

Goldin, H. (1941). *The Jewish woman and her home.* New York: Hebrew Publishing Co.

Gollay, E., Freedman, R., Wyngaarden, M., & Kurtz, R. (1978). *Coming back: The community experiences of deinstitutionalized mentally retarded people.* Cambridge, MA: Abt Books.

Green, H. (1983). *The light of the house: An intimate view of the lives of women in Victorian America.* New York: Pantheon Books.

Hagner, D. (1989). *The social integration of supported employees: A qualitative study.* Unpublished doctoral dissertation, Division of Special Education and Rehabilitation, Syracuse University, Syracuse, NY.

Hagner, D.C., Rogan, P., & Murphy, S.T. (1992). Facilitating natural supports in the workplace: Strategies for support consultants. *Journal of Rehabilitation, 58*(1), 21–34.

Halpern, A.S., Close, D.W., & Nelson, D.J. (1986). *On my own: The impact of semi-independent living programs for adults with mental retardation.* Baltimore: Paul H. Brookes Publishing Co.

Hedberg, B.L.T., Nystrom, P.D., & Starbuck, W.H. (1976). Camping on seesaws: Prescriptions for a self-designing organization. *Administrative Science Quarterly, 21,* 41–65.

Herman, S.E. (1991). Use and impact of a cash subsidy program. *Mental Retardation, 29*(5), 253–258.

Hill, B.K., Lakin, K.C., Bruininks, R.H., Amado, A.N., Anderson, D.J., & Copher, J.I. (1989, December). *Living in the community: A comparative study of foster homes and small group homes for people with mental retardation* (Project Report No. 28). Minneapolis: Center for Residential and Community Services, Institute on Community Integration, University of Minnesota.

Hill, B.K., Rotegard, L.L., & Bruininks, R.H. (1984). The quality of life of mentally retarded people in residential care. *Social Work, 29,* 275–280.

Hitzing, W. (1980). ENCOR and beyond. In T. Apolloni, J. Cappuccilli, & T.P. Cooke (Eds.), *Towards excellence: Achievements in residential services for people with disabilities* (pp. 71–93). Baltimore: University Park Press.

Hitzing, W. (1987). Community living alternatives for persons with autism and severe behavior problems. In D.J. Cohen & A. Donnellan (Eds.), *Handbook of autism and pervasive developmental disorders* (pp. 396–410). New York: John Wiley & Sons.

Hoggs, J., & Moss, S. (1990). Social and community integration. In M.P. Janicki & M.M. Seltzer (Eds.), *Aging and developmental disabilities: Challenges for the 1990s. (Proceedings of the Boston Roundtable on Research Issues and Applications in Aging and Developmental Disabilities).* Washington, DC: Special Interest Group on Aging, American Association on Mental Retardation.

Housing Technical Assistance Project. (1989). *Working with non-profit developers of affordable housing to provide integrated housing options for people with disabilities.* Washington, DC: Author.

Intagliata, J., Willer, B., & Wicks, N. (1981). Factors related to the quality of community adjustment in family care homes. In R.H. Bruininks, C.E. Meyers, B.B. Sigford, & K.C. Lakin (Eds.), *Deinstitutionalization and community adjustment of mentally retarded people* (pp. 217–232). Washington, DC: American Association on Mental Deficiency.

Jacobson, J.R., & Janicki, M.P. (1984, August). *Trends in staff characteristics in a large community residence system: 1980–1983.* Paper presented at the annual meeting of the American Psychological Association.

Janicki, M.P., Mayeda, T., & Epple, W. (1983). Availability of group homes for persons with mental retardation in the United States. *Mental Retardation, 21*(2), 45–51.

Johnson, T.Z. (1985). *Belonging to the community.* Madison, WI: Options in Community Living.

Jones, M.L., & Ulicny, G.R. (1986). The independent living perspective: Applications to services for adults with developmental disabilities. In J.A. Summers (Ed.), *The right to grow up: An introduction to adults with developmental disabilities* (pp. 227–241). Baltimore: Paul H. Brookes Publishing Co.

Kappel, B., & Wetherow, D. (1986). People caring about people: The Prairie Housing Cooperative. *Entourage, 1*(4), 37–42.

Klein, J. (1992). Get me the hell out of here: Supporting people with disabilities to live in their own homes. In J. Nisbet (Ed.), *Natural supports in school, at work, and in the community for people with severe disabilities* (pp. 277–339). Baltimore: Paul H. Brookes Publishing Co.

Knight, C. (1990). *Stigma: Stereotypes and scapegoats.* Columbus: Ohio Legal Rights Services.

Lachat, M.A. (1988). *The independent living service model: Historical roots, core elements, and current practice.* South Hampton, NH: Center for Resource Management in collaboration with the National Council on Independent Living.

Lakin, K.C., Bruininks, R.H., & Hill, B.K. (1986). Habilitative functions and effects of residential services. *Remedial and Special Education, 7*(6), 54–62.

Landesman, S. (1987). The changing structure and function of institutions: A search for optimal group care environments. In S. Landesman & P. Vietze (Eds.), *Living environments and mental retardation* (pp. 70–126). Washington, DC: American Association on Mental Deficiency.

Landesman-Dwyer, S. (1981). Living in the community. *American Journal of Mental Deficiency, 86*(3), 223–234.

Landesman-Dwyer, S., Berkson, G.B., & Romer, D. (1979). Affiliation and friendship of mentally retarded residents in group homes. *American Journal of Mental Deficiency, 83*(6), 571–580.

Langer, S. (1967). *Mind: An essay on human feeling.* Baltimore: John Hopkins Press.

Levy, P.H., Levy, J.M., Freeman, S., Feinman, J., & Samowitz, P. (1988). Training and managing community residence staff. In M.P. Janicki, M.W. Krauss, & M.M. Seltzer (Eds.), *Community residences for persons with developmental disabilities: Here to stay* (pp. 239–250). Baltimore: Paul H. Brookes Publishing Co.

Litvak, S., Zukas, H., & Heumann, J.E. (1987). *Attending to America: Personal assistance for independent living.* Berkeley: World Institute on Disability.

Lord, J. (n.d.). *Personal and family empowerment: Insights from the research literature.* Kitchener, Ontario: Centre for Research and Education.

Lord, J., & McKillop Farlow, D. (1990, Fall). A study of personal empowerment: Implications for health promotion. *Health Promotion,* 2–8.

McKnight, J.L. (1989, April). *Beyond community services.* Evanston, IL: Center for Urban Affairs and Policy Research, Northwestern University.

Mount, B., Beeman, P., & Ducharme, G. (1988). *What are we learning about bridgebuilding? A summary of dialogue between people seeking to build community for people with disabilities.* Manchester, CT: Communitas, Inc.

Nirje, B. (1985). The basis and logic of the normalization principle. *Australia and New Zealand Journal of Developmental Disabilities, 11*(8), 65–68.

Nosek, M.A. (1990). *Personal assistance services for persons with mental disabilities.* Houston: Baylor College of Medicine, prepared for National Council on Disability.

Nosek, M.A., Potter, C.G., Quan, H., & Zhu, Y. (1988). *Personal assistance services for people with disabilities: An annotated bibliography.* Houston: Independent Living Research Utilization, Research and Training Center on Independent Living at TIRR.

O'Brien, J. (1987a). Embracing ignorance, error, and fallibility: Competencies for leadership of effective services. In S.J. Taylor, D. Biklen, & J. Knoll (Eds.), *Community integration for people with severe disabilities* (pp. 85–108). New York: Teacher's College Press.

O'Brien, J. (1987b). A guide to life-style planning: Using *The Activities Catalog* to integrate services and natural support systems. In B. Wilcox & G.T. Bellamy, *A comprehensive guide to The Activities Catalog: An alternative curriculum for youth and adults with severe disabilities* (pp. 175–190). Baltimore: Paul H. Brookes Publishing Co.

O'Brien, J., & Lyle, C. (1986). *Strengthening the system: Improving Louisiana's community residential services for people with developmental disabilities.* Decatur, GA: Responsive Systems Associates.

O'Brien, J., & Lyle O'Brien, C. (1992). Members of each other: Perspectives on social support for people with severe disabilities. In J. Nisbet (Ed.), *Natural supports in school, at work, and in the community for people with severe disabilities.* Baltimore: Paul H. Brookes Publishing Co.

O'Connor, G.O. (1976). *Home is a good place: A national perspective of community residential facilities for developmentally disabled persons* (Monograph No. 2). Washington, DC: American Association on Mental Deficiency.

Ostroff, E., & Racino, J.A. (Eds.). (1991). *There's no place like home: Creating opportunities for housing that people want and control.* Seattle: Subcommittee on Housing, The Association for Persons with Severe Handicaps.

Page, S. (n.d.). *Introduction to cooperative housing.* Belchertown, MA: The Cooperative Initiatives Project.

Perske, R. (1988). *Circles of friends.* Nashville, TN: Abingdon Press.

Racino, J.A. (1988, March). Supporting adults with disabilities in individualized ways in the community. *TASH Newsletter, 14*(3), 4–5.

Racino, J.A. (1990). Preparing personnel to work in community support services. In A.P. Kaiser & C.M. McWhorter (Eds.), *Preparing personnel to work with persons with severe disabilities* (pp. 203–226). Baltimore: Paul H. Brookes Publishing Co.

Racino, J.A. (1991). Organizations in community living: Supporting people with disabilities. *Journal of Mental Health Administration, 18*(1), 51–59.

Racino, J.A. (1992). Living in the community: Independence, support, and transition. In F.R. Rusch, L. DeStefano, J. Chadsey-Rusch, L.A. Phelps, & E. Szymanski (Eds.), *Transition from school to adult life: Models, linkages, and policy* (pp. 131–148). Sycamore, IL: Sycamore Press.

Racino, J.A., & Heumann, J.E. (1992). Independent living and community life: Building coalitions among elders, people with disabilities and our allies. *Generations: Journal of the American Society on Aging, XVI*(I), 43–47.

Racino, J.A., & Knoll, J. (1986). Life in the community: Developing non-facility based services. *TASH Newsletter, 12*(9), 6.

Racino, J.A., O'Connor, S., Shoultz, B., Taylor, S.J., & Walker, P. (1989). *Moving into the 1990s: A policy analysis of community living for adults with developmental disabilities in South Dakota.* Syracuse, NY: Center on Human Policy, Syracuse University.

Racino, J.A., O'Connor, S., Walker, P., & Taylor, S.J. (1991). *Innovations in family supports.* Unpublished confidential research report.

Randolph, F., Laux, B., & Carling, P. (1987). Financing strategies for cooperatives. In F. Randolph, B. Laux, & P. Carling (Eds.), *In search of housing: Creative approaches to financing* (pp. 54–56). Burlington, VT: Center for Community Change Through Housing and Support.

Resolution on personal assistance services. (1991, September/October). Resolution passed by participants of the International Personal Assistance Services Symposium, Oakland, CA.

Schalock, R.L. (1983). *Sources for developmentally disabled adults.* Baltimore: University Park Press.

Seltzer, G.B. (1981). Community residential adjustment: The relationship among environment, performance and satisfaction. *American Journal of Mental Deficiency, 85*(6), 624–630.

Sherman, S., & Newman, E. (1988). *Foster families for adults: A community alternative in long-term care.* New York: Columbia University.

Shoultz, B. (1988). My home, not theirs: Promising approaches in mental health and developmental disabilities. In S.J. Friedman & K.G. Terkelsen (Eds.), *Issues in community mental health: Housing* (pp. 23–42). Canton, MA: PRODIST.

Shoultz, B. (1991). Regenerating a community. In S.J. Taylor, R. Bogdan, & J.A. Racino (Eds.), *Life in the community: Case studies of organizations supporting people with disabilities* (pp. 195–213). Baltimore: Paul H. Brookes Publishing Co.

Singer, G.H.S., & Irvin, L.K. (1991). Supporting families of persons with severe disabilities: Emerging findings, practices, and questions. In L.H. Meyer, C.A. Peck, & L. Brown (Eds.), *Critical issues in the lives of people with severe disabilities* (pp. 271–312). Baltimore: Paul H. Brookes Publishing Co.

Smull, M., & Bellamy, G.T. (1991). Community services for adults with disabilities: Policy challenges in the emerging support paradigm. In L.H. Meyer, C.A. Peck, & L. Brown (Eds.), *Critical issues in the lives of people with severe disabilities* (pp. 527–536). Baltimore: Paul H. Brookes Publishing Co.

Stainback, S.B., & Stainback, W.C. (1988). *Understanding and conducting qualitative research.* Reston, VA: Council for Exceptional Children.

Taylor, S.J. (1988). Caught in the continuum: A critical analysis of the principle of the least restrictive environment. *Journal of The Association for Persons with Severe Handicaps, 13*(1), 45–53.

Taylor, S.J., & Bogdan, R. (1989). On accepting relationships between people with mental retardation and nondisabled people: Towards an understanding of acceptance. *Disability, Handicap & Society, 4*(1), 21–36.

Taylor, S.J., Bogdan, R., & Racino, J.A. (Eds.). (1991). *Life in the community: Case studies of organizations supporting people with disabilities.* Baltimore: Paul H. Brookes Publishing Co.

Taylor, S.J., Lakin, K.C., & Hill, B.K. (1989). Permanency planning for children and youth: Out-of-home placement decisions. *Exceptional Children, 55*(6), 541–549.

Taylor, S.J., Racino, J.A., Knoll, J.A., & Lutfiyya, Z. (1987). *The nonrestrictive environment: On community integration for people with severe disabilities.* Syracuse, NY: Human Policy Press.

Turnbull, H.R., Garlow, J., & Barber, P. (1991). A policy analysis of family support for families with members with disabilities. *The University of Kansas Law Review, 39*(3), 739–782.

Warren, C.A.B. (1981). New forms of social control: The myth of deinstitutionalization. *American Behavioral Scientist, 24*(6), 724–740.

Williams, G. (1990). The movement for independent living: An evaluation and critique. In M. Nagler (Ed.), *Perspectives on disability* (pp. 248–258). Palo Alto, CA: Health Markets Research.

Wolfensberger, W. (1983). Social role valorization: A proposed new term for the principle of normalization. *Mental Retardation, 21,* 234–239.

Zirpoli, T., Hancox, D., Wieck, C., & Skarnulis, E. (1989). Partners in policymaking: Empowering people. *Journal of The Association for Persons with Severe Handicaps, 14*(2), 163–167.

Zola, I.K. (1987). The politicization of the self-help movement. *Social Policy, 18*(2), 32–33.

I

HOUSING, SUPPORT, AND COMMUNITY

2

"PEOPLE FIRST"

APPROACHES
TO HOUSING AND SUPPORT

Julie Ann Racino and Steven J. Taylor

Darwin and Glen live with Randy, their paid attendant, in an apartment in a cooperative housing project in Madison, Wisconsin. Darwin moved to the community in late 1985 after spending most of his life in a state institution. He is a pleasant and gentle middle-aged man who has many friends. These include coworkers he met at his supported employment position with the state Department of Health and Social Services, neighbors who also live in apartments in the co-op, and people who work for Options in Community Living, the agency that provides support for Darwin's living situation. He uses an electric wheelchair and a communication board. He communicates with picture symbols, and needs assistance with almost all his personal care. Darwin loves to share jokes, using his communication board and body language, and he especially enjoys pointing at the pictures of the people who work with him and laughing about something that happened the day before or that he hopes will happen soon (Center on Human Policy, November 1989, p. 1).

Debbie is a young woman who has a wonderful sense of humor, strongly believes in her religious convictions, appreciates and enjoys her family, describes herself as an independent voter, makes delicious sundaes, enjoys the band Blackwood, and wants a better and more interesting job. She is a sister, a daughter, a member of the Alliance church, a friend, a neighbor, a worker, a hostess, and a tenant. Since her aneurysm in 1975, she spent months in hospitals and has lived in a variety of "care and living facilities." Since July 1987, Debbie, with paid supports funded through North Dakota's Individualized Supportive Living Arrangements Program, has lived in her own apartment, which she decorated with the help of her mother. As Debbie

This chapter is based on the Center on Human Policy's policy analyses and technical assistance work in states and communities between 1985 and 1990. All policy analyses consisted of on-site interviews and observations, telephone interviews, and document reviews. All interviews and observations were based on an open-ended, qualitative research approach (Taylor & Bogdan [1984]).

We would especially like to thank the following people who participated in many of the program evaluations and policy analyses in states: Bonnie Shoultz, Pam Walker, Zana Marie Lutfiyya, Jim Knoll, Susan O'Connor, Rannveig Traustadottir, and Kathy Rothenberg.

explained, "I like everything compared to the other living situations" (adapted from Taylor, Bogdan, & Racino, 1991 pp. 116–117).

Darwin, Glen, Randy, and Debbie, as people who are leading the way with the support of others, are creating through their personal actions a vision of what life in the community can be for people with disabilities. Just like anyone, they wish to have full and meaningful lives, and as new opportunities arise, what they dare hope and dream continues to expand. Whereas each personal life picture is unique and constantly changing, in general, most people aspire to have a home of their own, a feeling of personal well being, financial and personal security, friendships and supportive relationships, self-expression, personal development, and ways to contribute to the lives and well being of others.

Today, some agencies are starting to listen more closely to people's dreams and hopes, and to recognize that their role is to support people—if, when, where, and how such help is desired—to have access to the opportunities and resources necessary to live fully in and be part of the community. This chapter presents some background on how this approach differs from the prevalent facility-based model still in existence in the United States, and discusses what this opportunity might mean in the lives of people with disabilities in their interactions with agencies.

THE CONTEXT FOR HOUSING AND SUPPORT

To understand present and future developments in housing and support, this section traces some of the key residential practice issues of the 1980s, the concept of facility-based services, and the movement to supporting people to live in "homes of their own." This selected history provides information about fundamental issues that must be addressed as efforts are made to develop and expand new "programs," such as supportive living and personal assistance.

"Residential Services" in the Early 1980s

During the early 1980s, the focus of the disability field was on issues such as the benefits and limitations of heterogeneous and homogeneous groupings; the optimal size of community facilities; site selection and neighborhood reactions; and quality assurance, which was primarily framed around issues of licensure and regulations. In the literature, distinctions were generally not made between facilities for children and for adults, and characteristics of ethnicity, age, and gender were largely ignored. The group home model was almost considered synonymous with residential services. More than 90% of the funding for residential services and related supports was in the control of a network of private and governmental agencies throughout the United States. Emphasis on skill teaching and behavior management, often drawn from developments in education, dominated the picture of what life in homes was about for people with disabilities.

The homogeneity-heterogeneity debate is one example of the underlying thinking reflected in this approach to housing, home life, and support for people with disabilities. It was common practice in states and communities for all people in a home or facility to be grouped by similar labels such as "challenging behaviors," "medical needs," or "social-emotional problems." Integrationists, however, argued that it would be preferable to have a group of people with a range of needs living in the same home to enhance people's acquisition of skills as well as their integration in the community. Both of these positions were based on the beliefs that: 1) disability was the primary characteristic to be considered in decisions regarding with whom people should live; 2) these decisions about groupings were primarily professional determinations, although people's preferences could be taken into account; and 3) housing was tied primarily to program versus human needs. Neither position was framed from the points of view of people with disabilities. The debate also focused upon the development of a universal rule that could be applied, sometimes with modification, regardless of the people, agencies, community, or society in question.

On the systems level, planning was based on community needs assessments and systems were constructed from a classic top-down approach. The primary aim was to increase the accessibility and availability of services on the local level and to do so based on principles such as accountability, cost-effectiveness (often framed in relationship to institutional costs), and equitable distribution. The systems primarily relied on disability-based models, which were considered replicable, with modification from one location to another.

Residential services were considered distinct from employment, education, and recreation services, and one of the "rules" in the field was to separate the "residential" provider from the provider of "day" services. While influencing each other, each life domain had its own specialists who framed issues in relationship to their area of expertise. Despite the tremendous growth in paraprofessionals involved with community living, no new discipline emerged and training continued under broader fields such as social work, special education, and rehabilitation.

These ways of thinking about people and the role of agencies and systems permeated all aspects of how "residential services" were "designed," "monitored," and "arranged"; how the people living in the homes were presented to society; how people with disabilities were treated in their interactions with agencies; and how systems were designed to meet people's needs. Therefore, changing one's thinking about these areas involves reconsidering all the aspects of residential services that are considered as "givens" in the field today.

This did not mean, of course, that other positive trends were not already prevalent during the early to mid-1980s. As Lakin summarizes (1988), a tremendous amount had been learned through research and practice on community living and quality of life. Areas such as social relationships, personal autonomy, and community participation also were increasing in importance.

Toward Smaller Facility-Based Services

During the late 1980s, while states such as New York were promoting a 12-"bed" prototype for group homes, other states had already developed smaller places for people with severe disabilities, ranging from one to three people in size. Examples include:

Maryland developed three-person "alternative living units" across the state and supported people with severe disabilities in these settings.

From 1982 to 1987, Connecticut increased the number of homes for one to three people, particularly for people with challenging behaviors or medical needs.

In 1983, Wisconsin limited the size of "living arrangements" under their home and community-based services Medicaid (HCBS) waiver to four people, unless an exception was granted.

Minnesota, through their HCBS waiver, limited the size of supportive living services for adults to places of no more than six people.

In 1985, Region V, Nebraska started moving from homes of five or six people to smaller size homes.

By the late 1980s, the general consensus of "innovative" service providers was that the greater the issues were in supporting a person to live in the community (e.g., an individual with multiple disabilities), often, then, the greater was his or her need to live with just a few people or even alone. They explained that the people who were most often viewed as needing to live in larger, specialized facilities, such as institutions and group homes, were often the very people who most benefited from the opportunities a smaller place offered. Providers shared their experiences that small size enabled people with disabilities to feel more secure and to have a greater sense of control over their life space. It also enabled staff to get to know people as individuals and to shift their emphasis away from "group management."

Based on the same model of services as larger facilities, small places can also become highly routinized and homelike instead of actually being homes. Consistent with the literature of the 1980s, community living in practice for people with severe disabilities tended to revolve around group home management and quality assurance, as opposed to more person-centered orientations. As trends toward smaller places continued in different states, it became noticeable that no matter what the size, whether eight, three, or even one person, the same "group home" model or way of thinking about people and their lives could still be applied.

Clustered Apartments

In the 1980s, it was common practice in many states to locate apartments in clusters. As a model, a cluster approach offered several advantages compared to traditional group homes, including: 1) less susceptibility to regimentation; 2) administrative and logistical advantages in locating and maintaining the apartment program; 3) greater physical integration in the community than most group homes; and 4) smaller size of living situations and, thus, greater likelihood that the people living together would get along with each other. From the vantage point of community integration, independent living, and related values, however, the cluster model has many drawbacks and disadvantages. These include (adapted from Taylor & Racino, November 1987, pp. 8–9):

1. Since a cluster model is a single location for a number of individuals, this automatically limits people's choices in housing options.
2. Many clusters are designed to be transitional in nature and people are uprooted when they learn new skills.
3. While more flexible than group homes and other congregate settings, clusters are often characterized by inflexibility, including neighborhood choice and number of roommates.
4. The clusters typically belong to the agency and are not considered the people's own homes.
5. The clusters lend themselves to a rigid distinction between staff, on the one hand, and clients on the other.
6. Since clusters are usually designed for groups of people, there is a tendency for them to become insular and self-reliant socially, thus inhibiting community integration.
7. The clusters are often operated in the same way as group homes, with a tendency to establish routines on the basis of the needs of staff and agency rather than individual preferences.

In other words, cluster apartment models, similar to group homes, tended to fit people into the program instead of promoting a nonfacility-based approach that started with the person first.

Characteristics of Facility-Based Services

Within this context of residential services, it was possible to identify eight characteristics of facility-based services that appeared important in distinguishing facilities from situations where people were living in their "own homes." These characteristics of facilities can also be found in many state "supportive living" programs, and include:

1. *Agency owned or rented facilities*   Since providers own or rent the residential settings, they ultimately control who lives there. As O'Brien and Lyle (1986) point out, under this arrangement, "the person is a guest in someone else's home."
2. *Licensed or certified facilities*   When agencies own or lease and operate facilities, licensing or certification are appropriate. However, by its nature, licensing tends to limit choices and places decision making in the hands of people who do not live there.
3. *Agency staffed*   Staff are hired, paid and supervised by the agency. Staff are employed by and accountable to the agency, not the people receiving services. The staff's relationship with the people is defined by conditions of employment set between the agency and the staff.
4. *Staffing ratios based on the group and not individuals*   In this model, to the extent that an individual has more or less supervision needs, she or he may not "fit into the program" and will be considered ineligible for the services or asked to leave.
5. *Linkage of housing and support*   Generally, people are required to live in the facility in order to obtain intensive support services.
6. *Core funding tied to facilities*   The funding is based on the facility and not the individual. Funding would not follow the individual if she or he moved to a new home.
7. *Weak relationship between funding and individual planning*   The rate setting and individual planning processes proceed relatively independently.
8. *Facility classification based on supervision needs*   Facilities are primarily classified as providing either 24-hour supervision or less than 24-hour supervision. (Taylor, Racino, & Rothenberg, 1988, pp. 51–53)

From 1985 to 1991, these facility-based characteristics continued to be a useful analysis framework despite the diversity across states in how community living arrangements are categorized and organized. These analyses provided a broader understanding of traditional community living arrangements, both their strengths and limitations, as they currently exist in the United States.

For example, in one study, facility-based models resulted in a poor distribution of fiscal resources, with some people getting less "supervision" than they needed and wanted, and others being "oversupervised." Simply changing policies, regulations, or legislation would not necessarily address this poor distribution because underlying issues, such as the tendency of providers and others to think in terms of levels of supervision and equating support with shift staffing, would be left untouched.

These characteristics, although helpful in understanding the nature of facilities and homes, indicate the accepted standards applied to housing and homelife for people with disabilities. They should not be interpreted to imply that in every situation a home would have the opposite characteristics. It is possible, for example, to have a home where support staff are employed by an agency. In other situations, some individuals may live in housing that is agency owned or leased. However, one would not anticipate agency staffing and agency ownership of homes to be standard practices for people with disabilities.

Foster or Family Care

Foster or family care options, which share fewer facility-based characteristics, tend to have unclear missions in most states, seldom distinguishing between the needs of children and adults. Policies seldom provide guidance on when adults should live with a family, including when: 1) the individual expresses a clear choice to live with a family, 2) the individual has a pre-existing relationship with an individual or family and expresses a desire to live in their home, 3) the individual desires the kind of companionship and close personal relationship found in a family, and 4) the individual has experienced long-term separation from the community and family members and may wish an opportunity to experience more traditional family life.

Any modifications of foster care systems to support adults in their own homes must start with an understanding of the current state of these systems in the country. These systems typically confuse the needs of children and adults. They also lack the following: adequate supports to ensure successful placements, mission statements that provide guidance to people supporting both children and adults, a permanency planning approach for children, and a coherent and unified approach. In addition, foster care systems often have unclear relationships between social services and developmental disabilities departments, and allocate insufficient resources to the operation of these programs.

HOUSING AND SUPPORT APPROACH

A housing and support approach has been pioneered on the local level by agencies such as Options in Community Living in Madison, Wisconsin; Centennial Developmental Services in Weld County, Colorado; Residential, Inc., Ohio; and other agencies now in their fourth or fifth year of an agency change process. Parents have also adapted this approach as a way to seek permanent housing and support for their child. Aspects of a housing and support approach can also be found on a regional and statewide basis, including in North Dakota's individualized supportive living arrangements (ISLA) program, Wisconsin's individualized services option (ISO) program, Michigan's supported independence program (SIP), and supports for adults in New Hampshire and Minnesota.

Numerous states have established demonstration projects or initiated new statewide efforts in the past few years, including Missouri, Arkansas, Maryland, Florida, Illinois, and Ohio. In 1991, the Health Care Financing Administration notified eight states that they will be permitted to cover "community supported living arrangements" under their state Medicaid plans: California, Colorado, Florida, Illinois, Maryland, Michigan, Rhode Island, and Wisconsin.

Characteristics of a housing and support approach were initially described as having these key elements: 1) a way of thinking focusing on people, not programs; 2) the separation of housing and support components so that people could obtain supports wherever they might live; 3) choice in housing, home location, and roommates; 4) opportunities for home ownership and leasing, if desired; 5) individualized and flexible supports; 6) assessments based on getting to know people; 7) services that would "build on natural supports"; and 8) choice by people with disabilities about who provides services.

Comparing Approaches

O'Brien and Lyle's (1986) work on systems change compared two contrasting strategies in residential services: a landlord strategy and a housing agent/personal support strategy. These strategies are highlighted in Table 1.

In 1988, this separation of housing and support was found to be a central feature of what was then called a nonfacility-based approach (Taylor, Racino, & Rothenberg, 1988). A manual prepared by Options in Community Living describes why it is important on the local agency level to separate housing from support:

> One agency should not provide both housing and support services. While we often advise and assist clients in finding, renting and furnishing their apartments, Options no longer becomes the lease holder or landlord for the client apartments. We want our clients to feel both control over and responsibility for their own living space. We also believe that receiving Options' services should not affect where clients live. Our clients have a greater choice in living situations and know the beginning, ending or changing of their relationship with us will not put them under any pressure to move. This policy also frees us from the time consuming responsibilities and sometimes conflicting relationships involved in being a landlord. (Johnson, 1985, p. 45)

Theoretically and practically, any housing arrangement can be matched with any one or more types of support options. For example, a person with mental retardation living in his or her own apartment or house can be supported by one or any combination of live-in roommates, on-call staff, neighbors, or friends. Table 2 illustrates a simple breakdown of housing and support options.

A contrasting example can also illustrate on the personal level why this separation of housing and support is important. In the traditional approach to residential services, two or three people who know each other and want to continue living together in the neighborhood where they grew up, could do so only if they need minimal paid support services. If any of the individuals would require more intensive services, he or she would need to move to an existing facility. This often results in people being separated and moving away from where they want to live and from the neighborhood and people with whom they are familiar. After these disruptions in their lives occur, service providers might then

Table 1. Contrasting strategies in residential services

LANDLORD STRATEGY

An agency acquires and manages the building.

Staff are employed by the agency.

Housing is offered along with other services such as instruction, supervision, and personal assistance in a tightly connected package. It is usually not possible for a person to refuse services and retain tenancy.

Usually the resident contributes only a small part to program costs from discretionary income. Most program costs are paid by a third party who may bundle several funding sources together to make up a daily per-person rate.

People often assume that different types of buildings match different levels of [disability]. The most able people live in apartments. The least able live in congregate health care facilities. The people in between belong in group homes.

People are "admitted" to a "bed" as "resident" or "clients" and receive "residential programming" or "active treatment." At the conclusion of their stay, they are "discharged" or "graduated" or "transferred to a more appropriate program."

An agency, not the people in residence, holds the property's lease, mortgage, or title, and owns most of the furnishings.

HOUSING AGENT/PERSONAL SUPPORT STRATEGY

An agency provides people with the help needed to locate, rent, and sometimes own their own homes.

People get only as much help as they need in negotiating and arranging payments, making necessary modifications, and acquiring furnishings.

People have opportunities to learn what they need to know to enjoy their homes in safety.

People whose physical abilities limit their ability to do things for themselves and people who have not yet learned what they need to manage safely have in-home assistance.

The agency joins with other local groups to influence the local housing market to offer suitable housing.

Money from programs for people with disabilities is directed toward two distinct purposes: personal support and housing subsidy. Housing subsidy supplements a person's own resources from wages, entitlements (such as SSI), and family resources. In some places, separate agencies or departments have been created which specialize either in housing or in personal support.

Each person an agency assists could have a different set of personal supports and a different mix of funds paying the rent or mortgage. Indeed the agency could easily offer personal support to people who live with their parents.

Reprinted from O'Brien, J. & Lyle, C. (1986). *Strengthening the system: Improving Louisiana's community residential services for people with developmental disabilities*, pp. 27–28. Decatur, GA: Responsive Systems Associates; reprinted by permission.

come in and help people to reconnect with the community and develop relationships.

On the state level, the separation of housing and support is also necessary because of the way in which service systems have been designed and the limits they place on opportunities for choice and ordinary living. This usually requires changes, which vary from state to state, to separate support and housing financing, and changes in pol-

Table 2.   Separation of housing and support

Housing options	Support options
Own home	Staffing (disability)
Parent's or guardian's home	Live-in
	On-call
Shared home	Other
Existing home and households	Paid roommates or companions
Cooperative	Paid neighbor
Corporation owned or rented	Personal attendant (can include a family
Home owned by a person with a	member)
disability	Live-in
Home leased by a person with a	On-call
disability	Physical adaptations or technological or
Home owned or leased by a parent or	communicative assistance
guardian	Stipends or cash subsidy
Home in trust	Unpaid neighbors, family, or friends
	Agency (employment)
	Live-in
	On-call
	Other

Adapted from Taylor, Racino, & Rothenberg, (1988).

icies, regulations, and legislation that may prohibit people from living in their own homes. In some ways, these changes are a response to the question, "What impediments must be addressed in each state to have supports available to people wherever they may choose to live?"

The separation of housing and support is not a vision of what should exist, but is simply the first step in starting to remove some of the barriers that are currently in place in all states, although in different forms. Of course, housing must be coordinated with supports on a variety of levels, but conceptually the design for such large scale arrangements is still unclear if using a bottom-up approach to service design. This separation of housing and supports is not a call to abruptly abandon what exists, which could cause harm in the lives of people with disabilities, but to introduce more flexibility and opportunities for individual choice for all people with disabilities. As with any other change, this will bring a new order of issues, which must be addressed carefully and thoughtfully with due attention and input from each person involved.

Key Values
and Assumptions

In 1989, a group of people representing a variety of perspectives, such as the independent living movement and community building in North America, developed a statement in support of adults to guide continued work in the area of housing and supports. Figure 1 represents the three

IN SUPPORT OF ADULTS LIVING IN THE COMMUNITY

Whereas children with developmental disabilities belong in families and public policy should support this right (Center on Human Policy, 1987), adults with developmental disabilities should have the opportunity to pursue the same range of lifestyles as nondisabled members of the community. This statement reflects principles to guide states, agencies, and organizations in supporting adults with developmental disabilities to live in homes, participate in community life, and pursue their individual lifestyles.

**Adults, regardless of ability, should have the right
and opportunity to live in a home of their own in the community.**

Adults should have the right and opportunity to live in typical, decent, safe, accessible, and integrated community housing.

States, agencies, and communities should ensure the availability of such housing for all of its citizens, including adults with disabilities. When necessary, government should provide housing subsidies for people whose incomes are insufficient to afford decent housing. Standards for evaluating the safety and decency of housing should be local housing codes.

Adults, whether married or single, should have choices about the neighborhood they live in, the style of community housing, and the people with whom they will live.

The preferences of each individual should guide all aspects of the selection of housing, including whether the individual will live alone, with their family, roommates, extended family, spouse, or friends. The role of government, agencies, and organizations is to determine how they can support the individual in meeting their needs and achieving their preferences.

Adults should have the same tenant and ownership rights and opportunities as other citizens, including the option to own or lease their own homes or apartments.

Government, agencies, and organizations must be guided by the principle that adults should have maximum choice and control of their lives, including their housing. Instead of requiring adults with disabilities to live in agency owned or leased facilities, adults should be supported to lease or own homes, if they so desire.

Adults should have the opportunity to live in housing free from the conflicting relationship of landlord and service provider.

Housing and support services should be provided by separate organizations so the individual's home is not jeopardized by a change in their relationship to the service provider. An agency might, however, assist people to locate housing, sign leases, negotiate with landlords, arrange architectural adaptations, and obtain subsidies.

Adults should have the opportunity to create a home of their own, reflective of their personal routines, values, and lifestyles.

Although the meaning of home is difficult to define, it includes the following features: a feeling of belonging and ownership, choice of who is invited in and who is not, an individualized or unique atmosphere or tone, a place where one's time is one's own, and a place where the person makes mutual or shared decisions about their home environment. The burden of proof must be on the government or other outside parties who seek to curtail or limit the choices in lifestyles of people with disabilities.

(continued)

Figure 1.   In support of adults living in the community. (Center on Human Policy, 1989.)

Figure 1. *(continued)*

All individuals should be entitled to the supports and personal assistance needed to live in their own home and participate fully in community life.

Adults should receive whatever personal assistance and supports they need to live fully in their own home and community with dignity, self-determination, and respect.

Personal assistance services could include interpreting, homemaking, mobility assistance, social support, medical assistance, transportation, personal hygiene, reading, recreation, and decisionmaking, among others. Services and supports should be provided in a way that maintains and/or strengthens the adult's personal relationships and social network.

Adults should have the option to live in their own homes in the community without risking the loss of material or personal assistance support.

Personal assistance and other supports should be available to adults with disabilities living in their own homes in the community. People, including those with severe disabilities, should not be required to live in an agency facility or to become impoverished to obtain support services.

Adults shall have maximum control over their personal assistance and other supports, with advocacy and support, and be independent of service agencies in making these decisions.

The concept of personal assistance is based on the principle that all people have a way of communicating choices and that all people are unique in their preferences. Thus, supports must be designed to be individualized and flexible, because people with similar needs may prefer different solutions. When people have difficulty expressing choices, independent facilitation should be available.

Adults have a right to determine who will provide personal assistance and supports.

Personal assistance and other supports can be provided by a variety of people, including paid staff, volunteers, neighbors, friends, and family members. Although each relationship will be unique, the adult retains the right to decide and negotiate who will provide these services, including hiring, firing, evaluation, and training of personal assistants.

All adults should have opportunities to participate in community life.

Adults with disabilities should have opportunities to be involved with ordinary people on a partnership basis and to develop relationships with neighbors, co-workers, and community members.

Community members can look for shared interests, share time and space with people, initiate relationships, and demonstrate a sense of sharing for each other's well-being. When government becomes involved, it should not disrupt existing networks and connections, but seek to support and strengthen relationships and help build connections with community.

Adults with disabilities are entitled to decent, safe, and affordable housing; financial security to meet basic needs; health and medical care; and community transportation, employment, and recreation.

Housing, recreation, health care, financial security, transportation, and employment are social issues that require community-based not disability-based solutions. Individuals with disabilities should have access to the personal assistance necessary to use these community resources. Government, human services agencies, community organizations, and people with disabilities should work together to ensure these basic needs are met for all people.

(continued)

Figure 1.   (*continued*)

Adults should have opportunities to contribute to the diversity and strength of communities.

Communities (towns, cities, suburbs, villages, associations) need to become more inclusive of all people, recognizing the unique contributions individuals with disabilities can and do make to community life. This diversity must include a . recognition and celebration of the differences between urban and rural life and people's ethnic and cultural heritage.

---

major themes and principles developed at the Center on Human Policy's policy institute on community living for adults: importance of living in one's "own home," personal assistance services and other supports, and the shift from being in to being part of the community. In the words of Gunnar Dybwad (Center on Human Policy, November 1989, p. 2), "Any of these concepts fully applied will challenge the service system as it today exists."

Whereas the field moved from "homelike" to "homes" in the 1980s, the 1990s will include more exploration of the meaning of "one's own home," such as the feeling of belonging and ownership that has been denied many people with developmental disabilities. The concept of personal assistance may be one way to start to think about support services for people with developmental disabilities and to increase the personal choices of people with disabilities in relationship to their support services. Finally, being part of the community means more attention to at least three distinct things: 1) participation in community places, 2) access to community services, and 3) friendships and social relationships.

In 1990, the Center on Human Policy hosted a policy institute on "support," which centered around three main issues: the meaning of support as experienced by people with disabilities, roles of allies and supporters, and issues in decision making and choices for people with severe disabilities. This institute addressed personal support and its inner meaning, which partially translated into the values of love, intimacy, compassion, hope, and courage. There has been a reluctance to discuss these issues for several reasons: they are considered religious, spiritual, or emotional instead of rational qualities; people with disabilities are sometimes not considered to possess these qualities; "technical" helping has been separated from "personal" helping; and there is a tendency to avoid areas that cannot be categorized and logically explained. To some extent, a housing and support approach also represents an attempt to reintegrate human values as legitimate parts of the discussion about the lives of people with disabilities. As Judith Snow explained (Center on Human Policy, 1990b), these discussions of personal support, love, and intimacy are difficult, which means we need to talk about them more, not less.

What a Housing and Support Approach Is and Is Not

Underlying the housing and support approach are several key concepts and assumptions that are important to bear in mind while reading the material in Part I.

It's Not *a New Program Model.*   A housing and support approach, although it shares some characteristics of models, is not an attempt to develop a new kind of program for people with developmental disabilities. Primarily, its importance is in helping people to think about, and consequently act, in ways that are more responsive to the needs and preferences of individuals with disabilities and their families.

It Does Not *Apply to Children Who Belong in Families.*   The approach as described here is developed primarily within a framework pertaining to the lives of adults, not children. As we have written elsewhere, children with disabilities belong in families (see, e.g., Taylor, Bogdan, and Racino, 1991). However, personal assistance is an issue that can apply to people with disabilities of all ages.

It Does Not *Imply a Change Only, or Even Primarily, in Services.* Although changes in services and systems on the local, state, and national levels are highlighted, this does not imply that these changes are the most critical ones in the lives of people with disabilities. Without more substantive personal changes in day-to-day interactions, systems changes often only remove some of the barriers that impede good things from occurring on the local level.

It Can Increase Choices and Options, But It Has Not *Shifted Control to People with Disabilities.*   At least as it exists in the United States today, a housing and support approach increases choices and decision-making by people with disabilities within a framework where agencies still maintain ultimate control and simply "allow" people with disabilities more choices and options.

It Will Not *in Itself Address Some of the Dilemmas in the "Helper–Helpee" Relationship.*   Because an actual power shift has not occurred in the relationships with agencies, people with disabilities are still placed in the position of being grateful for whatever decent options are available. This is one of the arguments for a move toward entitlement and direct cash subsidies.

It Is About a Change in How People with Disabilities Are Viewed and Approached.   A housing and support approach implies a change in how people with disabilities are viewed as well as a change in the nature of the relationship between organizations and people with disabilities. Because these reflect ingrained assumptions, changing to this approach takes time and will occur at a different pace for different individuals and agencies. These types of fundamental changes cannot be imposed or required, but must be addressed in many ways, including by placing more control in the hands of people with disabilities.

It Is About New Relationships Among People in Different Sectors. Many of the changes implied by a housing and support approach are about new relationships between the world of disability and local communities. Whether through new participation in housing associations or greater involvement with ordinary community members, these changes are an opportunity to forge connections with day-to-day communities.

It Provides an Opportunity To Connect with Other Groups that Are Experiencing Similar Issues. A housing and support approach provides a concrete opportunity for groups with diverse perspectives and needs to find common ground to make the changes that are necessary for all people to have decent housing and quality of life.

It Represents a Way of Getting Closer to Viewing the World from the Viewpoint of the Person. Given the dominance of the developmental disability system in the United States, a housing and support approach tries to refocus the attention of agencies from issues of home management and landlord concerns to attention on how people with disabilities view their own lives.

It Leads to a Need To Rethink All Aspects of What "Residential Services" Mean. Once housing and support are separated from each other, all aspects of how we have understood who the staff are, what organization roles are, how community and disability organizations relate to each other, and how systems are constructed and viewed need to be reconceptualized.

It Is a Way of Thinking that Can Be Applied Across All Service Areas (e.g., Recreation, Employment). Once housing is separated conceptually from support, it becomes easy to see the relevance of this approach across all areas of a person's life. Thus, support in its fundamental and service senses can be pursued across all life domains. For example, instead of supported employment, one can think about jobs with support; and instead of supported recreation, one can think about regular recreation with support.

It Will Require Careful Attention and Hard Work Over an Extensive Period To Make These Changes. Personal understanding about this approach (or approaches) continues to change both based on experiences in the field and on ongoing research. As the field has repeatedly learned, language and popularity of new concepts in the field often spread quickly, sometimes without the thoughtful attention to substantive change that requires persistent hard work over extensive periods.

While not all of the aspects discussed above are inherent in changing the mechanism or approach, all are potential opportunities presented by these change efforts to address fundamental issues in community life.

CRITICAL ISSUES IN HOUSING AND SUPPORT

Because of the increased popularity of supportive living, it is important to discuss three emerging issues: distinction between the development of supportive living programs and housing and support; distinction between supported housing and supportive living; and the lack of an overall vision uniting the areas of supportive living, housing, and personal assistance.

Distinctions Between Supportive Living and Housing and Support

Several distinctions need to be made between two major approaches to "supportive living." Supportive living is generally being approached in the field of disability by adding more elements of choice in services and housing while still maintaining the present nature of systems, agencies, and programs. These types of changes, as exemplified by the North Dakota Supportive Living Arrangements Program, have been important in several ways. First, these endeavors have indicated that it is feasible for agencies and systems to respond in more individualized ways to people with severe disabilities. Second, they represent an important direction toward greater recognition of the uniqueness of each person with a disability. Third, they are often accompanied by other efforts, such as greater attention to community connections and relationships. However, they are still fundamentally based on the same program view of "how things work" that is prevalent in the field today.

On a smaller scale, there is an effort occurring to change the nature of the relationship between agencies and individuals with disabilities and the people in their lives. This is a slower, more arduous process, which seeks to change the nature of agencies and systems and the role of community and agencies in relationship to people. This approach is less tied to specific program structures and more to the nature of the quality of life of people. Agencies that are in the process of such a change say they are just beginning to understand what this may mean. While often "fitting in" the category of supportive living, these efforts most closely resemble a housing and support approach.

Some of the conflicting information available in the disability field on concrete issues, such as how long change takes, reflects these two distinctly different approaches and goals. For example, the first approach can be accomplished as quickly or more quickly than programs that have been developed in the past, whereas the second approach requires much more extensive and ongoing efforts.

Distinctions Between Supported Housing and Supported Living

Supported housing is a term used for a similar approach in the field of mental health for supporting people to live in their own places. As it has developed throughout the United States, however, it has been primarily practiced as a housing initiative that provides new opportunities for decent, affordable housing, sometimes through the provision of rent subsidies, down payments, or money for apartment set-up. In contrast, *supportive living* in the field of developmental disabilities has proceeded primarily as a support initiative, often with an emphasis on modifying Medicaid home- and community-based waivers, and/or state financing sources to provide necessary supports in people's homes.

Housing and support issues in mental health are in many ways similar to issues faced in developmental disabilities services. Existing support funding often is more flexible, although less available, in the field of mental health than in the developmental disabilities field. Although housing is being pursued in the field of developmental disabilities, it has not been as integrated an effort as in mental health. For example, typically the organizations and individuals involved in this pursuit are not the same leaders as in the area of supportive living.

Lack of Vision To Unite Change Efforts

The people and organizations involved in housing, personal assistance, and supportive living, although overlapping, are generally proceeding without any unified vision of the future. This same disjointedness on the national front is also reflected on the state and local levels where each of these areas is typically addressed as a separate program initiative or project. Because personal assistance or technological supports and supportive living could actually reflect the same types of services provided in different ways, greater dialogue is needed about the vision of what community living will be like in the future, and how these services may fit in. For example, knowledge about personal assistance options can easily elicit questions about the use of a supportive living coach in Florida's Supported Independent Living Model. Also, greater knowledge about community housing options developed by housing organizations could broaden the possibilities of the Illinois Community Integrated Living Arrangements (CILA) approach. These efforts will be described in Chapter 7 of this volume.

MOVING TOWARD CHANGE

Several observations on the nature of change are helpful to keep in mind when reading this book. Fundamental change is slow and serendipitous. When it comes to complex human services systems, especially on the state level, it is impossible to predict with precision the outcomes of any new initiative. Every advance reveals new challenges; every solution creates its own set of problems. This is not to question attempts to change service systems; it is to suggest that there are no simple solutions to complex problems and that change can be an agonizingly slow and frustrating process. Because change is unpredictable, states, regions, and communities cannot control everything that happens within their borders.

In starting the change process from traditional residential services to a housing and support approach, the following two avenues are recommended as beginning steps: personal change strategies and identifying agency and systems barriers.

Personal Change Strategies

The most difficult aspect of change is the shift from the perspective of an agency to that of a person with a disability. The most important step in this approach is to begin to think in terms of individual people, their current life situation, and their hopes and dreams. A diagram from the Human Policy Press (Taylor, Racino, Knoll, & Lutfiyya, 1987) is presented in Figure 2 to illustrate the change from a continuum to an array of personal options. The person is at the center and paid (and unpaid) support strategies can be uniquely constructed to assist the individual in achieving his or her desired lifestyle.

In working with individuals and groups, it is critical to create a picture of a person's current and future life situations before introducing any issues about services and their roles. In other words, as illustrated in Figure 3, one of the key questions is if services might support a network of valued activities and places and people in a person's life. If so, then the question is how this might occur. This is particularly important in

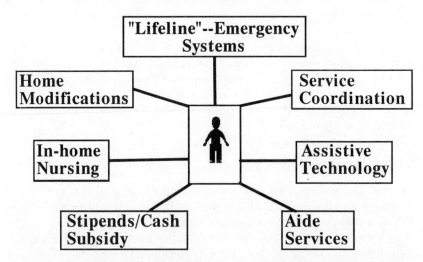

Figure 2.   Person-centered approach to housing and supports (paid services). (Modified from Taylor, S.J., Racino, J.A., Knoll, J.A., & Lutfiyya, Z. [1987]. *The nonrestrictive environment: On community integration for people with the most severe disabilities*, p. 12. Syracuse, NY: Human Policy Press.)

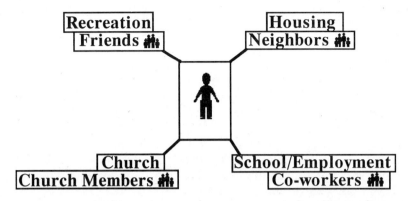

Figure 3. Person-centered approach to housing and supports (activities, places, and relationships).

assisting people to break away from thinking about what currently exists (e.g., place in a group home, funding under the Medicaid waiver for supportive living), and, instead, focusing on the person's life. It also allows for the consideration of nonservice or community options and strategies, including "informal" supports.

In a housing and support approach, it is important to have access and availability to what providers often call "individualized services"; in other words, to have a unique configuration of services available wherever a person may live that is flexible enough to change as his or her needs change. However, the basic goal of a housing and support approach is not the development of the "service packages," but improvement in the quality of life of each person.

Organizations have used a variety of strategies to assist in the personal value change process and to eliminate the personal constraints individuals may bring to any decision-making process involving people with disabilities. Common strategies include the use of values-based training such as Frameworks for Accomplishment (O'Brien & Lyle, 1988) and PASSING (Wolfensberger & Thomas, 1983), or the use of techniques such as personal futures planning (see Racino & Walker, chap. 3, this volume) as a training tool.

Identifying Agency and Systems Barriers

The identification of facility-based characteristics and the analysis of the problems with the continuum provide one way to start identifying key points for agency and systems change within any given state to allow the possibility for people with severe disabilities to live in their "own homes." Because each state is unique, the change process needs to start with an analysis within each state versus the use of standard solutions such as new program development or new legislation across the states.

By planning together with a small number of individuals (five or six) about their futures, it is possible to identify a series of changes in state-specific regulations, legislation, policy, financing, and training that would facilitate people obtaining the supports they need and want to live in their "own homes." Because the systems are all constructed on models reflecting old assumptions about people with disabilities, often layers of barriers are in place and need to be overcome, particularly in the "well-developed" systems. For example, changing a state disability policy on home living will not address issues about nursing practices acts that cover who can provide "medical" services. Changing foster care policies so adults can invite a provider into their home may uncover disincentives with IRS tax policies.

This approach to change reflects a "bottom up" approach, starting from the point of view of the person with a disability and his or her definition and experience of the system. Of course, a "bottom up" approach does not imply that each problem must be worked through on a person-by-person basis. It also does not relieve state and federal leadership personnel from their responsibilities. However, a series of individualized plans can be used to identify a range of systemic problems, such as the list in Chapter 1 that summarizes issues and barriers in housing and support.

Whereas in some ways it is ironic to promote the concepts of home and supports through the language of systems, the lives of many people with developmental disabilities are now inextricably tied to a service system that has driven how their lives are viewed and determined the options that are open to them. As a result, this book sometimes uses the language of that system, while also creating a picture of what it means to understand people with developmental disabilities as people first, and to view their lives as similar to our own.

Changes implied by a housing and support approach are very complex and involve all sectors of society. Many of the changes will take more than a decade, and all of us will need to be open to opportunities to make these necessary changes that will allow for more ordinary lives for people with disabilities.

BIBLIOGRAPHY

Arkansas Department of Human Services. (1988, May). *Waiver request Medicaid home and community-based services authorized by Section 1915 (c) of the Social Security Act, Alternative Community Services (ACS) Program: A community-based program providing alternative services to persons with developmental disabilities.* Little Rock, AR: Author.

Blystone, B., West, J., & Miller, T. (n.d.). *Supported Independence Program: Community services development.* Mt. Clemens, MI: Macomb-Oakland Regional Center.

Brown, F., Davis, R., Richards, M., & Kelly, K. (1989). Residential services for adults with profound disabilities. In F. Brown & D. H. Lehr (Eds.), *Persons with profound disabilities: Issues and practices* (pp. 295–331). Baltimore: Paul H. Brookes Publishing Co.

Brown, M.A., & Wheeler, T. (1989). Supported housing for the most disabled: Suggestions for providers. *Psychosocial Rehabilitation Journal, 13*(4), 59–68.

Bruininks, R.H., & Lakin, K.C. (Eds.). (1985). *Living and learning in the least restrictive environment.* Baltimore: Paul H. Brookes Publishing Co.

Carling, P.J. (1992). Community integration of people with psychiatric disabilities: Emerging trends. In J.W. Jacobson, S.N. Burchard, & P.J. Carling (Eds.), *Community living for adults with developmental and psychiatric disabilities.* Baltimore: Johns Hopkins University Press.

Center on Human Policy. (1985–1991). [Confidential field notes; organizational study]. Syracuse, NY: Author.

Center on Human Policy. (1989, May). *Policy institute 1989: Community living for adults summary.* Syracuse, NY: Author.

Center on Human Policy. (1989, November). *In support of adults living in the community.* Syracuse, NY: Author.

Center on Human Policy. (1990a). [Confidential field memos, Community Study]. Syracuse, NY: Author.

Center on Human Policy. (1990b). *The meaning of support in the lives of people with disabilities.* Proceedings of a Policy Institute on Support, Center on Human Policy, Syracuse University, Syracuse, NY.

Center on Human Policy. (1990, November). A home of their own. In B. Shoultz (Ed.), *Community living for adults* (pp. 1–2). Syracuse, NY: Center on Human Policy, Syracuse University.

Center on Human Policy. (1991). [Confidential field notes for policy study]. Syracuse, NY: Author.

Center on Human Policy, & Minnesota Department of Human Services. (1989, June). *Moving into the 1990s: Supporting individuals with developmental disabilities in Minnesota.* Proceedings of a planning retreat co-sponsored by the Center on Human Policy and Minnesota Department of Human Services.

Community Integration Project, Center on Human Policy. (1985). *Review of the literature on community integration: Report to NIDRR.* Syracuse, NY: Author.

Dever, R.B. (1988). *Community living skills: A taxonomy* (Monograph No. 10). Washington, DC: American Association on Mental Retardation.

Dowson, S. (1991). *Moving to the dance or service culture and community care.* London: Values into Action.

Florida Department of Health and Rehabilitative Services. (n.d.). *Developmental Services, Supported Living Project, Supported Independent Living Model outline.*

Ford, A., Davis, J., Messina, R., Ranieri, L., Nisbet, J., & Sweet, M. (1982). *Arranging instruction to ensure the active participation of severely multihandicapped students.* Madison, WI: University of Wisconsin-Madison and Madison Metropolitan School District.

Governor's Planning Council on Developmental Disabilities. (1987, January). *A new way of thinking.* St. Paul, MN: Author.

HCFA notifies CSLA winners. (1991, November). *New Directions, XXI*(11), 4–6.

Heal, L.W., Haney, J.I., & Novak Amado, A.R. (Eds.). (1988). *Integration of developmentally disabled individuals into the community* (2nd ed.). Baltimore: Paul H. Brookes Publishing Co.

Hill, B.K., Lakin, K.C., Bruininks, R.H., Novak Amado, A., Anderson, D.J., & Copher, J.I. (1989, December). *Living in the community: A comparative study of foster homes and small group homes for people with mental retardation* (Report #28). Minneapolis: Center for Residential and Community Services, Institute on Community Integration, University of Minnesota.

Hill, B.K., Lakin, K.C., Novak, A., & White, C. (1987). *Foster care for children and adults with handicaps: Child welfare and adult social services.* Minnesota: University of Minnesota.

Illinois Department of Mental Health and Developmental Disabilities. (n.d.), *Notice of proposed rules, Title 59: Mental Health, Chapter I: Department of Mental Health and Developmental Disabilities, Part 115: Standards and licensure requirements for community-integrated living arrangements; Subpart A: General provisions.*

Janicki, M.P., Krauss, M.W., & Seltzer, M.M. (Eds.). (1988). *Community residences for persons with developmental disabilities: Here to stay.* Baltimore: Paul H. Brookes Publishing Co.

Johnson, T. (1985). *Belonging to the community.* Madison, WI: Options in Community Living.

Knoll, J., & Racino, J.A. (1988). *Community supports for people labeled by both the mental retardation and mental health systems.* Syracuse, NY: Center on Human Policy, Syracuse University.

Koslowski, S. (1988). *Report on supported living workshop.* Hartford: Connecticut Office of Protection and Advocacy.

Lakin, C. (1988, December). *An overview of the concept and research on community living.* Paper presented at Leadership Institute on Community Integration for People with Developmental Disabilities, Washington, DC.

Lakin, K.C., & Bruininks, R.H. (Eds.). (1985). *Strategies for achieving community integration of developmentally disabled citizens.* Baltimore: Paul H. Brookes Publishing Co.

Landesman, S., & Vietze, P. (Eds.). (1987). *Living environments and mental retardation.* Washington, DC: American Association on Mental Retardation.

Lutfiyya, Z.M., Moseley, C., Walker, P., Zollers, N., Lehr, S., Pugliese, J., Callahan, M., & Centra, N. (1987, July). *A question of community: Quality of life and integration in "small residential units" and other residential settings.* Syracuse, NY: School of Education, Center on Human Policy, Syracuse University.

Missouri Department of Mental Health, Division of Mental Retardation and Developmental Disabilities. (n.d.). *Individualized supported living model.* Missouri: Author.

New York State Office of Mental Health. (1989). *Supported housing program implementation guidelines (draft).* Albany: Author.

O'Brien, J., & Lyle, C. (1986). *Strengthening the system: Improving Louisiana's community residential services for people with developmental disabilities.* Decatur, GA: Responsive Systems Associates.

O'Brien, J., & Lyle, C. (1988). *Framework for accomplishment: A workshop for people developing better services.* Decatur, GA: Responsive Systems Associates.

O'Brien, J., & Lyle O'Brien, C. (1991). Sustaining positive changes: The future development of the Residential Support Program. In S.J. Taylor, R. Bogdan, & J.A. Racino (Eds.), *Life in the community: Case studies of organizations supporting people with disabilities* (pp. 153–168). Baltimore: Paul H. Brookes Publishing Co.

Paine, S.C., Bellamy, G.T., & Wilcox, B.L. (Eds.). (1984). *Human services that work: From innovation to standard practice.* Baltimore: Paul H. Brookes Publishing Co.

Racino, J.A. (1988, March). Supporting adults with disabilities in individualized ways in the community. *TASH Newsletter, 14*(3), 4–5. [Reprinted in Racino,

J.A. (1989, August/September). Supporting adults with disabilities in the community. *Word from Washington,* 15–17].

Racino, J.A. (1989). *Individualized family supports and community living for adults: A case study of a for-profit agency in Minnesota.* Syracuse, NY: Center on Human Policy, Syracuse University.

Racino, J.A. (1991). Individualized supportive living arrangements. In S.J. Taylor, R. Bogdan, & J.A. Racino (Eds.), *Life in the community: Case studies of organizations supporting people with disabilities* (pp. 113–127). Baltimore: Paul H. Brookes Publishing Co.

Racino, J.A., & Knoll, J.A. (1986, September). Life in the community: Developing non-facility-based services. *TASH Newsletter, 12*(9), 6.

Racino, J.A., O'Connor, S., Shoultz, B., Taylor, S.J., & Walker, P. (1989). *Moving into the 1990s: A policy analysis of community living for adults with developmental disabilities in South Dakota.* Syracuse, NY: Center on Human Policy, Syracuse University.

Racino, J., Rothenberg, K., Shoultz, B., Taylor, S., & Traustadottir, R. (1988, October). *The service system's hidden places: Adult homes and room and board homes housing people with developmental disability and psychiatric labels in Onondaga County.* Syracuse, NY: Center on Human Policy, Syracuse University.

Racino, J.A., & Walker, P. (1988). *Supporting adults with severe disabilities in the community: Selected issues in residential services.* Syracuse, NY: Center on Human Policy, Syracuse University.

Ridgway, P., & Zipple, A.M. (1990). The paradigm shift in residential services: From the linear continuum to supported housing approaches. *Psychosocial Rehabilitation Journal, 13*(4), 11–31.

Rogan, P., & Racino, J. (1989). *Course outline for community services and systems change.* Syracuse, NY: Division of Special Education and Rehabilitation, Syracuse University.

Rucker, L. (1987). A difference you can see: One example of services to persons with severe mental retardation in the community. In S.J. Taylor, D. Biklen, & J. Knoll (Eds.), *Community integration for people with severe disabilities* (pp. 109–125). New York: Teacher's College Press.

Schalock, R. (1983). *Services for developmentally disabled adults: Development, implementation and evaluation.* Baltimore: University Park Press.

Shoultz, B. (1989, June). *Supporting individuals within their families or in homes of their own: The CAP-MR/DD Program in Raleigh, North Carolina.* Syracuse, NY: Center on Human Policy, Syracuse University.

Shoultz, B. (Ed.). (1990). *Annotated bibliography on community integration, revised.* Syracuse, NY: Center on Human Policy, Syracuse University.

Shoultz, B. (1991). Regenerating a community. In S.J. Taylor, R. Bogdan, & J.A. Racino (Eds.), *Life in the community: Case studies of organizations supporting people with disabilities* (pp. 195–213). Baltimore: Paul H. Brookes Publishing Co.

Smith, G.A. (1990, November). *Supportive living: New directions in services to people with developmental disabilities.* Alexandria, VA: National Association of State Mental Retardation Program Directors, Inc.

State of Minnesota Department of Human Services. (1987). *Home and community-based services waiver renewal request pursuant to Section 1915(c) of the Social Security Act for the period from July 1, 1987 to June 30, 1992.* St. Paul: Author.

Summers, J.A., & Reese, R.M. (1986). Residential services. In J.A. Summers (Ed.), *The right to grow up: An introduction to adults with developmental disabilities* (pp. 119–148). Baltimore: Paul H. Brookes Publishing Co.

Taylor, S.J. (1985). *Site visit report: Region V Mental Retardation Services, Nebraska.* Syracuse, NY: Community Integration Project, Syracuse University.

Taylor, S.J. (1987, July). *A policy analysis of the Supported Housing Demonstration Project, Pittsburgh, Pennsylvania.* Syracuse, NY: Center on Human Policy, Syracuse University.

Taylor, S.J. (1991). Toward individualized community living. In S.J. Taylor, R. Bogdan, & J.A. Racino (Eds.), *Life in the community: Case studies of organizations supporting people with disabilities* (pp. 105–111). Baltimore: Paul H. Brookes Publishing Co.

Taylor, S.J., Biklen, D., & Knoll, J. (Eds.). (1987). *Community integration for people with severe disabilities.* New York: Teacher's College Press.

Taylor, S.J., & Bogdan, R. (1984). *An introduction to qualitative research methods: The search for meaning* (2nd ed.). New York: John Wiley & Sons.

Taylor, S.J., Bogdan, R., & Racino, J.A. (Eds.). (1991). *Life in the community: Case studies of organizations supporting people with disabilities.* Baltimore: Paul H. Brookes Publishing Co.

Taylor, S.J., Lutfiyya, Z., Racino, J., Walker, P., & Knoll, J. (1986, June). *An evaluation of Connecticut's community training home program.* Syracuse, NY: Community Integration Project, Center on Human Policy, Syracuse University.

Taylor, S.J., & Racino, J.A. (1987, November). The clustered apartment model of services. *TASH Newsletter, 13*(11), 8–9.

Taylor, S.J., & Racino, J.A. (1987, December). Common issues in family care. *TASH Newsletter, 13*(12), 1, 4, 6.

Taylor, S.J., Racino, J.A., Knoll, J.A., & Lutfiyya, Z. (1987). *The nonrestrictive environment: On community integration for people with the most severe disabilities.* Syracuse, NY: Human Policy Press.

Taylor, S.J., Racino, J.A., & Rothenberg, K. (1988). *A policy analysis of private community living arrangements in Connecticut.* Syracuse, NY: Center on Human Policy, Syracuse University.

Turnbull, H.R., Turnbull, A.P., Bronicki, G.J., Summers, J.A., & Roeder-Gordon, C. (1989). *Disability and the family: A guide to decisions for adulthood.* Baltimore: Paul H. Brookes Publishing Co.

Walker, P. (1988). *Residential supports for adults with severe disabilities in Maryland.* Syracuse, NY: Center on Human Policy, Syracuse University.

Walker, P., & Salon, R. (1991). Integrating philosophy and practice. In S.J. Taylor, R. Bogdan, & J.A. Racino (Eds.), *Life in the community: Case studies of organizations supporting people with disabilities* (pp. 139–151). Baltimore: Paul H. Brookes Publishing Co.

Wisconsin Department of Health and Social Services. (1988). *Medicaid assistance (MA) community waivers manual.* Madison, WI: Author.

Wolfensberger, W. (1972). *The principle of normalization in human services.* Toronto: National Institute on Mental Retardation.

Wolfensberger, W., & Thomas, S. (1983). *PASSING: Program analysis of service systems' implementation of normalization goals.* Toronto: National Institute on Mental Retardation.

3

"WHOSE LIFE IS IT ANYWAY?"

LIFE PLANNING, CHOICES, AND DECISION MAKING

Julie Ann Racino and Pamela Walker

The real issue of personal support is: "Whose Life Is It? It's Still My Life!" Personal support means creating an environment where it becomes obvious I have gifts that are opportunities for other people. (Judith Snow, 1990, p. 4)

As Judith Snow explains above, the key question in personal supports is "Whose Life Is It?" In the disability field, issues, problems, and dilemmas are generally framed from the perspectives and interests of agencies and professionals. One major challenge is to bring to the forefront the viewpoints of people with disabilities.

This chapter introduces ways to move toward greater control by people with disabilities of their own lives. Specifically, this chapter discusses and highlights ways of understanding and getting to know people; how people have come together to plan and to challenge the narrow expectations for the lives of people with disabilities; critical decision-making issues in housing and support; and areas that service providers, planners, administrators, and others may face in joining in partnership with people with disabilities.

This chapter is based largely upon technical assistance work in 35 states, which included the use of life planning strategies, conducted between 1985 and 1991, and reviews of the literature on areas such as choice. Examples are also drawn from a national study of organizations supporting people with severe disabilities in the community.

The authors would like particularly to thank the following individuals for their work on technical assistance agreements on our behalf between 1985 and 1990: Wade Hitzing and Jack Pealer of Ohio, Karen Green-McGowan of Georgia, Beth Mount of New York, and Zana Marie Lutfiyya of the Center on Human Policy for their work on life planning; Gunnar Dybwad of Massachusetts, Cory Moore of Maryland, and Michael Kennedy, Susan O'Connor, and Bonnie Shoultz of the Center on Human Policy for their work on choices, decision making, and self-advocacy. Also, thanks are extended to Janet Duncan for her assistance in reviewing the literature on choice.

UNDERSTANDING WHO PEOPLE ARE

At the heart of a housing and support approach is a greater recognition of who people are in all their uniqueness and complexity. This section highlights the changing view of people with disabilities by society, the common experiences that people face, the importance of personal life histories, and the range of lifestyles of adults, including those with disabilities.

Historically, people with disabilities have been viewed in terms of being less able, different, and less valuable than other members of society. Often they have been defined solely in terms of their client role. Yet, people with disabilities have hopes and dreams, disappointments and sadness, and ways of understanding and relating with the world. They have a variety of capacities, interests, and commonalities with other community members. This is not to ignore that disability is a difference, but to bring to the forefront each individual's human complexity.

All people should be able to decide how they will live their lives. People with disabilities face the same decisions as anyone: the definition of self; the meaning of life; relationships with family, friends, and others who cross their path; daily routines and experiences; and opportunities that are seized, created, postponed, rejected, or simply let go.

Common Societal Experiences

People with disabilities also face other constraints in society. These include experiences of devaluation, medicalization, societal reliance on congregate and standardized care, and lack of choices.

Societal devaluation has resulted in people with disabilities being excluded from the mainstream of society. Defined as a burden, their disability has often been interpreted as a private social trouble requiring medical control and intervention. Social policy reinforces this perspective through the fiscal dominance of medical funding streams and of settings such as intermediate care facilities (ICFs) for people with mental retardation.

People with disabilities who rely on public support are at risk of congregate care, which tends to emphasize group over individual needs and segregates people away from society. Facing a pervasive lack of choices when forced to deal with service systems, people often need to exhaust personal, family, emotional, and financial resources in trying to obtain in-home services when they are needed. They may lose their legal rights or be placed in positions of forced choices, such as confinement at home without adequate supports or life in an institution.

Personal Life Histories

Whereas most people with disabilities share some common experiences, each person has a personal life history. In getting to know people's life histories, the following areas are helpful to consider:

Relationships with Others   By adulthood, people with disabilities may have a long history of relationships with families, people in the community, other people with disabilities, friends or acquaintances, and human services workers. These people, even if not currently in the person's life, form a network of past experiences that have influenced the person.

Places and Events   People experience a variety of places, sometimes institutional settings, schools, homes, stores, hospitals, recreation sites, and other community and human services settings. As with all people, certain places, such as where they grew up, may have personal meaning or memories.

Personal life histories include events that are important and meaningful to the person, such as birthdays. One man, for example, chose his own birthday because all records of this were lost in his institutionalization (Racino, 1991a). Events may be positive, such as a first job or award in school; or they may be negative, such as the death of a close relative.

Family and Personal Values and Heritage   People with disabilities hold a variety of values, including religious beliefs that influence their daily lives. Sometimes these philosophies are unstated but are reflected in a person's decision to rebel or be more passive.

People with disabilities, as with all people, are a product of a variety of influences, including gender, culture, and ethnic heritage. Whether through customs, beliefs, or traditions, they may wish to maintain certain traditions in their own homes. For example, when Thomas Salez[1] was growing up, he often listened to Arabic music with his Lebanese parents and sister. He still loves to listen and play drums along with it (O'Connor, 1991).

Personal Interests, Styles, Routines, and Tastes   People with disabilities have their own likes and dislikes, distinct personalities and styles, and personal interests and routines. Some people challenge the world boldly; others are cautious or gracious; still others may be private, quiet, or even reclusive. Some people may wish to dress conservatively, while others may want the latest styles.

Similarly, people with disabilities have their own preferred routines—when to go to bed, what to have for dinner, or when to eat. They also have preferences for how they spend their time, whether listening to a particular record, watching a sunset, or attending a sports

---

[1]All of the names of people used in examples are pseudonyms.

activity or cultural event. Derek Timmons, for example, follows movies and baseball, and is a Yankees fan. Although he has substantial physical disabilities and limitations in communication, everyone notices how excited he gets whenever his favorite team is ahead (Racino, 1991a).

For some people, their personal preferences will not be easily evident or well developed because of experiences such as institutionalization or living in facilities that have limited their exposure and opportunities to develop their own personal ways.

Disability and Socialization into Human Services   People with disabilities, by adulthood, often have a long history of interaction with the human services system, usually as first represented by the medical profession and schools. For some people, these interactions have affected their ability and willingness to trust.

People with disabilities, or those who care about them, are increasingly talking about the mental and physical abuse they may have suffered. Jerry Thomas, for example, paced all the time and vocalized loudly. His father explained that he had been kicked in the testicles so much during his stay in the institution that they had to be repaired surgically. As a moving target, he was less likely to be hurt (Racino, 1991a). These habits and experiences shade people's view of the world and must be heard, listened to, and to the extent feasible, understood.

A person's disability is also part of whom he or she is and accepting a person with disabilities means that these aspects of the person, whether incontinence, inability to walk due to a mobility impairment, or inability to read due to mental retardation, are acknowledged. Acceptance means accepting people for whom they are inclusive of the person's disability.

Lifestyles of Adults

Fundamental to understanding a housing and support approach is the belief that each individual person will relate with the world in a lifestyle that reflects his or her person as well as his or her interactions with others. One of the goals of services should be to assist people to live their lives in their preferred way. Whereas most adults live alone or with one other person, a variety of other alternatives also exist.

Although some would argue that this concept does not apply to people with the most severe disabilities, our low expectations and vision for people's lives and a "do whatever you want" attitude, which lacks genuine care and concern, have caused many of the major problems in their lives. Experience has repeatedly shown how often the disability field misjudges the capacities of people with disabilities (see Biklen's discussion of facilitated communication, 1990); therefore, it seems reasonable to start from a person first approach, acknowledging our incapacities to always determine what preferences, if any, the person has.

In thinking about community living for adults, it can be useful to examine a few possible lifestyles, including a variety of roommate relationships; living with parents or an extended family; marriage or other partner relationships, including children; and a variety of group living options, such as cooperatives, cohousing, or shared housing.

The relationships between adults and their roommates may vary tremendously. Some people may see each other as primarily sharing a physical place. Others may have a long-term commitment and share social routines and friends with each other. Still other roommates might develop joint routines, such as meals, food budgets, and rides to work, but keep essentially separate networks of friends. Each situation will depend upon the people involved and their changing life circumstances.

Some adults in our society continue to live with their parents. This is typically by their own choice, although these decisions may be highly influenced by life circumstances (e.g., finances, health of a parent). Adults with disabilities may continue living with parents because they have no other option or because the parents prefer this arrangement. In some cultures, adults may continue to live with their parents for most of their adult lives.

People with commitments to a similar lifestyle or cause sometimes choose to live together; for example, women's or "world peace" communities. Other options such as cohousing or cooperatives may offer the privacy of smaller places as well as opportunities for the closeness and support that a group may offer. These situations are typically based on common interests and can be multigenerational communities integrated by income levels, cultural and ethnic background, and disability. Whereas some adults may choose group living, one would not expect it to be the standard for people with disabilities.

Adults with disabilities have often been denied the right to marry and have children. In addition, parents with developmental disabilities are at high risk of having their children removed from their homes. Valued lifestyles for parents with disabilities and their children might include living in their own homes with support or temporarily living with other family members.

Some people will choose to live alone either temporarily or on a permanent basis. Single women, especially those who have disabilities, continue to be devalued, and written examples of single, healthy adult lifestyles are sparse. Living a valued single lifestyle may also mean opportunities to connect with other women for support, even if the actual living situation is not shared.

An important index of how much social control is exerted on people with disabilities is their option to participate in alternative lifestyles, such as gay and lesbian relationships, that are not generally accepted by mainstream culture. Discussing these controversial issues is important to understanding how agencies and parents are approaching issues of choice and support.

Elders are sometimes viewed as being unable to fulfill adult roles, and may be devalued in society and subjected to congregate care. It is important to look at a range of valued community roles and lifestyles when considering elders with disabilities rather than integrating them into segregated and devalued options.

APPROACHES TO GETTING TO KNOW PEOPLE

The process of getting to know each other is typically described from the perspective of an agency, which is trying to determine what, if any, services and help it is willing and/or able to provide or offer. In other words, the agency is in control of this process, which is an essential factor in understanding what occurs in these initial exchanges. The person with a disability is placed in the position of asking for help, and generally needs to be "grateful" for whatever is offered and given.

Comparing Approaches to Assessment

There are two primary types of assessment (i.e., the methods, techniques, and processes employed by agencies to get to know people) that are used in the field. Deficit-based and community assessments vary from each other in purposes, process, and design.

Deficit-Based Assessment   The most predominant form of assessment continues to be "deficit-based." Typically, there are three purposes for conducting such an assessment: 1) to measure a person's strengths and weaknesses in specific areas, 2) to determine whether the person meets an agency's entrance and exit criteria, and 3) to match individual characteristics and needs of the person to available services (Brost & Johnson, 1982). The results are then used to accept or deny people for services, place a person in a specific program setting or facility (e.g., day program or group home), and decide what skills they need to learn.

Community Assessments   In contrast, new approaches to assessment create a picture of the uniqueness of each person "in order to determine the forms of help the community needs to plan, arrange, provide, and monitor to meet his or her individual or human needs" (Brost & Johnson, 1982, p. 14). The assumptions underlying these new approaches to assessment include: all people can be served in the community if adequate supports are arranged, planning and supports must be unique for each person, and relationships with others are at least as important as learning specific tasks.

Typically, support organizations use some form of community assessments allowing their workers to get to know people as they go about their daily routines and community functions. This involves spending time with people in a variety of different places in the community and at home. In some, less formal, ways, these approaches build on the ecological inventories (Ford et al., 1984) that examine a person-environment match.

One note of caution is particularly important in thinking about community assessments. The underlying framework can still reflect a view of the world whereby people with disabilities come into contact with experts who will determine what they need and then "fix" their lives. In this approach, what is "fixed" might change (e.g., the number of friends), but the nature of the relationships with people with disabilities can remain unchanged.

Building Trust and Developing Relationships Another way to think about the process of people with disabilities coming into contact with agencies is to begin to view the situation from the person's point of view. For example, parents often have long histories of being undermined by the system and seldom believe that they are listened to or understood. When adults with disabilities start their interactions with agency workers, their life histories and previous interactions will influence these new relationships. The point called assessment can be a time to start to build trust, establish relationships, and form the groundwork of how people will approach problems, issues, and dilemmas together.

Learning About People's Preferences

In order to support people's lifestyle choices, agencies and others need to become more skilled in learning about people's preferences. The following are some strategies that have been suggested by individuals who are increasing their capacity to hear what people with disabilities are saying about their lives.

Listening Better Almost all people involved in a housing and support approach have said that the key is to better listen to people with disabilities, especially to what they want in their lives. As one person from New Hampshire (Racino, 1991a) described her work, "The most important thing is to really listen to what the people want [whom] we are providing support to." Listening means not only hearing what people want, but also acting upon those wishes and being in tune when things are not working.

Asking Another way to find out what the person's preferences and desires are, is simply to ask the person. At Project RESCUE, for example, staff members report that they begin by asking, "What would you like to work on that's important to you?" One staff member commented, "It's real hard to teach somebody something they don't want to learn" (Walker, 1991, pp. 173–174). Although it seems simple, many people with disabilities are seldom asked their opinions, much less have their responses taken seriously.

Spending Time Together For people who do not articulate their preferences, the agency may need to learn by observation and/or from others who know the person well. This will mean spending time together to figure out where and with whom a person may want to live, and drawing on the long histories of people who are committed to the person. People have many ways of indicating preferences—body posture, mood, or behaviors—although the preferences may necessitate a dimension of interpretation by others.

Creating Opportunities for New Experiences People may have had very limited experiences, which leave them undecided about their choices or what they like best. People who have never had many options in terms of choosing with whom to live may need to try out different things, such as living alone or with different types of people. Simply asking someone who has only lived in an institution whether they would prefer living in an apartment or a house makes little sense because they will not have the information to make this decision.

Expanding Opportunities for Communication One important development in the area of communication is the use of facilitated communication with people whose preferences were previously unknown. Through this type of support, people are able to communicate their preferences and have much greater input than most people ever imagined possible.

Making assistive technology for communication and opportunities to regularly use these devices available, can also increase people's opportunities for choice. In the Center on Human Policy's site visits across the United States, communication devices were often found to be in a state of disrepair, seldom used consistently across different life domains, and generally not used for communication with visitors.

Creating Safe Places for Speaking People with disabilities have many reasons to fear speaking up about what they want because they can easily be labeled as uncooperative, not ready, exhibiting behavioral problems, or incompetent to make informed decisions. A key aspect of promoting choice in daily lives is creating the space for disagreement and environments where it is okay to do so. People also need time to feel comfortable that their choices will be respected. For example, it took nearly 6 months before one man who spent most of his life in an institution felt comfortable taking a cookie from his kitchen counter.

A Person-by-Person Approach Each relationship must develop at its own pace; not everyone will experience the same degree of intimacy. Many issues need to be worked out about how people will build trust, create a mutuality, resolve problems with each other, and develop their relationship over time. Mistakes and misunderstandings are part of what occurs and should be considered a natural part of the relationship process.

Taking the Initiative   A person with a disability or their family or friends might gather together and invite one or two agencies to participate in a planning process, therefore helping the agencies construct the roles they might play. People with disabilities and their families can also make plans that seem suited to them, and then approach agencies to do their part (see Moore, chap. 8, this volume) or to respond more flexibly (see Racino, chap. 7, this volume). People with disabilities don't need to wait until agencies are ready to change; they can take the lead to make known what it is they want, need, and believe they have a right to expect. They can also pursue alternatives that do not involve existing agencies.

Learning Together   Staff, parents, and people with disabilities can help gather together the people who know the person—family, community members, friends, some professionals—to generate ideas with the person about places and people with whom to live.

LIFE PLANNING

Today, people are starting to come together in new ways to create a shared picture of a person's uniqueness, and to determine how all involved can help plan, arrange, and support a positive future for a person with disabilities. This is founded upon principles of choice, community participation, community presence, competence, respect, and valued social roles (O'Brien, 1987).

One of the most well-known tools or processes used by agencies to facilitate this change in vision is personal futures planning (Mount & Zwernik, 1988). Others include functional life planning (Green-McGowan, 1987), which is more commonly used with people with extensive medical needs, and the McGill Action Planning Systems (MAPS) (Vandercook, York, & Forest, 1989), which is used in schools. Although described differently, these types of processes are often part of the way agencies try to better listen to the people they support. Table 1 illustrates some of the ways support organizations describe these processes.

Personal futures planning, as described by O'Brien (1990), revolves around eight questions about the person's life, including the person's present life quality, environmental and personal influences on life quality, threats and opportunities to better life experiences, an image of a desirable future for the person, critical barriers to moving toward this desirable future, strategies for managing the barriers, next steps, and changes in the capabilities of service systems that could support such a personal future.

Personal futures planning is only one of many approaches to helping a group of people create a vision (Deshler, 1987), but it is an im-

Table 1.   Examples of life planning processes

Project RESCUE (Georgia)

Overall, in the development of goals and service plans, Project RESCUE staff members challenge themselves to figure out how best to help people acquire the things they want and desire to achieve. One of the ways they do this is by spending time as a staff "dreaming" with people about their needs and desires for the future and possible ways that Project RESCUE staff can help them work toward fulfilling these needs.

Residential Support Program, Centennial Developmental Services (Colorado)

To determine what kind of living arrangement would be appropriate for Mike, RSP organized a "life planning meeting." At this meeting, Mike and 19 people who know him shared their ideas; these people included family members, RSP residential support staff, his case manager, a few friends, his church minister, and others. Mike and Tim expressed an interest and willingness to live together, so the decision was made to look for a small house near the group home, so both men would be able to maintain contact with their friends there and continue to use community services and resources in the same neighborhood.

Residential, Inc. (Ohio)

The service planner does not just plan services; in fact, planning services may be the least important part of the role. Instead, the service planner makes at least a 1-year commitment to one or two people—although many have had much longer relationships—and assumes responsibility for assisting that person to attain and enjoy the "good life". . . Together, the person and the service planner create . . . a "vivid personal dream," a dream filled with details that are meaningful to the person. Then they work together to bring the dream to reality, including all kinds of people to share in the work.

From Walker, P. (1991). Anything's possible. In S. J. Taylor, R. Bogdan, & J. A. Racino (Eds.), *Life in the community: Case studies of organizations supporting people with disabilities* (pp. 171–183). Baltimore: Paul H. Brookes Publishing Co.; Walker, P., & Salon, R. (1991). Integrating philosophy and practice. In S. J. Taylor, R. Bogdan & J. A. Racino (Eds.), *Life in the community: Case studies of organizations supporting people with disabilities* (pp. 139–151). Baltimore: Paul H. Brookes Publishing Co.; and Shoultz, B. (1991). Regenerating a community. In S. J. Taylor, R. Bogdan, & J. A. Racino (Eds.), *Life in the community: Case studies of organizations supporting people with disabilities* (pp. 195–213). Baltimore: Paul H. Brookes Publishing Co. Reprinted by permission.

portant tool because it: 1) helps people confront the fact that not all issues can or should be addressed through services; 2) vividly creates a picture of the individual as a person first; 3) builds on the creativity and resourcefulness of the group; 4) places decisionmaking back into the hands of the person with a disability and the people close to the person; and 5) changes the fundamental question from, "How does the person need to change?" to "What can we all do to support these positive developments in the person's life?"

Emerging Issues in Life Planning

As experiences with life-planning processes have occurred across North America, with some small examples now in almost every state, the following comments are important to keep in mind:

Life Planning Will Take Time To Do Well   It is important to remember that usually none of the participants, including the facilitator, have had practice with this approach; the system still doesn't support this approach; participants may have limited capacity to respond immediately to what people want because of the multiple barriers that exist; and participants need to spend time building trust and working relationships with each other.

Life Planning Is Not Another Form of an Individualized Service Plan While the format of a life-planning approach may be followed, substantive issues such as power sharing, personal commitment to the person with a disability, and creativity are sometimes bypassed, thus undermining the process. In addition, if a life-planning process is rigidly and standardly applied across all people, or if the agency maintains control of all aspects, it will become another form of an individualized service plan.

Life-Planning Processes Provide Opportunities for Greater Involvement by People with Disabilities Life-planning processes increase the involvement of people with disabilities and others in their lives, but they remain primarily agency-determined in structure and participation. Materials that start from the perspective of the person are now beginning to appear (e.g., People First of Washington, n.d.). This includes such areas as how and if a person wants to establish a team or circle to support them, or if the person prefers a more person-to-person form of support.

The person's power and control are also limited by existing constraints such as their own poverty, limited life experience and knowledge of options, and the predominance of others (whether professionals or family and friends) who are all taking part in the decisions and may be making "best guesses" or exercising safety and caution as they contribute to the decision-making process.

Life Planning Is Not a Replacement for Committed Family Members, Friends, and Advocates Some agencies have found that even when using a life-planning process, those people whose "dreams" tend to be fulfilled or who have more positive, significant changes in their lives, tend to be those who are either vocal, persistent, or have a person(s) who is committed as their personal advocate. Consequently, it is recommended if a person does not have anyone who is personally committed to him or her, the first step must be to identify and support such a personal relationship (O'Brien & Lyle O'Brien, 1991).

Life Planning Is a Tool for Helping People To Change the Way They Think About and Approach a Vision of Life for People with Disabilities This is particularly important in moving to a "housing and support" approach that challenges "taken-for-granted" assumptions and encourages human services personnel and others to see the same range of possibilities in the lives of people with severe disabilities as they do in their own. It can be an opportunity for personal change for all the individuals involved; it is this personal change in how people with disabilities are viewed and approached that is essential. As Bogdan and Taylor (1987) have said about integration, once such a vision has actually occurred and is part of the assumptions of how people relate with each other, there will no longer be a need for such a planning process, which will then seem artificial and contrived.

Life-Planning Processes Can Be Used To Identify Agency and Systems Barriers   Close attention to a handful of personal futures plans can provide a tremendous amount of information on the barriers that currently exist in meeting the needs and preferences of people in a local community, agency, or system. Even though people have used life planning as a starting point for a variety of endeavors, such as developing a housing cooperative or personal support arrangements, this approach can be used to identify broader systems barriers that others may also face. For example, while a group may come together and find a way to tap into foster care funds to support one person to live in a place that the person locates and rents, on a systemic level, regulations, financing, and so forth may need to be modified so that such an option could be more easily available to other people. Life planning does not relieve administrators and planners from this role of removing systemic barriers that keep people from obtaining what they need and want.

CRITICAL DECISIONS IN PLANNING FOR HOUSING AND SUPPORT

This section examines three major areas: increased personal choices through a housing and support approach, the distinctions in decision-making between the traditional residential services and a housing and support approach, and the use of guides in determining personal preferences.

Increased Personal Choices Through Housing and Support

One of the most critical aspects of a housing and support approach is its emphasis on choice by the person with a disability. When housing is separated from support services, opportunities for personal choice are greatly increased. These include choices in the types of housing, location of housing, living alone or with others, deciding with whom to live, the types of support, support workers, and how support is provided. Choices in housing are highlighted below and choices on support are highlighted in Chapter 3 of this volume.

Types of Housing   In most communities, people live in apartments, condominiums, houses, cooperatives, housing projects, or mobile homes, not in specially built facilities designed or remodeled for groups of people with similar needs. People with severe disabilities should have the same range of typical housing options available to them as other community members, and any of these housing options could be called home for a particular person who chooses that style or type.

Location of Housing Homes should be in localities that make sense for the people who live in them. People have many rationales for choosing the neighborhood they want to live in. Some people want to live near family, their jobs, people they like, or particular kinds of community places or resources. Others may want to have some distance from particular people or prefer to live in sparsely populated areas where they have plenty of open space. People with disabilities should have choices about where in the community they prefer to live, and should be helped to find housing in areas that closely match their preferences.

For example, in Weld County, the Residential Support Program of Centennial Developmental Services assisted Mike and Ted to find a house in the same neighborhood as their group home, which allowed them the option to use the neighborhood shops with which they were familiar and where they were already known. Project RESCUE in Atlanta, Georgia, assisted a woman to find a one bedroom apartment, which she preferred over a studio, located near her grandmother so she could maintain close contact.

Living Alone or with Others Depending on factors such as racial and ethnic group membership, single adults in the United States sometimes live with one or two roommates of their choice or with family. Married people typically, although not exclusively, live in "homes of their own." People with disabilities, whether single or married, should be supported to live in homes by themselves, with roommates, with their parents or extended family, or with spouses, depending on their own interests and values. People making any of these choices should not face the risk of losing material support.

One of the most important factors for agencies to think about on this issue is the notion of choice as opposed to the application of a rule. One program, for example, formulated a rule that no one could live with more than one other person, thus reflecting the same way of thinking that resulted in the standardization of group home size.

Deciding with Whom To Live Some people have a clear idea about who they want to live with, if anyone, whereas others will need much more assistance with this decision. Sometimes a person may not know a specific individual they would like to live with, but may have some criteria for making these decisions. Some people will have strong preferences about whether or not they live with other people with disabilities. When help is desired, it is likely to involve staff thinking with the person about possible options, as well as inviting other people who know the person to assist with this process. The most important factor in people living together is a "good match" or compatible relationship between the people. Most people's economic situation may dictate that they share housing. However, with creativity and flexibility, agencies may be able to assist people who prefer to live alone to do so.

If a roommate will also be providing some support services (see Walker and Racino, chap. 4, this volume, for a discussion of this issue), the same types of issues about compatibility also apply. Considerations in selection might include: the age of the roommate, if this is important to the person with a disability; personal characteristics, habits, and needs of the roommate, and how compatible the people would be with each other; and shared interests, preferences, values, and living styles. Above all, agencies should remain flexible about possible roommates and involve the person with a disability in these decisions.

Comparing Decision-Making Processes for Residential Services

The traditional design of residential services and a housing and support approach vary on a number of different dimensions in the decision-making process. These include the content, process, and outcomes.

Content   Major decisions in the development of residential service programs include the size of the arrangement, the type of facility, the selection of the site, the level of disability, the number of staff, the general level of supervision, and the operating budget. These decisions require general information about the range of people who might reside in the facility. In a housing and support approach, all major decisions, including the housing and support plan, the budget, and the selection of roommates, if any, are based on information about a specific individual and important others in their lives.

Decision-Making Order   In the traditional process, significant decisions are made regarding housing and services before the person with a disability becomes involved. In the housing and support approach, no significant decisions are made without the person being involved. See Table 2 for a comparison of these two decision-making processes.

Decision Makers   In the traditional process, professionals decide on the types and locations of residential services and give the person a choice of existing alternatives based upon eligibility criteria. In a housing and support approach, the individual or their representative plays a significant role in determining the home location; the type of housing and modifications, if any; the support strategies; the roommates, if any; and the specific funding.

Decision-Making Process   In the traditional process, decisions are made by an interdisciplinary team based upon deficit-based assessments. In a housing and support approach, decisions are made on the basis of the person's direct input and community assessments, the func-

Table 2. Sample decision-making process

Facility based	Person centered
1. Community needs assessment	1. Assessment of individual's support and housing needs

2. Population
  −Level of disability
  −General supervision level (24 hour or less than 24 hour)
	2. Development of housing and support plan

3. Type of facility
  −Size of facility
  −Accessibility, special requirements
	3. Selection of support providers

4. Agency sponsorship	4. Selection of roommates (if any)
5. Fiscal negotiations for facility −Capital, start up, operating	5. Selection of specific home or apartment
6. Specific site selection	6. Negotiation of individual's funding
then	
7. Selection of specific people who meet eligibility requirements of facility	

From Racino, J. A., O'Connor, S., Shoultz, B., Taylor, S. J., & Walker, P. (1989). *Moving into the 1990s: A policy analysis of community living for adults with developmental disabilities in South Dakota*, p. 92. Syracuse, NY: Center on Human Policy, Syracuse University. Reprinted by permission.

tion of the team being to enable the person to meet his or her expectations.

Outcomes   The expected outcomes of the traditional process typically include an emphasis on increased scores on standardized assessments, the alleviation or remediation of skill deficits, or the capacity to move to a more inclusive environment. The expected outcomes in the housing and support approach focus on the quality of life of the individual based on decent community standards and determination by the individual.

Therefore, a housing and support approach represents a fundamental reordering of many of the aspects of the traditional residential services decision-making process.

Guides and Personal Preferences

Agencies, such as Options in Community Living (see Racino, chap. 5, this volume), have developed guidelines for their staff about what the agency wants to know about the people they support. Each question (see Table 3) is framed in terms of the person's preferences and feelings, and addresses key quality of life areas such as income, housing, safety, physical and/or mental health, appearance and/or hygiene, relationships with others, meaningful activities, mobility, and service provider issues.

Table 3.   A guide to what we want to know about people we support

Income

What are the person's feelings, preferences, comments about:
   a.   Options's involvement in budgeting/money management
   b.   Where he/she banks
   c.   The amount of money she/he has
   d.   The choices and decisions made about how money is spent
   e.   Changes he/she would like to make in how money is managed

Housing

What are the person's feelings, preferences, comments about:
   a.   Home
   b.   The neighborhood places (e.g., store, laundry, parks, and people)
   c.   Safety in the home/neighborhood
   d.   Landlord
   e.   The furnishings and belongings in his/her home
   f.   The choice concerning neighborhood, building, and roommate
   g.   Any changes she/he would like to make in her/his housing

Physical/Mental Health

What are the person's feelings, preferences, comments about:
   a.   Doctor, dentist, and other health care professionals utilized such as OT or PT (e.g., relationship, responsiveness, accessibility)
   b.   Current health status (e.g., weight, nutrition, exercises, smoking, medication)
   c.   Current mental health status (e.g., happy, depressed, upset, anxious)
   d.   The choices about which doctor or practitioners to use
   e.   Any changes he/she would like to make in these health related areas

Safety

What are the person's feelings, preferences, comments about:
   a.   Safety in the home
   b.   Knowledge of what to do in an emergency
   c.   Safety in the community
   d.   Any changes that would make her/him feel safer

Appearance/Hygiene

What are the person's feelings, preferences, comments about:
   a.   The way he/she looks
   b.   The way she/he dresses
   c.   The choices available about how he/she looks or dresses
   d.   Any changes she/he would like to make in appearance

Relating with Others

What are the person's feelings, preferences, comments about:
   a.   The relationship with family members
   b.   Friends (e.g., enough friends, a best friend, a boy/girlfriend)
   c.   Sexuality (intimate relationships)
   d.   Having people to do things with
   e.   The choices about who to spend time with
   f.   Any changes she/he would like to make in personal relationships

Meaningful Activities

What are the person's feelings, preferences, comments about:
   a.   Job (e.g., money, hours, type of work)
   b.   Recreational activities in and out of home

(continued)

Table 3.   (continued)

   c. Choices about work and recreational activities
   d. Any changes he/she would like to make in what is done

Mobility

What are the person's feelings, preferences, comments about:
   a. Method of transportation
   b. The ability to get to places he/she wants to go
   c. Adaptations (e.g., canes, walker, wheelchair) necessary to facilitate mobility
   d. The transportation choices available
   e. Any changes she/he would like to make

Service Provider Issues

What are the person's feelings, preferences, comments about:
   a. Attendant, paid roommate, or other direct service staff
   b. Options's services (choices about services, how it is provided)
   c. Other services received (e.g., vocational)

Options in Community Living. (1991). *A guide to what we want to know about people we support* (draft). Madison, WI: Author; reprinted by permission.

Florida's supportive independent living project (Florida Department of Health and Rehabilitative Services, 1989) provides another example of the kinds of areas that both people with disabilities and the agencies will want to consider in supporting people in their own homes. These include supports, community integration, housing, finances, use of guidelines, personal issues, and assumptions about agency roles.

In addition, there are several important issues to reflect on in deciding about the use of guidelines. While a guideline might be a helpful way to assist a new worker in becoming secure, the use of such guidelines is not necessarily a good way to talk with people about their lives. In particular, most people do not think in terms of words such as support, but respond better to regular conversation.

While people may be used to agencies intruding into their personal lives, some degree of intimacy and trust needs to be developed before personal areas are explored. It is inappropriate to do so in initial visits and meetings with people unless they raise these issues themselves. Guidelines often give the appearance that agencies will be responsible for addressing all these issues. In a number of situations, other community organizations or people, including the individual with a disability, may instead wish to assume some of these roles.

ISSUES AND DILEMMAS IN CHOICE

All people, no matter how severe their perceived disability, should be considered as having preferences. Because the issue of choice is fundamental to understanding a housing and support approach, the following discussion highlights some critical issues and dilemmas that continue to arise.

People with disabilities have been neglected, abused, and harmed in the name of choice. Choice is not a rationale for leaving people in conditions of poverty, hunger, or serious danger (O'Brien & Lyle O'Brien, 1991). As Judith Heumann explains in Chapter 11, even an expressed wish to die is often a cry for decent living.

Safeguarding efforts, however, can be a way of imposing middle class, mainstream cultural values and moral beliefs. People who are poor or relatively powerless in a culture are often subjected to standards and values that are considered a choice for others in society. The more a person's cultural and ethnic background and social class vary from the "norm," the more at risk the person is for such value imposition. In general, people with disabilities are held to stricter standards than others in our society.

Discussions about choice and safeguarding generally start with the presumption of incompetence or devaluation on the part of people with developmental disabilities, particularly mental retardation. Seldom is grave concern expressed about the extensive harm that can be caused by the curtailment of individual freedom. Current beliefs and processes also make it relatively easy for people with mental retardation to be judged incompetent to manage their affairs. In the same vein, parental choice often becomes confused with the choices of their adult children.

Agency accountability needs will, at times, conflict with personal choice. One of the reasons that people need personal advocates is because there are inherent conflicts between the interests of agencies and those of people with disabilities. While agencies can strive to minimize this conflict by placing people first in their decisions, this conflict remains and requires that safeguards be in place outside of the agency. It also means that any mechanism, including vouchers, that flow through an agency must be closely examined. Sometimes, simply distinguishing between the perspectives of an agency and the person instead of claiming that the agency view is in the person's best interest can create dialogue to discover other alternatives.

Choice in the lives of people with disabilities is currently being translated into a form of consumerism where services are "individually packaged" and one "shops and buys" both services and workers. This approach perpetuates the market view of people's lives, already predominant in some states, and detracts attention from the issue of the nature of relationships, power, and societal structures that can increase acceptance and support the opportunities for a range of lifestyle choices.

Personal choices are a part of day-to-day living for all of us, including people with disabilities. Self-advocacy, in contrast, is usually a more formalized way for people with disabilities to come together in groups for a variety of purposes, which can include social exchange, mutual self-help, opportunities for personal expression, and political undertakings. Participation in self-advocacy groups is also a matter of choice and agencies should not set up a "readiness continuum" for such participation.

Choice also must occur in the context of the relationships people have with each other and the mutual and shared decision making such relationships imply. Whereas a housing and support approach implies control of one's own life, such personal empowerment does not imply power over another person. The dynamics between personal empowerment and mutuality is a key issue today, not only in this approach, but in American society.

BIBLIOGRAPHY

Allan, Shea & Associates. (1988). *That's what friends are for: A guide for starting your own support group.* The NAPA Self-Reliance Project.

ARC of the United States. (n.d.). *Futures planning bibliography.* Arlington, TX: Author.

Atkinson, L. (1988). *Power and empowerment: The power principle.* Las Vegas: Falcon Press.

Baumgart, D., Johnson, J., & Helmstetter, E. (1990). *Augmentative and alternative communication systems for persons with moderate and severe disabilities.* Baltimore: Paul H. Brookes Publishing Co.

Biklen, D. (1987). The myth of clinical judgment. *Journal of Social Issues, 44*(1), 127–140.

Biklen, D. (1990). Communication unbound: Autism and praxis. *Harvard Educational Review, 60*(3), 291–314.

Biklen, D., Morton, M. W., Saha, S. N., Duncan, J., Gold, D., Hardardottir, M., Karna, E., O'Connor, S., & Rao, S. (1991). "I AMN NOT AUTISTIVC ON THJE TYP" (I'm not autistic on the typewriter). *Disability, Handicap & Society, 6*(3), 161–180.

Bogdan, R., & Taylor, S.J. (1987). Conclusion: The next wave. In S.J. Taylor, D. Biklen, & J. Knoll (Eds.), *Community integration for people with severe disabilities* (pp. 209–213). New York: Teacher's College Press.

Brightman, A.J. (Ed.). (1985). *Ordinary moments: The disabled experience.* Syracuse, NY: Human Policy Press.

Brost, M.M., & Johnson, T.Z. (1982). *Getting to know you: One approach to service assessment and planning for individuals with disabilities.* Madison, WI: DHSS-DCS.

Browder, D. (1991). *Assessment of individuals with severe disabilities: An applied behavior approach to life skills assessment* (2nd ed.). Baltimore: Paul H. Brookes Publishing Co.

Brown, S. (1991). *Independent living: Theory and practice* (draft). Oakland, CA: Research and Training Center on Public Policy in Independent Living, World Institute on Disability.

Center on Human Policy. (1990). *The meaning of supports in the lives of people with disabilities.* Proceedings of a Policy Institute on Support, Center on Human Policy, Syracuse University, Syracuse, NY.

Centre for Research and Education in Human Services. (1988). *Choices and obligations: A look at personal guardianship.* Kitchener, Ontario: Author.

Chamberlin, J. (1978). *On our own.* New York: McGraw-Hill.

Clark, P.G. (1988, September). Autonomy, personal empowerment, and quality of life in long-term care. *The Journal of Applied Gerontology, 7*(3), 279–297.

Coley, L., & Marley, R. (1987). Responding to the sexuality of people with mental handicap. In G. Horobin (Ed.), *Sex, gender and care work* (pp. 66–81). New York: St. Martin's Press.

Crawley, B., Mills, J., Wertheimer, A., Whittaker, A., Williams, P., & Bills, J. (1988). *Learning about self-advocacy series*. London: Campaign for Valued Futures for People Who Have Learning Difficulties.

Crossley, R., & McDonald, A. (1984). *Annie's coming out*. New York: Penguin Books Ltd.

Deal, A., Dunst, C., & Trivette, C. (1989). A flexible and functional approach to developing individualized family support plans. *Infants and Young Children, 1*(4), 32–43.

Deshler, D. (1987, Winter). Techniques for generating future perspectives. *New Directions for Continuing Education, 36*, 79–92.

Donnellan, A.M., Mirenda, P.L., Mesaros, R.A., & Fassbender, L.L. (1984). Analyzing the communicative functions of aberrant behavior. *Journal of The Association for Persons with Severe Handicaps, 9*(3), 201–212.

Driedger, D. (1989). *The last civil rights movement: Disabled People's International*. New York: St. Martin's Press, Inc.

Dunst, C.J., & Trivette, C.M. (1989). An enablement and empowerment perspective of case management. *Topics in Early Childhood Education: Families in Special Education, 8*(4), 87–102.

Dybwad, G. (1989, March). Empowerment means power sharing. *TASH Newsletter, 15*(3), 5, 8.

Ebert, G. (1990, September). *Panel presentation on "What are meaning, characteristics, and dimensions of support?"*. Policy Institute on Support sponsored by the Center on Human Policy, Syracuse University.

Edwards, J.P. (1982). *We are people first: Our handicaps are secondary*. Portland, OR: Ednick, Inc.

Florida Department of Health and Rehabilitative Services. (1989). *Supported living project: Supported independent living outline*. Tallahassee, Florida.

Flynn, M., & Ward, S. (1991). "We can change the future"—Self and citizen advocacy. In S. Segal & V. Varma (Eds.), *The future for people with learning difficulties* (pp. 129–148). London: David Fulton.

Ford, A., Brown, L., Pumpian, I., Baumgart, D., Nisbet, J., Schroeder, J., & Loomis, R. (1984). Strategies for developing individualized recreation and leisure programs for severely handicapped students. In N. Certo, N. Haring, & R. York (Eds.), *Public school integration of severely handicapped students: Rational issues and progressive alternatives* (pp. 245–275). Baltimore: Paul H. Brookes Publishing Co.

Fullwood, D. (1990). *Chances and choices: Making integration work*. Baltimore: Paul H. Brookes Publishing Co.

The G. Allan Roeher Institute. (1991). *The power to choose: An examination of service brokerage and individualized funding as implemented by the Community Living Society*. Downsview, Ontario: Author.

Green-McGowan, K. (1987). *Functional life planning for persons with complex needs*. Peachtree City, GA: KMG Seminars.

Green-McGowan, K., & Barks, L.S. (1985). *Assessment and planning for health professionals*. Peachtree City, GA: KMG Seminars.

Guess, D., Benson, H.A., & Siegel-Causey, E. (1985). Concepts and issues related to choice-making and autonomy among persons with severe disabilities. *Journal of The Association for Persons with Severe Handicaps, 10*(2), 79–86.

Hasazi, S.B. (1991). An exchange on personal futures and community participation: An interview with John McKnight and Ronald Melzer. In L.H. Meyer, C.A. Peck, & L. Brown (Eds.), *Critical issues in the lives of people with severe disabilities* (pp. 537–541). Baltimore: Paul H. Brookes Publishing Co.

Hayden, M.F., & Shoultz, B. (Eds.). (1991). Self-advocacy [Feature issue]. *IMPACT, 3*(4).

Houghton, J., Bronicki, G.J., & Guess, D. (1987). Opportunities to express preferences and make choices among students with severe disabilities in classroom settings. *Journal of The Association for Persons with Severe Handicaps, 12*(1), 18–27.

Illinois Planning Council on Developmental Disabilities. (1990, Summer). *Community Living Bulletin: Choice Issues.* No. 1.

Kapp, M.B. (1988). Forcing services on at-risk older adults: When doing good is not so good. *Social Work in Health Care, 13*(4), 1–13.

Kennedy, M., & Killius, P. (1987). Living in the community: Speaking for yourself. In S.J. Taylor, D. Biklen, & J. Knoll (Eds.), *Community integration for people with severe disabilities* (pp. 202–208). New York: Teacher's College Press.

Kishi, G., Teelucksingh, B., Zollers, N., Park-Lee, S., & Meyer, L. (1988). Daily decision-making in community residences: A social comparison of adults with or without mental retardation. *American Journal on Mental Retardation, 92*(5), 430–435.

Kittrie, N.N. (1971). *The right to be different: Deviance and enforced therapy.* Baltimore: Penguin Books.

Lord, J. (1984). The context of human services planning. In N.J. Marlett, R. Gall, & A. Wight-Felske (Eds.), *Dialogue on disability: A Canadian perspective. Volume I: The service system* (pp. 1–14). Calgary, Canada: University of Calgary Press.

Lord, J., & McKillop Farlow, D. (1990, Fall). A study of personal empowerment: Implications for healthy promotion. *Health Promotion,* 2–8.

Lovett, H. (1985). *Cognitive counseling and persons with special needs: Adaptive approaches to the social context.* New York: Praeger Publishers.

Manitoba Health Organizations, Inc. (n.d.). *Empowerment: A revolution in long term care.* Winnipeg: Author.

Matthews, G.F. (1983). *Voices from the shadows: Women with disabilities speak out.* Toronto: Women's Educational Press.

McKenna, C. (1986). *Self-advocacy in the lives of people with mental handicaps.* Thesis submitted to University of Manchester.

Miller, K.S., Chadderdon, L.M., & Duncan, B. (1981). *Participation of people with disabilities: An international perspective.* East Lansing, MI: University Center for International Rehabilitation.

Mohr, J. (1983). *Whatever you decide.* Venice, CA: Author.

Morton, J., Hughes, D., & Evans, E. (1986, Spring/Summer). Individualizing justice for offenders with developmental disabilities: A descriptive account of Nebraska's IJP model. *Prison Journal, LXVI,* 52–66.

Mount, B., & Zwernik, K. (1988). *It's never too early, it's never too late: A booklet about personal futures planning.* St. Paul, MN: DD Case Management Project, Metropolitan Council.

Nirje, B. (1972). The right to self-determination. In W. Wolfensberg, *The principle of normalization in human services* (pp. 176–193). Toronto: National Institute on Mental Retardation.

Nirje, B. (1985). The basis and logic of the normalization principle. *Australia and New Zealand Journal of Developmental Disabilities, 11*(2), 65–68.

O'Brien, J. (1987). A guide to life-style planning: Using *The Activities Catalog* to integrate services and natural support systems. In B. Wilcox & G.T. Bellamy, A comprehensive guide to *The Activities Catalog: An alternative curriculum for youth and adults with severe disabilities* (pp. 175–189). Baltimore: Paul H. Brookes Publishing Co.

O'Brien, J. (Ed.). (1990, October). *Effective self advocacy: Empowering people with disabilities to speak for themselves.* Minneapolis: Institute on Community Integration, Research and Training Center on Community Living.

O'Brien, J., & Lyle O'Brien, C. (1991). Sustaining positive changes: The future development of the Residential Support Program. In S.J. Taylor, R. Bogdan, & J.A. Racino (Eds.), *Life in the community: Case studies of organizations supporting people with disabilities* (pp. 153–168). Baltimore: Paul H. Brookes Publishing Co.

O'Brien, J., & Mount, B. (1989). *Telling new stories: The search for capacity among people with severe handicaps.* Lithonia, GA: Responsive Systems Associates.

O'Brien, J., O'Brien, C.L., & Schwartz, D. (Eds.). (1990). *What can we count on to make and keep people safe? Perspectives on creating effective safeguards for people with developmental disabilities.* Lithonia, GA: Responsive Systems Associates.

O'Brien, S., & Kelley, J. (1987). *Having a real say: A report on developing consumer participation within organizations for people who are intellectually disabled.* Australia: AMIDA Consumer Participation Project.

O'Connor, S. (1991). [Case study]. Syracuse, NY: Center on Human Policy, Syracuse University.

Options in Community Living. (1991). *A guide to what we want to know about people we support* (draft). Madison, WI: Author.

Orlansky, M., & Heward, W. (1981). *Voices: Interviews with handicapped people.* Columbus, OH: Bell & Howell Co.

People First of Washington. (n.d.). *People First self-advocacy goal: Participation in your individual service plan.* Tacoma, WA: Author.

People First of Washington. (1990). *A handbook for people thinking about moving.* Tacoma: Author.

People First of Washington, & Self-Advocacy Project, Rehabilitation Research and Training Center, University of Oregon. (1985). *Speaking up and speaking out: An international self-advocacy movement.* Portland, OR: Ednick Communications.

Perske, R. (Ed.). (1989). *Self-determination.* Minneapolis: Institute on Community Integration, University of Minnesota.

Perske, R., & Williams, R. (1984). *How we lived and grew together: An interstate seminar on self-advocacy for persons with developmental disabilities.* New York: InterServ.

Peter, D. (1991). We began to listen. In S.J. Taylor, R. Bogdan, & J.A. Racino (Eds.), *Life in the community: Case studies of organizations supporting people with disabilities* (pp. 129–138). Baltimore: Paul H. Brookes Publishing Co.

Peterson, N. (1981). *Our lives for ourselves: Women who have never married.* New York: G.P. Putnam's Sons.

Racino, J.A. (1988). [Macomb-Oakland and Wayne Community Living Services Supported Independence Program confidential field notes]. Syracuse, NY: Author.

Racino, J.A. (1991a). [Developmental Services of Strafford County, Inc., Dover, New Hampshire confidential field notes]. Syracuse, NY: Author.

Racino, J.A. (1991b). Individualized supportive living arrangements. In S.J. Taylor, R. Bogdan, & J.A. Racino (Eds.), *Life in the community: Case studies of organizations supporting people with disabilities* (pp. 113–127). Baltimore: Paul H. Brookes Publishing Co.

Racino, J.A., O'Connor, S., Shoultz, B., Taylor, S.J., & Walker, P. (1989, December). *Moving into the 1990s: A policy analysis of community living for adults with developmental disabilities in South Dakota.* Syracuse, NY: Center on Human Policy, Syracuse University.

Racino, J.A., O'Connor, S., Walker, P., & Taylor, S.J. (1991). *Innovations in family support.* Unpublished confidential research report.

Reichle, J., Mirenda, P., Locke, P., Piche, L., & Johnston, S. (1992). Beginning augmentative communication systems. In S.F. Warren & J. Reichle, (Eds.), *Causes and effects in communication and language intervention* (Vol. 1) (pp. 131–156). Baltimore: Paul H. Brookes Publishing Co.

Reichle, J., York, J., & Sigafoos, J. (1991). *Implementing augmentative and alternative communication: Strategies for learners with severe disabilities.* Baltimore: Paul H. Brookes Publishing Co.

Ridgway, P., & Carling, P. (1985). *A user's guide to needs assessment in community residential rehabilitation and community supports.* Boston, MA & Burlington, VT: Community Residential Rehabilitation Project, Center for Psychiatric Rehabilitation, Boston University, and Center for Change Through Housing and Community Supports, University of Vermont.

Rousso, H. (Ed.). (1988). *Disabled, female and proud! Ten stories of women with disabilities.* Boston: Exceptional Parent Press.

Salisbury, B., Dickey, J., & Crawford, C. (1987). *Service brokerage: Individual empowerment and social service accountability.* Downsview, Ontario: The G. Allan Roeher Institute.

Shoultz, B. (Ed.). (1989). *Community living for adults.* Syracuse, NY: Center on Human Policy, Syracuse University.

Shoultz, B. (1991). Regenerating a community. In S.J. Taylor, R. Bogdan, & J.A. Racino (Eds.), *Life in the community: Case studies of organizations supporting people with disabilities* (pp. 195–213). Baltimore: Paul H. Brookes Publishing Co.

Shreve, M., Spiller, P., Griffin, E., Waldron, N., & Stoltzman, L. (1988). *Consumer control in independent living.* New Hampshire: The Center for Resource Management, Inc., and the National Council on Independent Living.

Siegel-Causey, E., & Guess, D. (1989). *Enhancing nonsymbolic communication interactions among learners with severe disabilities.* Baltimore: Paul H. Brookes Publishing Co.

Sigafoos, J., Cole, D., & McQuarter, R. (1987). Current practices in the assessment of students with severe handicaps. *Journal of The Association for Persons with Severe Handicaps, 12*(4), 264–273.

Simon, B. (1987). *Never married women.* Philadelphia: Temple University Press.

Snow, J. (1990). *Panel presentation on "What is the meaning of support?".* Policy Institute on Support sponsored by the Center on Human Policy, Syracuse University.

Tanzman, B. (n.d.). *Researching the preferences of people with psychiatric disabilities for housing and supports: A practical guide.* Burlington, VT: Center for Community Change Through Housing and Support.

Turnbull, H.R., Turnbull, A.P., Bronicki, G.J., Summers, J.A., & Roeder-Gordon, C. (1989). *Disability and the family: A guide to decisions for adulthood.* Baltimore: Paul H. Brookes Publishing Co.

van der Eyken, W. (1991, September). Evaluating the process of empowerment. *Networking Bulletin: Empowerment and Family Support, 2*(2), 8–12.

Vandercook, T., York, J., & Forest, M. (1989). The McGill Action Planning Systems (MAPS): A strategy for building the vision. *Journal of The Association for Persons with Severe Handicaps, 14*(3), 205–215.

Vivona, V., & Kaplan, D. (1990, March). *People with developmental disabilities speak out on quality of life: A statewide agenda for enhancing the quality of life of people with disabilities.* Oakland, CA: World Institute on Disability.

Walker, P. (1991). Anything's possible. In S.J. Taylor, R. Bogdan, & J.A. Racino (Eds.), *Life in the community: Case studies of organizations supporting people with disabilities* (pp. 171–183). Baltimore: Paul H. Brookes Publishing Co.

Walker, P., & Salon, R. (1991). Integrating philosophy and practice. In S.J. Taylor, R. Bogdan, & J.A. Racino (Eds.), *Life in the community: Case studies of organizations supporting people with disabilities* (pp. 139–151). Baltimore: Paul H. Brookes Publishing Co.

Warren, C.A.B. (Ed.). (1981). New forms of social control: The myth of de-institutionalization. *American Behavioral Scientist, 24*(6), 721–846.

Weinburg, J.K. (1987, November). Aging and dependence: Toward a redefinition of autonomy. *Social Casework: The Journal of Contemporary Social Work,* 522–532.

Weinberg, J.K. (1988). Autonomy as a different voice: Women, disabilities, and decisions. In M. Fine & A. Asch (Eds.), *Women with disabilities: Essays in psychology, culture, and politics* (pp. 269–296). Philadelphia: Temple University Press.

Weiner, F. (1986). *No apologies: A guide to living with a disability, written by the real authorities—People with disabilities, their families and friends.* New York: St. Martin's Press.

Williams, P., & Shoultz, B. (1984). *We can speak for ourselves: Self-advocacy for mentally handicapped people.* Cambridge, MA: Brookline Books.

Williams, R.K. (1991). Choices, communication, and control: A call for expanding them in the lives of people with severe disabilities. In L.H. Meyer, C.A. Peck, & L. Brown (Eds.), *Critical issues in the lives of people with severe disabilities* (pp. 543–544). Baltimore: Paul H. Brookes Publishing Co.

Worth, P. (1989, May). The importance of speaking for yourself. *TASH Newsletter, 15*(5), 1–3.

4

"BEING WITH PEOPLE".

SUPPORT AND SUPPORT STRATEGIES

Pamela Walker and Julie Ann Racino

Everybody in this world today needs support of one kind or another. People need support to go ahead and do things whether this support comes from a good friend, parents, a social worker, or guardian. There is no person so independent in the world that they don't need anybody. We all need support, but with that support, we don't want somebody coming in and taking over our lives. (Michael J. Kennedy, 1991, p. 1)

SUPPORT

Although some excellent theoretical analyses exist (e.g., Bulmer, 1987), support has typically been discussed in the disability field in the United States by referring to several dimensions, such as paid and unpaid, or formal and informal. Yet, little information has been available on the practical level about the characteristics of formal and informal supports, the types of supports this refers to, their strengths and limitations, and the factors that might influence the relationship between them.

Human services workers tend to treat informal supports the same way they do formal services and to impose their agency roles and expectations on the community. Thus, the "interweaving of formal and infor-

This chapter draws largely on technical assistance work with states between 1985 and 1991, qualitative studies of organizations nationally supporting people with disabilities to live in the community conducted from 1985 to 1991, qualitative studies of the lives of individuals with disabilities and their families conducted between 1987 and 1991, and policy institutes on support held between 1987 and 1990.

The authors would particularly like to thank the following people who participated in our 1989 and 1990 policy institute on support: David Adler, Gunnar Dybwad, Lou Chapman, Cory Moore, Lynn Breedlove, Judith Snow, John O'Brien, George Ebert, Connie Lyle O'Brien, Judy Heumann, Frankie Lewis, Freeda Neumann, John Winnenberg, Gail Jacob, and Alex Henry, as well as other members of the Syracuse disability community, the Division of Special Education and Rehabilitation, and the Center on Human Policy.

mal supports" often results in the service system coopting the informal efforts, placing them under their control, or widening their net of influence in people's lives.

The term *support* is becoming popular in the language of the disability field. As Lynn Breedlove (1990), a strong advocate on behalf of people with disabilities, expressed at a 1990 policy institute on support, "The concept of support is not easy to dissect and break into parts. . . . With support, if the person doesn't experience the act as supportive, then the act was not one of support" (p. 10).

In thinking about the broad nature of support, the following is the view of one person who has been involved extensively in both self and parent advocacy:

> Support can be viewed in at least three ways: as an attitude, as a stance and in terms of the actions or form that support takes. *An attitude of support* involves a belief in people's judgment, as well as willingness to provide support when we disagree or think it will fail. *A stance of support* involves support from below, or acting as a supportive base, rather than guiding or controlling. It also . . . involves honesty and openness—to let the person you are supporting see how you feel, and know what your limitations are. *The actions of support* include: recognizing skills and abilities . . . listening . . . sharing feelings with the person . . . standing with the person, including taking risks together . . . the willingness to take criticism . . . the provision of physical, emotional, and intellectual support that does not unduly call attention to the person . . . not to cause harm; and helping only if it is wanted. Support is based on an understanding of people as people, on an understanding of the personal as well as technical aspects of helping, and on an understanding of the role of an ally or supporter. (Shoultz, 1990, p. 9)

Comparing "Formal and Informal Supports"

A basic understanding of the differences between informal and formal support will be critical as workers become more involved with people with disabilities in areas such as relationships, community associations, community places, and neighborhoods. Formal supports tend to be based on a bureaucratic mode of operation governed by rules and plans, whereas informal supports tend to be characterized by spontaneity and care based on personal ties versus instrumental reasons, such as performance of a job. Formal supports are often paid for and are provided by professionally qualified staff. Typically, when formal services are identified, examples include government and private social services agencies, and people in professional roles such as physicians and teachers. Informal supports are often equated with neighbors, co-workers, friends, acquaintances, and family.

Formal and informal supports often share overlapping characteristics. For example, a staff member may have a formal, paid relationship with an individual with a disability, but he or she can also develop a personal relationship that extends beyond the role of the job and continues over time. A neighbor may provide regular, formal help, such as telephoning each evening, perhaps even receiving some payment in return.

There are five trends regarding formal and informal supports, which are emerging in the field. First, disability organizations are beginning to encourage approaches that are less bureaucratic and provide greater opportunities for spontaneity to occur in the lives of people with disabilities. They are also encouraging relationships to develop between people with disabilities and workers.

Second, disability organizations are facilitating relationships between people with disabilities and community members. Sometimes this is pursued on what could be called "community" terms, based on an understanding of how communities function and how people associate with each other; and other times on "service" terms, expecting the community to abide by the bureaucratic rules and principles of service provision.

Third, disability organizations are entering into formal relationships with neighbors, co-workers, roommates, and others on behalf of people with disabilities. By entering into payment agreements and contracts with individuals, these roles and relationships may also be affected.

Fourth, community organizations and places are being approached to discover ways they can be supportive and accepting of all people, including people with disabilities. In neighborhoods, recreational places, or associational groups, ways of creating accepting and supportive environments are being explored by community members, sometimes in concert with disability organizations.

Fifth, people with disabilities, family members, and individuals who care about them, are coming together, sometimes through informal structures such as "circles of support." One function of these groups has been to attempt to influence the paid service system to be more responsive to the needs and wishes of the person.

While much is still unknown about the relationship of formal services and informal supports, government bodies and service agencies today are deciding how these will intersect. Without people outside the system monitoring and paying continued attention to emerging research findings, these well-meaning efforts could result in further intrusion into the lives of people with disabilities and a lessening of life quality.

Understanding the Concepts of Support and Supervision[1]

One of the important practical distinctions in examining the concept of support is to distinguish it from the residential services notion of super-

---

[1]Many of the ideas in this section are adapted from Taylor, S., Racino, J., & Rothenberg, K. (1989, January). "Supervision" in community living arrangements. *TASH Newsletter, 15*(1), 5–6.

vision. Commonly, in the United States, residential services fall into two general categories: those providing 24-hour supervision and those providing less than 24-hour supervision. Within a continuum-based service system, a recommendation that people require less supervision means that these people do not fit into licensed community living arrangements and are ready to move on to more independent living. The problem is defined not in terms of how the community living arrangements are staffed or supports are provided, but in terms of who should be placed where. This detracts attention from the basic question, "What support do people with severe disabilities need in the community?"

There are no simple solutions when attempting to resolve who needs "around-the-clock" support and who does not. However, whether a person will require 24-hour supervision will depend not only on the skills and characteristics of the person, but also on what other strategies are available besides on-site staff. The issue is not simply whether people may need some level of support, but how can support be provided in individualized and flexible ways. One of the major problems with current living arrangements is that support is often equated with the presence of paid, on-site, shift staff. As long as providers use shift staff as a matter of routine, many people will continue to receive more supervision than they need or is desirable.

Sample Decision-Making Framework   In examining the issue of supervision, it is critical that at least the following components be incorporated into the decision-making process:

1. A basic flaw in most processes is that staff ratios and supervision are determined separately from the individualized planning process. Decisions regarding supervision should be made in the context of the overall plan for the individual. There is no substitute for the reasoned judgment of those who have personal knowledge.
2. Another flaw is that they often use criteria unrelated to supervision needs to determine the level of supervision. Even though the lack of skills in areas such as eating and dressing may point to the needs for staff support during the course of the day, this is not necessarily related to supervision needs.

Table 1 provides one illustrative framework for determining the level of supervision a person may require. Although oriented toward nighttime support, it also could be used to make decisions regarding support required during the day. (This framework is not intended to be exhaustive [there are other considerations], but simply illustrative of some possibilities.)

Table 1. Sample decision-making framework for determining supervision and support

Step One

The person requires medical care or intervention during the night	**Yes**	Provide on-site support. Collect data and review on regular basis.
or	**No**	Proceed to Step Two
The person evidences behavior at night that if not immediately tended to would result in injury or harm to the person or others		

Step Two

The person is unable to recognize emergency situations or hazards.	**Yes**	Provide on-site nighttime support (staff or paid roommate). Collect data and review on a regular basis.
or		
The person evidences behavior at night that if not attended to within a reasonable period of time would result in injury or harm to the person or others.	**No**	Proceed to Step Three

Step Three

The person is unable to evacuate residence on his or her own.	**Yes**	Determine support strategy: 1. On-site nighttime support (staff or paid roommates) 2. On-call staff (nearby) 3. Paid neighbor 4. Emergency communication system—review on a regular basis.
	No	No nighttime support required. On-call support available.

Adapted from Taylor, S. J., Racino, J. A., & Rothenberg, K. (1988). *A policy analysis of private community living arrangements in Connecticut*, p. 84. Syracuse, NY: Center on Human Policy, Syracuse University.

SUPPORTING PEOPLE IN THEIR "OWN HOMES"

A housing and support approach is based on the philosophy that "whatever supports" are wanted and needed should be available, and supports should be individualized and flexible. Therefore, supports should be based on the individual's needs and desires, and should be able to be changed or altered (types of supports, levels of supports) without the person having to move.

Goals and Outcomes of Support

As implied by the continuum model, residential services have been directed to assist people to attain independence and to move to a more independent setting. People who were considered unable to do so might be consigned to an "indefinite" setting where very little was expected of them.

Today, some agencies are beginning to stress a different view—one of interdependence, which assumes that everyone needs some type of support in their daily life. For some people, this support will need to be long-term and ongoing, which should not preclude their opportunity to live in a home of their own. Whereas some people may never learn certain skills, they still can participate in the life of the community. For example, instead of spending inordinate amounts of time on tooth-brushing with a person who has been in these programs for most of his or her life, time can be better spent on opportunities to connect with other people in the community.

Individualized Supports

Each person needs and prefers a different combination of supports based to some extent on the range of existing informal supports in the individual's life and the lifestyle that she or he chooses to lead. Because disability is only one aspect to be taken into account, this approach is basically the same whether the person's primary disability is viewed as developmental disabilities, mental health, or head injury.

For one person, support may be provided by a paid roommate and other supplemental staff support, such as a paid attendant and relief staff. Another person may live in an apartment with a neighbor next door who provides nighttime emergency support as well as staff employed by a support organization who come in to assist with activities during the week. Yet another individual may share his or her home with one or more people, one of whom may be paid as a foster care provider. Table 2 includes three examples of individualized support strategies.

Flexible Supports

Flexible supports that can change over time as a person's needs change are critical to support people to live in their own homes. This can include changes in the type of staffing, the number of hours of staff support, or the specific people who provide support. For example, in Weld County, Colorado, when Lisa and Susan first moved into their apartment directly from the state institution, the agency had a staff apartment across the hall. However, over time, Lisa and Susan's situation changed so that 1) their skills and competencies increased, 2) new safety features such as speed dialing and emergency buzzer systems were available, 3) visiting nurses were able to provide certain services, and 4) they came to know neighbors who were now willing to provide some support. This example illustrates some of the different factors that can contribute to the number of hours of staff support needed or wanted.

Through Macomb-Oakland, Michigan's supported independence program, David was supported to live with a roommate, Alan. When the men no longer wished to share a home together, staff helped Alan find a

Table 2.   Examples of individualized supports

David Jeffries

David lives in his own apartment in the Midwest and obtains paid "come-in" support from agency-employed staff. He has two safety systems in his apartment. The FAST system is a button in his bedroom that rings at the medical center and contacts one of the four people on David's emergency list. If they are not available, an ambulance comes and the workers check the vial kept in his refrigerator. The vial contains emergency information including contact people and health data. David has a hearing impairment and uses a second emergency device called a silent pager. The telephone, fire alarm, and door are all programmed on this watch-type device that he wears on his wrist. The device shakes and a red light comes on next to the number so David can respond to the fire alarm, telephone, or door. His parents, family friends, relatives, and the landlord have good relationships with David and maintain close contact.

Ned Thomas

Ned shares an apartment in the Northeast with a "paid roommate" who provides emergency nighttime support. He also obtains ongoing day support from agency staff, whom he was involved in interviewing, hired specifically to work with him. He keeps in touch with his mother who is in a nursing home, and one of his brothers stops by when he is in town. Ned knows many of his neighbors and has relationships with several people at church and at the diner that he frequents.

Lisa Ayers and Susan Smith

Lisa and Susan share a wheelchair-accessible, two bedroom apartment in a Western state. A visiting nurse assists Lisa with her morning routine. Both Lisa and Susan have "primary" and "back-up" community support staff who spend time with them in their home and community. Once a week, a person from the local Association of the Blind comes to work with Susan. Both Susan and Lisa also have relationships with a variety of people, including Betty, the apartment manager, and two other women who live on the same floor, all of whom have agreed to be back up emergency contacts.

Adapted from Racino, J. A. (1991a). Individualized supportive living arrangements. In S. J. Taylor, R. Bogdan, & J. A. Racino (Eds.), *Life in the community: Case studies of organizations supporting people with severe disabilities* (pp. 113–127). Baltimore: Paul H. Brookes Publishing, Co.; Racino J. A. (1992). [Dover, New Hampshire field notes]. Unpublished confidential field notes; Walker, P., & Salon, R. (1991). Integrating philosophy and practice. In S. J. Taylor, R. Bogdan, & J. A. Racino (Eds.), *Life in the community: Case studies of organizations supporting people with severe disabilities* (pp. 139–151). Baltimore: Paul H. Brookes Publishing Co.

new place with another roommate, while David stayed in their old home. The agency was: 1) committed to supporting the people, not the specific place; 2) willing to invest the time and resources necessary for these changes; and 3) viewed their role as adapting to whatever changes the person was making in his or her life instead of life decisions being based on program needs.

Types of Support and How They Can Be Provided

There are many different types of support, some of which agencies may have a role in offering to the person. This section outlines some of these general areas of support services and some strategies to provide this support. Examples of types and areas of support include:

Live-in roommate
Support from a neighbor

Personal assistance
Peer support
Coordination
Adaptive equipment
Emergency back-up systems
Meals on Wheels
Homemaking and related tasks
Creating a family
Health care
Basic academic skills
Facilitation of decisionmaking and communication
Work related assistance
Appliances, home furnishings, and other goods
Income subsidy
Housing related assistance
Community connections, relationships, and social interactions

Live-In Roommate   Agencies may be in the position of providing live-in support. This might be a current agency staff member, someone hired by the agency, or a person who simply shares the home without payment. The most important area to address is that the people in the home be compatible and have what they view as a positive relationship with each other.

Support from a Neighbor   A neighbor may provide assistance, such as being accessible during the nighttime hours or being available in the event of an emergency. This may occur spontaneously as relationships develop, or the agency or person may specifically recruit a neighbor and provide some form of payment.

Personal Assistance   Traditionally, personal assistance has involved supports with a range of personal care needs, such as dressing, eating, bathing, toileting, positioning, and exercising. These tasks involve not only the physical work, but also the presentation of the individual as a valued adult member of the community. If a broad definition is used, personal assistance could cover a variety of different support services that promote involvement in home and community life. This could include assistance with daily activities such as leisure and work, assistance with speaking and reading, and safety and decisionmaking.

People with disabilities may hire, manage, and fire their own personal assistants with support; share responsibilities with other people, such as parents; or obtain these services through a home-health or support agency. Generally, people will be involved with several personal assistants to ensure back-up arrangements, which are a critical part of planning for personal assistance.

Peer Support   People with disabilities may want opportunities to share their concerns with people who have faced similar situations. This may include opportunities to freely associate with people with similar disabilities who share common experiences, assistance to identify and participate in community groups and associations that are concerned with related issues, and identification of other resources such as independent living centers that can offer a different perspective than traditional disability organizations offer.

Coordination   Arranging support services and communicating with the various agencies can take an inordinate amount of time and can be accomplished in a variety of different ways. Sometimes the person with a disability would like to do most of this or select someone he or she knows to assist them in these areas. At other times, he or she may prefer that some or all of these functions be done by paid support workers.

Adaptive Equipment   Another type of support is the use of adaptive devices or equipment, for purposes such as mobility, communication, safety and/or emergency devices, personal needs, and leisure interests. Some of these devices might be technologically sophisticated, but many are homemade, creative strategies, which may be as simple as use of a tape-recorded message. Telephones with programmed numbers, beeper or intercom systems, or a variety of generally available emergency devices have increased the options for people to have easy access to emergency services. The appropriate adaptive equipment gives people with disabilities, particularly those with severe disabilities, the ability to exercise more control and choice in their daily lives. Staff members' willingness to help people use this equipment is reflective of their willingness to support such increased control. Advocacy for funding of these devices is necessary, as is advocacy for repairs.

Emergency Back-Up Systems   In situations where a personal assistant or worker does not arrive or where unexpected breakdowns occur in transportation (e.g., one's wheelchair), emergency back-up systems need to be in place. The city of Berkeley, for example, has an emergency number that people can call to obtain such emergency assistance.

Meals on Wheels   Some people may want or need to look at alternatives to cooking all of their meals. Meals on Wheels, provided through formal organizations or through informal relationships, can provide a periodic option for obtaining nutritious meals without eating out or cooking in.

Homemaking and Related Tasks   Homemaking and related tasks include areas such as housekeeping, shopping, and banking. These are tasks that people may want to learn to do themselves, have someone else do for or with them, or make use of services available through commercial establishments (e.g., home delivery of groceries).

People may also need assistance to make their house into a home by personalizing their space; having some valued possessions that are not necessarily expensive items, but are personally treasured; and inviting others to visit. Assisting people with hospitality may also involve activities such as cleaning and cooking that can be accomplished through chore services, working alone, or with roommates and family.

Creating a Family   People with disabilities may need support within their home to create a sense of family and to acquire the social, personal, and technical skills for doing so. During courtship, marriage, and child raising, people with disabilities may need support to fulfill these roles within their home, if and how they desire.

Supports for parents with disabilities can include an array of family support services, including parent aides, homemakers, respite, technical and administrative support, recreation options for the child, support with education and medical services, and a range of other goods and services.

Health Care   People can access regular health services in the community, although help may be needed in advocating, scheduling, interpreting, and following through on health plans, and transportation. For some people, services such as in-home nursing may also need to be available; yet, many of these procedures can be taught to paraprofessionals or family and monitored by a health care professional.

Areas such as medication monitoring and administration of medications, including diabetes injections and medical procedures such as catheterization or tube feeding, can also be provided in a person's own home. In addition, many people can learn to monitor their health situation with support. Specialized areas such as mental health counseling, behavioral interventions, or assistance with drug or alcohol abuse can be obtained from a specialized service system or generic counseling organization, or they can be incorporated into the home environment.

Basic Academic Skills   Basic academic skills are typically taught through adult education programs, but they can also be taught in the context of daily living. Possible sites for learning these skills include cooperative extension, community colleges, adult literacy programs, adult education, and the YMCAs or YWCAs. Additional support can be obtained through disability specialists. For example, in Weld County, Colorado, the local Association for the Blind found someone to assist a person to learn Braille. In a locality where there are not many opportunities, people with disabilities may work with their allies to advocate for adult learning on a community-wide basis.

Facilitation of Decision Making and Communication   One of the most complex forms of support is assistance with personal decision-making. This includes assistance with one's legal rights in areas such as competency, independent facilitation to ensure that a person's wishes and needs are expressed and considered, and creation of opportunities for a range of experiences and choices in daily living.

Communication involves a variety of different types of support, including ways of positively including a person in conversations, especially when the person is "nonverbal." It may also involve assistance with communication devices and advocacy about those devices, as well as translating and interpreting the person's speech, gestures, and behaviors, particularly with strangers. It also means listening to the meaning of a person's behaviors and finding ways to respond to the requests and statements that these behaviors may reflect.

Work-Related Assistance People with disabilities may need support to discuss job and volunteer options, prepare for the work day, unwind from the events and stresses of the work environment, find leisure alternatives on holidays, and receive advocacy support for higher pay, better jobs, and more congenial work environments.

Appliances, Home Furnishings, and Other Goods People with disabilities often want basic goods as well as services. This may include helping a person to develop a credit history, obtain low interest loans, go to garage and house sales, or negotiate for exchanges or bartering agreements. In some cases, money that would have been spent on services could instead be allocated for goods that they may want and need to live a decent quality of life. One example is the purchase of a washing machine, which could allow a parent with a disability to spend time with his or her children and complete their homemaking tasks.

Income Subsidy Many people with disabilities live on low incomes and current government programs do not always provide adequate funding for basic needs such as food, clothing, and housing. Support may be provided by increasing the direct income of the person to meet their basic needs and advocating with and on behalf of people for changes in government policy to reflect this basic need.

Housing-Related Assistance Although housing should be separate from support services, support can be provided to assist people in locating or purchasing housing; signing leases; negotiating with landlords; arranging and paying for architectural adaptations; matching roommates; purchasing furniture and furnishings; obtaining housing subsidies; and advocating for change in local, state, and federal policies for accessible, affordable, and decent community housing.

Community Connections, Relationships, and Social Interactions People with disabilities often want to become more connected to neighborhoods and communities and obtain support to do so. This connectedness can be with family, friends, intimates, and community associations and organizations. Support may be needed in promoting a valued social role and in finding ways to contribute to communities. This means working from a belief that community members are willing to accept and include people with disabilities. Some community members may need some assistance or encouragement to do so; others will already have ways of including people with disabilities, although these efforts may be unnoticed, unrecognized, or undervalued by the traditional service system.

When and Where Supports Are Provided

When supports are individualized, people's daily routines fit their own rhythms and preferences. People can make individual schedules for the day, week, and year based on personal preferences, and can make spontaneous decisions about leisure activities. The severity of a person's disability has little impact on these decisions because a person can develop a personal schedule not dependent on group needs or an agency. People with disabilities and their support workers generally should negotiate, with support if needed, changes in personal schedules. Support services can be provided within the home and a variety of sites in the community ranging from grocery stores to libraries to sports arenas. Some people may prefer the same support worker at home, work, or a volunteer site whereas others would find this intrusive.

How Long Should Supports Be Provided?

As lives change, agencies and people should be prepared to assist for as long as necessary and adjust the level and types of supports to reflect the person's life circumstances.

Many people will need ongoing, long-term supports and it should not be assumed that the goal is to fade paid services. In fact, in places where services have been forced to decrease, two results are common: 1) providers may refuse to assist people with more severe disabilities to live in their own homes, or 2) providers may inflate initial costs to ensure adequate long-term funding.

For some people, it will be necessary, at times, to increase the availability of paid support services. This may occur because of changes in the person's life, in the lives of support workers or significant others, or changing situations in the environment. In these situations, agencies need the capacity to increase support hours and change support arrangements while still maintaining the person in his or her own home.

Initially, due to caution on the part of planners, supports may be more intense than necessary. For some people, supports may be reduced or formal paid services may be replaced with informal supports. Because agencies may be invested in replacing paid services with less expensive "informal services," people in the independent living movement have argued that paid services must be made available, and that decisions regarding the use of "informal supports" should be made by the person using them.

What Are Other Considerations in Support Strategies?

There are an infinite number of strategies that can be used to support people in homes in the community. In deciding on support strategies, the following considerations should be taken into account:

1. Adaptations can be used to assist with participation in activities. For example, people might use a stamp imprinted with their name to "sign" checks. A bit of creative thinking can also help; for example, in Weld County, one staff person made tapes of music and messages to assist a person to get through her morning routine.

2. Although people may need assistance with some activities, the relationship with the person assisting with these tasks and activities might be as important, if not more so. Therefore, in the course of routines, people may learn to know their neighbors, bank employees, store clerks, and others who are important in their daily routines.

3. Agencies have a tendency to find one solution that works well and apply it across the board to other people. Staff must actively work against this tendency, listening to the person and drawing on the creativity of all involved. For example, although it might be a good strategy to locate one apartment near the home of one of the staff members, this strategy should not be applied as a general principle.

4. Individualized does not imply that people should only live alone or with a paid roommate. Whereas many people may want to experience these options, agencies need to explore a variety of living situations comparable to those of adults in the community. Some people will want to live with several people, who may or may not be disabled.

5. Some people may prefer to obtain supports from different organizations; others may want the same organization to provide most services. The perspective of the individual person, including his or her need and desire for autonomy, security, personal confidence, and reliability will influence this choice.

6. During late adolescence, early adulthood, middle-age, and late adulthood, people may have different interests and needs. Age should not be used as a sole criterion, although consideration should be given to the effect age can have on the decisions of individuals.

7. Staff's attitude toward people and the trust that is built between them are critical in nurturing long-term, committed relationships. Staff must spend significant amounts of time gaining people's trust and developing a personal relationship.

8. One strategy for helping people develop community connections and relationships is to include them in staff's personal social networks, and use the staff's connections to identify other possible associations and relationships.

9. A small number of staff members who know the person well can help create support. More than one person in a support role protects the person from being alone if the one support person should leave. More than one staff member also provides variety and offers additional ideas for planning and decisionmaking.

10. If a person lives in poverty, issues of food, clothing, housing, shelter, safety, and securing more income may be priority interests.

11. People who are supported by organizations come from diverse ethnic, cultural, and racial groups. Support staff need to become familiar with the person's background and culture and seek to assist them in maintaining their heritage if the person expresses this desire.

PEOPLE WHO PROVIDE OR OFFER SUPPORT

Who Should Provide Support Services?

Supports can be provided by individuals employed by disability services, community or employment agencies, people employed by the individual with a disability, people acting on the person's behalf, a self-employed contractor, an individual who obtains services or goods in exchange for a subsidy, or a person freely offering support and services without reimbursement. Any approach to providing supports that sets up a standard staffing model (e.g., a supportive living coach for all people) limits individualization and flexibility and should be avoided. The key is to allow a variety of different options.

People providing supports may have a variety of relationships with a person with a disability, such as neighbor, relative, friend, family member, coworker, roommate, acquaintance, or other community member. Filling these roles, including that of family member, should not preclude people from being paid for personal assistance or other services. The choice of who will provide these supports should generally be left to the discretion of the person with a disability.

A court in Germany (Degener, 1991) decided that because women disproportionately provide personal assistance services within the family, denying payment to family members is equivalent to a form of gender discrimination. Issues of payment to family members are complex because there is a certain amount that family members typically do for each other. However, payment should be made available when family members perform activities beyond the typical scope.

Selecting Support Staff   People hired as support staff do not need special training or experience in the field of developmental disabilities. Even though this can be an asset, it could be a liability if it limits support staff's vision of what is possible for people with severe impairments who want to participate in community life.

People with disabilities, their allies, and their agencies are looking to hire support staff who are sensitive, compassionate, and committed to people, connected to the local community; energetic and creative; willing to listen to and learn from people with disabilities; and compatible with the specific individuals whom they will be assisting. The most important qualities in staff are the willingness to learn and the possession of values such as respect for the person, promotion of autonomy and choices, appreciation of people as individuals, and a spirit of mutual growth and learning.

People with disabilities, and at times their families, participate in the selection of staff. Some organizations, for example, may prescreen applicants and then involve the individual in the second interview. Some individuals with disabilities may develop and ask interview questions that are important to them. Yet, other people with disabilities may be present at the interview, even if they do not speak, to provide an opportunity for people who know the person to observe how the two people interact. Some people may hire staff directly and seek advice from an organization or others in their lives about what to look for in hiring.

Training and Supporting Staff   One valued and widely used method for staff training is modeling or mentoring by more experienced staff. This process can begin as early as the initial interview and be continued over the course of the staff's involvement with the person and/or agency.

People with disabilities and family members are also becoming involved in staff training with a growing assumption that training must be done by and for each individual. In contrast to competency-based training that is conducted irrespective of each individual, a person by person approach emphasizes learning about, from, and with each individual.

Values-based training can help staff to understand that the most important values in the lives of people with disabilities are similar to those of all people—friends, work, a job, a home, and family. On an ongoing basis, agencies or organizations can promote values through a variety of different mechanisms, such as participation in formalized values-based training, including Program Analysis of Service Systems (PASS), Program Analysis of Service System's Implementation of Normalization Goals (PASSING), and Framework for Accomplishment.

Organizations must invest in the support of staff. Staff members should know that their opinions matter and that they are respected both as people and for the contributions they make. Organizations can seek to empower the staff, to create a sense of ownership, to develop mutual trust and supportive relationships, and to maintain a participatory style of decisionmaking.

How Staff Roles Compare to Traditional Residential Roles

Traditionally, residential support staff have been viewed as direct service providers whose job is to carry out the individual's program plan, manage the household operations and routines, provide personal care, and develop caring relationships with all the people for whom they are responsible. Agency staff have related to people with disabilities in terms of a typical staff–client relationship, where the role of the staff member is to teach the person or do the caregiving. Thus, the staff person is the giver and the person with a disability is the receiver. The staff members who made decisions about people with disabilities were those who had the least amount of contact with them.

With individualized supports, the roles of residential support staff may be entirely different, even though some of the responsibilities and tasks may be the same. Agencies are beginning to reconceptualize the roles of staff. One agency may envision the essential role of support staff as discovering what the person wants and needs and assisting them to obtain it. In another agency, the support staff may "dream" with a person and support the person in realizing their dreams. Still another may speak of empowering the individual through support that encourages self- determination and control. The desired relationship is viewed more in terms of collaboration and mutuality where the person with a disability assumes a more directional role.

Throughout the field of disability, a number of trends are influencing the roles of staff, whether in residential, employment, recreation, or other areas. Figure 1 briefly highlights some of the current changes in the roles of staff.

From Professional Distance to Personal Relationships   Instead of promoting professional distance, support organizations speak of mutuality and reciprocity between staff members and people with disabilities. Personal relationship between staff and people with disabilities are encouraged and viewed as essential to working together. While it is acknowledged that not everyone will get along with each other, people with disabilities are viewed as having the right to support staff who get along with them.

From Service Focus to Informal Supports   Whereas service organizations have typically focused on the provision of paid services, greater attention is being paid today to the typical ways in which we all obtain

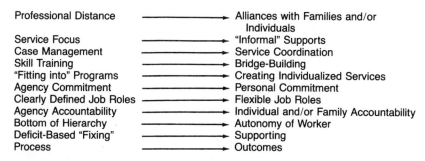

Figure 1. Changing roles of workers. (Adapted from Racino, J.A. [1990, December]. *Changing role of service workers*. Paper presented at the Annual Conference of The Association for Persons With Severe Handicaps, Chicago, IL.)

support. Whether through friends, family, co-workers, or roommates, organizations are exploring how people with disabilities can fully become a part of the community. Thus, staff need to understand more about communities, personal relationships, and other social network functions.

From Case Management to Service Coordination People with disabilities tend to dislike the term *case management*. Instead, service coordination implies conducting activities on behalf of an individual as opposed to something that is done to them. Many support organizations have internal roles similar to service coordinators. These typically are individuals who know the person well, try to meet their needs and desires, and who have authority in the use of resources on behalf of the individual.

From Skill Training to Bridge-Building The needs of people with developmental disabilities are often framed in terms of skill building. Today, it is more common for both management and support staff members to view establishing community relationships as part of their role. Staff members make efforts, both with and on behalf of the people they are supporting, to get to know neighbors, become known in local establishments, and participate in the community. One strong movement that emphasizes this changing role is *bridge-building;* Table 3 contrasts some of the assumptions between human services and community bridge building.

From "Fitting into" Programs to Creating Individualized Services Programs are generally designed so that people with disabilities need to somehow fit into them. Agencies are now looking at ways to start with the person first, and support staff are developing new skills to get to know people better and to assist in the creation of support options.

From Agency Commitment to Personal Commitment Most staff roles have required that people be committed first to the needs of the

Table 3.   Contrasting the basic assumptions between traditional human services and community bridge-builders

Traditional human services are breaking down because:	Bridge-builders seek to break old patterns by:
They often fail to support positive outcomes in the lives of people with disabilities.	Bridge-builders recognize and encourage the *capacities* and gifts of people with disabilities.
Traditional services focus on the disabilities of people with handicaps, and focus energy on the correction of these *deficits*.	Bridge-builders build community by establishing and *strengthening relationships* for people with disabilities.
Traditional services *segregate* people in congregate settings, and they *weaken* the natural ties people have to community life.	Bridge-builders often rearrange human service supports so people can live in their own homes, work, and contribute in community life.
Traditional services give power and decision making to professionals and other people paid to be in the lives of people, and all of these practices reinforce the *belief that community is rejecting, unsafe, and hostile* towards people with handicaps.	Bridge-builders learn to *take direction from people with disabilities* and the people who know them well.
These traditional service practices lead to *labeling, segregation, and dehumanization* of people with disabilities.	Bridge-builders believe in the *capacity of natural communities* to accept and include people with disabilities, and they believe that when community is responsive to one person, it becomes stronger for all of us.

From Mount, B., Beeman, P., & Ducharme, G. (1988). *What are we learning about bridge-building?*, p. 2. Manchester, CT: Communitas, Inc.; reprinted by permission.

agency and second to a group of people with disabilities. Support staff are now either directly working for an individual with a disability or making a commitment to the well-being of an individual. Whether the support staff is generally competent and caring is not as relevant as their personal relationship with the person they are supporting.

From Clearly Defined Job Roles to Flexible Roles   Instead of narrow job roles defined in detail by agencies, staff roles are becoming more flexible and responsive to the specific needs and requests of individuals with disabilities and families. These roles are defined in negotiations that include the person with a disability and the support worker and that may vary over time.

From Agency Accountability to Individual and/or Family Accountability   Although to a large extent support workers remain accountable to agencies, with personal assistance, support workers may be directly accountable to the individual. In addition, people with disabilities are included in assessing job performance, and in some places the primary criteria for job continuation is based on whether the support staff is best meeting the individual's needs.

From Deficit-Based Fixing to Supporting   Less emphasis is being placed on ways to "fix" people with disabilities and more emphasis is being placed on ways to support their participation and lifestyles. For example, support staff may acknowledge that incontinence is "part of who the person is" instead of seeing their primary function to "fix" this deficit so the person can be like everyone else. This is a particularly important orientation when incontinence is not manageable by the person.

From Process to Personally Defined Outcomes   Residential services have often examined the process that occurs (e.g., establishing a group home, passing site selection) as the sign of success. The focus of a housing and support approach includes constant attention to quality of life issues from the person's own perspective.

From Bottom of Hierarchy to Autonomy of Worker   Direct service staff have traditionally had the least power, seldom been represented, and taken direction from those in higher positions in the hierarchy. Greater credence is now being given to the importance of the individuals who work most closely with people with disabilities. They are the individuals who typically know the person best, who address the complexity of day-to-day life issues, and who are most intimately involved in critical issues.

Emerging Issues in Support Roles

This section highlights some of the current issues in the area of day-to-day "residential" support.

"Paid Neighbors" and "Paid Roommates"   Whereas organizations agree that the roles of "paid neighbors" and "paid roommates" are very different from paid staff relationships, they also are not the same as typical neighbors or roommates. One of the most critical issues to continue to examine is the nature of these relationships.

Some agencies actually refer to people as living alone when, in fact, they share a home with a "paid roommate." Fostering life sharing when payment exchanges hands is a challenge that will require efforts to promote the unique shared living that varies for every set of roommates. Ideally, relationships with neighbors should develop first and assistance with specific support, such as nighttime emergencies, should grow out of these relationships. Financial compensation may be offered because the assistance is more than what is typically expected of neighbors. Efforts must be made to make a "paid neighbor" relationship as comfortable as possible.

Foster Care in a Person's Own Home   Generally, state regulations for foster care or family care programs do not prohibit providers from moving into a home owned or leased by a person with a disability. This shared living alternative can be easily accomplished in most places because major changes are not necessary in regulations, undue attention is not drawn to the new option, and an existing financing mechanism is in place to fund basic costs.

Although this is a viable short-term strategy, many issues need to be addressed for the long term:

1. This option is different than traditional foster care where the person with a disability moves into the home of another; therefore, issues such as the exemptions from IRS tax payments for the support worker have not been addressed.

2. As state foster care regulations are modified, some "innovative" options have been treated more as traditional foster care situations, falling into parental and program patterns that are inappropriate for people living in their own homes.

3. Most payment systems for foster care tend to be based on levels of need and do not provide the individualization and flexibility characteristic of a housing and support approach.

4. Existing problems with foster care systems (as described in Racino & Taylor, chap. 2, this volume) are exacerbated by further confusion about the mission of foster care.

"Explicit" and "Implicit" Roles of Workers   Changing the explicit roles of workers to be more flexible and responsive to the preferences of individuals with disabilities may not result in any changes in the "implicit" or hidden roles. Although the new language may revolve around support and direction by the person with a disability, agencies still maintain the basic control and power in their relationships with people with disabilities.

If the emphasis within an agency is on living the "good life" as defined by the agency, workers may play the role of overseers, ensuring that people live their lives in accordance with these unstated agency rules. People from different ethnic groups, cultural backgrounds, races, or social classes would be at particular risk.

Workers may also enlarge the boundaries of their work beyond those agreed to by the person to offer input and comments beyond their defined scope. For people who are vulnerable, advice about areas such as sterilization and friendships can significantly and perhaps adversely affect people's lives.

Self-Directed Personal Assistance   Personal assistance schemes have typically been set up on the basis of three modes: 1) the independent provider mode where the person with a disability is in charge; 2) the agency mode where an organization, often a home health agency, selects, hires, and manages the personal assistance; and 3) a combination mode where a person with a disability may perform some of the functions, but an organization may perform others.

Whereas these three modes are also applicable to people with mental retardation, the field needs to move away from categorizing people as self-directing or non–self-directing. Instead, the focus should be on the preferred mode, which moves the power of selection from the assessors to the person with a disability and the people in their life. For example, under the independent provider mode, a parent, relative, or friend may assume the role that a person with a disability might have played, or work with the person to fill the coordination role.

Other emerging issues, including research on the nature of relationships and support roles, will continue to have many new implications for day-to-day interactions between support staff and people with disabilities. The key will be for everyone to remain open to learning from each other, and especially from people with disabilities, about what really matters.

BIBLIOGRAPHY

Baumgart, D., Brown, L., Pumpian, I., Nisbet, J., Ford, A., Sweet, M., Messina, R., & Schroeder, J. (1982). Principle of partial participation and individualized adaptations in educational programs for severely handicapped students. *Journal of The Association for Persons with Severe Handicaps, 7(2)*, 17–27.

Baumgart, D., & Ferguson, D.L. (1991). Personnel preparation: Directions for the next decade. In L.H. Meyer, C.A. Peck, & L. Brown (Eds.), *Critical issues in the lives of people with severe disabilities* (pp. 313–352). Baltimore: Paul H. Brookes Publishing Co.

Berkman, K.A., & Meyer, L.H. (1988). Alternative strategies and multiple outcomes in the remediation of severe self-injury: Going "all out" nonaversively. *Journal of The Association for Persons with Severe Handicaps, 13(2)*, 79–86.

Bogdan, R., & Taylor, S.J. (1989). Relationships with severely disabled people: The social construction of humanness. *Social Problems, 36(2)*, 135–148.

Bradley, V.J., & Knoll, J. (1990, November). *Shifting paradigms in services to people with developmental disabilities.* Cambridge, MA: Human Services Research Institute.

Braisby, D., Echlin, R., Hill, S., & Smith, H. (1988). *Changing futures: Housing and support services for people discharged from psychiatric hospitals* (Project Paper No. 76). London: King's Fund Centre, King Edward's Hospital Fund for London.

Breedlove, L. (1990, September). *Panel presentation on "What are the roles of allies and supporters?"* Proceedings of Policy Institute on Support sponsored by the Center on Human Policy, Syracuse University.

Brown, F. (1991). Creative daily scheduling: A nonintrusive approach to challenging behaviors. *Journal of The Association for Persons with Severe Handicaps, 16(2)*, 75–84.

Bulmer, M. (1987). *The social basis of community care.* London: Allen & Unwin.

Carling, P.J., Randolph, F.L., Blanch, A.K., & Ridgway, P. (1987). *Rehabilitation research review: Housing and community integration for people with psychiatric disabilities* (National Information Rehabilitation Center Review). Washington, DC: D:ATA Institute.

Center on Human Policy. (1989, May). *Policy Institute 1989: Community living for adults summary.* Syracuse, NY: Author.

Center on Human Policy. (1989). *A proposal for a Rehabilitation Research and Training Center on Community Integration for Persons with Mental Retardation by the Center on Human Policy, Syracuse University.* Proposal submitted to the National Institute on Disability and Rehabilitation Research, U. S. Department of Education, Washington, DC.

Center on Human Policy. (1990). *The meaning of support in the lives of people with disabilities.* Proceedings of a Policy Institute on Support, Center on Human Policy, Syracuse University, Syracuse, NY.

Chapman, L. (1990, September). *Panel presentation on "What are the roles of allies and supporters?"* Policy Institute on Support sponsored by the Center on Human Policy, Syracuse University, Syracuse, NY.

Condelucci, A. (1991). *Interdependence: The route to community.* Orlando, FL: Paul M. Deutsch Press.

de Balcazar, Y.S., Seekins, T., Paine, A., Fawcett, S.B., & Matthews, R.M. (1989). Self-help and social support groups for people with disabilities: A descriptive report. *Rehabilitation Counseling Bulletin, 33*(2), 115–158.

Degener, T. (1991, September). Untitled presentation at the International Personal Assistance Symposium, Oakland, CA.

DeGraff, A.H. (1988). *Home health aides: How to manage the people who help you.* Clifton Park, NY: Saratoga Access Publications.

Dixon, G.L., & Enders, A. (1984). *Low cost approaches to technology and disability.* Silver Spring, MD: National Rehabilitation Information Center (NARIC).

Donnellan, A.M., LaVigna, G., Zambito, J., & Thvedt, J. (1985). A time-limited intensive intervention program model to support community placement for persons with severe behavior problems. *Journal of The Association for Persons with Severe Handicaps, 10*(3), 123–131.

Ebert, G. (1990, September). *Panel presentation on "What are meaning, characteristics and dimensions of support?".* Proceedings of Policy Institute on Support sponsored by the Center on Human Policy, Syracuse University.

Emerson, R.M., Rochford, Jr., E.B., & Shaw, L.L. (1981). Economics and enterprise in board and care homes for the mentally ill. *American Behavioral Scientist, 24*(6), 771–785.

Ferguson, P., Hibbard, M., Leinen, J., & Schaff, S. (1990). Supported community life: Disability policy and the renewal of mediating structures. *Journal of Disability Policy Studies, 1*(1), 10–35.

Forest, M. (1989). *It's about relationships.* Toronto: Frontier College Press.

Forest, M., & Snow, J. (1983). The Joshua Committee: An advocacy model. *Journal of Leisurability, 10*(1), 20–23.

Gretz, S. (1988, September). About being a citizen. *The Developmental Disabilities Planner, 5*(2), 1, 4.

Hagner, D. (1989). *The social integration of supported employees: A qualitative study.* Syracuse, NY: Center on Human Policy, Syracuse University.

Hagner, D., Murphy, S., & Rogan, P. (1992). Facilitating natural supports in the workplace: Strategies for support consultants. *Journal of Rehabilitation, 58*(1), 29–34.

Halpern, A.S., Close, D.W., & Nelson, D.J. (1986). *On my own: The impact of semi-independent living programs for adults with mental retardation.* Baltimore: Paul H. Brookes Publishing Co.

Herman, S.E. (1991). Use and impact of a cash subsidy program. *Mental Retardation, 29*(5), 253–258.

Hitzing, W. (1987). Community living alternatives for persons with autism and related behavioral problems. In D.J. Cohen & A.M. Donnellan (Eds.), *Hand-*

book of autism and pervasive developmental disorders. New York: John Wiley & Sons.

Horner, R.H., Dunlap, G., Koegel, R.L., Carr, E.G., Sailer, W., Anderson, J., Albin, R.W., & O'Neill, R.E. (1990). Toward a technology of "nonaversive" behavioral support. *Journal of The Association for Persons with Severe Handicaps, 15*(3), 125–132.

Johnson, J.M. (1981). Program enterprise and official cooptation in the battered women's shelter movement. *American Behavioral Scientist, 24*(6), 827–842.

Johnson, T.Z. (1985). *Belonging to the community*. Madison: Options in Community Living and Wisconsin Council on Developmental Disabilities.

Jones, M.R., & Ulicny, G.R. (1986). The independent living perspective: Applications to services for adults with developmental disabilities. In J.A. Summers (Ed.), *The right to grow up: An introduction to adults with developmental disabilities* (pp. 227–241). Baltimore: Paul H. Brookes Publishing Co.

Kennedy, C.H., Horner, R.H., & Newton, J.S. (1989). Social contacts of adults with severe disabilities living in the community: A descriptive analysis of relationship patterns. *Journal of The Association for Persons with Severe Handicaps, 14*(3), 190–196.

Kennedy, M. (1991). [Personal interview]. In J.A. Racino, *Thoughts and reflections on personal assistance for people with mental retardation*. Paper prepared for the International personal assistance symposium, Berkeley, CA, September 1991.

King's Fund Centre. (1980, February). *An ordinary life: Comprehensive locally-based residential services for mentally handicapped people* (Project Paper No. 24). London: Author.

King's Fund Centre. (1988). *Ties and connections: An ordinary community life for people with learning difficulties*. London: Author.

Knoll, J., & Ford, A. (1987). Beyond caregiving: A reconceptualization of the role of the residential service provider. In S.J. Taylor, D. Biklen, & J. Knoll (Eds.), *Community integration for people with severe disabilities* (pp. 129–146). New York: Teacher's College Press.

Krauss, M.W., Seltzer, M.M., & Goodman, S.J. (1992). Social support networks of adults with mental retardation who live at home. *American Journal on Mental Retardation, 96*(4), 432–441.

Lambert, M. (1983). *Understanding social networks*. Beverly Hills, CA: Sage Publications.

Litvak, S., Zukas, H., & Heumann, J.E. (1987). *Attending to America: Personal assistance for supportive living*. Oakland, CA: World Institute on Disability.

Lovett, H. (1985). *Cognitive counseling and persons with special needs: Adaptive approaches to the social context*. New York: Praeger Publishers.

Lutfiyya, Z.M. (1990). *Affectionate bonds: What we can learn by listening to friends*. Syracuse, NY: Center on Human Policy, Syracuse University.

Lutfiyya, Z.M. (1991). "A feeling of being connected": Friendships between people with and without learning difficulties. *Disability, Handicap & Society, 6*(3), 233–245.

McKnight, J. (1987). Regenerating community. *Social Policy, 17*(3), 54–58.

McKnight, J. (1989a). *Beyond community services*. Evanston, IL: Center for Urban Affairs, Northwestern University.

McKnight, J. (1989b). *First do no harm*. Evanston, IL: Center for Urban Affairs, Northwestern University.

Meyer, L.H., & Evans, I.M. (1989). *Nonaversive intervention for behavior problems: A manual for home and community*. Baltimore: Paul H. Brookes Publishing Co.

Minnesota Governor's Planning Council on Developmental Disabilities. (n.d.). *Friends: A manual for connecting persons with disabilities and community members.* Minneapolis: Author.

Moon, M.S., Inge, K.J., Wehman, P., Brooke, V., & Barcus, J.M. (1990). *Helping persons with severe mental retardation get and keep employment: Supported employment issues and strategies.* Baltimore: Paul H. Brookes Publishing Co.

Mount, B., Beeman, P., & Ducharme, G. (1988a). *What are we learning about bridge-building? A summary of a dialogue between people seeking to build community for people with disabilities.* Manchester, CT: Communitas, Inc.

Mount, B., Beeman, P., & Ducharme, G. (1988b). *What are we learning about circles of support? A collection of tools, ideas, and reflections on building and facilitating circles of support.* Manchester, CT: Communitas, Inc.

Nisbet, J., & Hagner, D. (1988). Natural supports in the workplace: A reexamination of supported employment. *Journal of The Association for Persons with Severe Handicaps, 13*(4), 260–267.

Nosek, M.A. (1990). *Personal assistance services for persons with mental disabilities.* Houston, TX: Baylor College of Medicine.

Nosek, M.A., Potter, C.G., Quan, H., & Zhu, Y. (1988). *Personal assistance services for people with disabilities: An annotated bibliography.* Houston, TX: Independent Living Research Utilization, Research and Training Center on Independent Living at TIRR.

O'Brien, J., & Lyle O'Brien, C. (Eds.). (1992). *Remembering the soul of our work: Stories by the staff of Options in Community Living.* Madison, WI: Options in Community Living.

O'Brien, J., & Lyle O'Brien, C. (in press). Members of each other: Perspectives of social support for people with severe disabilities. In J. Nisbet (Ed.), *Natural supports in school, at work, and in the community for people with severe disabilities.* Baltimore: Paul H. Brookes Publishing Co.

O'Connell, M. (1990). *Community building in Logan Square: How a community grew stronger with the contributions of people with disabilities.* Evanston, IL: Northwestern University, Center for Urban Affairs & Policy Research.

Pearpoint, J. (1990). *From behind the piano: The building of Judith Snow's unique circle of friends.* Toronto: Inclusion Press.

Perske, R. (1988). *Circles of friends.* Nashville, TN: Abingdon Press.

Provencal, G. (1987). Culturing commitment. In S.J. Taylor, D. Biklen, & J. Knoll (Eds.), *Community living for people with severe disabilities* (pp. 67–84). New York: Teacher's College Press.

Racino, J.A. (1990, December). *Changing roles of service workers.* Paper presented at the Annual Conference of The Association for Persons with Severe Handicaps, Chicago, IL.

Racino, J.A. (1990). Preparing personnel to work in community support services. In A.P. Kaiser & C.M. McWhorter (Eds.), *Preparing personnel to work with persons with severe disabilities* (pp. 203–226). Baltimore: Paul H. Brookes Publishing Co.

Racino, J.A. (1991a). Individualized supportive living arrangements. In S.J. Taylor, R. Bogdan, & J.A. Racino (Eds.), *Life in the community: Case studies of organizations supporting people with disabilities* (pp. 113–127). Baltimore: Paul H. Brookes Publishing Co.

Racino, J.A. (1991b). Organizations in community living: Supporting people with disabilities. *Journal of Mental Health Administration, 18*(1), 51–59.

Racino, J.A. (1992). [Dover, New Hampshire field notes]. Unpublished confidential field notes.

Racino, J.A. O'Connor, S., Walker P., & Taylor, S.J. (1991). *Innovations in family supports.* Unpublished confidential research report.

Ratzka, A.D. (1986). *Independent living and attendant care in Sweden: A consumer perspective* (Monograph No. 34). New York: World Rehabilitation Fund.

Reinharz, S. (1984). Women as competent community builders. In A. Rickel, M. Gerrard, & I. Iscoe (Eds.), *Social and psychological problems of women.* New York: Harper & Row, Inc.

Rogan, P., & Racino, J. (1989). *Course outline for community services and systems change.* Syracuse, NY: Division of Special Education and Rehabilitation, Syracuse University.

Rusch, F.R. (Ed.). *Supported employment: Models, methods, and issues.* Sycamore, IL: Sycamore Publishing Company.

Sandys, J., & Leaker, D. (1988). The impact of integrated employment on leisure lifestyles. *Entourage, 3*(1), 17–23.

Shalock, R.L., Harper, R.S., & Carver, G. (1988). Independent living placement: Five years later. *American Journal of Mental Deficiency, 86*(2), 120–177.

Shoultz, B. (Ed.). (1989, November). *Community living for adults.* Syracuse, NY: Center on Human Policy, Syracuse University.

Shoultz, B. (1990). *Panel presentation on "What is the meaning of support?"* Proceedings of Policy Institute on Support sponsored by the Center on Human Policy, Syracuse University.

Shoultz, B. (1991). Regenerating a community. In S.J. Taylor, R. Bogdan, & J.A. Racino (Eds.), *Life in the community: Case studies of organizations supporting people with disabilities* (pp. 195–213). Baltimore: Paul H. Brookes Publishing Co.

Singer, G.H.S., & Irvin, L.K. (Eds.). (1989). *Support for caregiving families: Enabling positive adaptation to disability.* Baltimore: Paul H. Brookes Publishing Co.

SKIP of Maryland, Inc., & SKIP National. (1988). *Families to families: An introduction to the home care experience.* New York: SKIP National.

Smull, M.W. (1989). *Crisis in the community,* Alexandria, VA: National Association of State Mental Retardation Program Directors, Inc.

Snow, J. (1990, September). *The meaning of support as I experience it.* Presentation to Policy Institute on Natural Support sponsored by the Center on Human Policy at Syracuse University, Syracuse, NY.

Stack, R. (n.d.). *Technological adaptations to increase independence.* St. Paul: Minnesota Governor's Planning Council on Developmental Disabilities.

Stainback, S., & Stainback, W. (1990). Facilitating support networks. In W. Stainback & S. Stainback (Eds.), *Support networks for inclusive schooling: Interdependent integrated education* (pp. 25–48). Baltimore: Paul H. Brookes Publishing Co.

Strully, J.L., & Bartholomew-Lorimer, K. (1988). Social integration and friendship. In S.M. Pueschel (Ed.), *The young person with Down Syndrome: Transition from adolescence to adulthood.* Baltimore: Paul H. Brookes Publishing Co.

Strully, J., & Strully, C. (1985). Friendship and our children. *Journal of The Association for Persons with Severe Handicaps, 10*(4), 224–227.

Taylor, S.J. (1991). Toward individualized community living. In S.J. Taylor, R. Bogdan, & J.A. Racino (Eds.), *Life in the community: Case studies of organizations supporting people with disabilities* (pp. 105–111). Baltimore: Paul H. Brookes Publishing Co.

Taylor, S.J., Biklen, D., & Knoll, J. (Eds.). (1987). *Community integration for people with severe disabilities.* New York: Teacher's College Press.

Taylor, S.J., & Bogdan, R. (1989). On accepting relationships between people with mental retardation and non-disabled people: Towards an understanding of acceptance. *Disability, Handicap & Society, 4*(1), 21–36.

Taylor, S.J., Bogdan, R., & Racino, J.A. (Eds.). (1991). *Life in the community: Case studies of organizations supporting people with disabilities.* Baltimore: Paul H. Brookes Publishing Co.

Taylor, S.J., Racino, J.A., Knoll, J.A., & Lutfiyya, Z. (1987). *The nonrestrictive environment. On community integration for people with the most severe disabilities.* Syracuse, NY: Human Policy Press.

Taylor, S.J., Racino, J.A., & Rothenberg, K. (1988). *A policy analysis of private community living arrangements in Connecticut.* Syracuse, NY: Center on Human Policy, Syracuse University.

Taylor, S., Racino, J., & Rothenberg, K. (1989, January). "Supervision" in community living arrangements. *TASH Newsletter, 15*(1), 5–6.

Thousand, J., Burchard, S., & Hasazi, J. (1986). Field-based determination of manager and staff competencies in small community residences. *Applied Research in Mental Retardation, 7,* 263–283.

Traustadottir, R. (1991). *Supports for community living: A case study.* Syracuse, NY: Center on Human Policy, Syracuse University.

Ulicny, G.R., Adler, A.B., Kennedy, S.E., & Jones, M.L. (1987). *A step-by-step guide to training and managing personal attendants, Volume 1: Consumer guide; Volume 2: Agency guide.* Lawrence: Research and Training Center on Independent Living, University of Kansas.

Walker, P. (1989, November). *Family supports in Montana: Region III: Special Training for Exceptional People (STEP).* Syracuse, NY: Center on Human Policy, Syracuse University.

Walker, P. (1991). Anything's possible. In S.J. Taylor, R. Bogdan, & J.A. Racino (Eds.), *Life in the community: Case studies of organizations supporting people with disabilities* (pp. 171–183). Baltimore: Paul H. Brookes Publishing Co.

Walker, P., & Salon, R. (1991). Integrating philosophy and practice. In S.J. Taylor, R. Bogdan, & J.A. Racino (Eds.), *Life in the community: Case studies of organizations supporting people with disabilities* (pp. 139–151). Baltimore: Paul H. Brookes Publishing Co.

Warren, C.A.B. (1981). New forms of social control: The myth of deinstitutionalization. *American Behavioral Scientist, 24*(6), 724–740.

Wertheimer, A. (1986). *Images of possibility.* London: Campaign for the Mentally Handicapped.

Whitman, B.Y., & Accardo, P.J. (Eds.). (1990). *When a parent is mentally retarded.* Baltimore: Paul H. Brookes Publishing Co.

Wolfensberger, W., & Glenn, L. (1973). *Program analysis of services systems (PASS) 3.* Toronto: National Institute on Mental Retardation.

Wolfensberger, W., & Thomas, S. (1983). *PASSING: Program analysis of services systems' implementation of normalization goals* (2nd ed.). Toronto: National Institute on Mental Retardation.

5

"THERE IF YOU NEED AND WANT THEM"

CHANGING ROLES
OF SUPPORT ORGANIZATIONS

Julie Ann Racino

Unless staff members ally with the people they support to continually fight the negative effects of the human service(s) system, that system will crush the life out of all the people who rely on it for a living, both people with disabilities and staff people. (Options in Community Living, 1991, p. 79)

In the United States today, a massive system of community service providers has grown as state institutional populations have declined from 195,000 people with developmental disabilities in 1967 to 88,000 in 1989 (Lakin, 1991). Playing a critical role in the lives of people with developmental disabilities, these organizations control resources, often determine service access, and influence every area of people's housing, home life, and support services.

   This chapter sketches a picture of how organizations are striving to better support people with disabilities to participate in community life. It discusses the differences between traditional residential service agencies and support organizations, briefly describes how agencies organize to

   This chapter is based on qualitative studies of organizations, qualitative program evaluations, national telephone interviews with service providers, and technical assistance and training activities conducted between 1985 and 1991.

   The author would particularly like to thank the following people who contributed to the technical assistance work in states through consultations and study tours: Jay Klein, Gail Jacob, Sid Nichols, John Winnenberg, Jerry Provencal, Cheryl Martins, David Merrill, Terri Johnson, Nancy Rosenau, Julie Pratt, Lynn Rucker, Dennis Harkins, Marilyn Wilson, Steve Zivolich, and Pat Rogan. Thank you also to the following people at the Center on Human Policy who participated in telephone interviews with organizations nationwide: Ellen Fisher, Connie Barna, Jim Knoll, Pam Walker, Bonnie Shoultz, and Lori Gardiner.

provide support, highlights trends in organizational change, and raises issues agencies face in moving toward new roles.

RESIDENTIAL SUPPORT ORGANIZATIONS[1]

Options in Community Living, the Residential Support Program of Centennial Development Services, Inc., and Residential, Inc., are unique organizations. Each, however, is an excellent illustration of an agency that has significantly changed the way it supports people with disabilities. They are not perfect, but they are leaders in their willingness and ability to listen to people with disabilities, to stand with and by people, and to ensure that their actions match their values.

Options in Community Living (Madison, Wisconsin)

Options in Community Living provides support to 100 people, including some with severe and multiple disabilities, who rent or own houses and apartments throughout Dane County, Wisconsin. This private, nonprofit agency has moved away from a "clustered apartment" approach where people live in a cluster of apartments located in one apartment complex. Now, people live where they choose and with whom they choose (or by themselves) and receive supports at these locations.

Approximately 24 people served by Options employ live-in paid roommates or personal care attendants to provide full-time support, using a variety of Medicaid and state funding mechanisms. For these people, Options acts as a broker—assisting them to recruit, screen, hire, supervise, and, if necessary, fire their attendants. Options also provides support to about 75 people who do not require live-in assistance, but who may need intensive services and supports to remain in their homes. The agency has teams of "community support specialists" who provide support, case management, training, and other services.

The agency has chosen to remain small, and instead of expanding it has assisted in the formation of another agency to play a similar role within the Madison community. Options's 1985 book, *Belonging to the Community,* that describes their organization remains one of the best resources for agencies interested in learning more about this type of organization.

Centennial Developmental Services, Inc. (Weld County, Colorado)

The Residential Support Program of Centennial Developmental Services, Inc., provides support services to 56 adults with disabilities, in-

---

[1]The agency descriptions are adapted from Walker, P. (1990, August). Individualized supports for adults: Three residential support agencies. *TASH Newsletter, 15*(8), 12–13. Since the time of the site visits, each of these organizations has undergone numerous changes such as new team and management configurations.

cluding many who have significant impairments. This agency has moved from group home and clustered apartment arrangements to helping people live in their own homes with supports. The people, including those who have moved directly from institutions, live either by themselves or with others in apartments and houses; they receive significant, but varying, degrees of staff time and assistance.

Staff work in teams to assist people. Skills are taught within the context of typical daily routines and activities. A primary part of the staff role is to help connect and involve people in their neighborhoods and community. The agency tries to recruit staff who are connected to the community, and the staff then use their own connections to increase the social networks and relationships of the people they support. A strong sense of enthusiasm and spirit has been nurtured among the agency staff as a whole.

Residential, Inc. (New Lexington, Ohio)

Residential, Inc., located in a rural area in Ohio, has moved away from providing group homes and a semi-independent and independent living program. People supported by the agency told the staff that something was missing with the group homes and other residential settings. Based on this, the organization decided to work from the idea that people should have their own home—either by themselves or with others of their own choosing. Some of the agency staff joined together with other members of the community to form the Perry County Housing Association (see O'Connor & Racino, chap. 6, this volume), an organization designed to help promote increased opportunity for home ownership for all residents of the county.

The agency's administrative structure also changed. In the past, the staff who made major decisions about people's lives had little or no direct support experience with that person. The agency recognized a problem with this and changed to the use of "service planners." The agency emphasizes team support of people (trying to include at least one member of the team who does not work for the agency); helps people to maintain and expand their community supports; and assists people to learn and grow through relationships, rather than special programs. From this agency's perspective, a key factor in support and integration is finding people who are willing to make long-term commitments to others. A detailed case study of this organization is included in Chapter 13 of this volume.

COMPARING ROLES OF TRADITIONAL AND SUPPORT AGENCIES

In thinking about the roles of support organizations, it is helpful to first compare these organizations with traditional residential services as they

Table 1.   Comparison of service models

Options	Traditional residential services

Assumptions

Everyone can live in a home of one's own choice in the community, given appropriate support; no one should be forced to live in a segregated or congregate living situation based on the nature of his/her disability.

Readiness to live in a home of one's own in the community must be achieved in stages. Each stage or ability level corresponds to a different type of living arrangement. Because of their disabilities, some need to live in group homes, and others can live in apartments.

Readiness for living in a home of one's own in the community is not something that can be effectively predicted or produced by living in a protective, congregate, or segregated setting. People learn most easily when they have the daily opportunity and assistance they need to manage successfully in the actual environment to which they are trying to adjust.

Each living arrangement provides the training a person needs to progress to a new and different setting that will afford a higher level of independence.

The consumer of service is the best judge of his/her own needs and should direct his/her own life, make decisions, and manage his/her own affairs to the maximum extent possible.

The consumer of service is impaired in skills and judgment and should be granted increased privileges, autonomy, choices and integration opportunities only when he/she demonstrates readiness to handle them.

Agency Role

To provide a system of supports for as long as they are needed to enable the client to successfully live in a home of his/her own in the community and to gain more competence, control, and confidence with things in life that are meaningful to him/her.

To evaluate the strengths and weaknesses of a client, to identify needs and implement a program to remediate deficits, and to prepare him/her to move on to the next higher level of independence; to monitor his/her actions and development.

Helper, advisor, facilitator, advocate.

Landlord

Responsible agent for client's well-being and progress.

Service Design

System of support services designed around individual client needs and available to client wherever he/she lives. Flexible adjustment of services as needs change. Focus on environmental adaptations and supports.

Services attached to specific living environments, developed according to broad categories of need, and assigned to clients based on assessment to determine readiness for entrance or exit. Focus on client change vs. environmental accommodation.

(continued)

Table 1. (*continued*)

Desired Outcomes

Client's success in achieving a satisfying life in the community by combining individual resources with help from natural support systems and paid staff.	Improved scores on assessment scales, reduction or phase-out of staff supports, and/or client graduation to different settings or programs.

From Johnson, T. Z. (1985). *Belonging to the community*, pp. 46–47. Madison, WI: Options in Community Living and Wisconsin Council on Developmental Disabilities; reprinted by permission.

exist today. Table 1 includes a brief overview of the differences between Options in Community Living and traditional residential services.

Support organizations vary from most traditional residential service organizations in their underlying assumptions, agency roles, service design, and desired outcomes in the lives of people with disabilities. They are based on the principles of commitment to people instead of services and programs; to interdependence and quality living today, not a promise of quality tomorrow through movement and remediation; and to supporting people to live their own lives instead of assuming the primary responsibility for people's lives.

Organizational Roles[2]

Changed organizational roles can also be described in the following ways:

A major new role of the residential agency is to support Administrators of residential agencies and the state developmental disabilities offices that fund them traditionally view the residential agency as a provider (i.e., planner, organizer, controller, deliverer) of a set of services. From this perspective, the need to maintain efficient and effective service delivery, convenience, and accountability requires the organization to have control of decision-making authority over each person served. The person is often expected to adapt or subordinate his or her needs and wishes to fit the resources the agency makes available. When this is not possible, or when the person's needs change, she or he may be discharged or transferred to another setting.

Individualization, however, requires agencies to assume a supportive role. This role means that the agency assists the individual to fulfill his or her own hopes and wishes; recognize and develop skills and interests; attain personal wellness and safety; and participate fully in community life, which includes relationships with friends and family

---

[2]This section is adapted in part from Shoultz, B. (1990, April). Issues in providing housing and support. *TASH Newsletter, 15*(4), 6–7.

members. This assistance or support is given with direction from the person and with awareness and respect for his or her choices or preferences.

Another major role of a residential agency is to commit itself to the people it supports Residential agencies traditionally require individuals to fit agency criteria and may discharge or transfer people whose needs or wishes do not mesh with the agency expectations.

A new way of thinking, however, stems from the basic principle of personal and agency commitment to each individual. For example, Residential, Inc., an agency in southern Ohio, places major emphasis on recruiting and supporting staff who will make a personal commitment to one person with whom they work. This agency has a commitment to provide support for as long as it is wanted and to change the intensity or type of support as wants and needs change. Yet, agency commitment to the person, although it is necessary, is not viewed as enough. Each person also needs someone outside the agency who has a personal commitment to him or her; the agency must help to find that person or persons.

A new role of a residential agency is to take direction from people with disabilities Residential agencies traditionally decide what is in the best interests of a person based on professional decisionmaking. Agencies involve people with disabilities in service planning in order to obtain their input into agency-determined processes and decisions.

A new way of thinking is based upon placing the person first. This means restructuring organizations and organizational components, such as staffing and tasks, to support what people want to lead valued lives. Instead of basing decisions on what professionals or others in the hierarchy believe is best, the role of all organizational members is to listen better to people they support and to take direction from them. This may mean subordinating other tasks, such as budgeting, to ensure that the person's needs and wants are met. It can also mean creating an organization where one guiding question is, "What do people want in their lives and how can we help them to achieve it?"

Another role of a residential agency is to promote valued outcomes in people's lives Traditionally, residential service agencies have measured their accomplishments by the number of people making the transition to more independent settings and by improvement in habilitation related skills. Increasingly, valued outcomes are being defined, both in this and other countries, as some variation of O'Brien's (1987b) five accomplishments: competence, choice, respect, community presence, and community participation (see Racino & Taylor, chap. 2, this volume). These are often reflected in agency's mission statements (see Figure 1) and form the foundation for evaluations of a program's accomplishments.

Developmental Services of
Strafford County, Inc., New Hampshire

Agency Mission

Developmental Services of Strafford County, Inc., seeks to promote active and meaningful integration of people receiving its services into the life of the county's communities. This means that we support real people to live in real homes, work at real work, make real friends, and achieve active membership in community organizations.

In attempting to accomplish this mission we focus our attention on these five areas:
1. Physical placement in the community both at home and in the workplace
2. Enhancement of people's image and status as valued community members who are both productive and respected
3. Ensurance of people's rights and expansion of their self-determination and ability to make responsible and productive choices
4. Development of competence and skills both vocationally and in activities of daily living
5. Active, balanced social participation with other community members in an ongoing set of human relationships

The mission of the agency can only be accomplished with the active support of the wider community and with the active involvement of individuals in the community. Therefore, we do not seek to replace or supplant "natural" community supports, but, rather, to activate these supports. In order to allow people to participate in the life of the community and to establish wide-ranged and well-balanced relationships, DSSC must not undermine the community's capacity to care about all of its members. We must realize that although we cannot guarantee each person's personal happiness, we can ensure their right to pursue it.

Figure 1.   Sample agency mission statement. (Adapted from Developmental Services of Strafford County, Inc., [1988] One Forum Court, Crosby Road, Dover, New Hampshire 03820.)

A major new role is to support individuals in locating, purchasing, and controlling housing   Residential service agencies have traditionally played the role of landlord, owning or leasing the facilities in which people with developmental disabilities reside. As described in Chapter 4 of this volume, agencies can assist people in signing leases, negotiating with landlords, arranging and paying for architectural adaptations, matching roommates, purchasing furniture and furnishings, obtaining housing subsides, and advocating for change in local state and federal policies for accessible and decent community housing. This means new relationships with local housing organizations (as described in O'Connor & Racino, chap. 6, this volume), including working for the improvement of local housing codes.

WAYS OF ORGANIZING TO PROVIDE SUPPORT

As people move toward agency change there is a tendency to try to replicate management and programmatic structures of other organizations. Although most support organizations tend to be smaller in size, have more fluidity in design than traditional management structures, and are often less hierarchical, the key characteristics of support organizations revolve around their spirit.

Because "good agencies" are one of a kind, organizations should not strive to copy another agency (Bogdan & Taylor, 1987). Organizations can, however, learn by borrowing from each other and shifting their emphasis to developing the characteristics that "good" organizations share. These include keeping values alive, creating a spirit of self-reflection; guarding against bureaucracy; empowering, valuing, and supporting staff; and developing mutual collaboration and autonomy (see also Racino, 1991b; and Taylor, Bogdan, & Racino, 1991).

Keeping Values Alive   A philosophy, belief system, or world view permeates and guides the minute parts of the organization as well as the organization as a whole. Organizations keep their principles alive through the way people talk, act, and make decisions. Each action and decision is evaluated on the basis of: "Does this support a more valued life outcome for the person?"

Creating a Spirit of Self-Reflection   "Good" organizations continue to change and grow, are open to external evaluation and self-study, and continually appraise and revise their behaviors and invent their futures as well as survive them (Hedberg, Nystrom, & Starbuck, 1976). As O'Brien (1987a) describes, "good" organizations recognize their own ignorance, errors, and fallibility. They know that agencies are not perfect and that rational plans are often the bureaucrat's "unrealistic" dream.

Guarding Against Bureaucracy   Remembering that their purpose for existence is to support people to lead fulfilling lives, "good" agencies ensure that policies, regulations, financing, and technology do not take precedence over the lives of people with disabilities. They seek ways of minimizing the bureaucracy in people's lives and of meeting outside demands with minimal intrusion into the lives of people with disabilities.

Empowering, Valuing, and Supporting Staff   Support organizations seek to empower staff, create a sense of ownership, develop mutual trust and supportive relationships, and maintain a participative style of decision making. As Peters (1987) describes, it is important to get everyone involved in all aspects of the organization and to create an environment where accomplishments are recognized and celebrated.

Developing Mutual Collaboration and Autonomy   Promoting both personal autonomy and mutual decision making, these agencies encourage a range of solutions and strategies as long as basic values are maintained. This is one way of achieving organizational flexibility through personal empowerment.

A common question service providers ask is: "How do agencies organize to provide support?" The following sections describe learnings from support agencies and from other traditional agencies that are in the process of changing the way they have organized to provide support. (See also O'Brien, 1991.)

Ways of Organizing Staff

Residential support staff are deployed differently in support organizations than in conventional agencies. In traditional agencies, the staff who support people usually work according to a shift schedule, which is developed by the agency. Programs offering individualized support deploy staff in ways that make sense to the staff and the people who are supported. Several agencies have created a team concept where two or more staff members support a person and become very familiar with him or her. The paid staff work with the person to determine the types, times, and intensity of support needed or wanted. The agency sees one of its roles as supporting these individually negotiated arrangements. Staff act more as facilitators and as resources.

In traditional residential organizations, the greatest importance is placed on those highest in the agency's hierarchy. This is reflected in salaries, power relationships, status, and decision making. The new way of thinking includes redefining the relationships among organization members and recognizing the centrality of the person and those who best know and support him or her. Specific practices on the agency level include rotating administrative responsibilities among a group of people, increasing the decision making authority of the staff who know the people best, and minimizing salary and status discrepancies between roles.

In traditional residential agencies, staff are employed and accountable solely to the agency. Support organizations may assist people with disabilities to employ their own personal assistants or to use assistants employed by another organization, such as a home health agency. In these situations, the support organization has no direct employer relationship with the staff. Instead, the residential agency assumes the role of supporter to the person with a disability to hire, fire, and manage their personal assistants.

Another way of deploying staff that has been tried by many organizations is to hire specific people, sometimes called community connectors or bridge-builders, to facilitate relationships and community connections. The growing experience indicates that these functions should be integrated into all job roles rather than focused only in the jobs of designated individuals.

Ways of Thinking About "Management" and Leadership

Most residential managers are used to thinking in terms of units or residential sites. Changing to the role of a support organization challenges the definition of residential services and the role of agencies and "managers" in people's lives. A focus on individual people means re-thinking the "responsibilities" and the roles of people and the functions an organization will perform. It also means turning the organization upside down so that the needs and desires of people with disabilities drive the organization.

Support organizations, similar to those described by Peters (1987), have changed the roles of both top and middle management people. In particular, managers are viewed as leading through example and developing a broad vision. Leaders in support organizations use a participatory style that involves everyone and assumes that everyone can play a leadership role. Middle managers are seen as facilitators, on-call experts, and diffusers of good news. These organizations are exploring moving from residential directors, assistant directors, and other management staff to more explicit consultant roles.

Moving to a focus on the personal viewpoints of people can lead to a messiness of sorts. Typical ways of planning and coordinating services will need to change to promote more flexibility and spontaneity. It can be uncomfortable for many people in management roles who are used to feeling (not necessarily being) in control to rely on the judgment of people with disabilities and support staff, and to wait to resolve issues instead of choosing from clearly delineated options.

Ways of Thinking About "Eligibility and Termination"

Most residential service agencies are used to identifying, assessing, and screening people to determine if they are eligible for their services. If the person does not "do well," she or he can be asked to leave the program. This may mean that people are left to live on the street or in single room occupancies (SROs), room and board homes, shelters, adult homes, and other living arrangements that constitute the hidden service system in the United States.

People involved in support organizations are starting to look at ways to reconceptualize their roles in relationship to eligibility and termination. For example, "intake workers" who used to see their function as getting people into the service system are now finding ways to help people get what they need and want through informal means. This should not be confused with another traditional function of "intake workers," which is to deem people ineligible for needed and wanted services in difficult fiscal times. The support by some sectors to move from categorical eligibility, which perpetuates the need for professional assessments, to a system of more universal eligibility, would be another example of reconceptualizing these issues.

Making a personal commitment to people means that the agency moves away from "terminating" or "discharging" people from services.

Instead, the person, agency, and others may work together to change the person's support services, which might include changing the staff, the housing, or where and with whom the person lives. For some people this may mean a number of different options will be explored, always trying to listen closely to what the person is saying. Even if problems continue to occur, those associated with the organization strive to accept the person and distinguish between the needs of the person and those of the agency.

Ways of Promoting Quality on the Agency Level

Support organizations view rules, regulations, and accreditation standards as areas that must be met to maintain funding, but do not necessarily equate these with quality. In fact, most organizations note examples where these rules have interfered with the quality of life of individual people.

In general, support organizations are committed to high quality and try to develop multiple internal or external mechanisms to promote quality. For example, some organizations develop quality of life standards highlighting typical life areas, such as income, housing, autonomy and/or choice, and meaningful activities, or routinely change integration measures to focus staff attention on areas of relationships and participation in community life. Figure 2 provides a good example of quality of life standards developed by Options in Community Living.

Traditional residential agencies may appear more concerned about issues of liability than life quality of individual people. Most support agencies have found that there is no more risk in moving to a housing and support approach than already exists with their other services. Liability policies continue to cover mistakes that might occur as long as the organization has not acted negligently. To minimize agency risk, agencies sometimes continue to use a team process or other forms of decision-making consensus when first starting to make these changes.

Ways of Developing Proposals for "Supportive Living"

Private agencies in many states will be faced with the need to develop a proposal to submit to either their regional or state office describing how they will plan for services and supports in a "supportive living program." Basic components of such a proposal could include: 1) the philosophy and basic assumptions that the organization will ascribe to; 2) the anticipated benefits of this change to the person, the organization, and the state (see, for example, Table 2); 3) the expected internal changes to the agency, including a description of who the people are, the array of anticipated supports, the way in which staff will be deployed, and the expected changes in the agency itself; 4) the resources that will be necessary for the change process, including items such as training,

I. Autonomy/Choice
  A. Conditions that must exist to ensure that a person will not be at risk in the community.
    1. The person has opportunities to make decisions and express preferences in all areas of life. The right to make these decisions shall be respected by others in the person's life (e.g., service providers, parents, roommates). The person also has the right to refuse interventions initiated by providers.
    2. The person has a method of expressing preferences and a method of acting upon these preferences in all areas of life. For example, a person who has a physical disability and is nonvocal might use a communication board to express preferences and have a personal care attendant to act on those preferences. Preferences can be expressed in nonverbal ways, such as by a change in behavior.
    3. The person has access to information and experiences that assist the person in making decisions about his/her life.
    4. The person has people in addition to service providers for support and information needed to make decisions about his/her life (e.g., family, friends).

II. Personal Income
  A. Conditions that must exist to ensure that a person will not be at risk in the community:
    1. The person has a stable source of income that covers basic living needs, including shelter, food, transportation, clothing.
    2. There is effective management of this income to ensure that basic needs are met. (Support can be provided when needed through a double-signature bank account, representative payee, or assistance with budgeting.)
  B. Conditions that will further promote a valued lifestyle:
    1. There is sufficient income for items and activities that enrich one's life experience, such as vacations and other leisure activities, home decorations, and items that enhance one's personal appearance.
    2. The person is able to participate as fully as possible in decision-making about the use of personal income through the development of money and budgeting concepts and values that encourage financial responsibility.
    3. The person can maximize income through wise investments and purchases, and through subsidies for which the person is eligible.
    4. The person has a means of earning income through employment as a supplement to or in place of government benefits.

III. Housing
  A. Conditions that must exist to ensure that a person will not be at risk in the community:
    1. The person has housing that meets community building codes, is secure and has adequate heat, water and electricity.
    2. The person has the basic furnishings necessary for daily living, including a bed, chairs, table and lighting.
    3. The person lives in a neighborhood where she/he feels safe and where there is access to needed resources.
  B. Conditions that will further promote a valued lifestyle:
    1. The interior and exterior of the home is maintained in a safe, clean and attractive fashion.

(continued)

Figure 2.   Options in Community Living's policy on quality of life. (Options in Community Living, Inc., 22 North Second Street, Madison, Wisconsin 53704. Copyright 1987; reprinted with permission.)

Figure 2. (*continued*)

    2.   The person is able to exercise control over the home environment, including the choice of location, personalized furnishings and decor, and control of temperature and lighting.

    3.   The home furnishings are attractive and complete.

    4.   The person is able to have maximum influence over his/her housing situation through such means as participation in a tenant association, cooperative housing or home ownership.

IV. Physical and Mental Health

    A. Conditions that must exist to ensure that a person will not be at risk in the community:

       1.   The person's health is maintained through adequate nutrition, exercise, safe behavior, medical monitoring, and appropriate medications when needed.

       2.   The person receives prompt and up-to-date treatment for physical and mental health problems.

       3.   The person employs a personal care attendant if his/her physical disability limits the person's ability to provide self-care.

    B. Conditions that will further promote a valued lifestyle:

       1.   The person has established relationships with and easy access to health care providers (e.g., physicians, nurses, dentists, counselors, and therapists) who know the person and monitor his/her health needs on an on-going basis.

       2.   The person's lifestyle encourages wellness. For example, the person eats nutritious meals on a regular schedule and maintains an appropriate weight; does not smoke; does not drink in excess or use drugs; has coping mechanisms to relieve stress; has people to provide emotional support.

V. Safety

    A. Conditions that must exist to ensure that a person will not be at risk in the community:

       1.   Potential dangers in the person's environment are minimized. For example, his/her home is free of fire hazards and is locked and secure; the person does not walk alone on dark streets at night.

       2.   The person receives prompt and appropriate emergency services when needed, such as police, fire department, ambulance, crisis line.

VI. Appearance and Hygiene

    A. Conditions that must exist to ensure that a person will not be at risk in the community:

       1.   The person minimizes health-related problems through adequate personal hygiene and clothing choices that are appropriate for weather conditions.

       2.   The person maintains acceptable hygiene and appearance so as not to restrict where s/he can live, work and socialize.

    B. Conditions that will further promote a valued lifestyle:

       1.   The person has a choice of attractive clothing for different occasions.

       2.   The person maintains his/her hair in a manner that is becoming.

       3.   The person's hygiene and appearance serve to enhance self-esteem.

VII. Relating with Others

    A. Conditions that must exist to ensure that a person will not be at risk in the community:

       1.   The person has the means to communicate on a daily basis with

(*continued*)

Figure 2.   (*continued*)

primary people in his/her life. (This may include speech, signing and adaptive devices.)
2. The person has support people, including Options staff, with whom s/he is able and willing to maintain contact.
B. Conditions that will further promote a valued lifestyle:
1. The person has the means of communicating in such a way that encourages interactions with other members of his/her support system and community (e.g., clarity, assertiveness, appropriate affect).
2. The person has supportive relationships with family members that encourage independence.
3. The person has relationships with friends and peers that provide companionship, intimacy and support.
4. The person has the opportunity to responsibly engage in sexual relationships and marriage based on his/her personal beliefs and values.
5. The person's relationships include people who are nondisabled.

VIII. Meaningful Activities
A. Conditions that must exist to ensure that a person will not be a risk in the community:
1. The person has a daily routine that is designed around his/her needs and capabilities and that resembles as closely as possible a typical adult routine. Such a routine is likely to include vocational, domestic and leisure activities.
B. Conditions that will further promote a valued lifestyle:
1. The person's activities provide opportunities for personal growth and increase life satisfaction.
2. The person receives wages for work.
3. The person takes part in culturally valued leisure activities, such as parties, trips, concerts and shows.
4. The person's activities take place in community settings that are integrated with nondisabled people.
5. The person has the means of developing and achieving short-term and long-term goals (e.g., vocational planning, vacations, retirement).

IX. Mobility
A. Conditions that must exist to ensure that a person will not be at risk in the community:
1. The person has the means to move about his/her home and community environments to the extent necessary to satisfy basic needs.
B. Conditions that will further promote a valued lifestyle:
1. The person has physical access to a wide range of community resources for work, leisure, shopping, etc. Modes of transportation can include bus, car, bike, walking, vehicles equipped for wheelchairs.
2. The person, when needed, has adaptive devices that will enhance mobility, such as canes, motorized wheelchair, three-wheel bike.

study tours, and evaluations; and 5) the way the agency will address critical safeguards and accountability issues, such as the quality standards to be used and the way financing will be decided for each person.

Ways of Approaching Financing on the Agency Level

Many support organizations seek ways to modify, combine, or develop funding to meet the needs of individuals. Whereas all organizations are concerned with fiscal viability, support organizations first examine what is needed by people, then how the organization can seek or adapt funding to meet the individuals' needs.

Organizations differentiate between what they do and how they bill for it. For example, integrated community participation activities were billed by one agency as "behavior management" under the Medicaid waiver. Although these activities were accompanied by behavioral changes, people in the organization thought and talked about this as a way to help people get to know their community. The billing for behavioral management services was solely an administrative, bureaucratic mechanism.

In the area of community living, some financial sources, such as intermediate care facilities (ICFs), will not permit individualization and flexibility. These limitations are inherent in this facility-based program, and only limited opportunities for individual choice exist. In contrast, the home- and community-based Medicaid waiver allows for individualization to coexist, although somewhat uneasily, with Medicaid funding. Agencies should ensure their waiver allows for options such as support services in one's own home and an array of service (not facility) options. Sometimes it takes creativity for agencies to determine how to fund supports. For example, adults can be supported to live in their own place through the use of "adult family care" funding streams because state regulations and licensing seldom prohibit such options.

Agencies and others need to move away from thinking about funding streams as the solution to the problems of daily living for people with disabilities. Although a government program such as the Medicaid home- or community-based services (HCBS) waiver or the new federal Community Supported Living Arrangements (CSLA) may provide new financial avenues, a program category of "supportive living" is not the "answer" or the "solution." On the agency level, people need a vision of what they are trying to accomplish with and on behalf of people with disabilities and must continually ask: "How can the CSLA or HCBS help this vision to occur in practice, and in which ways does it hinder this vision?"

Setting Up and Defending Agency Budgets for State Proposals
Many agencies will be faced with developing proposals to submit to regional and state offices. Some important principles to keep in mind are:

No "individual" budgets can be developed without individual plans—a person's budget must be directly tied to what that person needs and wants.

No individual caps—anyone can be supported to live in their own home, and agencies should ensure that certain people will not be excluded by the application of a per person cap.

Table 2.   Supported living

Benefits to Participants

1. People have increased opportunities to establish and develop relationships with non-paid community members.
2. People have increased continuity with staff. Paid staff tend to make personal commitments to participants.
3. People have significantly more opportunities to use community resources and settings.
4. People are much more likely to experience the living arrangement as a *home* instead of a program.
5. People live in quality housing in typical neighborhoods without exciting the neighbors by moving in "12" adults.
6. People have more control over their money. They are likely to increase their consumer power in the community.
7. People have more control over the small as well as the life-defining decisions that are made on their behalf.
8. People have support to develop and express personal preferences. Programs are typically designed to fit the unique characteristics of each person.
9. People with complex behaviors are likely to experience more positive programs and supports.
10. People are likely to have futures rich in opportunities for continued growth and self-expression.
11. The numbers of critical incidents and crisis situations decreases significantly.
12. People grow beyond the expectations of family and staff.

Benefits to Agency

1. Decrease in level of stress for staff and decrease in staff turnover.
2. Increase in the staff's sense of personal responsibility for the program.
3. Staff are likely to have greater opportunities for creativity, responsibility, and personal fulfillment.
4. Provides a flexible method of meeting individual needs on an as-needed basis.
5. Provides a method of responding to changes in a person's life (e.g., illness, behavioral problems) without a change in placement.
6. Provides a wide variety of living environments suitable to meet an individual's habilitation and environmental needs without being "hamstrung" by unnecessary regulatory restrictions.
7. The agency becomes more deeply interwoven into the social fabric of the community.

Adapted from Orleans ARC. (n.d.). *Supported living: Benefits to participants.* Albion, NY: Author; reprinted with permission.

Averaging costs over people—at least initially, the agency can average costs over different people, especially individuals moving from settings where some people are already getting more or less support services. However, as long as averaging is the employed method, control of distribution of resources will be retained by the agency.

Defending individual costs—agencies will at times be called upon to defend the costs of individual support plans. It is important to be able to compare the costs of previous living arrangements to those in this approach. Comparisons should be done across a group of people or by "true" person-by-person costs, not by comparing an individual's budget with the average group home or institutional cost.

Demonstration proposals across groups should include the broadest array possible of support services, especially categories such as stipends and the purchase of goods, to allow for the person-by-person individualization that will be necessary.

Mechanisms for paying for increased support needs—agencies must assume in their fiscal planning that some people's support needs will increase at times.

Coordination of housing and support—on the agency level, both housing and support service financing should be explored to ensure that these are coordinated for each individual involved. Pursuing "separate projects" in these areas on the agency level is problematic from the person's viewpoint.

Ways of Meeting State Expectations in Changing Times

Given that it will take time for the larger system to adjust to changes, people at the local level will continue to receive contradictory messages and expectations from regulators, funders, and other key outside forces. As one example, state agencies monitor progress in programs on skill acquisition. This is a dilemma for agencies who wish to assist people to learn and develop additional competencies, but who do not believe that people should be constantly programmed or trained in their homes and daily lives. In Weld County (Walker & Salon, 1991), the issue is handled this way:

> Formal programming . . . is highly integrated into normal, daily living routines. . . . For funding purposes, staff must document progress on certain program goals . . . however, . . . programming is flexible, not forced, and can be reevaluated and/or redesigned according to a person's needs or abilities. (p. 33)

Agencies adopting this approach will come into conflict with a number of existing and outmoded regulations, policies, and legislative initiatives. One of the indicators of their success will be their capacity to maintain their vision and use their creativity to influence the larger systems.

ORGANIZATIONS AND CHANGE

In the United States, there are many different kinds of organizations involved in residential service provision for people with developmental disabilities. Depending largely upon the state, local agencies that provide services might be: 1) private nonprofits that are responsible to their own boards of directors; 2) private for-profits that are locally based or part of a regional or national "chain"; 3) quasi–public-private, in-state regional organizations that may directly provide services and/or contract for them with private providers; 4) state-regional offices that may directly provide and/or contract for services; and 5) county offices that could also directly provide some services.

Some of these organizations may be solely residential service providers; others are multi-service agencies providing a range of services from vocational to residential, recreational, and family support. Even an organization that provides only residential services may do so for different population groups, such as mental health and developmental services. In addition, some intentional communities, such as L'Arche, may be funded as private, nonprofit organizations; others may be a loose-knit collection of people at different sites. Organizations also vary tremendously in size from 12 or fewer people to those that assist 1,000 or more people.

In moving to a housing and support approach, it is important to become familiar with organizations other than those providing residential services to people with developmental disabilities. These include independent living centers, which are consumer-controlled organizations, home health agencies, which sometimes provide personal assistance services; and community "generic" social service agencies.

Organizational Trends

How an organization, its staff, and board of directors will understand a housing and support approach depends on their knowledge of different trends in the field and the starting point for agency change. Following are a few important trends that influence agency level change.

Residential, Vocational, Educational, and Family Support How professionals and service providers view the world depends largely on the way in which they center the frame of their world. A review of the literature in residential, vocational, educational, and family support fields indicates an interest and awareness of the need to build bridges across disciplines. Yet, each frames the problems and solutions by placing their particular field in the center. In general, there is a trend toward the blurring of boundaries across disciplines and some movement toward a more holistic view. However, change strategies must start from the particular perspective that an agency uses as a framework.

Supported Employment and Supportive Living The literature on conversion to a supported work organization from a sheltered workshop provider can be a helpful starting point for residential agencies involved in change. It delineates some basic principles of organizational change that can be a useful introduction to the local agency change process.

Yet, the supported employment area is based primarily on models, even as it moves away from a standard job coach model toward the use of coworker strategies and "natural supports." Basic principles and examples described earlier, such as control by the individual of their job coach (i.e., personal assistance) and determination of the support configuration are seldom discussed. Also, the change literature appears to presume that the nature of organizations will remain essentially the same.

A rule-based approach continues to predominate in supported employment and in supportive living. For example, in debates on issues such as integration versus paid work, the assumption seems to be there is an answer that could be applied across the board to all people (see Racino & Taylor, chap. 2, this volume). People continue to be moved into paid or integrated community participation systems, which generally are constructed separately from each other and assume an "all or none" orientation.

People with severe disabilities, for whom supported employment could be particularly beneficial, have been virtually excluded from this option in some states. Supportive living providers can learn from their counterparts about how and why this occurred and guard against the same scenario.

Generic and Disability Agencies People within the disability field distinguish between the disability system and the generic system. In fact, the disability agencies typically see part of their role as helping people with disabilities access these generic services. From the perspective of individuals with disabilities and families, however, all these organizations form a network of potential resources that can be actively used for their own purposes.

Disability agencies, at times, fear integration of "their" clients into the generic system. They believe they can respond better to the needs of people with disabilities or that the existing generic services are devaluing to people. This way of thinking often results in reverse integration with a disability agency inviting others to participate in their program instead of assisting people with disabilities to be part of the community process. Another, more positive outcome could be the creation, as a community, of more valued generic services.

AGENCY CHANGE

One of the first steps for organizations that wish to make changes is a critical re-examination of their values. This usually leads to two major insights: 1) a realization that they must change the way they are organized to provide supports to people, not just the size of their facilities; and 2) a process of listening more carefully to what each person wants, with a subsequent attempt to help the person attain this goal.

Why Change?

One of the most important questions to address in examining the issue of agency change is "why?" People involved with the organization—boards of directors, staff members, people with disabilities and their families, and to some extent, funders and community members—need to believe that change is important to improve the quality of life of people with disabilities and that it will not jeopardize the agency itself.

Change can be a very sensitive area, particularly for people who may have founded the organization and devoted their personal and professional interests and careers to developing residential services. Even the mildest criticism can be taken as an attack on their work, moving people from the position of being "white knights" to people who often, with the best intentions, remain in controlling positions.

Parents, too, may be skeptical that a son or daughter could live in a place of their own when this had previously been equated to an apartment with inadequate or no support services. People with disabilities may echo the words of professionals who tell them they are not ready to live their life while it passes before them.

The following strategies have proven to be effective vehicles for providing information to everyone involved in deciding whether change is important.

Study Tours   Building on the principle that "seeing is believing," visits to other places that have undertaken this change continue to be one viable strategy. Even a small group that includes at least one parent, a person with a disability, administrators, board members, and funders can become an important force not only for agency change, but also for broader regional and state change. Of course, people can also learn lessons that are not applicable in their own state system, which sometimes introduces new problems by borrowing inapplicable techniques, mechanisms, or political compromises.

Brief Information Articles and Stories   For those who cannot visit, brief accounts of personal stories and information about other agencies, their accomplishments, and the difficulties they have encountered, can help people to believe that: 1) it can be done, 2) it is possible for us to do it, and 3) it matters that this change occurs.

People tend to learn best from others in similar roles or who have had similar experiences. Telephone conversations with parents and providers from other locations are another inexpensive way to facilitate personal exchange and alleviate personal doubts. On-site consultations are also helpful.

Personal Life Planning   An agency's approach to life planning can also be a way to convince skeptics of the personal importance of agency change to the lives of people with disabilities. By identifying agency barriers as part of the process, a framework for agency change can also be developed. Starting a process of obtaining feedback from people with disabilities and encouraging candid responses can also provide information to help answer the "why?" question.

Ways of Reframing Questions

One of the most important areas in approaching change is to begin to reframe questions from the point of view of an agency to that of an individual. The following are some examples selected from the discussions of the planning committee for the TASH Support Strand, Supports for Community Living: Assisting People to Live in Homes They Control (November, 1990):

Making a House a Home
Agency: What do staff need to know to promote a feeling of home and home ownership?
Person: What can I do when I am not comfortable where I live?

Supporting Personal, Neighborhood, and Community Connections
Agency: How can we promote the development of friendships and relationships in the lives of people with disablities?
Person: How and where can I meet people? Who might have some good ideas about this?

Ways of Organizing to Support Participation in Homes and Communities
Agency: What changes do agencies need to make to move from traditional residential to support organizations?
Person: How can I get the help I need from the places that are funded to support me?

Simply changing the questions to a different viewpoint allows for a broader range of solutions, making it clear that: 1) the disability organization is not the only possible supporter, 2) the questions asked by individual people do not always correspond with those asked by agencies, and 3) all the agency questions imply some form of control and ownership by agencies of both the problem and the solution.

Common Questions About Agency Change

Although many residential managers or directors have skills in maintaining what exists or creating new programs, they often have little experience in making major agency changes. Sometimes, for example, people will naively believe that simply changing to an individualized life planning process will result in agency change. At other times, directors may not be able to undertake a process that seems as if they are dismantling their own work. In this situation, the person's contribution may be simply to step aside to allow others to move forward with what is needed to improve the life quality of people with disabilities.

Many of the questions that staff members raise about a housing and support approach revolve around the following areas: issues and dilemmas that have always been integral to residential services (e.g., parent choice versus that of the person with a disability); fears about what change will mean (e.g., Will I still be needed and treated fairly?); "how to" questions about the basic approach (e.g., how to individualize; financing for these options); and basic values and concerns (e.g., normalization and person-centered approaches). (See Table 3 for specific exam-

Table 3.   Commonly asked questions in agency change process

Change

How do we get beyond the traditional mind-set of "group homes" (eight beds, 24-hour supervision)?

How can we talk about group homes without the group home staff feeling attacked and feeling devalued?

It seems that we need to not only educate each other about smaller and individual supports and living situations, but also potential funding sources. How do we do this?

Parents and Choice

How do we help parents become more comfortable with the choices that their son or daughter has indicated that they would like to make?

Where do we draw the line between parental interaction, or parental restrictions, and the desire—or *right*—of a person with severe disabilities to adult activities and interpersonal relationships such as dating, sexual activity, or even community integration?

What suggestions do you have for assisting a person with severe disabilities who is not very communicative to make choices?

Support

How do we offer real individual support options with limited staff time available?

What are some safeguards so that our service doesn't fall into the trap of claiming to provide individual supports, yet those "individual supports" are the same for everyone?

What strategies are there to get nondisabled persons to be roommates with persons with disabilities?

Housing

How do we encourage persons to purchase their homes instead of being in the position of always having to rent an apartment?

At what point do we compromise to (help) persons find affordable housing in a geographical area that is very high priced?

How do we take advantage of grants or projects such as a HUD 202 Project?

Old Concepts

Age appropriateness—Is it appropriate or "fair" for us to "remove" activities or concepts that our residents may find very rewarding/enjoyable (i.e., arts and crafts such as painting, coloring, cutting items out to hang on the walls)?

Transition—What if a person does not want to be in a less restrictive setting (i.e., not want to move from the group home to the supervised apartment)?

Independence—We say that people should become independent but do we really want people to be independent rather than initiating and maintaining an interconnectedness with the community?

Selected from list submitted by Community Services Board, VA (1990).

ples.) Most people, in other words, do not directly raise questions about what changes might mean for the agency; instead, they assume that these changes can be accomplished without changing the organization's present structure in any substantial way.

Targets for Change

It is important to differentiate individual, agency, and systems changes. The individual change process is often described as "a light bulb" being turned on. The time frame and circumstances seem unpredictable, and the most one can do is offer opportunities for the experience to occur. For some people, change will occur in moments; for others, it will take many years. Most agency change can be approached more systematically than systems change, which is unpredictable because of the complexity involved. Common organizational development techniques can help foster agency change; however, these processes are not well known by residential agencies.

In 1986, Racino identified the key targets for change as: 1) attitudes, including those of professionals, policymakers, administrators, human services groups, parents, people with disabilities, and neighbors; 2) service design, particularly in quality of life standards, flexible and individual supports, individual needs assessment and plans, consumer-directedness, and personal commitment and case management; 3) staff roles, recruitment, training and support, design or organization of staffing, and evaluation; 4) management role definition, dispersed services management, agency structure and design, and creative scheduling; and 5) quality assurance and financing (which will be discussed in more detail in Chapter 7 of this volume). These remain key areas, although the desired changes might be expressed better as changing the nature of the relationship between agencies and people with disabilities, agencies and communities, agencies and systems, and within agencies.

Ways of Promoting a Positive Change Environment

Residential organizations can learn about change by examining the processes followed by others both within and outside the disability field. In organizational terms, change strategies typically include:

Providing information and education (Gardner, Chapman, Donaldson, & Jacobson, 1988)

Exercising power (in this case the power of vision by listening, reflecting, and learning through action)

Understanding the organization's culture (what the organization is about)

Redefining the mission

Building commitment and leadership through participation, ownership, personal commitment, and group support

Identifying and overcoming barriers to change, both internal (e.g., structures, policies, practices, and people) and external

Seeking resources for change (new coalitions and groups)

Validating and maintaining change through the use of experts and consultants

Formalizing change through practices and policies, from demonstration to agency change

Maintaining change as an ongoing process within the agency

At the early stage, four factors appear to be very important in promoting a positive agency environment for change: 1) creating an environment where it is okay to make mistakes; 2) promoting a feeling of ownership on the part of all people involved; 3) developing a commitment to a set of values, sometimes through more formal training; and 4) developing an approach to continual learning, recognizing that without such a process things do not remain the same, but move backwards.

An evaluation of Alternative Living, Inc., (see Walker, chap. 14, this volume, for a description of this organization) delineated 10 factors as important conditions leading to positive agency change (Mount & Caruso, 1989). These include:

1. Agency leadership and commitment
2. Listening to people and standing by them
3. "Busting" the constraints of existing service models
4. Responding to the interests of all stakeholders
5. Developing a new mission
6. Willingness to risk disorder
7. Tapping the capacities of all the staff
8. Use of external facilitators to get started
9. Developing pilot programs and demonstrations
10. Proceeding slowly

Often, the barriers faced in the change process are old concepts and assumptions, which people often maintain without realizing it. Independence, in the sense of being on one's own, is a good example of a concept that is difficult to change and that permeates the values of many agencies. Other concepts, such as transition, mental age, adults viewed as children, and "normal" as the meaning of normalization, also can be transferred to a new form of service if fundamental values of the organization are not explored and challenged. Agencies may also try to accomplish too many surface changes too swiftly without addressing substantive issues. In addition, they may neglect agency change in lieu of focusing only on individualized planning. There is also a tremendous amount of pressure on some agencies to become leaders, which can result in a reluctance to share problems and issues from which we all can learn.

Ways for Agencies To Affect System, Community, and Societal Change

It is important that agencies recognize the impact that the system, community, and society have on people's lives. When agencies realize they can't do it all, they will better recognize what they can do: make a stand with people and strive to make changes with them on all levels, and make efforts to find others within the disability field and the community who will make the same commitment to alliances.

Societal Issues   Agencies need to recognize and acknowledge social forces that have an impact on the people they support. These include poverty and the oppression people experience based on race, gender, culture, and social class, as well as disability.

Service Issues   Agencies must also acknowledge that service systems can hurt as well as assist people. Alliances with people mean fighting together to address the negative features of systems.

Community Issues   Agencies are also constrained by local resources and community services. These include: housing, transportation, personal assistance, recreation/leisure, health care services, and adult education opportunities. Agencies need to recognize that many of these are broader community issues, not just disability issues, and that they must advocate for these within the context of the larger community. Agencies must also recognize the capacities of regular community members and their contributions to relationships with people with disabilities.

CONCLUSION

Traditional residential agencies have major challenges before them—to create changes within as well as to change their relationships outside the organization. In the coming years, organizations will be faced with even more fundamental questions about their role as people with disabilities and families assume greater control of resources.

BIBLIOGRAPHY

Area Agency for Developmental Services, Region VI. (1985). *Quality assurance policy.* Merrimack, NH: Author.

Bedeian, A.G. (1986). Contemporary challenges in the study of organizations. In J.G. Hunt & J.D. Blair (Eds.), *Journal of Management 12*(2), 185–201.

Bellamy, G.T., Rhodes, L.E., Mank, D.M., & Albin, J.M. (1988). *Supported employment: A community implementation guide* (pp. 139–159, 209–228). Baltimore: Paul H. Brookes Publishing Co.

Bennis, W. (1978). Organizations of the future. In W. Watemyer (Ed.), *Classics of organizational behavior* (pp. 281–293). Oak Park, IL: Moore Publishing Co.

Biklen, D. (1987, December). *Small homes: A case study of Westport Associates.* Syracuse, NY: Center on Human Policy, Syracuse University.

Bogdan, R. (1987, December). *"We care for our own": Georgia citizen advocacy in Savannah and Macon.* Syracuse, NY: Center on Human Policy, Syracuse University.

Bogdan, R., & Taylor, S.J. (1987). Conclusion: The next wave. In S.J. Taylor, D. Biklen, & J. Knoll (Eds.), *Community integration for people with severe disabilities* (pp. 209–213). New York: Teacher's College Press.

Brown, L. (1985). Democracy in organizations: Membership participation and organizational characteristics in U.S. retail food cooperatives. *Organizational Studies, 6*(4), 313–334.

Center on Human Policy. (1985, 1991). [Confidential field notes on organizational studies]. Syracuse, NY: Author.

Community Integration Project. (1986, April). *Programs demonstrating model practices for integrating people with severe disabilities into the community.* Syracuse, NY: Center on Human Policy, Syracuse University.

Drucker, P. (1990). *Managing the nonprofit organization.* New York: Harper Collins Publishers.

Gardner, J.F., Chapman, M.S., Donaldson, G., & Jacobson, S.G. (1988). *Toward supported employment: A process guide for planned change.* Baltimore: Paul H. Brookes Publishing Co.

Goldberg, G.S. (1980, June). New directions for the community service society of New York: A study of organizational change. In *Social Service Review* (pp. 184–219). Chicago: University of Chicago.

Hage, J., & Aiken, M. (1980). Program change and organizational properties. In H. Resnick & R. Patti, *Humanizing social welfare organizations: Change from within* (pp. 159–182). Philadelphia: Temple University Press.

Hagner, D.C., & Murphy, S.T. (1989, July/August/September). Closing the shop on sheltered work: Case studies of organization change. *Journal of Rehabilitation,* 83–89.

Hedberg, B.L.T., Nystrom, P.D., & Starbuck, W.H. (1976). Camping on seesaws: Prescriptions for a self-designing organization. *Administrative Science Quarterly, 21,* 41–65.

Johnson, T.Z. (1982). *A report of the assessment of Options in Community Living by means of program analysis of service systems (PASS).* Madison, WI: Options in Community Living.

Johnson, T.Z. (1986). *Belonging to the community.* Madison, WI: Options in Community Living.

Johnson, T.Z., & O'Brien, J. (1987, July). *Carrying Options' story forward: Final report of an assessment of Options in Community Living.* Madison, WI: Options in Community Living.

Karan, O.C., & Granfield, J.M. (1990). *Engaging people in life: A report on one supported living program in Connecticut.* Connecticut: University Affiliated Program.

Klein, J. (1992). Get me the hell out of here: Supporting people with disabilities to live in their own homes. In J. Nisbet (Ed.), *Natural supports in school, at work, and in the community for people with severe disabilities* (pp. 277–339). Baltimore: Paul H. Brookes Publishing Co.

Lakin, K.C. (1991). Foreword. In S.J. Taylor, R. Bogdan, & J.A. Racino (Eds.), *Life in the community: Case studies of organizations supporting people with disabilities* (pp. xiii–xv). Baltimore: Paul H. Brookes Publishing Co.

Lutfiyya, Z.M. (1991). "Mighty prophets of the future." In S.J. Taylor, R. Bogdan, & J.A. Racino (Eds.), *Life in the Community: Case studies of organizations supporting people with disabilities* (pp. 227–241). Baltimore: Paul H. Brookes Publishing Co.

Martin, P.Y. (1990). Rethinking feminist organizations. *Gender & Society, 4*(2), 182–206.

Mount, B., & Caruso, G. (1989, September). *New dreams, new lives, new directions for Alternative Living, Inc.: A report on the initial outcomes, findings, and implications of the Citizenship Project.* Annapolis, MD: Alternative Living, Inc.

O'Brien, J. (1987a). Embracing ignorance, error, and fallibility: Competencies for leadership of effective services. In S.J. Taylor, D. Biklen, & J. Knoll (Eds.), *Community integration for people with severe disabilities* (pp. 85–108). New York: Teacher's College Press.

O'Brien, J. (1987b). A guide to life-style planning: Using *The Activities Catalog* to integrate services and natural support systems. In B. Wilcox & B.T. Bellamy, *A comprehensive guide to The Activities Catalog: An alternative curriculum for youth and adults with severe disabilities* (pp. 175–189). Baltimore: Paul H. Brookes Publishing Co.

O'Brien, J. (1991). *More than just a new address: Images of organization for supported living agencies.* Lithonia, GA: Responsive Systems Associates.

O'Brien, J., & Lyle O'Brien, C. (1991). Sustaining positive changes: The future development of the Residential Support Program. In S.J. Taylor, R. Bogdan, J.A. Racino (Eds.), *Life in the community: Case studies of organizations supporting people with disabilities* (pp. 153–168). Baltimore: Paul H. Brookes Publishing Co.

O'Brien, J., & Lyle O'Brien, C. (Eds.). (1992). *Remembering the soul of our work: Stories by the staff of Options in Community Living, Madison, Wisconsin.* Madison: Options in Community Living.

O'Brien, S. (1986). Supported independence program: MORC creates a new community alternative. *Transition, 14*(1), 1.

Options in Community Living. (1987). *Options policy on quality of life.* Madison, WI: Author.

Orleans ARC. (1991, June). *Supported living proposal.* Albion, NY: Author.

Peter, D. (1991). We began to listen. In S.J. Taylor, R. Bogdan, & J.A. Racino (Eds.), *Life in the community: Case studies of organizations supporting people with disabilities* (pp. 129–138). Baltimore: Paul H. Brookes Publishing Co.

Peters, T. (1987). *Thriving on chaos: Handbook for a management revolution.* New York: Harper & Row.

Peters, T.J., & Waterman, R.H. (1982). *In search of excellence: Lessons from America's best-run companies.* New York: Harper & Row.

Racino, J.A. (1986, June). *The community integration project: Resources and research on community integration.* Presentation at conference, "To Join with Others," Waterbury, Ct.

Racino, J.A. (1988a). *Individualized family supports and community living for adults: A case study of a for-profit agency in Minnesota.* Syracuse, NY: Center on Human Policy, Syracuse University.

Racino, J.A. (1988b). *Memorandum: S.P., Inc., Idaho: Future directions and issues* (confidential). Syracuse, NY: Center on Human Policy, Syracuse University.

Racino, J.A. (1988, March). Supporting adults in individualized ways in the community. *TASH Newsletter, 14*(3), 4–5. (Reprinted in *Word from Washington,* August/September 1989, 15–17).

Racino, J.A. (1991a). Individualized supportive living arrangements. In S.J. Taylor, R. Bogdan, & J.A. Racino (Eds.), *Life in the community: Case studies of organizations supporting people with disabilities* (pp. 113–127). Baltimore: Paul H. Brookes Publishing Co.

Racino, J.A. (1991b). Organizations in community living: Supporting people with disabilities. *Journal of Mental Health Administration, 18*(1), 51–59.

Racino, J.A., & Merrill, D. (1989, January). *Residential supports for children with severe disabilities in northeast South Dakota.* Syracuse, NY: Center on Human Policy, Syracuse University.

Racino, J.A., O'Connor, S., Shoultz, B., Taylor, S.J., & Walker, P. (1989, December). *Moving into the 1990s: A policy analysis of community living for adults with developmental disabilities in South Dakota.* Syracuse, NY: Center on Human Policy, Syracuse University.

Racino, J.A., O'Connor, S., Walker, P., & Taylor, S.J. (1991, August). *Innovations in family supports.* Unpublished confidential research report.

Rappahannock Area Community Services Board. (1990, May). *Questions on supportive living.* Fredericksburg, VA: Author.

Rogan, P., & Racino, J.A. (1990, Spring). *Community services and systems change* [Course readings]. Syracuse, NY: Syracuse University, Division of Special Education and Rehabilitation.

Rucker, L. (1987). A difference you can see: One example of services to persons with severe mental retardation in the community. In S.J. Taylor, D. Biklen, & J. Knoll (Eds.), *Community integration for people with severe disabilities* (pp. 109–125). New York: Teacher's College Press.

Sarason, S.B. (1971). *The culture of the school and the problem of change.* Boston: Allyn and Bacon.

Shoultz, B. (1990, April). Issues in providing housing and support. *TASH Newsletter, 15*(4), 6–7.

Shoultz, B. (1991). Regenerating a community. In S.J. Taylor, R. Bogdan, & J.A. Racino (Eds.), *Life in the community: Case studies of organizations supporting people with disabilities* (pp. 195–213). Baltimore: Paul H. Brookes Publishing Co.

TASH. (November, 1990). *Supports for community living: Assisting people to live in homes they control.* Washington, DC: Author.

Taylor, S.J. (1986). *Community living in three Wisconsin counties.* Syracuse, NY: Center on Human Policy, Syracuse University.

Taylor, S.J., Bogdan, R., & Racino, J.A. (Eds.). (1991). *Life in the community: Case studies of organizations supporting people with disabilities.* Baltimore: Paul H. Brookes Publishing Co.

Taylor, S.J., Racino, J.A., Knoll, J.A., & Lutfiyya, Z. (1987). *The nonrestrictive environment: On community integration for people with the most severe disabilities.* Syracuse, NY: Human Policy Press.

Taylor, S.J., Racino, J.A., & Rothenberg, K. (1988, July). *A policy analysis of private community living arrangements in Connecticut.* Syracuse, NY: Center on Human Policy, Syracuse University.

Tjosvold, D. (1987). Participation: A close look at dynamics. *Journal of Management, 13*(4), 739–650.

Traustadottir, R. (1987). *"The answer to my prayers": A case study of the CITE Family Support Program, Cincinnati, Ohio.* Syracuse, NY: Center on Human Policy, Syracuse University.

Villa, R.A., & Thousand, J.S. (1990). Administrative supports to promote inclusive schooling. In W. Stainback & S. Stainback (Eds.), *Support networks for inclusive schooling: Interdependent integrated education* (pp. 201–218). Baltimore: Paul H. Brookes Publishing Co.

Walker, P. (1990, August). Individualized supports for adults: Three residential support agencies. *TASH Newsletter, 15*(8), 12–13.

Walker, P. (1991). Anything's possible. In S.J. Taylor, R. Bogdan, & J.A. Racino (Eds.), *Life in the Community: Case studies of organizations supporting people with disabilities* (pp. 171–185). Baltimore: Paul H. Brookes Publishing Co.

Walker, P., & Racino, J.A. (1988). *Supporting adults with severe disabilities in the community: Selected issues in residential services.* Syracuse, NY: Center on Human Policy, Syracuse University.

Walker, P., & Salon, R. (1991). Integrating philosophy and practice. In S.J. Taylor, R. Bogdan, & J.A. Racino (Eds.), *Life in the community: Case studies of organizations supporting people with disabilities* (pp. 139–151). Baltimore: Paul H. Brookes Publishing Co.

Warrimer, C.K. (1984). A sociology of organizations. In C.K. Warrimer, *Organizations and their environments* (pp. 3–25). Greenwich, CT: JAI Press, Inc.

Wildavsky, A. (1972). The self-evaluating organization. *Public Administration Review, 32,* 509–520.

Yoe, J.T., Carling, P.J., & Smith, D.J. (1991). *A national survey of supported housing programs for persons with psychiatric disabilities.* Burlington, VT: Department of Psychology.

6

"A HOME OF MY OWN"

COMMUNITY HOUSING
OPTIONS AND STRATEGIES

Susan O'Connor and Julie Ann Racino

I was still feeling that my life was being controlled and wondered why I couldn't move into a place of my own (M. Kennedy, personal communication, June 1990).

This statement by Michael Kennedy has been similarly expressed by other people with disabilities who have spent much of their lives in either institutions or group homes. In these places, their lives have often been controlled, for the most part, by people who are paid by agencies to work with them. As housing has become a major issue in this society, people with developmental disabilities, along with other Americans, are beginning to demand access to regular homes—places that they can call their own (Carling, 1989; Tanzman & Yoe, 1989).

This chapter discusses ways of understanding the meaning of a "home of my own," presents a brief overview of today's social and policy issues in the area of housing, builds on suggestions from Chapter 5 for agencies that have typically provided services under one roof to begin to change their role in the area of housing, and suggests strategies for people with disabilities to have access to existing resources to support more personal control of their housing.

This chapter is based primarily on reviews of the literature, telephone interviews conducted with key informants, and training and technical assistance work in states, although some examples are also cited from our qualitative research studies. In particular, the reader is referred to: O'Connor, S., & Racino, J.A. (1989, November). *New directions in housing for people with severe disabilities: A collection of resource materials.* Syracuse, NY: Center on Human Policy, Syracuse University.

A particular note of thanks to the TASH (The Association for Persons with Severe Handicaps) Housing Subcommittee members who shared their insights and work in this area: Bill Mitchell of Washington, D.C., Elaine Ostroff of Massachusetts, Sara Page of Connecticut, Ginny Harmon of Michigan, Diane Cuthbertson of New Jersey, and Jay Klein of New Hampshire.

FROM AGENCY FACILITIES TO A HOME OF MY OWN

As described in Chapter 1, the traditional approach in the human services field to providing housing for people with severe disabilities and elders has been to develop segregated, congregate settings with the intent of providing for all people's needs under one roof.

A number of human services agencies have undertaken a change to decrease their control and ownership of housing and subsequently increase the control and ownership on the part of people with disabilities. This change has meant no new acquisitions of group homes or clustered apartment sites and no new disability agency ownership of property. If the agency cannot terminate ownership, it may look for alternative uses such as renting agency-owned apartments to nondisabled community members. The change also has resulted in the need for new roles in relationship to community housing, as introduced in Chapter 5 of this volume. For people supported by the agency, it has meant assisting people to move into homes and apartments they choose. Sometimes this results in the closing of group homes or a reduction in their size. On an individual basis, it has meant assisting the person to decide where he or she would like to live and with whom.

People with disabilities wish to live in homes like everyone else. Usually people living in a home determine the routines; create the home atmosphere; make decisions about who will enter and live there; develop their own rituals and celebrations; and have a feeling of ownership, whether legal (e.g., mortgage or lease) or simply in spirit and practice. Home, for the most part, is a place where a person belongs and feels at ease. Unlike the presentation of home by many professionalized organizations, home is not primarily a classroom. It is the base from which many people gather strength and reach out to participate in other aspects of community life. It is the site of privacy and companionship. Home is "a feeling as much as a place—safety, love, some laughter, tears, a place of belonging" (Cheatham & Powell, 1986).

A Brief History of Home

The meaning of home has shifted through the years and varies, to some extent, in different cultures. Changes in lifestyles and perceptions of the roles of people in a society influence how home is viewed. The meaning of home varies based on a number of dimensions including gender, ethnicity, culture, and social class. Religion may also influence home and home life, for example, through festivals, rituals and prayers, foods for religious customs, home decorations, home games and songs, gift exchanges, and changes in home routines.

The following extract presents a written history of home and house that particularly highlights the appropriation of the word home to facilities or other settings.

The history of common words illuminates the meanings humans attach to home and house.

The word *home* arises from a Sanskrit root (k'semas) that identifies a safe place to lie down: a separation of outside from inside, defined by a threshold. This sense of safety is elaborated into the social realm through the Gothic (haimo) to mean village and the Old English and Middle English definition of home as a village with its included dwellings. So people are secure at home when they are part of a larger social unit, such as a village or neighborhood.

From about 900 AD, the word home has referred to the center of family economic life; a place where one properly belongs with important people; and where one finds refuge, rest, or satisfaction. To be away from home is to be out of one's element. To be at home means to be at ease and prepared to receive visitors. In some games, home defines the goal and place where a player is safe from attack.

At root, the word house is associated with possession, with having, and thus with a family of terms referring back to the Latin domus (such as domicile, domesticate, and domain). Just to have a house means to possess symbolic and legally recognized authority to include or exclude and to have a say. That which is housed is orderly, proper, and familiar. That which is outside housing is undomesticated, strange, and very likely dangerous (Danto, 1990).

By 1550, English law created a new task for the word house by naming the workhouse a place for the enclosure of the poor under the external control of local authorities. Such houses disciplined their inmates by sheltering them without offering them the status of guests, the authority of householders, or the security of those who are at home. It is the split of shelter from authority, embodied in the workhouse, that defines the sense and quality of the housing generally available in today's state controlled apartment clusters, group homes, institutions, and nursing homes. Not until the 1850's was the word home appropriated to identify an institution intended to provide refuge for the destitute.

Today, people with severe disabilities and their allies search to restore the older, deeper meanings of home and house, and to extend their meaning to people who have historically been, at best, subordinate members of other men's households. (O'Brien, 1991, p. 3)

As O'Brien argues, today there is a need to "restore the older deeper meanings of home and house." This search is not just about a disability movement; it also reflects a societal need to restore the value placed on the home. In the 1850s, while women were relegated to the separate sphere called "home," this place was considered central to our culture. One hundred years later, the political, religious, social, and emotional meanings of home have diminished (Matthews, 1987). These changed meanings of home are part of a larger cultural problem that particularly affects people for whom home provides the necessary supportive base for meaningful societal participation.

Critical Dimensions of Housing, Home, and Household

As described in the introduction to this book, a distinction has been made among housing, which includes the types of housing a person has access to and its legal dimensions through rental, private, and cooperative ownership; home, as a physical place with social, personal, and control dimensions; and household, which reflects decision making across household members and the establishment of the household (see Table 1). Each of these dimensions is discussed further on the following pages.

Table 1. Dimensions of housing, home, and household

Housing

Legal ownership/tenancy	Styles or types	Household
Rental by person with disability	Condominiums	Adequacy of household income
Private ownership by person with disability	Duplexes	Decency of housing and allocation of space
Private ownership by parents or others on individual's behalf	Trailers/Mobile homes	Decisionmaking across household members
Cooperative ownership equity or nonequity	Flats	Household maintenance and routines
Joint rental or ownership, including by person with disability	Apartments in complex	Relationships among household members
Agency ownership on behalf of individual	Single "family" home	Transformation of wages and goods into household use
Disability agency ownership	Apartments attached to houses	Household rhythms and task distribution
	Multiple family homes	Home atmosphere
	Cooperative sites	Negotiation of personal boundaries

Home

Physical Place	Social	Personal	Control
Place of housework	Feeling of belonging, love, and togetherness	Privacy	Home design and adaptations
Place of leisure	Companionship and social network	Personalized to one's tastes	Finance management
Place of learning	Physical presence of others	Self-identity	Home and household management and decision making
Place of convalescence, death, and birth	Relationship between social roles in and outside home	Religions and cultural rituals	Relationships with neighbors, kin, and others
Place of courtship, marriage, and sexual experience	Games, songs, and forms of home play	Daily routines, styles, and interests	Support services and service providers
Place to raise and nurture children and family	Base for friendships and out of home activities	Personal safety and comfort	Home location; ownership/tenancy
Place of culture and education for family and visitors	Offer hospitality	Home atmosphere, pace, and space preferences	Household members
Place to practice religion and cultural traditions		Personal values (e.g., stability)	Access and departure
Place to promote health and daily routines		Respect and dignity	Home rituals and routines
		Reflection of lifestyle	Sense of ownership
		Security	

In many respects, these distinctions reflect similar dimensions to those delineated by O'Brien (1991): ownership—tenancy, individual, or cooperative equity; sense of place—personalized time and space, engagement in household activities, safety and comfort, security of tenure, base for outside activity, means to offer hospitality; and control—choice of place to live, choice of people to live with, control of necessary assistance.

Housing

Legal Ownership and Tenancy Legal ownership and tenancy are important aspects of housing because they legally provide people with disabilities the right to remain in their home. Home and cooperative ownership, as opposed to tenancy, can offer opportunities for building financial equity and can give the homeowner the opportunity to make changes in the physical place without seeking permission from landlords.

However, it is important not to assume that the ideal for everyone is individual or joint home ownership. In fact, some people may prefer cooperative living, which provides some of the benefits of home ownership. Others may prefer the flexibility that leasing offers. To address the barriers to home ownership, a variety of strategies must be used, including addressing the public attitude that people must become materially impoverished to obtain support services. Given the number of barriers in place for home ownership, many people with disabilities will be renting or leasing places.

Styles and Types of Housing For some people, the style of housing may be as important or more important than the issue of technical ownership. For example, in one family, all adult members grew up and moved into condominiums. Being able to follow this traditional family pattern was more important to one woman with disabilities and her family than the legal dimensions involved. Some people feel more secure in an apartment complex that limits access to the buildings, whereas other people may be more concerned about the layout of the place.

Home

Physical Site The literature has reflected a very narrow view of homes and home life for people with disabilities (Racino, 1989). Between 1985 and 1987, for example, the disability literature emphasized the development and operation of service settings as opposed to supporting people in stable homes. Table 1 lists some ways of thinking about home as a physical place. Learning and housework, two areas stressed by service agencies, are only one part of what occurs in homes.

Social, Personal, and Control Dimensions of Home Homes are very complex environments and researchers are still trying to understand the diverse aspects involved. The social dimensions of home include emotional feelings, such as belonging and love; the presence and companionship of others in the home; the relationship of social roles in and outside the home; and forms of social play, expression, and hospitality. Home also has many dimensions that reflect individuality. These include: privacy, personalization to one's taste, self-identity, personal safety and comfort, daily routines, styles and tastes, and personal values. Control dimensions involve all aspects of home life; support services and technical aspects of housing are one small part. Other important aspects are relationships, home and financial management, and an actual sense of ownership.

Household

The most complex areas of home life are decision making across household members and the actual establishment of a household. Critical dimensions involved include the adequacy of household income, the decency of housing and allocation of space, maintenance and routines, personal relationships among household members, transformation of wages and goods into household use, household rhythms and task distribution, and negotiation of personal boundaries.

A "Home of My Own"

It is becoming increasingly common in the disability field to use the term a "home of my own" to refer to a variety of different options. Yet, there is still little understanding about how people with disabilities experience the different dimensions of home, housing, and household. Sometimes people with disabilities, whose lives have often been controlled by agencies, may experience a change in even one dimension (e.g., legal ownership, more personal control) as being "a home of my own." For some people, ownership and control, especially in contrast to following state- or agency-mandated rules, privacy, and relationships with housemates, may be the critical dimensions. For others, independence from support agencies that still maintain substantial control over many aspects of home life may be most important. As options and experiences grow, it is reasonable to anticipate that people's expectations for homes and home life may also increase.

POLICY AND SOCIAL CONTEXT OF HOUSING

This section moves from a discussion of home to housing, starting with an overview of the national community housing situation and related key legislation.

Housing in Today's Society

Since the 1970s, the United States has witnessed a noticeable decline in home ownership, affordable and available rental units, and an increase in the number of people who are homeless. Between 1978 and 1985 the number of poor households rose 25% from 10.5 million in 1978 to 13.3 million in 1985, while the number of rental units costing $250 or less has declined from 9.7 million units in 1970 to only 7.9 million units in 1985 (Lazere & Leonard, 1989).

Describing present trends, Schwartz, Ferlauto, and Hoffman (1988) list the four demographic trends that will pose the greatest challenge to housing policy in the 1990s: 1) the increase in the number of people 75 and older; 2) the sharp upturn in the number of single people living alone and single-parent, female-headed households; 3) the increase in young families buying homes; and 4) the large concentration of poor families that is expected to increase by almost 6 million in the 1990s.

From the points of view of 4,127 surveyed Americans with disabilities, housing affordability, availability, and accessibility are major problems in their lives (de Balcazar, Bradford, & Fawcett, 1988). The major "consumer-identified dimensions" of the problem are: the extreme shortage of accessible, affordable housing; eligibility requirements and regulations that keep people with disabilities who live with family or attendants from living in public or subsidized housing; lack of compliance by builders to laws, codes, and accessibility modifications; and unawareness or lack of interest by managers and directors of public housing to the needs of disabled tenants.

The Legislative Context

The 1980s saw a diminished role by the federal government in the provision of housing. Reductions took place in: new construction of housing; funding to local governments for low and moderate income housing; federal tax incentives to the private sector to produce rental housing; and assistance to the elderly, people with disabilities, American Indians, and farmers. Overall, housing expenditures were cut more in the 1980s than any other federal activity. Housing and Urban Development (HUD) funding diminished 57% from 1980 to 1987 (Schwartz et al., 1988).

The two major pieces of federal legislation affecting housing in this country, including housing for people with disabilities, are the National Affordable Housing Act and the Fair Housing Amendments.

National Affordable Housing Act   In an attempt to provide a framework for a national housing policy, the National Affordable Housing Act (NAHA) was introduced in both the House and Senate in 1988 and passed in 1990. This comprehensive legislation provides a renewed housing policy that could ultimately bring suitable housing within reach for a wider number of people. The legislation gives states and local governments more flexibility to design affordable housing strategies while emphasizing the involvement of local organizations and private industry in the area of housing. It also requires the development of a 5-year plan, the Comprehensive Housing Affordability Strategy (CHAS), to define how federal housing funds will be spent.

The legislation includes a variety of programs that could benefit people with disabilities. These include:

HOPE (Home ownership and Opportunity for People Everywhere)—encourages opportunities for low income people.

HOME Program—used for rental assistance, rehabilitating and creating access, and developing affordable housing in local communities.

Community Development Block Grant (CDBG)—funds housing, human services, economic development, and other activities benefiting low and moderate income people.

Supportive Housing for Persons with Disabilities (the "811 Program")—replaces Section 202 and provides capital grants and rental subsidies for housing for people with disabilities.

While these are important steps to expand housing, continued advocacy is necessary to ensure that financing is available for integrated, individually controlled housing.

Fair Housing Amendments of 1988   Another piece of legislation that has an impact on housing for people with disabilities is the Fair Housing Amendments Act (FHAA) of 1988. The passage of FHAA offers people with disabilities protection under the federal fair housing law and prohibits discriminatory housing practices, whether intentional or not, based on disability and familial status (Brady, 1989; Center for Accessible Housing, 1991). This law is designed to permit people with disabilities to live where they want regardless of the views or prejudices of neighbors, governments, or the real estate industry. Under this act, discrimination includes refusing to make reasonable accommodations in rules, policies, practices, and services when they are necessary in offering people equal opportunity to live in a dwelling and to have "full enjoyment of the premises."

NEW DIRECTIONS IN HOUSING FOR PEOPLE WITH DISABILITIES

Within this national housing context, people with disabilities are starting to explore ways to gain greater control of their own housing. The idea of new directions in housing for people with disabilities is an exciting one. Much of what is needed is already in place in the general housing market; the key is to learn how to begin using what already exists.

A housing and support approach requires a change in the way people and organizations think about housing and housing roles. Often disability organizations are only generally familiar with their community housing situation. One of the initial steps is to explore local housing situations to determine which housing strategies would be most appropriate to pursue. In order to select these strategies, it is important to ask the following questions:

1. Is housing available and affordable?
2. Is housing available, but not affordable?
3. If housing is affordable, is the standard for housing a decent one?
4. Is housing accessible?

Such an initial analysis of the local housing market is necessary before any other housing actions are taken. Even though there is a national housing crisis, some localities may have an abundance of housing and the particular community barriers must be examined. With knowledge of the housing situation, organizations and people with disabilities can: 1) pursue options on a person-by-person basis, 2) work together to advocate for and join with others to develop options that are not currently available, and 3) develop interim strategies that can increase the control of housing by people with disabilities.

Some strategies that have been used to promote greater control by people with disabilities over their housing include: the development and/or participation in cooperatives, the purchase of homes through housing associations, the use of trusts and housing subsidies, housing modifications, and creative use of funding sources. Other areas, which are used by the community-at-large but remain largely unexplored in the field of developmental disabilities, include land trusts.

Housing Associations and Cooperatives

Opportunities for housing used by people with disabilities in the United States and Canada include housing associations and cooperatives (see Table 2). Individuals involved with human services are joining together with community members to develop or influence local housing associations to include people with disabilities.

Cooperatives are often defined as housing collectively owned and operated by and for the mutual benefit of the people who live there. Cooperatives may be formed or supported by a housing association. Housing associations are community, not disability, organizations that help finance and provide assistance in housing. They may develop long-term management support services to co-ops and create long-term stability in housing options. Housing associations use a number of strategies to increase available low and moderate income housing, including

Table 2.   Examples of housing cooperatives and associations

Prairie Housing Cooperative[a] is a non-profit housing association that is operated by people with disabilities and without disabilities throughout Winnipeg, Canada. The cooperative has established several "clusters" of houses in which nondisabled neighbors and housemates offer practical support to members with disabilities. This particular cooperative was established in 1982 in Winnipeg and by 1986 included 20 households or 60 people, 12 of whom had disabilities.

Common Thread Housing Cooperative[b] is a new 16-unit, mixed income cooperative in Connecticut. It has four wheelchair-accessible units planned for families with children and people with severe disabilities who require live-in assistants. The co-op is designed to foster a sense of community with the four buildings arranged around a courtyard and a community room provided for meetings, recreation, and shared meals. As a limited equity co-op, residents will invest $500 and 200 hours of work for a total of $1,500. Upon leaving the co-op, the members receive interest on their initial investment.

Madison Mutual Housing Association[c] is a small housing provider with 206 scattered site units in which 400 individuals reside in Madison, Wisconsin. The organization represents as diverse groups as possible in their housing, including people of different generations, incomes, household compositions, racial and ethnic backgrounds, and ability levels. (For more details, see Racino, chap. 12, this volume.)

[a]Adapted from O'Connor & Racino (1989).
[b]Adapted from Co-op Initiative, Inc. (1991).
[c]Adapted from Racino, J. A. (1991).

mixed income housing. They make homes available to people who otherwise would not be able to afford them.

How Cooperatives Work   Unlike ownership of a single dwelling, cooperatives are owned by a cooperative corporation where all members own a share. Within the co-op structure, the cooperative corporation owns or leases the project, including the land. The corporation is owned jointly by the stockholders who are residents of its land and buildings. The corporation collects monthly payments from each shareholder to cover operating costs. Because of the mutual ownership, cooperative members are interested in carrying out maintenance as well as being part of the day-to-day operations (Lewis & Sullivan, 1988).

Many cooperatives are owned by low and middle income people. Many have been constructed using government loans; some, especially for lower income people, are sponsored by local and state funds as well as Section 8 funds (see section on vouchers and subsidies, pp. 150–151, this chapter). Certificates and housing vouchers may be used because cooperative members own a share of the cooperative corporation and essentially lease rather than own. The cooperative itself is financed under a mortgage based on property value.

Benefits of Cooperative Living   Cooperatives can provide a number of benefits aside from ownership. Members get to know each other because they share an active part in the upkeep of the cooperative. Cooperatives offer individuals the opportunity for joint ownership as well as the following benefits:

People are part of decision-making processes that provide a sense of community.

People develop pride in their homes and are part of, for the most part, a stable community where there are a number of opportunities for people to interact and have friendships.

People earn equity because the money they invest may appreciate.

Cooperatives provide affordable long-term housing.

Cooperatives offer control, security, community, and equity, all of which are very new to people with disabilities (Page, n.d.).

Financing Cooperatives   Financing options for cooperatives take on a variety of forms. Funds are available through HUD, and the Farmers Home Administration (FmHA) under the rural Cooperative Housing program. Debt financing sources include:

Mortgage insurance
National Cooperative Bank
Federal National Mortgage Association
State and local government agencies
Home ownership assistance programs
HUD rental rehabilitation loan

Equity financing sources include:

Foundation and religious organizations
Local Initiative Support Corporation and Enterprise Foundation (Mitchell, 1991b)

A challenge within the disability field is for state agencies serving people with disabilities to find ways to redirect funds that would typically be used for upgrading traditional housing settings such as institutions and group homes into community housing, such as cooperatives (Randolph, Laux, & Carling, 1987).

Common Issues and Dilemmas   The following are issues and dilemmas that are arising in the United States as disability organizations explore the inclusion of people with disabilities in cooperatives.

Cooperatives as Community, Not Disability, Efforts   Although disability organizations can support the development of cooperatives, they generally do not have the broad-based community and housing focus necessary for the success of such an endeavor. Developing and maintaining a functioning cooperative requires a heavy investment of time and resources that disability organizations could better invest in the critical issue of support. Housing is typically handled better by housing organizations.

Integration Through Housing Associations   Some co-ops have a reputation of bringing diverse groups of people together and promoting multigenerational and ethnically and racially integrated communities, whereas others are designated for specific populations (e.g., senior citizens). Cooperatives that view their mission as promoting and living together in a more integrated society are those that are most likely to share a common agenda with disability organizations supporting the full inclusion of people with disabilities.

Cooperatives as an Underutilized Resource   Cooperatives are one of the many options that should be more vigorously pursued for and with people with disabilities. Other options, such as cohousing, a concept borrowed from Sweden, are also starting in the United States and can be another opportunity for people with disabilities to have both the independence and mutuality that are often missing in today's society. In the United States, human services organizations and people with disabilities and their allies are just beginning to recognize the potential for integration by collaborating with housing organizations.

Lack of Balance in Community Organizations   When community organizations are responsive to people with disabilities, there is often a tendency on the part of the disability community to refer a disproportionate number of people to this option. At times, this leads to a congregation of people with disabilities and can transform the community image of a generic agency to that of a specialist service.

Housing Trusts

One method of promoting home ownership as well as future security for people with disabilities is through the use of trusts, which are growing in popularity. There are multiple types of trusts and this section provides an overview of housing trust funds and briefly highlights community land trusts, living trusts, trust programs for families, and private trusts.

Since 1985, housing trust funds have grown from seven such funds across the nation to more than 34 with at least 15 more being developed (Brooks, 1989b). Housing trust funds are sources of revenue (e.g., real estate tax sales, interest on real estate escrow accounts) that are committed to the purpose of providing low and moderate income housing. They are usually established through revenue committed by legislation on a city, county, or state level. Funds usually become available through loans and grants to municipalities, nonprofit development corporations, private developers, individuals, and other organizations. The main commitment is to new construction, rehabilitation, or other housing services including rental subsidies (Brooks, 1989a).

Brooks (1989b) describes five major characteristics of housing trust funds:

1. Ongoing—provide an ongoing source of revenue dedicated to the provision of housing.

2. Production oriented—allocate revenue directly to support construction or preservation of housing.
3. Targeted—commit collected funds to providing low and moderate income housing.
4. Permanent—come into existence by ordinance, legislation, or policy of a unit of government and require government action to be dissolved.
5. Local—locally funded and controlled using nonfederal financial sources and programs to supplement federal support.

The most critical element in the development of a housing trust fund, as Rosen (1987) describes, is that of securing public consensus and support. He suggests that a task force be convened to look at overall community needs, review programs, and make recommendations. This task force should be made up of community members ranging from local officials to developers and realtors, financial community neighborhood groups, and appropriate service providers (Rosen, 1987). Such an approach would be an excellent way for disability rights activists and organizations working on issues of disability to make their housing needs known as well as educate broader community members about issues related to people with disabilities. Some argue that the national housing crisis in this country leaves no choice but to establish such trust funds.

Family Trust Programs   In the United States, a number of agencies involved in disability issues have worked toward establishing trust fund programs for families. One example is the Virginia Beach Trust Program (Field, 1982) in Virginia. The public and private sectors collaborated and formed a private nonprofit association that was initially designed for parents wanting to set up support trusts for their children with disabilities. At the request of some parents, provisions have been added for housing trusts. Although such trusts have been used to set up group homes, this movement toward the development of trusts could be a good vehicle to begin looking at ways to use the trust funds to develop more integrated housing.

Private Trusts   With the establishment of private trusts, a family can appoint a trustee who acts for the beneficiary. The family home, for example, then can be set aside legally for the person with the disability, although the management falls on the trustee. In this situation, as with all trusts, one key is making certain that the person is able to maintain eligibility for various other forms of assistance programs they might receive.

Community Land Trusts   Another largely untapped area, but one being looked at more and more in the area of housing, is that of community land trusts. Community land trusts are based on a commitment to remove community land from the market to provide a variety of community development activities, including the construction of new housing, rental housing, and housing cooperatives, and the rehabilitation of existing structures (Institute for Community Economics, 1986). The goal of such trusts is to promote ecologically sound land use and practices and to preserve long-term affordability of housing.

Trusts can be used for a range of options that could include people with disabilities and assist them to procure secure living options for themselves and their family members. One particular caution is the establishment in some states of a national trust where individual needs are computerized, which can lead to another programmed way of providing services. In addition, trusts can be used to simply replicate traditional patterns of residential living for people with disabilities. Little is known from a research perspective about these trusts, whom they will benefit, and how they work.

Housing Vouchers and Subsidies

Both vouchers and certificates provide assistance to low and moderate income renters to reduce their rental payments and allow them to live in decent homes. A housing subsidy is simply financial assistance given to an individual, organization, or government entity for the purpose of housing or related costs.

Types of Vouchers and Subsidies   There are many types of housing subsidies, including: federal "Section 8" subsidies; "bridge" subsidies through state, regional, or county offices responsible for people with disabilities; and housing subsidies determined on an individual needs basis (e.g., in conjunction with home- and community-based Medicaid services waivers).

Most frequently used is the "Section 8" voucher or certificate provided through the federal HUD program and administered by local housing authorities. People using these certificates or vouchers are required to contribute a maximum of 30% of their adjusted monthly income to rent. HUD then pays the landlord the difference between what the renter pays and the Fair Market rent. This program is very much in demand, but it is encumbered by long waiting lists in communities across the United States.

Several states and counties, through their departments of mental retardation, have also initiated a voucher housing subsidy model. In Connecticut, for example, the Department of Mental Retardation offers such a subsidy with similar requirements to the Section 8 subsidy. It is used after all other possibilities have been exhausted, and, in addition to rent, it can cover security deposits, utilities, and costs related to maintenance. The program also provides information on locating homes though the use of real estate agencies and other community resources.

An example on the county level is the concept of a "bridge program" like the one in Central Virginia where the county community services board, with support from the state Mental Retardation Services Division (MRSD), works closely with the local housing authority to expand housing subsidy opportunities. The division devised a way to fund individuals identical to the Section 8 program. The program acts as a bridge offering individuals financial support while they wait for Section 8 funding, which can take up to 3 years.

On the state level, the North Dakota Division of Developmental Disabilities uses a state housing subsidy in conjunction with their home- and community-based Medicaid waiver program. This subsidy can be used flexibly to cover a variety of housing-related costs; therefore, for example, a person is able to live alone who might not otherwise be able to afford to do so. The housing subsidy is paid for through state funds and supplements an area not covered by the federal program.

Areas To Consider   In thinking about housing subsidies, the following areas are important to consider.

When Housing Subsidies Should Be Used   Housing subsidies are used by people who wish to rent places and who would like the flexibility to be able to move to other locations. This strategy is often chosen when housing is available in a community, but not affordable, or when start-up costs would preclude the rental of a decent place. While housing subsidies by disability organizations are an effective short-term strategy, on a long-term basis national housing policies and financing need to ensure that these subsidies are more generally available for people, including individuals with disabilities.

Lack of Federal Subsidies for Individuals   In the Center on Human Policy's national work, Section 8 subsidies were one of the most unanimously valued programs across states on the local level. However, when negotiations occur on the federal level, preferences of individuals with disabilities are often subsumed to the preferences of agencies and organizations. Inadequate funding and advocacy continues to be placed into expanding these individual subsidies that foster consumer control.

Safety and Decency in Housing   All organizations, no matter what population group they support, should work toward safe and decent housing for all citizens. When local housing codes exist, they should be applied to people with disabilities who own or rent homes. When codes do not exist, quality of life standards (see Racino, chap. 5, this volume) should apply to guide agencies that assist people with disabilities in locating housing. Although state agencies should require certification of any apartment or house owned or leased by an agency, people's own homes should not be certified or licensed.

Housing Modifications

Housing designs are not consistently based on a standard of adaptability; however, housing could be easily converted to meet the specific accessibility needs of individuals or families with disabilities. Even newer housing may require modifications. Currently, inaccessible homes can sometimes result in people needing to rely on personal care attendants simply to help them to get around their own places. Simple renovations, such as roll-in showers, lowering of kitchen cabinets, and side-by-side refrigerators may support someone who otherwise might need to rely on paid services (*Co-op Initiative News*, 1990).

Financing Options   Although there is no single funding source available on the national level for home modifications for accessibility, several resources might provide financing on the local state levels. These include:

Community Development Block Grant
Tax-exempt bonds
Section 8 rental certificates
FmHA Section 504
Landlord financing
Loans for accessibility programs (state) (Mitchell, 1991a)

Two major federal housing sources that have been used on the local level are the community development block grant funding and tax exempt bonds. People supported by a state's home- and community-based Medicaid services waiver (HCBS) may also have access to financing for accessibility needs in the home, such as wheelchair ramps, lifting devices, shower modifications, protective covers, and kitchen work space modifications.

Other options to consider (Mitchell, 1991a) include: Section 8, which allows landlords to make accessibility modifications and pass the cost on to the public housing authority; FmHA Section 504, which is a low interest loan program to assist homeowners in making modifications to their homes; individual negotiations with landlords; and low interest accessibility loan programs, such as the one sponsored by the Co-op Fund of New England, for people with disabilities who are moving into co-ops, mutual housing, and other innovative home ownership options.

Emerging Issues   Two major issues today with home modifications are the continued use of inaccessible housing designs and the lack of experience of contractors with home modifications.

Adaptable Housing Design   Builders and the construction industry continue to base their standard housing designs on models that exclude people with accessibility needs. People with disabilities and their allies need to influence the trade to move toward such standards as universal heights for light switches and the design of homes that can be visited as well as lived in by people with disabilities. Without such standards, these renovations can be costly.

Inexperience with Modifications   Many contractors remain inexperienced with home modifications and without vigilance and assistance from people with disabilities and disability organizations, modifications may be done in ways that do not adequately meet the needs of the people who will live there. People need to create opportunities within their local communities for builders, architects, and others involved in rehabilitation and construction to gain the skills necessary to ensure that changes are done inexpensively, responsively, and within reasonable time frames. Local independent living centers are often a good resource in this area.

Funding Sources

Financing is a key issue in developing the kinds of housing options described in this chapter. Within the disability field, there are specific sources that can assist in moving toward more individualized housing for people with disabilities. They range from federal, state, and local initiatives and programs to tax credits and community options developed by individual agencies, to the use of cooperatives as previously described.

Within the structure of the human services system, funding sources on a national level for services to people with disabilities have come through loans, grants, or special programs such as those provided by HUD. Because many people with disabilities have low incomes, they qualify for most low income loan programs (Randolph et al., 1987). (Additional information on the types of funding available can be found in Skarnulis, E., & Lakin, C. [1990].)

While funding is very complex, several areas are critical to address as initial steps.

Financing for People, Not Organizations   Many federal funding programs targeted specifically for people with disabilities do not provide the flexibility to allow for more individualized development. Some funds, such as HUD 202 funding, have been used to construct facilities that isolate people from other community members and place the locus of control out of the hands of the individual and into the hands of the agency. In addition, using such funds has kept agencies bound to long-term mortgages, often leaving their hands tied when they want to move to a variety of housing options. Greater attention must be paid to how fiscal strategies could be used by people with disabilities, in conjunction with families and allies, to attain greater control over their housing.

Current Mortgages on Agency Facilities   As with the conversion of sheltered workshops to supported work agencies, existing facilities are also an important component of change in some states to support people in their own homes. In most states, major strides can be made without immediately addressing the question of existing, specially built facilities with long-term mortgages. Also, many agency facilities are leased or agencies can find options for other uses (e.g., alternative use plans are required as part of FmHA mortgage). The most problematic situations are those where HUD 202 mortgages have been used or where local community organizations have invested heavily in the financing of the group homes. Although HUD 202 mortgages can be transferred to another group, such as the elderly, caution must be used to ensure that people with disabilities are not supported at the expense of the congregation and segregation of others in our society.

Specialist versus Generalist Issues   The issue of set asides (i.e., allocation of units for certain groups) is one example of a situation where a special interest group, people with a certain disability, often seek to ensure that housing is available for their needs. Set asides are one way to remedy a situation where people with disabilities have been systematically excluded. However, this can create competition and division between groups for scarce housing resources and can limit flexibility on the local level to meet people's needs.

Roles of Bankers, Builders, Realtors, and Developers   Because people with disabilities have been segregated from society, bankers, realtors, and builders may not have the training or background on issues that can benefit people with disabilities. Similar to any process, it will take time to develop the training and investment of people in these issues, but the current demand can be expected to increase people's interest in gaining this knowledge and expertise. People in the disability field need to begin fostering these relationships and supporting these new roles.

COMMUNITY RESOURCES

A multitude of organizations, agencies, and people have been involved in developing our housing stock and looking at creative, cooperative, and individual ways to offer housing to all people. People in the field of disabilities must begin to understand how people with disabilities can be included in the vast housing networks and resources available.

As people with disabilities, together with family, friends, and human services professionals, pursue efforts to make community integration a reality, people in the disability field must join with other community members and use resources that are beyond the present scope of the disability network. These include already established community networks around the development of cooperatives, low income housing, and specific interest groups. (See Appendix A to this volume for a listing of some of these organizations.)

One example is the Women's Institute for Housing and Economic Development, which has already been working toward providing better housing. This is a nonprofit organization providing economic development expertise and technical assistance, information, and education to women, and has a wealth of information that may be of interest to women with disabilities and agencies supporting them. The National Association for Housing Cooperatives is an excellent resource for information on development, funding, and education. Other organizations such as Habitat for Humanity, an ecumenical Christian housing ministry, have worked internationally to build houses in communities. Habitat for Humanity has recently written a statement of purpose that specifically acknowledges that their ministry includes people with disabilities. These, in addition to a number of other housing and economic development organizations provide excellent information not yet fully pursued by people with disabilities and human services professionals.

Partnerships between the housing and disability communities can begin to educate the broader public on issues that affect people with disabilities. Building these networks is crucial to ensure that the needs of people with disabilities are addressed in regular housing instead of continuing to be viewed under the purview of the specialty disability system. Demonstration projects to improve coordination of government departments concerned with housing and support, such as Australia's Shelter Victoria Housing and Intellectual Disability Project, can help build the necessary bridges between the housing and disability communities. Such efforts are critical to ensure coordination of housing and supports once these responsibilities are separated into the two sectors.

MOVING FORWARD WITH HOUSING

Building alliances between the disability field and other community organizations, such as housing associations and community development, offers the potential for greater creativity in generating solutions that will enhance all members of the community. Some specific strategies that could be pursued to build stronger alliances include:

Joint advocacy efforts on housing issues that promote choice in integrated housing, such as the "mobile Section 8 program" and housing vouchers.

Better use of resources by the disability field, such as the expertise of real estate agents in understanding the financing issues involved and of community developers in understanding the nature of communities.

Advocacy for state legislation to make all housing adaptable.

Inclusion of people with disabilities and their families in local, state, and national housing efforts.

Joint efforts with other groups, such as low income housing coalitions

and the elderly, to develop a greater supply of decent, affordable, and accessible housing in communities throughout this country.
Development and highlighting of statewide and local projects inclusive of people with severe disabilities.
Exploration of ways to coordinate housing, which is provided by housing organizations, with support services provided by other organizations.

FUTURE ISSUES AND DILEMMAS IN HOUSING AND HOME

Future directions in housing for people with disabilities can no longer be viewed as an issue to be solved by those involved in disability issues alone. Housing is a community issue and building bridges between the housing and disability fields is becoming increasingly important to promote and encourage new networks on housing issues and increase the awareness of housing organizations to include people with disabilities. Given the importance of housing as an issue in this country today, it is critical for people with disabilities to be part of accessing and planning for equal housing opportunities. The ultimate challenge lies with society to create communities that provide access to all citizens.

For people with disabilities, a house or place of their own in the legal and physical sense helps lay the groundwork for creating a home and becoming valued members of their communities. As Gunnar Dybwad (personal communication, April 1990) shared, "Just the fact we are talking about people with mental retardation living in condominiums and owning places is an accomplishment. Who would have thought this would be possible 10 years ago?" Similar to other aspects of a housing and support approach, a change in how agencies relate to people with disabilities is critical, as is the promotion of roles such as neighbors, tenants, home owners, and contributors. Whether coming together to share home life, to create a sense of belonging and ownership, or to work together to contribute to solutions of community issues, a housing and support approach offers an opportunity for us all to come together in new ways and with new hopes and expectations for what is possible for our communities and our future.

BIBLIOGRAPHY

Ardinger, R.S. (n.d.). *Fair Housing Amendments Act of 1988: How the new law works and protects persons with disabilities.* Columbia, MD: Ardinger Consultants and Associates.
Barnes, A. (1986). *Black women: Interpersonal relationships in profile: A sociological study of work, home and community.* Indiana: Wyndham Press.
Brady, P. (1989, February/March). Fair housing final regs published. *Word from Washington,* 18–20.

Brazil, R., & Carle, N. (1988). An ordinary home life. In D. Towell (Ed.), *An ordinary life in practice: Developing comprehensive community-based services for people with learning disabilities* (pp. 59–67). London: King Edward's Hospital Fund for London.

Brooks, M. (1989a). *A guide to developing a housing trust fund.* Washington, DC: Center for Community Change.

Brooks, M. (1989b). *A survey of housing trust funds.* Washington, DC: Center for Community Change.

Carling, P. (1989). Access to housing: Cornerstone to the American dream. *Journal of Rehabilitation, 55*(3), 6–8.

Carling, P.J., Randolph, F.L., Blanch, A.K., & Ridgway, P. (1988). A review of the research on housing and community integration for people with psychiatric disabilities. *NARIC Quarterly, 1*(3), 6–18.

Center for Accessible Housing. (1991). *The Fair Housing Amendments Act of 1988: Provisions relating to discrimination based on disability.* Raleigh, NC: Author.

Center on Human Policy. (1987). *Annotated bibliography on community programs for people with severe disabilities.* Syracuse, NY: Author.

Center on Human Policy. (1989). *Policy institute 1989: Community living for adults summary.* Syracuse, NY: Author.

Cheatham, A., & Powell, M.C. (1986). *This way day break comes: Women's values and the future.* Philadelphia: New Society Publishers.

Cooperative Housing Foundation, & National Association of Housing Cooperatives. (n.d.). *Cooperative housing: People helping each other.* Silver Spring, MD, and Alexandria, VA: Authors.

Co-op Initiative, Inc. (1991). Innovative model housing cooperative in Manchester. In E. Ostroff & J.A. Racino, *There's no place like home: Creating opportunities for housing that people want and control. Participants' reference book.* Seattle, WA: The Association for Persons with Severe Handicaps, Community Living Committee, Subcommittee on Housing.

Co-op Initiative News. (1990). Hartford, CT: Co-op Initiatives Project.

Covert, S. (1990). *A facility is not a home: A report on the housing symposium.* Durham: University of New Hampshire.

Danto, A. (1990). Abide/Abode. In L. Taylor (Ed.), *Housing: Symbol, structure, site.* New York: Cooper-Hewitt Museum.

de Balcazar, Y.S., Bradford, B., & Fawcett, S.B. (1988). Common concerns of disabled Americans: Issues and options. *Social Policy, 19*(2), 29–35.

Field, P. (1982). *A guideline for developing a community trust program.* Virginia Beach: The Virginia Beach Trust Fund Program for Developmentally Disabled People and Their Families.

Goldin, H. (1941). *The Jewish woman and her home.* New York: Hebrew Publishing Co.

Gramlich, E. (1991, June). *Comprehensive housing affordability strategy (CHAS): A citizen's action guide.* Washington, DC: Center for Community Change.

Housing & Intellectual Disability Project. (1988, February). *The need for coordination between the Ministry of Housing (MOH) and Community Services Victoria-Office of Intellectual Disability Services (CSV-OIDS).* Collingwood, Victoria, Australia: Author.

Housing Technical Assistance Project. (n.d.). *Building partnerships.* Washington, DC, and Upper Marlboro, MD: Housing Technical Assistance Project, Association for Retarded Citizens and National Association Home Builders National Research Center.

Housing Technical Assistance Project. (n.d.). *Volume I: The development process; Volume II: The financing mechanisms.* Washington, DC, and Upper Marlboro,

MD: Housing Technical Assistance Project, Association for Retarded Citizens and National Association Home Builders National Research Center.

Housing Technical Assistance Project. (1989). *Working with non-profit developers of affordable housing to provide integrated housing options for people with disabilities.* Washington, DC, and Upper Marlboro, MD: Housing Technical Assistance Project, Association for Retarded Citizens and National Association Home Builders National Research Center.

Institute for Community Economics. (1986, June). *The community land trust: A new system of land tenure.* Greenfield, MA: Author.

Johnson, M. (1989). Housing for all. *The Disability Rag, 10*(1).

Kappel, B., & Wetherow, D. (1986). People caring about people: The Prairie Housing Cooperative. *Entourage, 1*(4).

Kron, J. (1983). *Home-psych: The social psychology of home and decoration.* New York: Clarkson N. Potter, Inc.

Lawrence, R.J. (1987). What makes a house a home? *Environment and Behavior, 19*(2), 154–168.

Lazere, E.B., & Leonard, P.A. (1989). *The crisis in housing for the poor: A special report on Hispanics and blacks.* Washington, DC: Center on Budget and Policy Priorities.

Lewis, T., & Sullivan, J. (1988). Housing cooperatives threatened with thousands of dollars in delinquent taxes and penalties. *Housing Cooperative Journal,* 3–5.

Luxton, M. (1980). *More than a labour of love: Three generations of women's work in the home.* Ontario, Canada: Women's Educational Press.

Marcus, H.B. (1985). *Yours, mine and ours.* Washington, DC: National Association of Housing Cooperatives.

Marcuse, P. (1989). The pitfalls of specialism: Special groups and the general problem of housing. In S. Rosenberry & C. Hartman (Eds.), *Housing issue of the 1990s.* New York: Praeger Publishers.

Massachusetts Housing Partnership and the Adaptive Environments Center. (1991). *A consumer's guide to home adaptations.* Author.

Matthews, G. (1987). *"Just a housewife": The rise and fall of domesticity in America.* New York: Oxford University Press.

Matthews, G.F. (1983). *Voices from the shadow: Women with disabilities speak out.* Toronto: The Women's Educational Press.

Mental Health Law Project. (1988). *The impact of the fair housing amendments on land-use regulations affecting people with disabilities.* Washington, DC: Author.

Mitchell, B. (1990, July). Obtaining financial support for housing for people with mental retardation. *ARC Facts.*

Mitchell, B. (1991a). *Financing home modifications for accessibility.* Washington, DC: Author.

Mitchell, B. (1991b). *Financing sources for cooperatives.* Washington, DC: Author.

National Association of Housing Cooperatives. (1977). *Cooperative housing: People helping each other.* Washington, DC: Author.

National Housing Institute. (n.d.). *Shelterforce.* Orange, NJ: Author.

O'Brien, J. (1991, August). *Down stairs that are never your own: Supporting people with developmental disabilities in their own homes.* Lithonia, GA: Responsive Systems Associates.

O'Connor, G. (1976). *Home is a good place: A national perspective of community residential facilities for developmentally disabled persons.* Washington, DC: American Association on Mental Deficiency.

O'Connor, S., & Racino, J.A. (1989). *New directions in housing for people with severe disabilities: A collection of resource materials.* Syracuse, NY: Center on Human Policy, Syracuse University.

O'Connor, S., Racino, J.A., Kennedy, M., & Taylor, S.J. (1990, June). *New directions in housing for people with disabilities.* Unpublished manuscript.

Ostroff, E., & Racino, J.A. (1990, November). *There's no place like home: Creating opportunities for housing that people want and control: Participants reference book.* Seattle: The Association for Persons with Severe Handicaps (TASH) Housing Subcommittee.

Oxford English Dictionary (2nd ed.). (1983). Origins, NY: Greenwich.

Page, S. (n.d.). *The Co-op Initiatives Project.* Belchertown, MA: Page Associates.

Paterson, A., & Rhubright, E. (1988, September). *Housing for the mentally ill: A place called home* (Human Services Series, Vol. 13, No. 26). Denver, CO: National Conference of State Legislatures.

Pressman, A., & Pressman, P. (1980). *Integrated space systems: Vocabulary for room languages.* New York: Van Nostrand Reinhold Co.

Racino, J.A. (1989). *Annotated bibliography on homes and women with disabilities.* Unpublished literature review.

Racino, J.A. (1991). Individualized supportive living arrangements. In S.J. Taylor, R. Bogdan, & J.A. Racino (Eds.), *Life in the community: Case studies of organizations supporting people with disabilities* (pp. 113–127). Baltimore: Paul H. Brookes Publishing Co.

Racino, J.A. (1991). *Madison Mutual Housing Association and Cooperative: People and housing building communities.* Syracuse, NY: Center on Human Policy, Syracuse University.

Racino, J.A., O'Connor, S., Shoultz, B., Taylor, S., & Walker, P. (1991, May). Housing and support services: Some practical strategies (Part II). *TASH Newsletter, 17*(5), 16–17.

Randolph, F.L., Laux, B., & Carling, P.J. (1987). *In search of housing: Creative approaches to financing integrated housing.* Burlington, VT: Center for Community Change Through Housing and Community Support.

Raynes, N., Sumpton, R., & Flynn, M. (1987). *Homes for the mentally handicapped.* London: Tavistock Publications.

Ridgway, P. (Ed.). (1988). *Coming home: Expatients view housing options and needs.* Burlington, VT: Center for Community Change Through Housing and Support.

Ridgway, P., & Carling, P.J. (1987). *Strategic planning in housing and mental health.* Burlington, VT: Center for Community Change Through Housing and Support.

Rosen, D. (1987). *Housing trust funds.* Chicago: American Planning Association.

Rosen, D. (1988). Affordable housing: The American day dream. *Business and Society Review, 67,* 67–70.

Schwartz, D.C., Ferlauto, R.C., & Hoffman, D.N. (1988). *New housing policy for America.* Philadelphia: Temple University Press.

Sheen, T.M. (1988). *Attorney handbook: Estate planning for persons with disabilities.* Elmhurst, IL: Illinois Self-Sufficiency Trust.

Shoultz, B. (Ed.). (1989, November). *Community living for adults.* Syracuse, NY: Center on Human Policy, Syracuse University.

Shoultz, B. (Ed.). (1990, November). *Annotated bibliography on community integration, revised.* Syracuse, NY: Center on Human Policy, Syracuse University.

Shoultz, B. (1991). Regenerating a community. In S.J. Taylor, R. Bogdan, & J.A. Racino (Eds.), *Life in the community: Case studies of organizations supporting people with disabilities* (pp. 195–213). Baltimore: Paul H. Brookes Publishing Co.

Siegler, R., & Levy, H.J. (1986). Brief history of cooperative housing. *Cooperative Housing Journal,* 12–19.

Skarnulis, E., & Lakin, C. (Eds.). (1990). Consumer controlled housing [Feature issue]. *IMPACT, 3*(1).

Szenasy, S. (1985). *The home: Exciting new designs for today's lifestyles.* New York: McMillan Publishing Co.

Tanzman, B., & Yoe, J. (1989). *Vermont consumer housing and supports preference study.* Burlington, VT: Center for Community Change Through Housing and Support.

Taylor, S.J., Bogdan, R., & Racino, J.A. (Eds.). (1991). *Life in the community: Case studies of organizations supporting people with disabilities.* Baltimore: Paul H. Brookes Publishing Co.

Taylor, S.J., Racino, J.A., Knoll, J.A., & Lutifyya, Z. (1987). *The nonrestrictive environment: On community integration for people with the most severe disabilities.* Syracuse, NY: Human Policy Press.

Taylor, S.J., Racino, J.A., & Rothenberg, K. (1988). *A policy analysis of private community living arrangements in Connecticut.* Syracuse, NY: Center on Human Policy, Syracuse University.

Tilly, L., & Scott, J. (1978). *Women, work, and family.* New York: Holt, Rinehart, Winston.

Werner, C.M. (1987). Home interiors: A time and place for interpersonal relationships. *Environment and Behavior, 19*(2), 169–179.

Wilcox, R. (1987). *Community sponsorship of housing cooperatives.* Alexandria, VA: National Association of Housing Cooperatives.

Wolf, J. (1990). Out of mind, out of sight? From housing discrimination to public accommodations legislation. *Journal of Disability Policy Studies, 1*(2), 99–110.

7

"OPENING THE DOORS"

THE STATE ROLE
IN HOUSING AND SUPPORT

Julie Ann Racino

Bureaucracies are run by well meaning people who often are caught in rules, procedures and ways of doing things that other well intentioned people have put in place.
When rules stand in the way of full citizenship, they can be adapted, modified or
changed. Think always with creativity and innovation, and above all, start by focusing on the individual rather than the system.
(Cory Moore and Ralph Moore, RTC on Community Integration, 1988, p. 5)

The movement of people from institutions in many states has been
accompanied by a growth in the community services systems, although
to differing extents from state to state. During the 1980s, the complexity
of the service systems, the nature of society's regulatory environments,
and the pace of change have resulted in structures and mechanisms that
often do not and cannot respond well to the needs and desires of people
with disabilities and their families.

This chapter briefly reviews critical dimensions of state systems,
highlights state approaches to housing and support, describes changing
roles of state disability departments, and discusses critical issues in moving toward a housing and support approach, including ways of thinking
about planning, "case management," quality assurance, financing, and
change.

The Center on Human Policy is in its second year of a 5-year study of state systems
change and practices in community integration and deinstitutionalization. This chapter,
however, is based on technical assistance and training (including policy analyses) conducted from 1985 to 1990 in several states and does not reflect the findings of this
forthcoming study.

The author would particularly like to thank Gary Smith, John O'Brien, Steve Taylor,
Frank Laski, Bonnie Shoultz, Gunnar Dybwad, the late Ben Censoni, Jerry Provencal,
Nancy Rosenau, David Towell, Charlie Lakin, Paul Carling, and John Lord for their direct
and indirect contributions to our work in the policy and change area.

THE STATE CONTEXT

No two state systems are alike and their political environments vary tremendously from each other. Therefore, to some extent a state must be approached uniquely when discussing state change strategies.

One critical dimension on which states vary and that is crucial to a housing and support approach is centralization or decentralization of control. Some states, such as New York, are heavily state controlled, even though regional offices exist throughout the state. Many of the important decisions about services, such as how rates are established and services are defined, are determined by the central offices with little influence from local communities.

Other states, such as Nebraska, have more power at the regional level; although there is a push in this state to move toward more centralized control. States such as Wisconsin give substantial decision-making authority to counties. Such comparisons of states are important because some aspects of a housing and support approach require a more decentralized, local form of control.

State systems also vary on other dimensions. A few of the dimensions relevant to changing to a housing and support approach include:

Degree of centralization and decentralization
Relationship of state office of developmental disabilities with other state
     departments
Nature of relationship between department and governor
Commitment to community versus institutional services as evidenced by
     financial and demographic measures
Presence and strength of advocacy groups independent of service provi-
     sion and community and institutional parent groups
Legislation and court cases on deinstitutionalization and integration
Nature of the state political system, legislature, and state political values
Nomenclature, financing, and structure of community service system

How States Approach Housing and Support

In the mid- to late 1980s, a series of developments on the state level contributed toward policies and practices that could better support the integration and participation of people with disabilities in community life. These included initiatives for supporting people to live in homes of their own.

Promoting Choice   On the state level, one of the precursors of a support approach is Michigan's Supported Independence Program, which cut across the fields of developmental disabilities and mental health. It was one of the first state initiatives that explicitly indicated that staff should move instead of people, and required that people with disabilities be involved in the selection of where they would live and with whom. The program had a number of limitations, including some difficulty in obtaining approval for 24-hour support services and the potentially damaging fiscal tradeoff of tying the reimbursement rate to the unit instead of people. Table 1 provides highlights and issues of this program based on a site visit in 1987.

Table 1.   Michigan supported independence program

Principles of the Program
(from Michigan Department of Mental Health Services Standards, 7/31/87)
1.   The program must provide the participants with as much autonomy as possible.
2.   The program must be designed to meet the needs of the participant, i.e.: location, type of residence, staff support, etc.
3.   The program must be flexible and responsive to changes in the participant's needs, particularly with regard to staff support. Providers must be able to add, or withdraw support as the participant and his/her I-team deem appropriate.
4.   The participant is an active member of the I-team. His/her preferences for living situation, roommate arrangements, employment are very seriously regarded.
5.   The residence (home, apartment) is that of the participant(s), not the staff or provider. Professional staff should observe the same courtesies they would entering anyone else's home.
6.   Each site will serve no more than 3 people.
7.   Wherever possible, the person's current I-team should continue to provide support services in their new residence.

Additional Highlights
1.   The contract rate is based on the recipient's utilization of approved service categories and may be adjusted as services change.
2.   Exceptions request mechanism also used for the supported independence program to increase added support when needed.
3.   Program has made extensive use of home modifications to adapt places to meet the needs of individual people.
4.   Assessments include a focus on: client training needs and needs for supervision/assistance, staff training needs, needs for specialized or adaptive equipment, recommended type and frequency of service contacts, recommended staffing, and needs/recommendations for special services.

Issues
1.   Plans are developed for individual people, but cost centers become the home; aspects of contracting process (e.g., 95% occupancy rate) based on group as opposed to individuals.
2.   Greater availability for people with severe physical disabilities as opposed to severe intellectual limitations; person must be able to live in the community without "continuous supervision" as opposed to supports.
3.   Team recommendations tend to lean toward oversupervision initially.
4.   A variety of implementation issues, including assisting state personnel and private providers to change to a new approach.
5.   Initial lack of a mechanism for a participant to change to a new provider during the contract period if so desired.
6.   No provision for the person hiring their own attendant; all staff are hired by the provider.
7.   Little emphasis on building on "natural supports" in the community.

Based on site visit in fall 1987 and review of statewide guidelines for the supported independence program.

From Taylor, S. J., Racino, J. A., & Rothenberg, K. (1988, July). *A policy analysis of private community living arrangements in Connecticut.* Syracuse, NY: Center on Human Policy, Syracuse University; pp. 65–66. Reprinted with permission.

Moving to a Closer Tie of Funding, Assessment, and Planning
Wisconsin, through its Community Integration Program (CIP) Waivers
and Community Options Program (COP), was a state leader in developing an individualized planning and funding process through their Medicaid waiver mechanisms. The counties could average costs across people
so that each person could obtain varying amounts of supports in different combinations. It was also one of the first states to work indepth with
counties (or regional structures) to develop local capacities for individualized planning of support services, instead of the traditional residential
services model.

As early as 1986, Wisconsin's assessment process was individualized and integration-oriented and included informal supports, personal preferences, and social participation. The purpose of the assessment
was to gather current, valid information about a specific person and his
or her environment in order to determine what services, supports, and
other environmental modifications would be necessary to enable the
person to live and participate in the community with as much dignity
and value as possible.

Creating State Policies in Support of Community Life   Connecticut
has made several important contributions toward a housing and support
approach. The mission statement of the Department of Mental Retardation is a concise, yet excellent, guide, which was skillfully tied to some
evaluation instruments (see Rammler, 1986, for a review of day programs). The statement is as follows (Connecticut Department of Mental
Retardation, 1986):

> The mission of the Department of Mental Retardation is to join with
> others to create the conditions under which all people with mental
> retardation experience:
> *Presence* and *participation* in Connecticut town life
> Opportunities to develop and exercise *competence*
> Opportunities to make *choices* in the pursuit of a personal future
> Good *relationships* with family members and friends
> *Respect* and *dignity*

The Minnesota, Pennsylvania, and Connecticut developmental disabilities councils have also played major roles in advocating for policies in
support of community integration and inclusion. Minnesota maintained
a state and national leadership role in promoting "A New Way of Thinking" (Governor's Planning Council on Developmental Disabilities, 1987).
Pennsylvania paved the way in supporting local "bridge-building" and
community participation efforts. The Connecticut Developmental Disabilities Council was one of the first to include personal assistance in its
plan and to approach these issues on a cross-disability basis.

Promoting Flexibility and Individualization in Systems   Connecticut also developed a temporary support services fund, which was used

to pay for time-limited services to keep people in the community. As described by regional staff and providers, these funds were used successfully to obtain additional staffing to respond to crises, to provide intense support services for people with challenging behaviors, and to fund nursing care for people experiencing or recovering from acute medical conditions. It is similar to Michigan's exception payment mechanism that allows for built-in systems flexibility in existing services.

Minnesota was one of the first states to develop local capacities for planning individualized or customized packages of support services. This is the precursor of the market economy approach to housing and support, which is now apparent in other states' plans for supporting adults. Reflective of societal values, this market approach holds some of the same problems for disability services as it does for society-at-large.

Promoting Supportive Living as a Feasible Systems Strategy   The Individualized Supportive Living Arrangements Program (ISLA) in North Dakota broke myths about the feasibility of supporting people on a person-by-person basis. Although there were a number of philosophy and practice issues related to its implementation, North Dakota showed that many more options for choice, including selection of roommates and places to live, could be accomplished in a time frame that need not exceed that usually involved in traditional residential services development. This could be done without compromising what was considered the "accepted level of quality in the state." It also illustrated how state funding could be used for decent, affordable housing and combined on a person-by-person basis with the Medicaid waiver.

Developing State Supportive Living Programs   States are developing discrete supportive living programs: two of these are highlighted here because they are based on similar philosophical principles but very different service designs.

The Illinois Community Integrated Living Arrangements (CILA) Act was passed on August 30, 1988, and provided the statutory base to promote the development of community integrated living arrangements based on a customized array of support services for individuals. Although in many ways this was a positive step in Illinois for expanding community services, the CILA program excludes many people with severe disabilities, particularly with medical, psychiatric, or challenging behaviors. Its service array includes facilities; standards and licensure bear many similarities with traditional quality assurance approaches. The CILA was followed by the development of the Community Supported Living Arrangements (CSLA) Option, with Illinois selected as one of the eight states to participate in the federal CSLA program. Because of per person funding limitations, it is likely that people with the most severe disabilities will continue to be excluded.

Another example is Florida's Department of Health and Rehabilitative Services' Supportive Independent Living program, which is described as a person rather than a program model. By design it is stronger than the Illinois proposal on aspects of personal control over supports; it seeks to change the roles of staff in relationship to people with disabilities and to be more inclusive. The determination of a standard model, in this case an independent living coach, basically places limitations on choice and control by people with disabilities. The program has approached most "residential" issues in creative and responsive ways.

Changing State Policy To Support People Living in Their Own Homes Maryland was one of the first states to develop regulations directly related to supportive living. However, other states throughout the country, ranging from Arkansas to Connecticut to Idaho, made changes in policies and regulations earlier to allow people to live in their own homes. This included changes in their Medicaid waiver application (Arkansas), waivers in state nursing practices (Idaho), and changes in state policy (Connecticut). Today, states, such as New Hampshire, are developing distinct policy statements on supportive living. However, it is still unclear whether these efforts will work to the benefit of people with disabilities.

Encouraging Agency and Systems Change The developmental disabilities councils in states such as Maryland have used their grants to encourage agencies to rethink the way they approach people with disabilities. Other states, such as New York, have focused more on distinct housing initiatives and training of parents and people with disabilities, emulating Minnesota's Partners in Policymaking.

Local agency programs in states such as Ohio and Colorado created the examples and the environment necessary for broader systemic state policy and program change. Through their work in listening to people with disabilities, they identified ways systems had a negative impact on people, and provided potential avenues for state policy changes that might make it easier for other agencies to respond to the desires of people with disabilities.

Separating and Coordinating Housing and Support Michigan (1991) has pursued housing policy statements delineating principles based on housing and on support, thus beginning to define the department's role in both areas. These include:

Individuals shall have choice in selecting where and with whom they live.

Units shall be both *in* and *of* community. Housing units must be scattered throughout a building, a complex, or community in order to achieve integration.

Public and private housing, subsistence, and support subsidies shall be maximized.

Supports shall be rendered in-home versus requiring out-of-home placements to receive same and/or progress to a different level of support.

Support services shall give attention to the consumer's need for assistance in assuming responsibility for management of his or her home.

Generic services and support shall be maximized.

These changes are important because they move away from a "supportive living program" to an effort to redefine how housing and supports will be approached.

Promoting Choice in "Case Management" If pressed to point to a solid system of *case management*, Macomb-Oakland Regional Center, Michigan, is an organization that has created an environment where the role of case managers in family support is based on relationship-building with families and being with people when they are needed and wanted. It is this characteristic, not "choice" per se, that appears to be most valued by parents and people with disabilities. Family support programs for children with technological assistance needs, such as those in Maryland, demonstrate the importance of choice of a case manager, including the options for parents (and by extension, people with disabilities), to be able to perform all or some of these "case management" functions if she or he chooses to do so.

Supporting Community for All New Hampshire, through its 1991 closure of Laconia, its only state public institution for people with developmental disabilities, and the concomitant development of decent community services, played a major role in moving discussion away from the institution-community debate. The story of this institutional closure is one of a person-centered approach to both people with disabilities and staff, and illustrates how such an approach may be key for larger changes to occur.

Changing Roles of State Departments in Housing and Support

As the field moves toward new paradigms of support, the roles of state departments also are continuing to change. A few of these roles are described below.

One new role of state disability departments is to separate housing and support services and to explore new ways to work with state housing departments. This separation aspect will involve unbundling the financing between housing and services, which varies from state to state; changing legislation, regulations, and policies that may prohibit people from living in their own homes; and separating, on the local level, the role of housing and support organizations.

Housing and support must also be coordinated with each other at the levels of the individual, the agency, and the state. This means new roles for state offices of mental retardation/developmental disabilities that must learn about and make new connections with the state housing department. Most states have a need for a project, such as one conducted in Australia, where the barriers to coordination are explored and strategies pursued from both the disability and housing sides (Housing and Intellectual Disability Project, 1988).

Another new role of state disability departments is to identify and address impediments in their own systems that stand in the way of full community participation, including adults living in their own homes. Even if funding and services are available, other barriers may prohibit certain groups of people from living in their own homes. For example, state Nursing Practice Acts may require certain professional qualifications for staff that virtually end up excluding people with medical needs from living in a regular home. People with physical disabilities who need daily assistance with medications, catheters, injections, and ventilators are also being prohibited from living in the community due to these same types of restrictions (Kennedy, 1991).

States can explore options to allow individuals to be trained, and have these options approved on an individual basis to provide necessary medication and other in-home supports to a specific person. Other states have addressed this issue through revised regulations or waivers granted by the nursing boards; a regional and national strategy has not yet been pursued.

A new role of state disability departments is to become more familiar with generic services in their state and to explore new ways of coordination across different disability groups. State departments tend to be insular in their approach, usually competing with other departments for limited state resources. Although coordination has always been a stated, yet seldom practiced value, the future quality of life for people with developmental disabilities requires these efforts to occur. The solutions to many disability issues will not and cannot come from the field of developmental disabilities alone.

As one example, planners in the disability field must change their role to become more integrated into regular planning processes for housing, neighborhood service-based initiatives, recreation, and other nondisability systems. This needs to be done in a more collaborative approach, such as by mutual resource sharing, with concern for all population groups. Another example is that the costs must be shared for supports for people with dual labels if they are to be supported in community life.

Departments must change their roles to view the problems with generic systems such as personal assistance as *their* problems, instead of assuming that their only role is to integrate people in these other systems. This will take time; fundamental changes that are necessary to improve people's quality of life must not be sacrificed for short-term surface changes.

Disability departments should support providers in gaining experience in developing individualized and flexible supports. In many states, individuals with severe disabilities are served within congregate settings. Except for people with mild disabilities, many have limited experience in supporting adults in more individualized and flexible ways. States, particularly with a private provider system, must play a role in assisting providers to obtain this expertise. These roles can include encouraging and supporting creativity on the part of providers, addressing systems barriers as they are identified through the development of individualized plans, making possible the use of nontraditional support, ensuring the adequacy of funding and resources, and working together to translate from demonstrations to broader service networks. One of the major barriers to overcome in most systems is the lack of trust between providers and the central and/or regional offices.

Disability departments must promote decision making on the part of people with disabilities and take direction from this constituency. Policies seldom differentiate between the views of people with mental retardation and those of family members. All state policies need to be reviewed to ensure that people with disabilities have an opportunity for choice, and that they will be adequately informed of and involved in all issues related to their lives. People's right to be informed should not be abridged by the need for support in decision making or the presence of a guardianship arrangement.

Providers will need assistance in issues related to the implications of liability policies and tax laws on personal choice. This will require stances on the parts of states to work with providers to see these barriers as issues of mutual concern. For example, the *independent provider mode* of personal assistance, which is the form of personally controlled assistance, is now in jeopardy in some states. These problems need to be seen as fundamental to personal control, not as simply program or fiscal concerns.

As agencies need to learn to take direction from people with disabilities, state systems also need to learn how to respond to this new constituency, instead of to the agencies and others who have previously played this role. In moving to a family driven system, states are placing people with disabilities in the role of self-advocates, instead of examining the changes that a person-centered system implies for all processes in state government, such as regulatory, legislative, and program initiatives.

MOVING TOWARD HOUSING AND SUPPORT ON THE STATE LEVEL

This section describes some ways to start thinking about housing and support today and raises some initial issues that must be addressed in moving toward the more extensive changes that will be required on a long-term basis. This section does not create a vision for the future, but seeks to introduce the reader to basic information that will be necessary for a more broad-based discussion that must involve people with disabilities, parents, and others who have traditionally been excluded from these issues.

Attending to the Basics

A housing and support approach requires attention to basic issues that reflect concern about the state of systems, not about the readiness of people with disabilities. Issues will vary from state to state, but some areas to consider before moving to this approach on a large-scale basis are:

The availability of values-based training on an ongoing basis for new staff involved in "the systems." When people are still debating the value of relationships between people with and without disabilities, the importance of home, and whether institutions or homes are better, making a move toward a housing and support approach will most likely result primarily in language and procedural changes.

Basic mechanisms to encourage quality and protect the rights and safety of people with disabilities. State attention must be given to circumstances that may involve systems that are either corrupt or out of control, or where basic rights mechanisms are not operational.

Mechanisms for decentralized decision making. Aspects of the housing and support approach require decision making on the local level, and effort must be made to address this type of politically difficult change over the next decade.

Adequate financing of community services to ensure that people get at least the minimal supports they need and want. Some systems are inadequately funded and a housing and support approach can be used to place people with disabilities in hidden jeopardy if mechanisms are not in place to make this lack of fiscal support visible.

Many of these issues go beyond the field of developmental disabilities and require radical political change in some states in how citizens who are poor, represent minority groups, or have disabilities are treated. The difficulty of these issues can no longer be used as a rationale for not beginning the decade or more of work that will be required for some of these changes to occur.

Ways of Thinking About Planning

A housing and support approach requires a different way of thinking about the relationship between individual and systems planning. The traditional approach to planning has been a top-down approach with the assumption that major policy and legislative changes would be implemented on the local level by those in the field. In contrast, a housing and support approach recognizes the uniqueness of people, localities, and communities, and moves up through the system to the changes that are necessary in each different system to support the local efforts. Because of the cumbersome nature of many systems, even five to six well-pursued individualized plans can identify systems issues that can take many years to address.

State government typically deals with "private troubles" or "individual problems" in one of three ways. The first option is to address the problem only for the one individual—this perpetuates the illusion that the traditional system responds to individual's needs and wants. The second option is to create a demonstration—often done without any plan to move to broader system changes. The third option states and the federal government prefer is to create a new program—this is often done without addressing the problems in what already exists, often layering another level of regulation or legislation as part of the solution.

State disability departments need to learn how to systematically use the experience of individuals and demonstrations to move toward broader systemic changes. This means attending to the barriers in existing systems and the larger political environment, not simply developing new programs and models. For example, one individualized plan can create an opportunity to examine the role of the state's foster care program, particularly for adults, and to explore the issues of personal control by people with disabilities as a matter of state policy.

Several common planning errors in moving toward this approach are: 1) to assume that regional and/or state budgets can be projected and planned through a system of identifying actual individual needs; 2) to fail to recognize the diverse purposes of needs assessments, including indicating to the legislative and the executive branches that state agencies are acting in a reasonable and accountable way; 3) to confuse the importance of the process of planning with the product, which in turbulent times may not be viable by the time it is implemented; and 4) to fail to recognize what it is we do and do not know, instead of embarking on major changes that disrupt people's lives to do whatever is the latest innovation (i.e., supportive living) without attention to the basics.

Ways of Thinking About Supportive Living Programs

To understand the way in which *supportive living* is developing on the state level, it is useful to compare discrete initiative programs across states. Although states differ from each other, all of the programs represent distinct views on what supportive living is (from the viewpoint of the system), even when using similar sets of principles. Even though specific mechanisms can vary to accomplish the same goals, people with disabilities should not be denied the right to home living based on where they live in the United States. Table 2 provides an example of how to begin to review and compare these initiatives.

One role all people can play is to expect policymakers to clearly answer the types of questions addressed in Table 2. For example, if people with the most severe disabilities are excluded from supportive living in a state, how will they be provided with the option to live in their own home? This is a social policy question, not solely a program, professional, or fiscal concern.

Ways of Thinking About Medicaid Waivers and Other Financing

As expressed on the agency level in Chapter 5, "good" organizations place people with disabilities ahead of financing and technology. This, of course, does not mean they ignore resource limitations, which will continue to be an ongoing issue in systems. This section presents some ways of starting to think about financial issues from a person-first perspective.

Financing from an Individual's Perspective   In its supportive living

Table 2.   Comparing state initiatives: Selected questions

Purpose/outcomes   Do the philosophical principles represent values such as interdependence, community participation, and community for all?

Exclusion criteria   Are people with the most severe disabilities included (through eligibility, available financing, or in-home supports)?

Definitions of key items   What are the state's definitions for home, service array, residential continuum, facility, supports, and community participation?

Service options   What is the array of allowable services and how does this fit in with other state- and generic-funded services? Are they limited by existing options or service categories?

Who can provide services?   Who can (or cannot) be paid to provide support services? What are staff roles and to whom are they accountable?

Housing options   Are there any limitations on where and with whom people can live?

Options for service coordination   Do people have a variety of options about who will perform these functions and the kinds of functions that will be included?

Control of services   How much control do people with disabilities have over all aspects of their services, including the planning process? Who makes final decisions when disagreements occur?

Control of housing   Are tenancy and home ownership options?

Control of informal support/services relationships   Who decides the relationship between informal aspects of the person's life and the role services will play?

Separation and coordination of housing and support   How is housing separation and coordination accomplished?

Definition of quality   How is quality defined and who defines it?

Financing   Is the financing adequate to support people with the most severe disabilities?

manual (n.d.), the Ohio Department of Mental Retardation and Developmental Disabilities has one of the clearest state illustrations of how to think about funding from the perspective of individual people. As stated in the manual, "each service and support required to enable an individual to live in a setting of his or her own choosing is identified, and then payer sources are determined" (p. 10). Although this is not substantially different than the Wisconsin approach, the illustration (see Figure 1 as an example) is helpful and includes generic as well as disability funding sources. Planners should evaluate the implications of program initiatives by using an individual perspective with a range of people, including people with the most severe disabilities.

The Role of Medicaid and the Waivers   Table 3 includes a brief summary of common questions asked about Medicaid, which is the primary program in the United States for funding residential programs for people with developmental disabilities. Whereas intermediate care facilities are not a feasible financing mechanism to move to a support approach, the Medicaid waivers and optional state plan services have been comparatively useful tools. However, without substantial reform on the federal level in Medicaid, limitations will continue to be placed on the possible opportunities for individualization and flexibility on the local levels even in these more flexible sources.

Within federal constraints, including those related to the medical assistance nature of Medicaid, both the waivers and the Community Supported Living Arrangements Program (see Table 4) can offer some new opportunities for people with disabilities to live in their own homes. Whereas many of the states' home- and community-based waivers and community supported living arrangements programs include aspects that can support greater individualization and flexibility

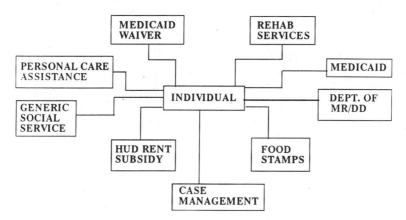

Figure 1. Supported living concept funding sources. (Adapted from Ohio Department of Mental Retardation and Developmental Disabilities [n.d.].)

Table 3. Common questions about Medicaid

Why is Medicaid important for community living?

Title XIX of the Social Security Act, Medicaid, is the primary program in the United States for funding residential programs for people with developmental disabilities. Depending upon the state, the federal government shares 50% to approximately 78% of the cost of these services.

What are intermediate care facilities?

These settings are designed to provide health and rehabilitation services based on the concept of active treatment. Enacted in 1971, ICFs generally are large public or private congregate or institutional settings.

Can ICFs/DD funding be used for "individualized" supports?

In 1977, federal regulations explicitly authorized the funding of "small ICF/MR" facilities for 15 or fewer people. Approximately 20% of the "small facility care" in the United States is provided through ICFs. However, ICF funding has proven to be inflexible in addressing individual needs that are nonmedical in nature.

What is the Home- and Community-Based Medicaid Waiver?

The Medicaid home- and community-based services (HCB) waiver program was enacted in 1981 as Section 1915(c) of the Social Security Act. It offers the states considerable flexibility to develop a state specific plan for small community services that could be approved by the federal government. The plans need to be cost neutral, which means they cannot cost the federal government more money than they would have spent without the waiver.

How many Medicaid waiver programs exist in the United States?

By 1990, there were 150 waiver programs of different kinds targeting elders, people with physical disabilities, developmental disabilities/mental retardation, and people with HIV infection. Two thirds of the waiver spending in 1990 went toward services for people with developmental disabilities; by December 1990, 43 states were offering full-scale HCB waiver programs.

What services are offered by states in their MR/DD waiver program?

Services offered by states include: case management, day habilitation, prevocational services, supported employment, residential services, personal/care/in-home supports, respite care, therapies/specialty services, assistive devices/adaptive aids, home modifications, and transportation.

Can waivers be used for people who have not lived in institutions?

In some states, the waiver supports the "diversion" of people from institutional or other ICF placements; thus, people "at risk" in the community as well as people living in the institution may be eligible.

Can waivers be used to support people in more individualized ways in the community?

To some extent, some states used their waivers for people with developmental disabilities/mental retardation primarily as a fiscal strategy to assist in moving money from institutional to community services. Others also saw the waiver as a vehicle for systems change in the community, developing more flexible, person-centered opportunities. However, Medicaid funds continue to be less flexible than state financing sources.

What optional services are available to states in their Medicaid plans?

As of 1981, case management, personal care (or personal assistance), habilitation services, and eligibility for disabled children (TEFRA) have been critical in supporting people with developmental disabilities in the community.

(continued)

Table 3. (continued)

In 1988, 23 states provided personal assistance as a Medicaid personal care option. Nine states specifically used this option for people with mental retardation and related conditions. However, some of these options were used to supplement programs instead of the modes of individual delivery typically characteristic of personal assistance.

This material is adapted from Lakin et al. (1989); Litvak (1991); and Smith (1991).

than traditional residential services, neither of these funding streams should be considered the "solution" to supporting people to live in their own homes.

Each waiver and CSLA application should be reviewed and evaluated, as illustrated in Table 5, to see which aspects support a more individualized approach and which might need to be changed or supplemented in other ways. These programs also must be examined in conjunction with other state programs and financing because what appears to be an inflexible approach in one state might not be in another one. (For more information on the use of the Medicaid waivers for supportive living and the community supported living arrangements, the reader is referred to Smith [1990, 1991].)

Financing for Personal Assistance Proposed financing strategies for personal assistance all have relevancy to and should be better coordinated with discussion of financing for developmental disabilities services in the United States. As an initial step, state developmental disabilities policymakers should become more familiar with the personal assistance programs in their states and begin to explore ways to better

Table 4. Common questions about Community Supported Living Arrangements

What are Community Supported Living Arrangements?

The newest (1990) optional state plan service is called the Community Supported Living Arrangements (CSLA). These are services that are intended to assist persons to live in their own homes or continue to live with their families in order to promote independence, integration, and productivity. Congress limited this option from two to no more than eight states with total payments of no more than $100 million from fiscal year 1991–1995.

What services are included?

CSLA service categories include personal assistance, training and habilitation, 24-hour emergency assistance, assistive technology, and other support services, such as home or environmental modifications and transportation. These are the same types of services that could be available under a state's HCB waiver program.

Why is CSLA important from the state perspective?

This option has four critical federal policy features: 1) decoupling eligibility from the "need for institutionalization," 2) providing an alternative service principle to active treatment, 3) stating a clear federal policy to support people in their own homes and in families using federal dollars, and 4) the possibility to tailor services based on individualized needs and circumstances.

Adapted from Smith, G.A. (1991, January).

Table 5.   Minnesota home- and community-based Medicaid waiver

Separation of Housing and Supports
1.   Supports can be provided in a person's own rented or owned home as well as in an agency facility or an adult foster home.
2.   A person can live in a variety of kinds of housing and still receive support.
3.   A person can be involved in locating and selecting the home.
4.   A person can live alone or with others and can have a choice of roommates.

Home Ownership
1.   Does not encourage this to occur, but allows for providing services in a person's own home either leased or owned under certain circumstances.

Individualized Supports
1.   A range of different services can be provided to adults in and out of their home, including recreation/leisure, behavior programming, community integration, menu planning and dietary, budgeting, counseling on sexuality, bus training, safety/survival skills, home maintenance, and community orientation. Additionally, nursing, psychological-care, personal care, occupational therapy, communication consultation, behavior consultation, and related services are available.
2.   Plans and budgets are developed for individual people; an average cost across people served must be maintained at the county level.
3.   Amount, frequency, and duration of services is dependent on the needs of individuals.
4.   Services are determined through an individual planning process.

Flexible Supports
1.   Contracts can be renegotiated between the private agency and the county during the course of the year.
2.   Workers can be hired on temporary contracts to perform services for as long as people need those specific services.
3.   Times when supports are provided can be changed dependent on the person's schedule and needs.
4.   Amounts of different supports may vary over the course of the year.

Availability for People with Severe Disabilities
1.   This is both a deinstitutionalization and a diversion waiver; designed for people at ICF/MR level of care; respondents indicate that some of the people with the most severe disabilities may not yet be served.

Choice in Support Providers
1.   The county can contract with different providers for different services that a person may need or one provider can offer a number of different services; input of the person may be solicited before decisions on providers are made.

Issues
1.   Stringent informal criteria used for determining when supports will be provided in a person's own home; less than 5% of supports are offered in a person's own home.
2.   Available only through the waiver.
3.   No mechanisms available to allow for people to hire their own attendants or to grant money to person/family for purchases.
4.   A variety of implementation issues, including maintenance of average cost at county level and change in thinking of provider community from ICF/MR model.
5.   Still results in "boxes" of services; supportive living services are generally 24-hour support and are funded through the Medicaid waiver; if a person needs substantially less support, must be funded as semi-independent living through state/county funds.

Information based on a site visit in August 1987, a telephone interview with a Medicaid waiver manager in May 1988, and a waiver application.

From Taylor, S. J., Racino, J. A., & Rothenberg, K. (1988, July). *A policy analysis of private community living arrangements in Connecticut.* Syracuse, NY: Center on Human Policy, Syracuse University; pp. 64–65. Reprinted by permission.

coordinate on the state level. (A good resource on potential strategies for PAS financing on the state and federal levels is Litvak [1991].)

People committed to full community participation for all will find allegiance with those groups that are asking Congress to move money from institution to home care, permit people on low fixed incomes to become eligible for Medicaid without having to deplete budgets and sell homes, and revise policy and financing to promote home care over institutional care (Center for Independent Living of North Florida, Inc., 1992).

Individualized Funding In the United States, the term *individualized funding* is used primarily to refer to money that could follow a person wherever they move instead of being tied to a setting. However, the funding generally flows through an agency and is not controlled by the person with a disability. This is in contrast to the Canadian use of this term to refer to cash subsidies or money that is intended to go directly to the person and/or their family.

The primary issue in thinking about individualized funding is who controls decision making, not solely whether the funding can be used in different settings. Experience to date in North America indicates that much greater attention needs to be given to existing power relationships between agencies and people with disabilities and among service provider, funding, and other "independent" organizations. Otherwise, these strategies can result in more interference of the service system in their lives and/or simply add another layer of workers involved with the problem.

Cash Subsidies and Entitlements Because of the conflicts between agency accountability and personal choice, direct cash subsidies and entitlements that are under the control of people with disabilities can help remove some of the stigma of asking for help, enable people to plan on a long-term basis, and remove some of the social control exercised through the requirement of specific types of worker involvement. Instead of using the need for support as a rationale to force worker or agency control, entitlements or direct cash subsidies offer an important opportunity to rethink the current systems of case management and payees that typically allow for little input by people with disabilities. One option to explore is adding a supplement to the SSI payment (see Heumann, chap. 11, this volume, for more information).

Ways of Thinking About "Case Management"

One of the critical aspects of a person-centered approach to housing and support is the role of the "case manager" (people with disabilities almost universally dislike this term), service coordinator, or service broker. From a systems perspective, the location of these individuals in the system has been viewed as critical with the main concern being that these roles must be independent from service provision. The debate on this issue has tended to reflect the rule that one must be either for or against independent case management.

At least three elements are often neglected in the discussion about the way in which a "case management" system should be designed. First, whereas some functions of service coordination, such as advocating and evaluating, require an independence from service provision, other elements, such as coordination, may not require this. A more functional analysis of the role is necessary as we move toward a system that is based more on choice and support. Second, the power relationship between families, people with disabilities and their service coordinators vis à vis the service providing and funding agents is at least as essential as the location issue. Examples of a lack of attention to this issue resulting in more funding being spent for more workers have already occurred. Third, differences among state systems cannot simply be ignored or minimized. Independent case management has already been used as a rationale to decrease local control and safeguards and increase state control under the rubric of personal choice. Although there are no simple solutions to these issues, the discussion on independent case management needs to take into account these kinds of concerns and be more integrated with an understanding of how greater choice may have an impact on the definition of these roles.

Ways of Thinking About Quality Assurance

Quality assurance, including its role in new supportive living programs, is one of the most strongly debated issues on the state and federal level, with some people advocating a minimal government role and others the need for more extensive oversight. People base their positions on factors such as: the degree they believe that regulations and similar mechanisms can or cannot control harm to people with disabilities; the trust they place in agencies, families, and people with disabilities; their respective valuing of potential protection from harm and loss of personal freedom; their own role in relationship to oversight; and their view of the role of government in the lives of individual people.

Although many issues about quality and safeguards exist throughout state systems, one critical feature in discussing a housing and support approach is the strong pattern of overregulation that seems to exist in this country. As Taylor (1992) explains, regulations represent the bureaucratization of values and reflect the abuses of the past. More importantly, they circumscribe the potential for the future, place control and power in the hands of the regulators instead of people with developmental disabilities and their families, direct attention to concrete and tangible things, and trivialize the most important things in life.

Because of this, states and the federal government should consider the following directions for regulatory reform, which is a critical aspect of their roles in quality assurance:

Keep regulations to a minimum and confine them to concrete health, safety, and related issues. This is particularly imperative in supporting people in their own homes.

Consider regulatory reform only in linkage with system reform. Distinguish between the regulation of facilities and promoting life quality in one's own home.

For homes leased or owned by people with disabilities, apply local housing codes as the housing standard.

Ensure that families and individuals with disabilities have clear-cut rights and due process mechanisms, including the recourse to pursue damages in situations of harm.

Support a variety of informal mechanisms to promote the quality and responsiveness of services, including agency self-evaluations, consumer surveys, self-advocacy, and citizen advocacy.

As an interim measure, consider the development of individualized quality plans as part of individualized planning processes for people living in their own homes.

Ways of Thinking About Change

In moving to a housing and support approach, how one thinks about change is a critical base to deciding about strategies and reforms. This section shares some important distinctions about the nature of change, the different kinds of change, and the relationship between systems change and individual life quality. All of these areas require further exploration and research in order to better understand state decision making.

Fundamental change, as defined here, is change that improves the life quality of people with disabilities. Service systems cannot and should not provide everything that people need and want. When people with developmental disabilities rely exclusively on service systems, they cannot become part of their communities. Fundamental change in people's life quality does not occur simply because legislation is passed, a new program is financed, or policy is changed. Changes are necessary not only in systems on which people rely, but also in people's relationships, communities, and societal assumptions about how people should live together.

Societal change, as opposed to systems change, means addressing the disability-based assumptions that permeate our daily lives. Nora Groce's *Everyone here spoke sign language: Hereditary deafness on Martha's Vineyard* (1985) is a wonderful example of how a disability, such as deafness, can be easily accepted and not treated as a negative difference in people. Every change, including systems change strategy, needs to be examined on the basis of whether it brings people closer to a society in which disability is accepted as a matter of routine, not as a cause for stigmatization. Strategies that have short-term effectiveness, but move us away from this goal, should not be pursued.

The changes that are needed will require that people work from different directions, whether through the avenues of housing, community regeneration, legislative and policy analysis, program evaluation and research, or advocacy and training. At this time, many states are trying to balance three systems: an institutional system, a traditional community system, and another emerging "support" or person/family-driven system. It is also unclear what the future "systems" will look like, which can be stressful for the people who created or are involved with the existing systems.

In thinking about change, the following change strategies are shared as ones that others have found personally or professionally meaningful, including those in leadership roles on the state level. They are as applicable to a housing and support approach as they are to any other reform initiative. They include: rewarding creativity and innovation; making a personal commitment; taking risks and recognizing opportunities; promoting leadership by parents and people with disabilities; learning from pilot innovations; a person-by-person approach; grassroots organizing; role of policy, legislation, and financing; efforts outside the disability system; the role of technical assistance; building coalitions; and community relationship building and networking. Each of these strategies is discussed briefly on the following pages.

Rewarding Creativity and Innovation   Many states stifle creativity. They create an atmosphere in which bureaucratic compliance is rewarded and innovation and risk taking are punished. Just as states can inhibit innovation and creativity, they have the ability to foster these things. States can also create incentives and disincentives, thus encouraging or discouraging positive changes from happening. However, they cannot mandate meaningful lives for people with developmental disabilities.

Making a Personal Commitment   As a society we have come to believe that services, techniques, and strategies can substitute for human caring and commitment. There is no replacement for personal commitment, and leadership can and must be exercised by people at all levels. People in state roles can and must both exercise leadership and make possible opportunities for others to do so.

Taking Risks and Recognizing Opportunities   Sometimes change is stifled by personal or professional fear; other times it is stifled by unclear vision. Leadership involves the willingness to take risks on behalf of people with disabilities—professionals and policymakers in this field need to remember for whom they are really working. Leadership means developing the capacity to hold onto a vision in day-to-day reality and to notice and seize opportunities for change as they arise.

Promoting Leadership by Parents and People with Disabilities A common strategy being used to create change is a version of Partners in Policymaking, a strategy developed by the Minnesota Developmental Disabilities Council, to educate parents and people with disabilities about state-of-the-art practices and to increase leadership capacities. Similar strategies have played a role in creating family support legislation in New Hampshire; versions that include people with disabilities and that are cross disability in nature are particularly valuable.

Learning from Innovations Piloting innovations is a classic change strategy, even for large scale endeavors. It works out the basic problems that could get in the way, or even undermine an effort, if unaddressed. Demonstrations also provide examples of what is possible. A mutual commitment to work through issues found on the individual and agency levels can also hasten larger scale change.

A Person-by-Person Approach Some of the largest state changes started on a person-by-person basis with a gradual shift in state policy over many years. In any area of the United States, for example, a few people can decide that they will work together to support someone who is in jeopardy of admission to an institution to remain in the community.

Grassroots Organizing A variety of action strategies can be used to make issues visible and to shift the content and frame of debate. These include demonstrations, letter writing, public hearings and fact finding, media and communication networks, symbolic acts, lobbying, boycotts, and legal action (Biklen, 1974). In the most successful states, policymakers have formed an alliance with their constituencies, privately encourage and support such activities, and respond to the pressure to move toward fuller integration.

Role of Policy, Legislation, and Financing Some state barriers on housing and support can be addressed by simply reinterpreting legislation, revising regulations or policies, or making other relatively minor modifications. Other broader social policy changes, such as the need for a new approach to United States family policy and national health care will take a longer time. On the state level, often the key is to have a vision of what people are trying to accomplish (e.g., all people living in their own homes) and to notice and grasp the opportunities for change.

Going Outside the Disability System Whether through support for training, public information, or interdepartmental relationships, states need to foster policy and relationships inclusive of people with disabilities rather than specifically for people with disabilities. This may mean taking what appears to be short-term "losses" for long-term gains. It also means exploring ways that disability systems can contribute, as well as be recipients of, public goods.

The Role of Technical Assistance What states need more than technical advice is ongoing support and thoughtful advice, such as: help in setting a direction and encouragement to stay on course, advice in struggling with difficult problems, information on what has and has not worked at other places, an independent look at what is being done, a fresh perspective to bring to bear on current issues, validation of good ideas and honest criticism of bad ones, and openness to dialogue.

Building Coalitions   States can build coalitions with new groups holding common concerns, such as elders and people with low incomes. Organizing around issues such as personal assistance, housing, family policy, and child welfare can offer new opportunities for more valued options for all people.

Community Relationship Building and Networking   States can use incentives to promote local efforts to develop relationships between people with and without disabilities, and can act as a model of ways to collaborate with different sectors of the community. New issues and coalitions will demand better skills in listening, the need to learn each other's language, respect for each other's views, and a common understanding and vision.

The next decade will pose many challenges to people who are concerned about maintaining the right for all people to live and participate in the community. We can no longer afford to be pitted against one another, but must unite around common interests and expand our efforts at education, advocacy, and research. Together we can work to overcome the barriers within ourselves, our communities, agencies, systems, and societies that prohibit decent home living and community life.

BIBLIOGRAPHY

Apolloni, T., Meucci, S., & Triest, G. (1981). *Monitoring the quality of life experienced in living arrangements: A guide to citizen participation.* Sacramento: California State Council on Developmental Disabilities.

Attendant Care Action Coalition. (1987). *Independent living brokerage: A new model of service development, coordination and delivery.* Canada: Author.

Bersani, H.A. (1989). *Assuring residential quality: Issues, approaches and instruments.* Syracuse, NY: Center on Human Policy, Syracuse University.

Biklen, D. (1974). *Let our children go: An organizing manual for advocates and parents.* Syracuse, NY: Human Policy Press.

Braddock, D., & Fujiura, G. (1990). *Politics, public policy, and the development of community services* (Public Policy Monograph Series, No. 47). Chicago: University of Chicago at Illinois, Institute for the Study of Developmental Disabilities.

Braddock, D., Hemp, R., Fujiura, G., Bachelder, L., & Mitchell, D. (1990). *The state of the states in developmental disabilities.* Baltimore: Paul H. Brookes Publishing Co.

Bradley, V.J., Ashbaugh, J.W., Harden, W.P., Stoddard, S., Shea, S., Allard, M.A., Mulkern, V., Spence, R.A., & Absalom, D. (1984). *Assessing and enhancing the quality of services: A guide for the human service field.* Cambridge, MA: Human Services Research Institute.

Bradley, V.J., & Bersani, H.A. (Eds.). (1990). *Quality assurance for individuals with developmental disabilities: It's everybody business.* Baltimore: Paul H. Brookes Publishing Co.

Center for Independent Living of North Florida, Inc. (1992, February). Independent living services pages: "White paper on personal care." *ACCESS,* 14–15.

Chin, R., & Benne, K.D. (1972). General strategies for effecting changes in human systems. In G. Zaltman, P. Kotter, & I. Kaufman (Eds.), *Creating social change* (pp. 233–254). Holt, Rinehart & Winston, Inc.

Coleman, J.S. (1973). Conflicting theories of social change. In G. Zaltman (Ed.), *Processes and phenomenon of social change* (pp. 61–74). New York: John Wiley & Sons.

Connecticut Department of Mental Retardation (1986). *Mission Statement.* Hartford, CT: Author.

Connecticut Developmental Disabilities Council. (1990). *1990 report on supported living.* East Hartford: Author.

Department of Health and Mental Hygiene. (n.d.). *Application for Section 1930 of the Social Security Act, Community Supported Living Arrangements (CSLA) Services for Individuals with Mental Retardation and Developmental Disabilities.* Baltimore: Author.

Florida Department of Health and Rehabilitative Services. (1990, October). *Supported living: The Florida initiative.* Tampa: Author.

Governor's Planning Council on Developmental Disabilities. (1987, January). *A new way of thinking.* St. Paul, MN: Author.

Groce, N.E. (1985). *Everyone here spoke sign language: Hereditary deafness on Martha's Vineyard.* Cambridge, MA: Harvard University Press.

Hazel, R., Barber, P.A., Roberts, S., Behr, S.K., Helmstetter, E., & Guess, D. (1988). *A community approach to an integrated service system for children with special needs.* Baltimore: Paul H. Brookes Publishing Co.

Health and Welfare. (1987, November). *"I am who I should be already": A report on the proceedings of the National Symposium on Brokerage/Individualized Funding.* Ottawa, Ontario: Author.

Hemp, R., Braddock, D., Bachelder, L., & Haasen, K. (1990, April). *Creative financing of community services: The state agency perspective* (Public Policy Monograph Series, No. 51). Chicago: University of Illinois at Chicago, Institute for the Study of Developmental Disabilities.

Hogan, M.F. (1987). *Comparing model mental health systems: A review of the Dane County (Wisconsin), Massachusetts and Rhode Island Systems.* Paper presented at the Refining Vision and Promotion Action Conference sponsored by the National Institute of Mental Health.

Housing and Intellectual Disability Project. (1988, February). *The need for coordination between the Ministry of Housing (MOH) and Community Services Victoria—Office of Intellectual Disability Services (CSV-OIDS).* Collingwood, Victoria, Australia: Author.

Illinois Department of Public Aid. (1991). *Application for Section 1930 of the Social Security Act, Community Supported Living Arrangements (CSLA) Services for Individuals with Mental Retardation and Developmental Disabilities.* Springfield: Author.

Kaufman, J., Lichtenstein, K.A., & Rosenblatt, A. (1986). Service coordination: A systems approach to medically fragile children. *Caring, 62,* 42–46.

Kennedy, J. (1991, September). Personal assistance services: Program policy issues. In Research and Training Center on Public Policy in Independent Living, InfoUse, & Western Consortium for Public Health, *Personal assistance services: A guide to policy and action.* Oakland, CA: Authors.

Koslowski, S. (1988, December). *Report on supported living workshop.* Hartford, CT: Author.

Knoll, J., Covert, S., Osuch, R., O'Connor, S., Agosta, J., & Blaney, B. (1990). *Family support services in the United States: An end of decade status report.* Cambridge, MA: Human Services Research Institute.

Kregel, J., & Wehman, P. (1989). Supported employment: Promises deferred for persons with severe disabilities. *Journal of The Association for Persons with Severe Handicaps, 14*(4), 293–303.

Lakin, K.C., Jaskulski, T.M., Hill, B.K., Bruininks, R.H., Menke, J.M., White, C.C., & Wright, E.A. (1989, May). *Medicaid services for persons with mental retardation and related conditions.* Minneapolis: Center for Residential and Community Services, Institute on Community Integration, University of Minnesota.

Lippert, T. (1987). *The case management team: Building community connections.* St. Paul, MN: Metropolitan Council.

Litvak, S. (1991, September). State and federal funding sources for PAS. In Research and Training Center on Public Policy in Independent Living, InfoUse, & Western Consortium for Public Health, *Personal assistance services: A guide to policy and action.* Oakland, CA: Authors.

Lord, J., & Pedlar, A. (1991). Life in the community: Four years after the closure of an institution. *Mental Retardation, 29*(4), 213–221.

McWhorter, A., & Kappel, B. (1984) *Mandate for quality.* Downsview, Ontario, Canada: The G. Allan Roeher Institute.

Meyers, J.C., & Marcenko, M.O. (1989). Impact of a cash subsidy program for families of children with severe developmental disabilities. *Mental Retardation, 27*(6), 383–387.

National Association of Developmental Disabilities Councils. (1990). Forging a new era: The 1990 reports on people with developmental disabilities. *Journal of Disability Policy Studies, 1*(4), 15–42.

National Association of Private Residential Resources. (1991, November). *Supported living monograph.* Annandale, VA: Author.

National Development Team. (1989). *Services for people with learning difficulties living in Hereford and Worcester.* England: Author.

New York State Housing Task Force, Mental Health Planning Advisory Committee. (1988). *Housing task force issue paper.* Albany: Author.

O'Brien, J., & Lyle, C. (1986). *Strengthening the system: Improving Louisiana's community residential services for people with developmental disabilities.* Decatur, GA: Responsive Systems Associates.

O'Brien, J., & Lyle O'Brien, C. (1991, May). *Learning from implementing the residential services guidelines.* Lithonia, GA: Responsive Systems Associates.

O'Brien, J., Lyle O'Brien, C., & Schwartz, D.B. (1990, January). *What can we count on to make and keep people safe? Perspectives on creating effective safeguards for people with developmental disabilities.* Lithonia, GA: Responsive Systems Associates.

Office of Disability. (1988). *Disability, society, and change.* Sydney, Australia: Author.

Ohio Department of Mental Retardation and Developmental Disabilities. (n.d.). *The supported living reference manual.* Columbus: Author.

Provencal, G., & Taylor, R. (1983, December). Security for parents: Monitoring of group homes by consumers. *The Exceptional Parent,* 39–44.

Racino, J.A. (1991a). [Confidential policy research field notes, New Hampshire]. Syracuse, NY: Author.

Racino, J.A. (1991b). *Life in the community: "A home of my own with the supports I need or want."* Paper presented at International Symposium on Personal Assistance Services, Berkeley, CA.

Racino, J.A. (1991c). *Thoughts and reflections on personal assistance services: Issues of concern to people with mental retardation.* Paper presented at International Symposium on Personal Assistance Services, Berkeley, CA. (Reprinted in *Disability Studies Quarterly, 12*(1), 81–86, Winter 1992).

Racino, J.A., O'Connor, S., Shoultz, B., Taylor, S.J., & Walker, P. (1989). *Moving into the 1990s: A policy analysis of community living for adults with developmental disabilities in South Dakota.* Syracuse, NY: Center on Human Policy, Syracuse University.

Rammler, L. (1986). *A guide to program quality review of day programs* (2nd ed.). Hartford, CT: Connecticut Department of Mental Retardation.

Research and Training Center on Community Integration. (1988, November). *From being in the community to being part of the community: Summary of the proceedings and recommendations of a Leadership Institute on Community Integration for People with Developmental Disabilities.* Syracuse, NY: Author.

Region V Mental Retardation Services. (n.d.). *Safeguards: A system for monitoring service quality.* Lincoln, NE: Author.

Regional Mental Handicap Advisory Group. (1989, February). *Services for people who are mentally handicapped: A guide to quality assessment.* England: Author.

Richardson, A., & Higgins, R. (1990, April). *Case management in practice: Reflections on the Wakefield case management project* (Working Paper No. 1). England: Nuffield Institute for Health Services Studies, University of Leeds.

Robinson, G.K. (1990). *Choices in case management: Current knowledge & practice for mental health programs.* Washington, DC: Mental Health Policy Research Center.

Robinson, G.K. (1991, March). Changing the system: The Ohio experience. In *Policy in Perspective, 1*, 3–4.

Rothman, D.J., & Rothman, S.M. (1984). *The Willowbrook wars: A decade of struggle for social justice.* New York: Harper & Row.

Schalock, R.L. (Ed.). (1990). *Quality of life: Perspectives and issues.* Washington, DC: American Association on Mental Retardation.

Smith, G. (1990, November). *Supported living: New directions in services to people with developmental disabilities.* Alexandria, VA: National Association of State Mental Retardation Program Directors, Inc.

Smith, G.A. (1991, January). *Community Supported Living Arrangements: A guide to Section 1930 of the Social Security Act.* Alexandria, VA: National Association of State Mental Retardation Program Directors, Inc.

Smith, G.A., & Aderman, S. (1987, July). *Paying for services.* Alexandria, VA: National Association of State Mental Retardation Program Directors, Inc.

Smith, G.A., & Gettings, R.M. (1991, January). *The HCB waiver program and services for people with developmental disabilities: An update.* Alexandria, VA: National Association of State Mental Retardation Program Directors, Inc.

Smith, H. (1989). *Collaboration for change: Partnership between service users, planners and managers of mental health services* (Managing Psychiatric Services in Transition Working Paper, No. 6). London: King Edward's Hospital Fund for London.

Tarmon, V. (1989). *Client to consumer: An assessment of individualized funding projects in the United States.* Toronto: Social Planning Council of Metro Toronto.

Task Force on Personal Assistance Services. (1991, October). *Recommended federal policy directions on personal assistance services for Americans with disabilities* (draft). Washington, DC: Consortium for Citizens with Disabilities.

Taylor, S.J. (1979). *Negotiation: A tool for change.* Syracuse, NY: Center on Human Policy, Syracuse University.

Taylor, S.J. (1986, March). *Some thoughts on quality assurance.* Syracuse, NY: Center on Human Policy, Syracuse University.

Taylor, S.J. (1987). *A policy analysis of the Supported Housing Demonstration Project, Pittsburgh, Pennsylvania.* Syracuse, NY: Center on Human Policy, Syracuse University.

Taylor, S.J. (1992). The paradox of regulations: A commentary. In C.S. Holburn (Ed.), Symposium for *Mental Retardation, 30*(3), 185–190.

Taylor, S.J., Lutfiyya, Z., Racino, J.A., Walker, P., & Knoll, J. (1986). *An evaluation of Connecticut's community training home program.* Syracuse, NY: Center on Human Policy, Syracuse University.

Taylor, S.J., Racino, J.A., & Rothenberg, K. (1988) *A policy analysis of private community living arrangements in Connecticut.* Syracuse, NY: Center on Human Policy, Syracuse University.

Towell, D., & Beardshaw, V. (1991). *Enabling community integration: The role of public authorities in promoting an ordinary life for people with learning disabilities in the 1990s.* London: King's Fund College.

Towell, D., & Kingsley, A. (1989). *Elements in a strategic framework for developing local psychiatric services* (Managing Psychiatric Services in Transition Working Paper, No. 3). London: King Edward's Hospital Fund for London.

Turnbull, H.R., III (1988). Ideological, political, and legal principles in the community-living movement. In M.P. Janicki, M. W. Krauss, & M.M. Seltzer (Eds.), *Community residences for persons with developmental disabilities* (pp. 15–24. Baltimore: Paul H. Brookes Publishing Co.

United Cerebral Palsy of Indiana, Inc. (1986, July). *Final report of the Residential Task Force.* Indiana: Author.

Vail, J. (1989, September). *Housing and supportive services* (Publication No. 450–89–104). St. Paul: Metropolitan Council.

Whittaker, A., Gardner, S., & Kershaw, J. (1990, March). *Service evaluation by people with learning difficulties.* London: King's Fund Centre

Wieck, C. (n.d.). *Resource materials: A variety of approaches to outcome evaluation.* St. Paul, MN: Author.

Wieck, C., Nelson, J., Reedstrom, C., Starr, J., & Stone, N. (1989). *Quality assurance resources: Instruments, organizations, and publications.* Arlington, NJ: ARC-US.

Wolfensberger, W., & Zauha, H. (Eds.). (1973). *Citizen advocacy and protective services for the impaired and handicapped.* Toronto: National Institute on Mental Retardation.

Zirpoli, T.J., Hancox, D., Wieck, C., & Skarnulis, E. (1989). Partners in policy-making: Empowering people. *Journal of The Association for Persons with Severe Handicaps, 14*(2), 163–167.

II

PERSPECTIVES

8

LETTING GO, MOVING ON

A PARENT'S THOUGHTS

Cory Moore

I have been a professional in the field of disabilities for more than 18 years, but here I am writing from the perspective of a Parent. (The capital "P" distinguishes me from the parent of a typical child, although, happily, I hold that distinction as well.) I am writing, then, from my own experience and from the thoughts and reactions to events that have evolved over time. My outlook has changed in the harsh light of some happenings and with the unexpected delights of others. And the odyssey is not yet over.

To understand a Parent's perspective on housing and support for his or her adult son or daughter, it is vital to acknowledge the years of growing with that son or daughter. Feelings and history cannot be discounted. Unlike the professional who makes decisions based on today's realities and written records from the past, every Parent has a storehouse of vivid memories that influence all judgments. I share but a handful of those memories.

BEGINNINGS

Leslie Ellen is my middle child. (Her sister Laurie is 2 years older; her brother Ken is 3 years younger.) Leslie's birth, 27 years ago, was a complicated one; it was a double-footling breech delivery (baby's feet precede the head during delivery). Immediately following her birth, she was rushed into intensive care. I held her for the first time shortly before an operation in her 70th hour of life revealed that a kidney had not formed properly and had to be surgically removed.

Those early days were traumatic. Yet, already showing her skills as a survivor, Leslie recuperated quickly. She was discharged from the hospital when she was 9 days old and came home to be mainstreamed into her family. However, the nightmare was only temporarily over. She was indeed a sweet and adorable baby, but different in so many ways from her sister Laurie. Leslie was quiet and too placid; her cry was relatively soft, her demands few. The days passed as they do with the care of two small children, but they were not punctuated by the frequent and awesome delights that Laurie's infancy had offered. There seemed little change in Leslie beyond those of physical growth. Her head continued to need support through days, weeks, and months. She stayed in one position wherever she was placed and didn't seem particularly frustrated by her inability to move even short distances. Her eyes followed movement, but they were crossed. Yet, she reacted to the loving, nuzzling games I played with her; she seemed to enjoy being held and cuddled; she laughed at funny noises and to my forehead touching hers in the same game my mother had played with her babies.

Leslie rolled over for the first time when she was 3 months old and I breathed more easily; the growing fears were quieted. The comfort was brief because she did not turn again. Each time we went for her monthly checkup I mentioned my concern to her pediatrician and he was able to subdue my anxiety for a while. He told me I was unfairly comparing Leslie to her precocious older sister. "Just look at her eyes," he said. They were (and are) beautiful eyes—large, twinkly, alert; although at that time, they were still crossed.

When Leslie was 7 months old, we finally were given the necessary referral to a neurologist. It was a numbing and one-sided interview. He went far beyond my suspicions; his was a complete and total rejection of my lovable, adorable infant. "Brain-damaged" was his descriptor. He amplified, "She will never learn to sit, walk, talk, or take care of herself." If "pressed to define her IQ," he would "estimate it at about 15 to 20." He advised us to seek "a residential school for the sake of the family." (He also asked us if he could perform a tissue biopsy on her leg muscle for a research project in which he was engaged.)

Parents know all too well the depression and grief, the bitter questioning, and the mourning that follow such a diagnosis. Isolation, emptiness, loss, and failure are the emotions that plague those early days. We get through those beginnings somehow; we adapt, we reorganize, and we move on.

Leslie moved on, too—with us and beyond us. We did not take the neurologist's advice; Leslie stayed with us. Furthermore, his damning prophecy proved less than accurate. It is true that Leslie Ellen has multiple disabilities—for those to whom labels matter, my 27-year-old daughter carries several, including mental retardation, physical disability, and speech impairment. She uses a wheelchair and she takes daily medication for migraine and seizure control. Emotionally, she is prone to extremes in behavior, often demanding and intolerant. She is also charming and insightful. She can surpass my wildest expectations, but not understand my simplest question.

Despite my advocacy for integration, Leslie attended segregated public schools and graduated to a sheltered workshop. Just after her 19th birthday, emulating her older sister who "run away from home when she be 18" (actually, Laurie had left for college), Leslie moved from our family home to a group home. She lived there for 5 years. Today she lives, again at her own request, in her own apartment with a typical, same-age roommate. She has a very special boyfriend who also spends his daytime hours at the sheltered workshop. Now, I have new pictures to add to my collection.

I see her taking the key out of her wallet to open the door of her own home. I remember watching her peel a carrot to pack in her lunch—it took more than 20 minutes, but her look of pride was far more important than the ticking clock. I smile when I think about the time she arrived home for a weekend visit with several suitcases and said, "I have brought you my laundry."

I shake my head in wonder at a more recent happening. Leslie was gazing intently at a photograph of her friend Alan. She sighed deeply. "I really love that man," she said quietly. "He is my honey."

LETTING GO

Leslie's first move from her family home took place in August 1983. Parent needs were met—there was ample time for an in-home information-sharing session with the placement director about Leslie's interests, likes and dislikes, and special needs. There was time for family members to meet with staff and learn the administrative structure of the program as well as the answers to the human considerations that are of most interest to us. There was time for us to meet other Parents and give and receive support in this transitional phase. Most important, there was time to structure a gradual moving-in program for Leslie, based on how we thought she would best handle this exciting and potentially upsetting change.

The house was new and the staff was enthusiastic while making their own adjustments. The residents moved in individually to make the process easier on everyone. (How easily I use the labels *staff* and *residents*. At that time I accepted those labels; it was the way things were. I no longer appreciate the designations. People with disabilities should live with supportive companions and friends; the depersonalization of *staff, residents, clients,* and *group homes* cannot substitute for living in one's own home with people of choice.)

Leslie's acceptance of her move to the group home, despite some pullbacks and occasional doubts along the way, was relatively easy, for which I feel incredible gratitude. I cannot be certain that the separation was less traumatic for Leslie than I expected. Certainly, there was pain for her. During the months following her first request for a move, she had expressed frequent desire for a new setting. Yet, in the weeks after she learned that she would actually be moving, her behavior became difficult and even outrageous. I finally challenged her, "Leslie, you're not just mad at your brother. Something else is bothering you, isn't it? Are you worried about moving into the group home?" She broke into tears and clung to me. "I love you, Mommy," she cried. "I not want to lose you." It is often hard to believe that this child of mine has mental retardation; her emotions are so clearly on target. She does need help in reaching them appropriately, but will there always be someone to help her understand and express them?

What is it like when the time comes to let go? For my generation of Parents, who defied the doctors advising institutionalization and who kept our sons or daughters at home when public schools had not yet opened their doors, the feelings can be intense. There is elation, certainly, when the opportunity for a new life for ourselves as well as our children is presented. There is also disbelief and fear. No matter how prepared we think we are, we are never ready. For me, there was an additional feeling of inadequacy—Why were we selected? Am I doing something wrong? There were spinning thoughts: How do we prepare Leslie? What will be expected of us? How will her brother and sister react? There was also concern for all the others who had not been given this news. Would they think we were receiving preferential treatment? In our case, I knew, with humbling and heartbreaking understanding, that it was because of Leslie's multiple disabilities that she was one of the chosen. Her new group home was initially meant for six adults who have *both* physical disabilities and mental retardation. It was not Leslie's father's many volunteer hours or the years that I had spent on the staff of the agency serving her that ensured my child's entry into the program. Instead, it was her inability to walk independently; few on the long waiting list shared that distinction.

The adjustment for all of us took time. Initially, for me, there was a profound reaction. For two nights after her move, I lay restless through long, sleepless hours. When I did doze off, I soon awoke startled, certain I'd heard a cry from Leslie's room. The third night I woke from a dream I could not remember, sobbing uncontrollably. Wide awake, I moved from my bed and sat in the dark, huddled alone in a chair in the living room where years before I had held my small daughter and wept silent tears. The sun eventually rose and my shaking subsided. The next night, I slept peacefully until the morning alarm.

There are times, even today, when ambivalent feelings surface.

When Leslie leaves after a weekend visit, I feel deep sadness. I also feel that sadness when her brother and sister depart to more distant places, but the emotions around Leslie are more complicated. My concern for her future is always with me. Adjusting to this major life change, letting go, carries stress beyond the typical or the expected.

PRIORITIES, EXPECTATIONS, AND REALITIES

Parents at a residential support group meeting share their everyday concerns with one another; for example, mattresses are wearing out prematurely because staff members don't think about turning them periodically or using mattress covers. Other housekeeping details also get cited and the consensus is that counselors need training in house management. These Parents are concerned that staff members are experimenting, learning the "how to's" of maintaining a household, and that their sons and daughters are losing out in the process. Are mattresses actually the issue? Or are they symbols of a deeper worry? Sometimes Parent worries are truly significant and sometimes the concerns expressed mask feelings that have never been resolved.

At the same meeting, one mother talks about how "really nice" it is that her daughter has to be reminded by staff to call her parents. This mother has always felt it appropriate for her children to move away from home when they reached adulthood. She is also the one who suggests reframing—pretending that our families are similar to ones in which kids are away at college, making it possible to adopt the notion that no news is good news. Not every Parent can handle the separation issue with this degree of ease.

Another mother speaks of her need to find out what happens in her son's life, her yearning for him, and her desire to hear about more of his daily happenings. She has not found it easy to create the communication channel she seeks. She also acknowledges that distancing oneself from one's child happens in subtle ways and with time, but it does happen.

There is heart-stopping poignancy in another mother's quiet statement, "I'd breathe for him, if I could." This, tempered by the reality, "But I'm getting older. How can I keep getting him in and out of the tub?"

Exactly what are Parents looking for in a supervised living arrangement for our sons and daughters whose needs are so special? There are some things we must insist on that cannot, under any circumstances, be compromised. Health and safety issues are nonnegotiable. A home must be safe, and all the medical and health needs of our particular child must be met, totally and competently. We should be able to expect that our child's welfare need not depend on our involvement. We may need to explore this area and get answers to our specific questions to assure ourselves of the highest level of confidence in the program and the people who lifeshare with our sons and daughters.

Beyond these basic and absolute requirements, there are others. Concerns and worries are exacerbated if our child cannot make decisions or clearly voice his or her own needs. Will this home further our child's quality of life and contribute to his welfare? Will he be content? Will she be comfortable? Is the home a happy place both to live in and to visit? Are there opportunities for choice of clothing, religious affiliation, recreation, food, program alternatives, room furnishings, and house rules? Is there individual help and supervision as well as encouragement of independence? Are our children supported in their needs and wishes? Are we?

At one time, some of us looked to a move to a group home as the best of all solutions. Our hopes for the differences that community programming could make were probably unrealistically high. To see problems occur or little progress effected in community settings results in additional depression and anxiety. Once again we ask ourselves, "Will there never be an answer?"

Expectations must be tempered with reality. A group home, no matter how special, is not a panacea. Group home staff will have no more answers to make everything right for our sons and daughters than doctors, therapists, teachers, or even we, their Parents, do. In addition, Parents have developed certain patterns and standards with and for our children that seem to be the only justifiable ways of handling daily routines. We have become rigid in our habits. Even when we acknowledge that other ways of thinking and doing and new perspectives offered by a different set of people may work, and even though we recognize that the challenge of adjustment may stimulate new tolerance in our sons and daughters, we are not always able to change our emotions along with our understanding. We don't appreciate seeing patterns and adjustments that we have shaped come undone. Sometimes we reenter the grief cycle of hopeless despair when routines we painstakingly put in place are so easily ignored. We, the Parents, must be the ones to compromise, and we find that painful.

Staff may regard Parents as overprotective, sometimes with reason. Often, unwittingly, Parents discourage independence. This is our child, the child we have tended and cared for since birth, and it takes courage and a new way of thinking not to infantalize a child you've nurtured through the years, a child who still needs care. There is fear in entrusting that care to others. Emotional bonds press tight. We, as Parents, eventually realize that we have little control over letting go of our typical children. We can resist or allow, we can make it difficult or easy for them and for ourselves, but it is our children who effect the separation, leaving us only to react to it. We, as Parents, have a much more difficult road to walk because our children often cannot effect their separation, despite how much they may desire it. We hand over the control, not to our children, but to others—agencies, bureaucracies, and providers. We cannot choose the people who will be most directly in charge of helping to create a new life for our child. Often we have little to say about where and with whom our children will live. Yet, these are the most vulnerable of our children; the ones we have ministered to and advocated for, the ones we understand and whose words and actions we can translate.

Our questions sometimes seem silly and can often be overwhelming: Where will my child live? Will she be surrounded by the sorts of possessions she is used to? Who will live with my child? Will the people she lifeshares with understand and care? Will the food be what she likes? Will someone comfort her during a midnight thunderstorm? How will I know when something wonderful, frightening, exciting, or dangerous happens?

Leslie has always had a clear notion of the sort of person she most enjoys. In addition, she has always made her attitude quite clear toward those whom she doesn't like. I have almost always understood—and usually agreed with—her choices. It is not easy to articulate the difference between a roommate and a counselor, between a staff person and a friend. Yet, family members, like Leslie, "know one when we see one." Parents truly hope that the professionals who are making decisions with and for our sons and daughters are aware of the gravity of their responsibility. They must also be aware that the people in their charge are individuals, with their own opinions, ideas, choices, and dreams. We don't always see that happening.

We are challenged, in large and small ways. Agencies and human services providers are not always responsive. Quality of life issues seem to take second place to budgets and administrative decisions. There are reports, written and verbal, that sound strange or inaccurate, clothing that disappears, or a casual acceptance of a cough or a rash. Parents wonder if staff really know when a child is sick or unhappy, if attention is paid to the little signals that we can read so well.

Feelings, all sorts of feelings, are intense. There is joy, relief, guilt, fear, and apprehension. A significant loss has occurred in our life. There is no longer the need for the intensity of the daily commitment. One Parent noted, "I've never had so much free time; yet, I'm not energized." Many of us have provided 24-hour care for many years. We have lived the days of constant, never-ending vigil. Now, we feel like the parent of a toddler who has disappeared in a crowd instead of the parent of an adult who is secure in his or her own home.

SYMBOLS

At another meeting, a discussion among several counselors and Parents of adults with severe developmental disabilities who live in a group home focuses on nail-cutting. Parents list this as a priority; counselors feel indifferent. There are more significant daily responsibilities for counselors that have an impact on the house and all of its residents. One Parent suggests that when we visit we can take care of the nail-cutting chore. This pragmatic approach is not an acceptable solution for most Parents. It is clear that cutting nails is symbolic of something far greater than a grooming need. A mother suggests that ignoring such details illustrates a lack of sensitivity on the part of the counselors. Another comments that good care and good attitudes on the part of the counselor sponsor a feeling of dignity and value for a "resident." Parents and counselors agree that good personal hygiene is a necessary constant. The discussion seems to mask a larger issue that eventually surfaces. The words are quiet, but the pain is clear—"I feel such disappointment," a mother says. "I had looked to a group home as the solver of all the problems. If this agency that promised so much can't do it, who *can?*"

What, then, is it that Parents *really* want? We want our sons and daughters to be happy, content, well-nourished, and well-cared for. We want their daily routine to be stimulating and exciting, but not overly demanding. We want their homes to be furnished to *our* taste, well-equipped, and well-kept. We want the people who interact with our children to be attentive, sensitive, and caring. We want them to be perfect versions of ourselves—a surrogate family who will do everything we ever did for our children *plus* everything we didn't do; a caring circle of friends who will love our children as we do *and* encourage their growth far beyond any realistic potential. In short, we really want the impossible.

Our feelings are intricately bound in our expectations. Again and again we realize that no one will take the same care of this child as we have. The years of nurturing, feeding, dealing with professionals, teaching, medicating, transporting, and loving have been demanding, draining, and constant. There is guilt in feeling that it may not have been enough and guilt in turning the life of this child over to others. There is also guilt in feeling relief when we do, and that leads to anger and disappointment when nails don't get clipped.

I think about the ways I allow myself to magnify happenings and nonhappenings out of proportion at times. Leslie's tape recorder needs batteries; does her roommate *really* care about my child and her interests? Her hair has grown too long; is anyone looking at her, paying attention? While I am still part of my child's life, I can trim her hair, buy the batteries, and cut her nails. If she never gets her favorite meal, I can provide that special treat. If her home is not kept clean, I can think about giving her a hand vacuum cleaner or a monthly housekeeping service as a present.

Taking ownership of the short-term solutions makes far more sense than focusing on negatives and investing them with symbolic overtones. We can change those things that distress us and still recognize the greater good that has come from this experience. This approach, however, can never answer the fright of looking ahead to the days when we won't be around to create solutions.

HOW INVOLVED IS INVOLVED?

Parents experiencing the trauma and the challenge of separating from their adult sons or daughters ask the same questions: "How involved should I be?" "How involved *can* I be?" "He really likes a snack before bed," says one mother, "Dare I ask?"

The years of growing for many of our sons and daughters who are now adults were years of exclusion. Parents have not yet had enough experience with true parent/professional teaming to be at ease with mutual planning. We often were awed and intimidated by the professionals who surrounded our children. We felt angered by them, patronized by them, misunderstood. We still feel the scars from our encounters with doctors who told us to institutionalize our children and then added to our guilt if we rejected the idea by restating the negative effects our decision would have on our families. There are valid reasons why some Parents stay locked in a trap, still protesting, afraid, unable to deal with professionals who we feel do not understand us, who seem insensitive to the Parent perspective, and who, we assume, cannot deal effectively with our sons and daughters.

Some Parents deliver mixed messages. One mother I know proclaims she wants to be *informed* of problems in her son's living arrangement, but she doesn't want to be bothered with them. She hasn't the energy to be part of any solution; yet, she doesn't want to be left out. We want others to do it all, but we are angry and upset with any sign of mismanagement. Tactful sharing is necessary to establish and continue mutual respect. This is a dilemma for Parents and a dilemma for staff.

MOVING ON

Leslie did well in the group home. I learned with delight of the three questions she asked each time she interviewed a potential counselor: "Are you a boss?" "Do you tell jokes?" "Are you a nice person?" However, feelings change and 3 years after Leslie had moved into the group home, she startled everyone at her interdisciplinary team meeting by announcing that she wanted her own apartment. "I not want to live in the group home anymore. There be too many people and too much noise. There be too many rules. And Susan be a pain of the neck!"

Leslie shared 3 years of living with 5 other adults with disabilities (who ranged in age from 32 to 54 years old), and a number of counselors who moved in and out according to staff schedules. She understood, without expressing it, that being assigned housemates is not feasible. Common sense should govern. People should live together because they know and like one another, not for the convenience of an agency.

Leslie rebelled against regulatory requirements such as the monthly fire drill. When the dreaded bell rousted Leslie out of bed at 2 A.M. one cold February morning, she got into her wheelchair and rolled to the front door to prove that she could get out in case of a fire; however, she refused to actually go outside. The next day, a distraught counselor called me to report the incident. Leslie got on the telephone to explain why she had stopped at the front door. "Mom," she sighed, "it be *dark* outside. It be *cold* outside. When it be *summer*, I go outside!" Another illustration of common sense that is shadowed by rules and regulations.

Although Leslie really wanted to move to an apartment of her own, she understood without our prompting that she needed someone there for transportation and to help her with daily living. Because of her multiple disabilities, her father and I felt that it would be wise to have the agency already in place as a backup for the time when we are no longer around. We didn't want Leslie's brother and sister to have the responsibility; they don't even live in the area.

With Leslie as our guide, a plan took shape. Leslie's need for a physically accessible living arrangement and 24-hour individual support was a new venture for the agency that had been sponsoring her group home life. They put Leslie's name on waiting lists at two apartment complexes. Two years later, she was still waiting. She had become impatient and unpleasant, making certain that everyone around her was as committed to her leaving as she was. We felt frustrated, unable to make the sleeping elephant of bureaucracy lumber on. We had labored for a long time under the illusion that the agency was in control and would move things along, but when we checked the two apartment complexes we found that one was not accessible and the other had not had an available accessible unit for more than 10 years. Therefore, we decided to buy a reasonably priced accessible condominium in a lively neighborhood with neighbors of all ages and a mixture of cultures. The small, well-planned apartment has two bedrooms and a sofa bed in the living room for sleepover guests or the "respite counselor" who comes in two weekends per month. There are two bathrooms—one of which is wide, long, and accessible. The kitchen sink and counters are low. A back door on the ground level leads into a pleasant sunroom.

After we found the condominium, we had to find a roommate. We ran the following ad in a small, weekly newspaper: "Unique opportunity to be a friend, roommate, and advocate for a spirited young woman with developmental disabilities. Room and board and . . . a monthly stipend. To arrange an interview, call . . . " The first person to respond was a first grade teacher exploring opportunities for personal growth and possible new career options. I participated in the initial interview required by the agency and realized that we did not need to look any further. Leslie was not included in that interview, but she confirmed my reaction when the two young women met a few days later.

Beth has a degree in psychology, but no background in special education and no training in rehabilitation. She has common sense and the ability to explore new territory in creative ways. Beth was Leslie's guide to the larger community while they lived together for 18 months. She and Leslie are the same age and her friends formed Leslie's new circle of friends. Together they "hung out," shopped, partied, and enjoyed leisure time. It was the best of all arrangements, better than anything I had anticipated. What was most exciting was that Beth never viewed herself as heroic or extraordinary. She helped me confirm that Leslie and other individuals who have been labeled can truly be valued by people outside their immediate families. It is a feeling that I needed to trust.

Leslie can do many things for herself, but there are times when she must have the assistance of someone else. She can operate a microwave, but does not measure ingredients in a recipe accurately. She can do her own laundry, but has trouble folding clothes. She transfers from her wheelchair to her bed and to the toilet, but needs someone to help her in and out of the bathtub. Her roommate will always have to spend time encouraging Leslie to deal appropriately with day-to-day frustrations and problems. In her shared apartment, Leslie can have this support, and usually without having to wait for it.

Leslie's reaction to her new arrangement was typically Leslie. The third day after the move, she confided, "It much easier to wake up happy." At the end of a week, she proudly observed, "In this house, *I* am a staff!"

PEOPLE

For all its positives, the setting in which Leslie lives is an artificial structure. She actually wanted a place of her own. She will always have to share her place with a roommate/helper, one who may not necessarily be her first choice. Support is necessary for this young person so that her health and safety will not be compromised; the support is predicated on what agencies can offer. The community in which Leslie lives seems to be a place that would offer natural supports: neighbors, a community pool, and an active civic association. Leslie cannot become connected with these supports without someone else setting up connections; however, her roommate may feel shy or awkward about sponsoring friendships. As a person who believes in the goodness of most people and the possibilities that a community can offer, it is difficult for me to acknowledge the need for creative and often elaborate solution finding every step of the way.

Today, Leslie wants to live with a man who wishes to share his life with her. Bureaucracies and family members can block or at least make their choice difficult. Three months of weekly sexuality counseling for Leslie and Alan were arranged. According to the professional counselor working with them, the sessions were "reality based." Beyond the functional information about what sex is and how it is done, using graphic rubber representations that Leslie found "confoosing," she and Alan were asked to grapple with solutions as to what would happen if and when they no longer want to lifeshare. How many people without disabilities are required in the wonderful warm days of early love to solve the problem of a potential break-up in order to live together? "Reality" for Leslie and Alan should certainly include setting up appropriate support for future problem solving *when* problems arise. "Reality" should not be used to prevent problems by denying quality of life.

Adults, all adults, should be able to make choices. When those adults must rely on others for everyday care, their vision of what they want for themselves can too easily be ignored or compromised. As a Parent who believes in the value of my child and knows the gifts she has to offer, it is draining and discouraging to recognize how many others do not share my perception.

There are people outside the field of disability who are still unable to accept the "Leslies" of this world as neighbors. They fear any involvement beyond accepting a package from the postman. They haven't known "Leslies" in their families, on their school buses, or in their classrooms. There are people outside the field of disability who accept and are comfortable with the "Leslies," but who are leading busy lives of their own. They pass up the opportunity to add a new acquaintance to their activities, particularly a person who will take added time, physical effort, and creative planning.

I cannot fault these people, although their rejection of Leslie leaves me with a deep feeling of sadness. I understand too well that even those people in the field of disability often do not see my daughter as a person of value. I remember calling the group home one day and asking for Leslie and a new counselor answered, "There's no one here by that name." "Of course there is," I said, a bit testily. "She lives there." "Oh," was the response, "you're talking about one of the clients." When I first raised the issue of Leslie sharing an apartment with counselors who would supervise others in the apartment complex on a drop-in basis, Leslie's program coordinator explained to me why the arrangement couldn't work. "You see," he said patiently, "the free room and board for staff is a real perk, but if they had to live with Leslie, it wouldn't be a perk."

Certainly the bottom line for Parents is "Does this child matter?" A decent home and a dignified life must also offer affection and respect. Caring goes beyond the fundamental issue of dignity around the issues of how our children present themselves, the clothes they wear, the care taken in what they eat, and how they are fed if they can't do this for themselves. The "job" must be more than a job for Parents to feel completely comfortable; it is lifesharing in its most basic and far reaching aspects. In good community-based programs, there is involvement and dedication. People who have chosen to be where they are must get satisfaction from what they do. A Parent like me—an incurable optimist, although I am increasingly understanding of the realities—starts with high expectations of the people who choose, as their jobs, to live with my daughter. Unfortunately, the quality of counselors as well as the quality of people enlisted from the community can vary considerably. Leslie has had many experiences in her 8 years of living away from her original family home. There were exceptionally caring people in the group home setting as well as punishing, angry people. Leslie has lived with three roommates in the 3 years she has been in her own apartment; one of them—a short-timer—was both verbally and physically abusive. That raises still another thorny issue. I did not pay close attention to the significant messages my daughter was trying to give me during this phase. I wanted so much for the second roommate relationship to work well. I was at a point in my life that was draining and I worked to make things better for Leslie rather than recognize how irretrievably bad they were. I don't forgive myself, but I do understand. If I missed what my verbal child was trying to communicate, what must it be like for Parents whose children cannot talk? The part of me that still wants to live forever to ensure Leslie's continued well-being becomes more and more aware of how little protection I can give her. It is difficult to live with hope when it is so often challenged.

JUDGMENTS

During our years with our children, we deal with the judgments of others. The issue of residential life makes Parents deal with even more judgments. There is a "myth of abandonment" often alluded to by Parents of children with disabilities. It is encouraged by the misconceptions of a world that doesn't yet appreciate the rights of all people. After

Leslie's first move, which took place when she was still attending public school, a new therapist in her school program attended a meeting at which I was present. I was later told that she had asked another participant who I was. Her reaction to the answer was shock, "Her *mother?* If Leslie has a mother, why is she living in a group home?" I felt defensive, judged, seen as a Parent who doesn't really care or who cannot handle what should be my responsibility alone.

Even a report that same year from a school psychologist discussing Leslie's "significant gains in developing more appropriate adult-to-adult social skills . . . self-confidence and maturity" touched a raw nerve. Although I fully understood that a setting that can have consistent expectations of adult behavior is not usually one's original home, I felt as if the years preceding had not been handled well—that I should have done more. It takes very little to make a Parent feel guilty for past, present, and future failures.

More painful was a team report by a group studying normalization that interviewed Leslie and her housemates. Asked why she was in the group home, Leslie replied, "My mother want me to live here." The team report referred to family rejection on the basis of Leslie's words. I suffered my feelings silently. I am secure in the knowledge that Leslie's decision and our decision was exactly right for Leslie and for the rest of us. Leslie was, even in the group home setting, usually happy. She showed signs from the beginning of profiting from the move.

Moving on should be a right of adulthood. It is not a punishment, not an admission of failure on anyone's part. Once, not so long ago, we Parents were made to feel guilty when we did not institutionalize our children; in today's world, we are made to feel guilty if we seek out-of-home placement. With dwindling resources, band-aid services are currently being patched together to keep adult sons and daughters with their original families. It is not a fair solution for anyone.

PERMANENCE

The issue of permanence is another source of considerable Parent anxiety. We know, of course, that nothing is permanent, that the problems never end, and that there is no single solution. Yet, knowing is different from wishing, hoping, and wanting. Leslie has helped me to understand fully that her life, as everyone's life, should be a series of choices and decisions based on her interests and desires, and that those interests and desires are not static or permanent. She must continue to be empowered to choose her own life goals. Some of us, particularly those of us who never accepted institutions as an answer, looked to the group home as the setting that would truly make a difference. Now, we recognize that congregate living based on administrative convenience is little better than institutional living. Some of us have taken the next step, guided by our own understanding of what should be; some of us, like me, have been led by our children to that recognition.

When I meet friends again after a time, they ask about Leslie. "Is she still living in the apartment?" Their use of the word "still" reminds me that the arrangement is precarious, subject to change, that *any* arrangement is precarious, not permanent. Again, the worries intrude.

OPPORTUNITIES AND RISKS

Life in the community does not come without risk. Even as we weigh the significant possibilities of growth, the cultivation of personal responsibility and independence, the value of integration, companionship, participation in decision making, skill development, a weaning from psychological dependence, a more normalized existence, we are still scared. It is far easier for roommates and job coaches to allow risks than Parents. Protection of our sons and daughters often becomes a way of life for us; we understand their lack of judgment, their lack of coping skills, and their vulnerability. Leslie's experiences with her family and her friends have ensured her trust in people.

Once Leslie had moved into her own place, the only remaining hurdle to full inclusion in her community was her placement in a sheltered workshop. Those of us who advocate for Leslie's full citizenship want to see her engaged in doing things on a daily basis that make a difference to her and to others. Leslie worked briefly in the activities department of a nursing home. Her job was, in her words, "to make people happy." She loved what she was doing. Transportation was by taxi—another proof of her growing independence. On the seventh day of employment she was assaulted by a cab driver. Although she suffered no physical injury, she was victimized in a way that terrified her, threatened her spirit, and robbed her of her desire to be part of the real world. For many months, she no longer wanted to work in the community.

All of us—people with disabilities, families, friends, advocates, and society—pay a price when community living involves such risks. I am a believer in community and what it can offer to our "Leslies." I believe in the gifts our "Leslies" can offer to the community as well. But events such as the one I have described cause even me to question my previously unshakable conviction. I know that risk taking is inherent in community life. I know, too, that dreadful things can happen in the most protected of settings. As a professional and as a Parent I will not stop working toward the fullest possible life in the community for Leslie and her peers. However, I do it now with more caution, more understanding of the true risks, more recognition of just how vulnerable my grown child is.

A FINAL NOTE

Sometimes I miss Leslie Ellen with an intensity that is overwhelming, just as I miss her sister and brother, but I respect her need for a life of her own and I am glad. I remember the phone ringing in April of the year after her first move. "Mom," said Leslie's emphatic voice, "I have something important to tell you. I want you to pick me up on Friday for Easter." I assured her that I had marked the calendar. "And," she continued, "I want to be at 6805 for my birthday" (August 4). "Absolutely," I replied, "Wouldn't think of celebrating your birthday without you." The message was not finished, "And I want to come to your house for Christmas." "Certainly," I laughed, "but what about Thanksgiving?" Her voice was exasperated; I could picture her shaking her head in disgust. "Mom," she said, "I have told you. I want to be at your house for Easter, and for my birthday, and for Christmas. Thanksgiving you can give to yourself!" That I do, my lovely daughter. For all the years past, for the wisdom you have given me, for the directions you have been responsible for, and for the new learnings to come, I am thankful, indeed.

9

TURNING
THE PAGES OF LIFE

Michael Joseph Kennedy

My name is Michael Joseph Kennedy. I am 30 years old, I have cerebral palsy, and I am one of four children. Because services were not available to assist my family and me, I was forced to spend 15 years of my life in institutions. I would like to share with you my transition from institution life to living in a real neighborhood and owning my own home.

FROM INSTITUTION LIFE
TO MY OWN HOME AND NEIGHBORHOOD

I started living in the West Hemington Nursing Home when I was about 3 years old. I was scared, and I knew I was in for a rough, long struggle. I lived with children with various disabilities, and I had no say about my life at all. I did not like the nursing home because of the treatment the residents received. I will never forget these experiences, although I try to, because we were not treated with the respect due to any human being. Because we had physical impairments, many of us were also assumed to be, and thus labeled, mentally retarded. I believe that no matter how people are labeled they should be given basic rights such as decent treatment, education, and the right to live in the community.

Later I was moved to the Central Developmental Center in New York State where I received much of the same treatment as at West Hemington. For instance, I was put in the shower under ice cold water, sometimes for as long as an hour. This was in retaliation for my com-

All names of places and people used in this chapter are pseudonyms.

I would like to take this opportunity to say thank you to my immediate family—Pat and Joe Kennedy, Kevin Kennedy, Lynn Flint, and Robert Kennedy—for their support and encouragement. Thank you also to Burt Blatt, Doug Biklen, Steve Taylor, and other members of the Center on Human Policy for giving me the opportunity to show my talents in my work.

plaints about staff members abusing residents. I was also hanged upside down in a doorway with rope around my ankles because I slapped another resident who smashed my model airplane for the third time. I complained to staff about it, but they could not be bothered to intervene.

I later moved to the Owago Developmental Center where I lived from 1979 to 1982. Residents were not respected and were not given choices or freedom. Some people were abused; although, it was better than at Central.

Moving to Supported Apartments

In 1982, I heard about a new supported apartment program being started by a private, nonprofit agency, and I wanted to be a part of it. After wanting to get out of the institution for years, I finally saw my opportunity. In August of that year, I moved into an apartment in the city where I lived for 6 years with three roommates who also had disabilities. It was a great improvement over Owago Developmental Center where I had lived with 20 people. What I liked most was that the apartment was in the community. I was viewed as belonging to the community and could experience being around people without disabilities.

A supported apartment might be a much better place than an institution; however, thinking about it now, it would have been best if I could have moved directly to my own place with the support I needed. With supports, I could have made it. In the apartment I learned a lot about living in the community and made new friends. After a while, however, I began to feel very restricted in my growth, and I felt that my life was still being controlled. I was not making decisions for myself. For example, I traveled a lot for my job, which involved presenting, training, and writing about self-advocacy for people with all types of disabilities, and many times when I came home from a trip, plans had been made without asking me. I also had to leave the apartment every day, even if I was tired after a consulting trip for work (although the staff did occasionally make exceptions, if I made arrangements ahead of time).

The staff at the apartment were excellent. They did all they could to create a homelike atmosphere. However, since the program was funded by Medicaid, staff had to develop and submit things such as personal goals for all the residents. The staff people did realize some of the state requirements were ridiculous and a waste of time, but they were unsuccessful in getting any changes made. They even went so far as to challenge Medicaid to cite them for violations instead of fulfilling certain requirements.

During my fifth year at the apartment, I began to feel strongly that I was ready to leave, so I talked with our administrators about how the apartment had no more purpose for me. Although on a much smaller scale, the apartment still retained some institutional features because of the Medicaid funding. For example, whenever I wanted to go somewhere, I had to tell everyone where I was going and when I would be coming home. I am an adult and I am capable of using my own judgment regarding these issues. At the apartment, I didn't have any privacy and wasn't truly free to make my own choices. I decided I was ready to move on because I had experienced everything I was going to at this place.

Moving to My Own Home

I actually moved into my own house on September 30, 1988, with my friend Dan, who had worked with me at the supported apartment, and Dan's roommate, Jeff. Neither of my roommates had disabilities. We rented a house on the northeast side of the city from our landlord (also a friend of mine who had worked at the supported apartments). She bought a house she thought could easily be made accessible for me and my wheelchair. My name was on the lease for the house and our neighborhood was one that we chose for ourselves.

The agency that ran the supported apartments had been working for a few years to start a service offering individualized support for adults. They wanted a service that would combine a home and the supports necessary to assist a person with a disability to live there. A service finally was started in October 1988, using the state "family care" funding stream. I was the role model for other people with disabilities who also were to be part of this program.

The unique thing about this situation is that the agency did not set this up for us. Dan, Jeff, and I decided the kind of house and the neighborhood we wanted to live in, and our landlady helped us locate the home. While the agency was very supportive of our decision to live together in this particular house, the choice was the result of the three of us working together. Even when the agency's own consultant advised them not to go with this house because accessibility would be costly, they backed us and did a lot of work to make it accessible. Also, because the landlord is my friend, she was very supportive and worked on improving it by doing things such as enlarging the bathroom.

When I moved, I considered myself very fortunate to be able to maintain my services such as visiting nurses, doctors, dermatologists, and therapists. This was my decision. Basically, I did not need to start over again and could keep working with the same people whom I was comfortable with and knew about my background. The only new people who actually worked with me were the aides who assisted me with personal hygiene and other aspects of daily living.

What Is Different in My Own Home

The differences between living in my own house with roommates and previous living situations are numerous and immeasurable. These are a few examples:

It Was Important To Be Trusted   I started to be responsible for paying my own share of living expenses when I moved into a house with roommates. Previously, I had never been trusted with responsibilities; it was always assumed that I could not be responsible for myself because I have disabilities.

My Mom Felt More at Home   Another difference is that my mother, who lived more than 200 miles away, was able to stay at my house for the weekend. She could never do that before because we did not have room, and she wouldn't have felt comfortable. For the first time in all these years I was able to host my mother in my own home.

Sometimes I Just Need My Own Space   If I wanted to be alone I could go into my room or, for that matter, anywhere in the house without anyone asking, "What's wrong?" Staff may not have meant it, but they would get pushy and make me feel like I had to talk about it right then whether I wanted to or not. In my own home, Dan, one of my roommates, said, "I'm here whenever you want to talk about this," but did not place demands on me. Just having that kind of control over my own space was quite an accomplishment. In the supported apartment the agency said that I had that control, but I really didn't have the authority.

I Like People To Ask Me What I Want   When I lived in the supported apartment, people such as doctors would always ask the staff what I needed because they figured the staff would have more information about me than I had about myself. Once I moved into my own house, they needed to deal directly with me about any of their questions and concerns.

It's My Life   Chris Smith, my social worker, and I had an understanding. I could ask her questions about things that were new to me and advice about the easiest way to handle situations. She, however, would not do anything without talking to me. When the program was first introduced to me, I said I would do it only on one condition—that nothing was to be done without me present or informed about what was going on. For example, people from Social Security would call and want Chris to make decisions. She would say, "I'm not doing anything until I check with Michael."

I Hate Service Plans   I did not want to waste my valuable time doing service plans, and I wanted to get out of the structure of the state. Everyone sets goals for themselves, but how many people go home and write them down? It makes me feel kind of degraded in a sense. I was not going to come home from work and do goals for 3 hours with verbal prompts. When I get out of work, I just want to relax like everyone else.

I Want To Make All of the Decisions that Directly Affect Me   Being responsible for my life led to having control over my life. I had equal say in everything that happened regarding our house and I made all the decisions that directly affected me. In the institution and the supported apartment my decisions were all made for me, often without my consultation. In my former living situations, activities such as recreation were decided by majority vote. In my own home, I could go out when and where I wanted without asking anyone's permission.

When I lived at my family's home, my mother taught me to choose—what I wanted for dinner, when to take a bath, whether to go out or stay home, what clothes I wanted to wear, and when to get up. These are basically everyday things that a person without a disability does—the basic rights every individual should have. I did not have these choices when I lived in the institution and the supported apartment.

I Like Being Part Owner of a Van   Having a van was another big accomplishment because it was the first time I could really say I owned anything. The experience was similar to teenagers receiving their first car; they feel like they're on top of the world. I like not having to depend on the state for transportation (although the state Office of Vocational Rehabilitation paid for the lift).

Dan and I decided together that we would like to have a vehicle so we could get out and do things without having to pay for a bus. We bought it from the landlady who sold it because she was not going to use it anymore and she knew we were looking for an affordable van. We had an understanding that if Dan got sick or died, the vehicle would be left to me.

I've Always Liked Pets   When I was growing up I didn't see my dog a lot; my parents kept him on the farm they owned. In the institution and apartment, I could not keep a dog. In the house, Dan kept his two dogs, which were good companions to both of us. If I was home alone and someone tried to break in, the size of the dog scared them off or gave them second thoughts.

I believe that when you get an animal and give it a home, it's your responsibility to make sure the animal gets proper care. If you are not going to give it love and commitment, then why would you buy the pet? We had to put our dog to sleep because we were spending astronomical amounts of money on medications. We tried everything we could to keep her alive. We buried her in a pet cemetery right next to her mother.

I Want My Independence   Living in the supported apartment was important to my independence. I knew I was not able to do some of the physical work, but I could use my voice to direct people on how I wanted my house set up. I was lucky to find three good aides to work with me. With the aides, I tried to break my routine down into simple instructions. I worked with each individual very closely. I also left it open so that they could ask questions if they were unsure. If they were not clear, they needed to tell me and be specific.

I Shared a House with Friends   Dan and Jeff assisted me with everyday needs, but I saw them as typical roommates sharing a home. On paper, Dan was my "careprovider," but he said he would have done it without being paid. Jeff was there for moral support. They respected me, and I respected them.

Dan and I basically hit it off when we met, and we seemed to understand each other. We had disagreements like everyone else, but for the most part we tried to work together and help each other. We had a lot of the same interests, such as growing up in the country. Just because we shared a house, I did not feel I had the right to tell him what to do and he didn't tell me what to do.

Once I got to know Jeff, he opened up, and through the course of 2 years, we grew to be good friends. Jeff was skeptical because he had never been around a person with a disability. Through my work, he began to see that people with disabilities are people, too, and have the same wants, needs, and rights as everyone else. He will help fight now, donating money to the cause, but he will not demonstrate or do hands-on care. It was hard for him, and he had to readjust some of his life. Jeff told me, "Regardless of disability, they're people just like me. (Before) I didn't even know people with disabilities existed." Jeff learned by getting to know me. He learned we did not want anything more or less— just to be as equal as everyone else.

Moving to Georgia

In 1990, my roommate Dan and I went to Atlanta, Georgia, to a national conference of the American Association on Mental Retardation (AAMR). Dan has a sister-in-law, nieces, and nephews who live in Georgia, but he did not stay in contact with them after his brother died and his sister-in-law remarried. Dan decided to look them up. They invited us to come out for 4 days after the conference. During those 4 days, I saw such a change in Dan. He was relaxed, natural, and very comfortable. I met his family and felt as though I had known them for 10 years; that's how relaxed I was. They kept asking us, "Are you going to move down here?" Dan had thought about moving before, but did not because of his mother who died 2 years before.

I talked with Dan about moving South. I also had relatives there and liked the warm weather and climate. One day Dan came home from work very frustrated and said he wanted to move to Georgia. He asked if that was okay with me, and I said it was fine. We planned to move in April 1991, but moved it up to September 1990, deciding if we were going to move we needed to simply do it instead of talk about it.

Later on, we welcomed Jeff, our roommate, to go with us. When he decided to come, we were shocked because he was born in upstate New York and had never lived outside of the city where he had been born. We didn't know how long Jeff would stay, but we agreed to help him get back home if he didn't like it. Jeff and Dan had been together a lot longer than Dan and I had been friends. When we decided to go to Georgia, Dan became the happiest person in the world; it was time for a change.

We started to make arrangements with people in Georgia. I had written letters to two people I knew and to the independent living center. Dan called his sister-in-law two times a week to make arrangements for buying a mobile home and we started to save the down payment for it. Dan's relatives helped us find our house; they did all the legwork. We were in contact with them quite a bit.

I was excited with the new surroundings and a new venture. I hoped to get down there and work for the independent living center and eventually start my own consulting firm. These last 2 years I have achieved two of the main things I wanted out of life, although I can't explain how it happened: renting a house and moving South to a house I could own. I had no idea it would happen quite like this; I couldn't believe it. I guess it was meant to be.

HOUSING AND SUPPORT

In this section, I share what I have learned about setting up a house, renting and owning a house, picking a neighborhood, getting supports, working with aides, and making decisions and living with roommates. This might give other people an idea about how to accomplish this.

Setting Up a House

It is important for people with disabilities to be involved in setting up housing. With me, it was just a matter of a porch lift and some adaptive equipment, but other people may need more. The government should add funding so that people can get the equipment they need. I found out if I put the lease, lights, and phone in my name, I could get a discount. It helped out a great deal.

It is important for the individual to be in control of the process, including where they want to live and the neighborhood they want to live in. Agencies should work together with people to determine the best way for each individual to be more independent. It is important not to make people feel pressured; they should feel comfortable calling the agency if they are having trouble.

Working Together

It is important to always have the individual with a disability involved in setting up the living situation. They know what they want and need, but may not know how to get it. When people move, they have a lot of questions. It is important that the person understand every aspect, even if the worker has to explain it a hundred times. Staff need to use language that is easy to understand.

It is important for the agency not to present themselves as if they know everything. We all make mistakes, and people learn by making them. If someone is not verbal, the individual has to feel comfortable enough, and the agency must be confident enough, to figure out how to do this together.

Picking a Neighborhood

People do not need to move away to own or rent a house. If kids grow up in a particular neighborhood, it would be nice if they could still live in that neighborhood. Agencies could set up programs and supports so that people can stay in the neighborhood they have lived in all their life, where they know people and people know them. Professionals and parents need to think about this.

Renting and Owning a Place

The most important reason to have leases in the person's own name is for the sense of responsibility. The house can be rented by the person, not an agency, with the difference being a sense of control and the right to do what the person wants. When the lease is in his or her name, the person can feel comfortable making changes without checking with the agency or taking the chance the agency will not like it. Professionals sometimes think people with disabilities cannot own or rent; they do not think people with disabilities have the capabilities to take on such a challenge.

Owning instead of renting is important for several reasons. An individual should be able to own a home without worrying about losing the home to pay for services. Also, if a person goes to family care, the family usually owns the house, but it does not need to be that way. If people own their home, it gives them something of their own to work for. People do not need to worry that the landlady will sell the home, leaving them without a roof over their head. It is something people can enjoy for years to come unless they decide to move. Owning a home makes a difference; it is an incentive to move ahead. It is good not to live under the terms of an agency.

Getting Supports

Today, everybody needs support of one kind or another. People need support to go ahead and do things, whether this support comes from a good friend, parents, a social worker, or a guardian. Everybody needs people, not people to say they are doing right or wrong, but people who will listen. Even if people are independent in what they do, they will always need friends with whom to cry, laugh, and joke. There is no person in this world so independent that they don't need anybody. We all need support, but with that support people don't want someone coming in and taking over their lives.

Working with Aides

It is also important to have backup systems for aide services. If an aide calls in sick at the last minute, there should be an emergency number to call. A person would be in a critical situation to get things done if the aides could not come. This happens.

With some home health agencies, people have the option to choose aides. It is important to get aides that people feel comfortable working with and can trust. Screening is a very important process to see if it will work for both parties. What is also important is to hire staff who will listen to the person's wants and needs, and who have a sense of humor and can laugh with the person, even through the hard times.

The independent living center recommended to always ask for as many aide hours as possible because 99 times out of 100 the funding agency will give you less. It is like selling furniture; people negotiate. This is a very key factor, one of the very first things people need to learn.

People might want to do some research to compare agencies and then go with the one that will best meet their needs. I needed an aide service available to help me get dressed and ready for work. Also, I needed someone to assist with doing some light housekeeping and to be with me until my ride or bus arrived. If I needed to go to the restroom, I had support to do that. An aide's job is different with each individual.

Aides' hours need to change when a person's work schedule changes, which is often a problem for the aide service offices. They're not used to having someone whose schedule changes, and it can create a problem for the agency. I needed to have set work hours instead of changing the hours around because the aide services didn't allow for flexibility or arrange for backups when aides were sick. These are common problems people experience working with aides.

Also, any person with a disability should consider having a device called a Lifeline, which can be worn on the wrist or around the neck. A Lifeline is an emergency system for people with disabilities and elders. It is patched into the emergency room of a hospital so a person living alone can quickly call for help. The government should allocate adequate funding for this device. This is a very useful piece of equipment, not only for people with disabilities, but for everybody.

Living with Roommates

A roommate may need support, too. One way to do this is to set up a system where two or three aides come in so that your roommate can get a break and have time away. When people live together they can like each other a lot, but every now and then people get under each other's skin. It's good to find a roommate with similar interests because it makes things go smoother. Dan and I found a lot in common—music, old cars, living in the country, and being around people. Age has nothing to do with it; Dan is a lot older than me. No matter what the person's disability, if they like being around each other and want to be there, that makes a big difference. Because people get along at one time doesn't mean they are always going to get along well together. People can end up having differences of opinions. Not everyone will live together forever.

MORE THAN HOUSING AND SUPPORTS

Living in the community is more than housing and support. This section discusses my own experiences in helping other people, believing in myself, and breaking old habits.

Helping Other People

I see myself as being just like everyone else if given the opportunities to get the supports I need. What I enjoy in my work is being able to help other people—it is my satisfaction. It is nice to get awards and be recognized, but that is not why I do my work. I see myself as a role model, and I try to set a good example for other people. I hope they will have the instinct to go ahead and advocate for their own rights. I am happy knowing all people with disabilities can live and work as independently as they possibly can. My meaning of independence is that people have supports, friendships, and guidance.

Believing in Yourself

The first thing people have to do is to believe in themselves—each person is important. People do not need to live up to other people's standards, and each individual must believe in what is right for them. People must not be afraid that if it does not go right the first time, it is not going to work. Everything takes time and people must not stop from doing what is right for them because of how others perceive them. I could have very easily shut myself off from the rest of the world.

My parents gave me a lot of guidance when I was living at home. There were times when I wanted to give up, but my mother said, "No way I'm going to let you give up." They never felt sorry for me and I didn't need to feel sorry for myself. They never treated me differently than anyone else. Even at my lowest point, and there were times when I was really at a low point, they said, "Let's talk about what you can do and can give back to the community or the world." A person can either be bitter about what happened or can use it to make him- or herself a better person. I believe God put me on this earth with this disability for a reason, but only He knows the purpose. As that old saying goes, I believe nobody is to question why we are the way we are.

A lot of people say, "I don't understand why you're not bitter." I say, "What good would that do me?" I had to learn the hard way that being bitter is not a good thing. In my mother's life, there were times when she would get upset and frustrated because she didn't know what to do—keep me at home or put me in an institution. At that time, she was a new mother with no supports. While it bothered me to go to the institution, I also knew where she was coming from. To this day, she blames herself that this happened to me, but she knows deep down inside that there was nothing we could have done. There is no use in dwelling on the bad situations.

What I want is for people with disabilities and professionals to see that no matter how severe or minor a disability is, they need to make people feel like they are somebody unique. Everyone has talents of one sort or another. It takes time, but service providers, parents, and consumers need to work together. Everyone goes over some rocky roads in their lives, whether disabled or not.

Breaking Old Habits

It was hard for me at first to make my own decisions. I would ask Dan questions that I really did not need to ask him, basically asking permission. Then I realized it is my house, too; but it was hard to get out of the pattern. Because it was a habit I had to teach myself to get out of, it took me a good 2 years to break it. Dan would sit down and say, "You're 28 years old. You don't need to ask me to do this or that." I did not think about it because for so many years I had to ask. I was always skeptical about asking friends over because I was not sure how Dan would react. He told me, "You pay the rent here. You can invite anybody you want to invite."

One other habit that was hard for me to break was to trust people, even Dan, as nice as he could be. Dan got offended one time and said, "Don't you trust me?" I explained, "It's not you, it's just that for a lot of years, I could not trust people, and you get into a pattern and you don't trust. Not that I want to be that way. It's a pattern, a habit I got into."

Money is another issue related to trust. I could have had a roommate who would rip me off and I would not have known it. I won't give everyone the authority to help me write out those checks. I don't want this kind of job in everyone's hands; I just want one person helping me who works together with me.

When we purchased a home, we worked together. No decisions were made without Dan or without me. If we could not come to an agreement, we sat down and worked out a compromise we both could live with, which is what I call working it out together. There are going to be shades of the institution that I need to overcome—to make decisions, to trust people, and break old habits. I just need time to make these changes; it could take 1, 5, or 15 years, I don't know. Change takes time.

Who would have thought I would own my own vehicle or my own home? When you have lived in institutions, you kind of wonder, "Am I going to do something with my life?" I've come a long way because I believed that I could.

EPILOGUE

Since this chapter was written, I moved from Georgia to northern New York to live next door to my family. I liked Georgia; it just did not work out, but I am glad I tried it. I did not know until I actually tried it whether it could work out or not. Now, I have my own place and I live alone. I would never have been able to do that without these past few years. But that is another story.

10

PERSPECTIVES OF A SUPPORT WORKER

David Adler

This is a story about my experiences with Luke. I was his attendant, and in the 7 months I worked for him we became close friends. He died on Wednesday June 29, 1988, a few days after the wheelchair lift in his van malfunctioned and dropped him on the ground. Luke taught me a lot and I am still learning some of the lessons.

THE STORY BEGINS—COMING TOGETHER

Luke's entrance into my life was as unexpected as his exit. In December 1987, I had just started work at a Supportive Service Living Unit (SSLU)[1]. It was a few weeks after having finished my first stint working with Judith Snow, the first person in Canada to obtain individualized funding; she was also the person who taught me the importance of story telling. I was called by a friend who worked at the local independent living center and who knew I was unhappy working at the SSLU. She wanted to tell me about a job opportunity she thought would suit me better. Luke had fired his attendant and urgently needed a new one. Also, his wife was no longer there to give him the support she typically provided; she had left him for another man—his full-time attendant.

From the time I started working with Luke, I had a regular 8:30 A.M. to 5:00 P.M. Monday to Friday shift because he only had funding for 8 hours a day on weekdays and 4 hours on the weekend. His funding

---

This chapter is dedicated to Matt Van Geffen.

The name Luke is used as a pseudonym in this chapter; all other names are true.

[1]In an SSLU there are usually 12–15 accessible apartment units in a large building that have been adapted for people with physical disabilities. These units have attendant services provided to them from an office in the building. (For more information on attendant services in Ontario and other parts of Canada, see the appendix at the end of this chapter.)

217

was based on the assumption that his wife would be around in the evening and provide any needed attendant service. Therefore, his attendant care budget was inadequate for his suddenly altered circumstances. He had friends come over to help him in the evening and do most of the overnights (they were there for security in case Luke needed anything, but they could sleep during that time), although for the first few weeks I usually did one overnight, which was unpaid, and one half-day on the weekend about every other week. His plan was to get a roommate to live in the second bedroom of his apartment in exchange for putting him to bed and being there at night. The spare room had belonged to his 5-year-old daughter, but when his wife moved out she took their daughter with her.

ON BEING AN ATTENDANT

Some of the tasks of an attendant are the same whether in an SSLU or under individualized funding, where the person receiving the attendant service has direct control over that service. These mostly involve hygiene, such as toileting, bathing, and dressing; as well as food preparation, clean up, and possibly feeding. (This list is general; not everyone needs all of these services, nor is the list exhaustive.) The major difference between individualized funding and an SSLU is that the duties of an attendant in the SSLU basically end with hygiene functions. However, in individualized funding the job can entail many other things: driving, office work (typing, filing), traveling, going to social occasions, and even blowing out birthday candles (a task I shared with another attendant at Judith Snow's 41st birthday). The list of jobs an attendant can do in an individualized situation is limited only by the scope of activities of the employer.

There is also one important aspect of the job that needs special mention—availability. One of my jobs is to be available and ready to work, even though I might not actually do anything for my employer for extended periods of time. This may mean sitting nearby, but out of the way as Judith gives a talk, waiting in case she wants a drink, or sitting and reading in Luke's apartment while he worked on his computer. This also highlights another part of the job—learning to disappear. My services may be required, but not necessarily my presence. However, this job is more than a list of duties, as you will see.

RELATIONSHIP

The rest of the picture of working as an attendant can be encapsulated in one word—relationship. I believe the relationship is the most important aspect of doing attendant service. The formation of a relationship is essential for the attendant to give good service and for the person with the disability to receive the quality attendant service they want. Everything that went on between Luke and me was because of our relationship with each other; it started at my job interview.

Although we had met casually once or twice when I was Judith's attendant, my arrival at his apartment was the first time we really talked. We took an immediate liking to each other—a prerequisite for doing one-to-one attendant service. If the two people don't like each other at some level, then there is no chance for the relationship to form. Who would want to be in a one-to-one employment situation with someone they disliked? So liking each other was the first step in forming our relationship. The next and most important step happened on my first day of work. Luke let me into his life and I let Luke into mine.

Luke saw me as more than just a body that he called on when his body needed a little help. He accepted the fact that I was a person and that I would be part of his life while I was in his presence. Also, I saw him as more than a boss, as more than someone who told me what to do. This major step involved Luke talking to me and taking me into his confidence about his life, which also meant that I was willing to listen and respond as a person and not just an employee.

I realized the situation was unusual and that realization fostered the speed at which our relationship formed. Luke was very upset about his wife leaving; he needed to talk and this probably made it easier for him to let me into his life. Also, I was a ready ear and to some extent a captive audience, but I was also a willing audience. If I had just been an employee, talking to me would not have been very satisfactory because I would have only been listening out of politeness or a sense of duty. My willingness to listen came out of my willingness to let Luke into my life.

INTIMACY

My willingness to listen is also needed because it allows the relationship to reach a natural state of intimacy. For Luke and me that natural state was a close friendship. In other situations, as with Judith, it is less clear whether we are really friends or not, but the openness of each person to the other allows for the essential intimacy that is required to let the two people work with each other.

Using the word intimacy is always a problem because it seems to have so many meanings. I suppose the type of intimacy that occurs between the two people in an attendant service situation has its own meaning—the sense that both people feel comfortable with the closeness necessitated by the performance of the job. However, I cannot think of any other word that describes how I feel when I am doing attendant service and I am connecting with the other person at some emotional level. At that point, I am not working for Luke or Judith, we are doing the job together. If this intimacy does not develop, the work will be unsatisfactory for the employee and the service will be unsatisfactory for the employer.

A traditional idea of intimacy always present in attendant service is physical intimacy. One of the common jobs of the attendant is to help the person with bathing, dressing, and toileting, and this obviously involves touching the person who is receiving the service. Being comfortable with the physical intimacy of handling the person's genitalia is really important. If either person is uptight about doing that then it quickly becomes an uncomfortable situation. The attendant must maintain an appropriate detachment to guard against inappropriate familiarity. Conversely, the person receiving the service shouldn't see this intimacy as sexual. This does not mean that the attendant should not be caring in his or her touching or that the person does not appreciate a caring touch. When a mutual relationship exists, intimacy develops that allows the attendant to show care, and the person with the disability to receive it, even in something as simple as the quality of the touching.

I remember once asking Luke if all the touching he received from various people made him feel good. I was thinking of the idea that people do better if they have a certain number of hugs each day. I wondered if the touching Luke received while receiving attendant service could be counted toward that healing type of touching. He said it depended on the individual attendant. Some did the job, but they treated the touching as nothing more than physical manipulation; he said they could just as well have been lifting a sack of potatoes instead of him. He also said some people's touch did make him feel good; he told me I "touched good." That made me feel really good. He knew I cared for him even though I never told him. I am glad he knew because I didn't realize how much I did care until he died. At least one of us appreciated how much I cared when it was happening.

MUTUALITY

Attendant service is more than a simple exchange of service for money; it is more for both people involved. Luke received more than just an extra set of arms and legs and I received more than money. This mutuality is important because without it the two major tools in making the job work—control and negotiation—will lead to conflict instead of mutual satisfaction.

As with any job there has to be control by the employer; however, because of the unique relationship between the employer and employee, the issue of control manifests itself differently than in any other job. The facile view would be that I would give up control of myself while I am working because I am nothing more than a tool for my employer to live his or her daily life. And to some extent this is true. I am trained by my various employers to go through their daily routines the way they want them done. They know more about their particular physical needs than anyone else possibly can. However, I am a thinking, feeling human just like they are and I expect acknowledgment of that. That is where mutuality becomes important. Mutuality encompasses all I have been talking about; it allows the possibility of working *with* the other person, not just for them. If each person receives mutual benefits then control becomes a side issue. It only has to be used when there is a situation where negotiation will not work.

NEGOTIATION

Negotiation is the main tool for the working relationship between two people. Both people want to work things out so that they each believe they have benefited. One instance that sticks in my mind occurred around New Year's Day when I worked for Luke. I had agreed to work New Year's Day because I had taken Christmas off. I then learned some good friends of mine were having a party on New Year's Eve and I wanted to go. However, I realized either I would have to leave the party really early or stay late and go to work tired, which I wouldn't intentionally do. Also, Luke's roommate wanted to go out, but he was committed to being around from 11:00 P.M. on so that Luke could go to bed. We negotiated. The end result was that Luke and I went to the party. I agreed to put him to bed and do the overnight so that his roommate could go out. In addition, he said I could leave at my regular time the next day regardless of when we woke up.

The example may appear a bit banal, but it is worth examining. If I had not had the relationship with Luke that I did, I would never have thought of asking him to the party, which was his major benefit from the negotiation. Although it may seem that I lost nothing by making the agreement, I also compromised. I went to the party, which I otherwise would not have done, but I agreed to leave when Luke wanted to (which turned out to be later than I would have). I restricted myself to one drink, partly because I knew I had to work later and partly because I was driving Luke's van. Also, I had to help Luke at the party and I had to sleep at his place and not my own. I did get to see my friends and I still had a good time, and that outweighed everything else. In addition, the arrangement enabled Luke to give his roommate the night off. It is easy to see how a negotiation coming out of a sense of mutuality works better than control by one person in the traditional employment situation.

This example does not deal with the problem of being asked to do something that I don't want to do. If I am asked, I can still refuse and my various employers can do one of several things: listen to my reasons and decide if I have what they see as a valid reason to refuse the request; they can ask someone else to do it; we can discuss what I am willing to do and see if we can negotiate an agreement; or they can simply say they are the boss, and if I don't do it I will be fired. If the latter happens I can either decide to do it or I can quit. None of this is particularly unusual, except the last scenario of firing and/or quitting, which is not very likely because of the mutuality. My employers do not want to lose an employee they have trained and whom they value; I don't want to quit a job where I have made such an investment. Both of us have a vested interest in working it out. The presence of the relationship creates a strong foundation on which to work. If there is mutuality, there is not really an issue of control because we are working together.

CONFLICT RESOLUTION AND SUPPORT FOR THE ATTENDANT

Mutuality helps to resolve conflicts. Sometimes, however, we need a little help, and someone for the attendants to talk to is also useful. Judith has a more formal arrangement than most. She has irregular staff meetings to discuss issues that may come up between her and her attendants or among attendants. At these meetings we always have someone from her support circle (the group of friends she uses to support her in getting the services she wants) present to keep things in line and to assist in any negotiation that needs a little refereeing. Either Judith or any of her staff can request a meeting. This mechanism helps deal with any minor conflict before it escalates. It works on the premise that sometimes an outsider can and will help everyone keep things in perspective, which can be difficult when you work so closely with someone. Judith's staff meetings usually quickly turn into a social event. In the last one we had, almost all of the complaints were about Judith's van being uncomfortable; unreliable; and, worst of all at the time, having a broken stereo. The stereo was fixed and she started working on raising funds for a new van. The staff meetings also provide support for the attendants in dealing with issues that arise in their work.

In the case of Luke, the support for me was informal. When I became frustrated about something I would go to the friend who helped me get the job. She would listen and then remind me what my job was about. That was all I seemed to need to keep in line.

RESPONSIBILITY AND RISK

In providing attendant services I sometimes face the problem of being asked to do something or help with something that I see as potentially dangerous to the person I am working with. Risk taking is part of providing services; we all do it, but rarely think about it. There is always a risk of an accident when driving a car, but we see it as an acceptable risk. After all, living is more than just sitting at home and breathing. The same is true of someone with a disability except there are more things that are risky and the level of acceptable risk is higher. This is because a person with a disability is generally more physically fragile than a person without a disability and is more dependent on technology to maintain independence.

For Luke, to participate in the community meant doing things that were potentially risky—using the wheelchair lift in his van for instance. I don't know if he realized it was a potentially lethal device if it failed, but he was probably aware at some level that there was a risk involved. Judith is well aware of the risks of using a lift. Her lift is the same make as Luke's, and she knows how he died, but to her the chance of an accident is worth the risk because otherwise she would just have to stay at home. I know the risks too, and I wish Judith didn't have to use the van. I realize it is not my role to tell Luke or Judith what risks they can take. It is their life and I have no right to refuse to do anything I am asked to do unless I see it as unacceptable to my well-being or I may be liable for the outcome. The most I can do is point out a potential risk if I feel strongly about it. I can do this because it is in the context of a relationship. Also, because of the relationship I would feel comfortable telling them what I think if they want to do something that I would consider really stupid, as I would with any friend.

However, there is one risk that my employer should not have to be exposed to and that I can make sure they avoid while I am working— hazardous attendant service. I touched on it in the story about New Year's Eve when I said I would neither go out knowing I would have to go to work tired nor would I have more than one drink if I would be doing attendant work. I have a responsibility to my employer not to put them at an unnecessary risk. I am responsible for the physical well-being of another human life; if I do something wrong I could, at least, cause inconvenience or pain, and, at worst, cause serious injury. I am not saying that I don't make careless mistakes, but I should not do the job if I feel I am diminished in my ability to do it properly, whether intentionally from not getting enough sleep or unintentionally from illness. If I am going to be a good attendant then I must care for the person I am working for; if I care for the person then I cannot help but be aware of their physical vulnerability and the potential for me to cause injury. This sense of responsibility for the other person is always with me and is one of the stresses in the job; stress is one of the down sides of this work.

STRESS

The feeling of responsibility is only one of the potential stresses in the job. Some of the others may be a constantly shifting schedule, such as I have with Judith; being in uncomfortable situations with no choice as to whether I can leave or not; conflict with my employer; boredom with the work; long drives; and traveling (especially by air). Most of these can be overcome and may not be very different from stresses experienced in other jobs. However, there is a certain amount of base level stress arising from the nature of the work. I think it comes from always being at someone else's beck and call whenever I am on duty, even if I am not actively working. For example, I have found I frequently don't sleep soundly when I do overnights because I am afraid I won't hear my employer if I am called. One thing I am careful to do is that when I am given a break, I really take a break. If I can, I will take my breaks somewhere else, even another room, to give both me and my employer a break.

Another major source of stress, and potential mishaps, is boredom. The job is sometimes very boring. It is sometimes hard to give my full attention to something such as the morning rising routine that I have done hundreds of times, and I am sure that my boss may be just as bored. Usually, talking to each other helps, but sometimes one of us isn't in a talkative mood. As with boredom in any job, I cope with it as best as I can. When I realize it is there, I make an extra effort to pay attention to try and forestall any mistakes.

Stress can also arise from the issue of value, albeit indirectly. When I say value, I don't just mean monetary value although that is also part of it. Value has to do with feeling valued, feeling that what I do is worthwhile. Feeling valued is a bit more complicated than it may at first appear. I believe I am valued by the person to whom I am providing service. Given the existence of the relationship between me and my employer in an individualized funding situation, I am more aware of this than when I am working in an SSLU. Many times all I need to feel good about the situation is for the person I am working for to acknowledge the fact that they value me. Certainly, better pay would help also, but that is set by the amount of funding from government, not the person, so there may be little they can do about that.

BEING VALUED

When I am working in an SSLU I feel less valued by the people I am working for even though I am better paid. I think that arises from not having as clear of an acknowledgment of how they value me. I know that people who treat me like a person as opposed to a machine make me feel better about the job. They usually get better service, too. I am not talking about a big thing. When I say, "treat me like a person," I am just talking about getting a "Hello, how are you?" when I come in, a thank you when I leave, and maybe a little small talk. Also, I want to have the general feeling of being welcome. If I feel welcome in their lives, no matter how briefly, I feel better about what I am doing and I am more open to doing a better job.

However, I also realize that the nature of the SSLU may make this difficult. The set up, rather than the person, may tend to generate the feeling of not being welcome. Tenants may have several people a day coming into their apartment that include new staff being trained or relief staff whom they see infrequently. This constant flow of new people can lead to tenant burnout; they stop interacting with new attendants because they are tired of expending the energy every time management hires new people. This also highlights another major difference between an SSLU and individualized funding—the tenants have no say in who provides their service in an SSLU. As I already said, the first thing that needed to happen between Luke and me was to realize that we liked each other. People in an SSLU can be stuck with having to deal with an attendant they don't even like and there is nothing they can do about it.

ATTENDANT CARE AS A "REAL JOB"

Part of the value issue arises when I leave the world of disability and go into society at large and see how my job is viewed by other people. It is sometimes hard to feel good about a job that is not recognized as a "real" job either by society or by the bureaucrats who determine my level of pay.

I also realize that most people don't know what attendant service is. This is apparent when I am in a social situation and I am asked about my job. Saying, "I am an attendant to a person with a physical disability," usually results in the response, "So you're a nurse." I then have to explain what my job is and that I am not a nurse. There is nothing wrong with nursing, but it is a different job than being an attendant.

I sometimes feel frustrated that the importance, difficulty, and rewards of my very real job are not recognized. I know the issue of the job being "real" has to be discussed because it is a big issue both inside and outside the field of disability.

I am aware that many people take a job as an attendant while they are waiting for their "real" job, the one they are qualified for or the one they want as a career, but that shouldn't make this job any less real. I know I took my first attendant job, which was in an SSLU, because there was not any work in my field of environmental chemistry in the recession of the early 1980s. Fortunately for me, I was not too intent on getting a job in my field and I found the attendant service interesting work, partly because I had never been exposed to people with disabilities before and partly because it was a welcome change from the academic work I had been doing. (I had done more than 4 years of postgraduate research.)

The manner in which I received my first attendant job is illustrative of the issue of the "reality" of the job. I didn't seek work as an attendant because of some noble motive; I happened to bump into an acquaintance of mine at a meeting. I jokingly asked him if he knew of any work I could do, and he told me about his part-time work at an SSLU. He gave me a 5 minute description of the job and the name of the person I should talk to. So the next day I phoned, I had an interview the same afternoon, and I was hired a few days later. I had no training and had never really thought of disability issues at all. It was a job and it sounded okay. My only qualification was that I impressed my prospective employer with the right attitude toward the work—a willingness to do the job.

TRAINING

One of the main issues involved with attendant service is how people learn about the work. Most of the people I know heard of it through other attendants or because they know someone with a disability. I think very few people think of going into attendant service because they are interested in the job and want to train for it specifically. The job doesn't have a label such as nursing, which is a "real" job because you go to school and get a piece of paper that says you are trained. The issues of training and certification are very important if attendant service is going to be perceived as a "real" job.

One difficulty revolves around training. There is a school of thought among some of the more traditional service providers that community colleges in Ontario, Canada, should have a certificate program in attendant service. This has never happened mainly because of the objections of some of the more vocal supporters of independent living and some of the more progressive SSLU's. When I heard that there were moves to offer this course, I was also strongly against it.

The primary reason for my opposition is that the attendant is trained by the person he or she is helping in that person's needs. These people know more about their limits and needs than anyone else. I don't have to know that there are more than 40 neuromuscular disorders classified as muscular dystrophies; however, I do need to know what are the particular needs of the people I am working for. Sure, there are some common things, but knowing what "is likely" to be present with someone labeled as having muscular dystrophy (MD) is not really going to help me deal with any particular person. In fact, Judith and Luke both have MD, but the only thing they had in common was that they both had somewhat swollen, sensitive feet. Also, since Judith had surgery, this is no longer the case.

I also worry about some sort of official training because of the likely medicalization of attendant service. The reason I always make it clear that I am not a nurse is because there is an important distinction between the two jobs; that is, who is in control in the job, rather than the particular tasks performed. In nursing, direction is given by a doctor for procedures to be done to a third party. The doctor assumes the nurse has the appropriate expertise to carry out the orders and the patient submits because they are under the care of the doctor. Any discussion on the treatment itself is between the doctor and the patient. In attendant service, the person who receives the service trains the attendant and expects the attendant to learn the expertise on the job. The person who receives the service decides what they need and directs the attendant. The person who hires an attendant is looking for someone who has the right attitude, not someone who knows about particular procedures.

I think the danger of having medical training is that the attendant may start to think they know more than their employer and, therefore, have a better way. This goes against the main thrust of attendant service; that is, self-directed care by the person receiving the service.

I cannot say strongly enough that the real qualifications for the job are the right attitude, basic people skills, and a willingness to listen. These are things that the person hiring, whether an individual or a manager in an SSLU, can determine just by talking with the person. The prospective attendant will learn very quickly if the work is for them after only a few hours on the job. In the 11 years of hiring attendants with individualized funding, Judith has only fired one person. I believe Luke only fired two— one was the man who ran off with his wife and the other provided good service, but was not punctual (a problem in any job).

RECOGNITION AND BENEFITS

I realize there is a need for some recognition of the profession; therefore, I will make a proposal regarding the issue of certification, a type of apprenticeship system. Briefly, it would work like this: A person is hired by an SSLU or an individual, and if after an appropriate period of probation (3 months is common now), the person is doing the job well in the opinion of whoever is receiving the service, the attendant will be allowed to join an attendant's association. In the event that the attendants move on to working for different people, they will receive pay commensurate with their experience as recorded by their association. I realize that there would be more details to work out, but the main idea would be to make the job properly recognized while allowing the people receiving the service to maintain control over that service.

When I started to work for Luke, his Order In Council, which paid for my services, was administered through the Muscular Dystrophy Association (MDA). I submitted invoices to MDA for the hours I worked and they would send me a check. Basically, they were bookkeepers. The disadvantage of this system was that I was seen, for tax purposes, as an independent business person; therefore, I received my entire pay without any deductions. I had to make sure I saved enough money for my taxes, and I could not receive standard benefits such as unemployment insurance and Workers' Compensation, which would provide me with money if I injured myself at work and had to take time off. Given the nature of the work, I was concerned with the lack of benefits. I knew there was always the chance of injury and I had been on compensation before due to work-related injuries. MDA did not want me as their employee because they did not see me as working for them. They also claimed that there was not enough money to take into account the employer's contribution to the benefits. (Judith's attendants are technically employees of the organization that handles her funds, so this problem does not arise.)

In the end, after a certain amount of discussion and an increase in funding because of the new fiscal year, Luke was set up as the legal employer of his attendants. He opened a special bank account into which MDA deposited the necessary amount of money each month. He would write my paycheck, make all of the source deductions, and send checks to the appropriate government departments for the benefits and taxes.

This was very important for two reasons. First, Luke was given direct control over his support funds, and, second, I was treated as a "real" employee. If I am treated as a "real" employee it helps me feel as though I am doing a "real" job. Providing benefits also indicated that Luke cared about his employees and wanted them to be treated properly. Luke would probably not have pursued this issue if he had not cared. His willingness to go after the benefits was good, even if it had not turned out as well as it did.

POLITICIZATION AROUND DISABILITY

When I started my first attendant job in November 1984, I expected that I would do the job for a while and then move on to something else. Yet, every time I was out looking for a job I kept coming back to attendant service. Something kept drawing me to it.

I knew that once I had done the work it was easy to get another job doing the same thing; however, I also believed that it was a worthwhile job and if I was going to take a job to just get by I might as well do something politically correct. I kept coming back to the work again because of my growing politicization about disability issues. I knew I had no business talking about these issues publicly because the people with the disabilities were more than capable of doing so themselves; I was not going to fall into the trap of paternalism. Attendant service allowed me to show my support for people with disabilities.

Sandra Carpenter, a friend of mine, was responsible for my political awakening around disability issues. She lived at the first SSLU that I worked in and has been active in the independent living movement in Canada for years. When I met her, she was working for the Centre for Independent Living in Toronto. Sandra is the friend who suggested I work for Luke and was my informal support while I did the job. She made me comfortable with advocating attendant issues on my own behalf while I worked for Luke; Sandra, along with Judith, also encouraged me to advocate on Luke's behalf after his accident.

THE STORY ENDS—THE LAST WEEK

I have talked about many of the issues that have come up in my years as an attendant. If what I do sounds rather clear, it isn't. When I talk about relationships I suspect it sounds professional, but the distinction between doing the job and being friends, even just being friendly because we work together, is all very fuzzy. The distinction became even fuzzier after Luke fell off his lift one Wednesday evening.

The accident happened after I had left his place for the day. He had been out with a friend for coffee and the van lift malfunctioned as he was getting out of it behind his apartment building. He was rushed to the hospital with severe head injuries.

I found all this out the next morning when I arrived at work. I knew something was wrong when I walked into the apartment and his electric wheelchair was in the living room; it was usually left next to his bed to recharge the batteries. I assumed the chair was broken. I walked into his bedroom and the bed was still made from the day before. Then his roommate told me what had happened. It really was one of the worst moments of my life. He and Luke's friends had decided not to call me the night before because they felt there was nothing I could have done that night, and at least one person should be reasonably coherent the next day.

I went straight to the hospital and promptly found out they wouldn't tell me anything because I was not family. All I knew was what I could see—Luke was unconscious in the neurosurgical intensive care unit. I called Sandra and the MDA and they each sent someone over to talk to the hospital staff about my role. The nurses, doctors, and other staff then saw me as a resource to find out about Luke's needs and abilities. Also, his friends saw me as a way to find out what was happening; through all of this I was leaning heavily on Sandra and Judith for support.

I don't want to go into more detail because of another aspect of this work—confidentiality. I decided to tell the story about Luke and me because it is my story; he can't tell it any more. However, at this point, Luke's story starts to involve many more people and issues that I am not willing to share indiscriminately in print. The story of Luke and me becomes the story of Luke and many people, with me near the center of it all because I was his attendant. I don't want to risk abusing that position by writing about something I would not have learned if I had not been in that position. So, I decided to just set the scene for the last week of Luke's life.

I was there that week because I was his attendant and I knew he was terrified of being in the hospital. I went beyond my role as his attendant; I became his advocate. I did it because of the relationship we had formed that was so essential to our working together. I wanted to do it because the "working" relationship had grown into a friendship.

When he died, his mother was holding one of his hands, I was holding the other—I was deeply honored that his family welcomed me to stay at that time.

There was some unexpected fallout from my experience with Luke when I was working with Judith more than 2 years later. I realized I had not been willing to let Judith into my life and therefore was not as good an attendant as I could have been. This reluctance arose out of fear. I felt such pain when I lost my friend Luke that I was shutting Judith out of my life. I was afraid that if I got close to her and she died, even though I had no reason to think she would, I would be devastated again. When I realized what I was doing, I allowed Judith into my life. I know that what can grow out of this is probably one of the greatest benefits of the job. Although I still miss my friend Luke, it is better that I miss him than not to have known him at all.

APPENDIX

BACKGROUND INFORMATION
ON ATTENDANT SERVICES IN ONTARIO, CANADA

There are three major forms of administration of attendant services in the province of Ontario, Canada. These include: individualized funding, supportive services living unit (SSLU), and the outreach attendant care program.

Individualized Funding

With individualized funding a person has direct control over his or her attendant service. Funds are provided to a person to hire his or her own attendants and be responsible for scheduling, pay sheets, and all other aspects of being an employer. However, the money does not go directly into that person's bank account; it is usually funneled through a community-based organization that writes the actual paychecks and does the bookkeeping.

A person with a disability can obtain individualized funding for attendant service through several mechanisms, including an Order In Council (OIC). An OIC is a special piece of legislation coming from the Ontario Cabinet; in Spring 1992 only about 15 people had OICs for attendant service in the province. An individualized funding pilot project is planned that may initially involve up to 500 people.

Supportive Services Living Unit (SSLU)

One of the typical ways attendant services are provided is in a Supportive Services Living Unit. An SSLU is where 12–15 accessible apartment units are located in a large building. These units have attendant service provided to them from an office in the building. The tenants who require service book it ahead of time or phone when they need help, which they get if the attendant is not away on another booking. In general, the attendant services are only provided within the building.

In an SSLU, the service is attached to the building not the person. An SSLU limits the choice of housing for a person with a disability. The person has to live in the building where the SSLU is located to get attendant service. If that same person had individualized funding he or she would have greater choice in accommodation because the attendant service could go wherever he or she is. With individualized funding, a person may live wherever he or she wishes, limited only by the level of physical accessibility required for their living space.

Outreach Attendant Care Program

The other typical way of funding is the Outreach Attendant Care Program where attendant service is provided to people on an in-home visitation basis. The attendants are hired by a central agency that is the actual employer and they work with a number of people requiring service. Consumer control can vary in an outreach program depending on how it is set up; however, it has many similarities with SSLU.

11

A DISABLED
WOMAN'S REFLECTIONS

MYTHS AND REALITIES OF INTEGRATION

Judith E. Heumann

DEVELOPING A PERSONAL FOUNDATION

From the time I was disabled with polio at the age of 1 1/2 years until I was 3 years old, I was in and out of the hospital. I recently learned that when I was 2 years old, a doctor told my parents that I should be institutionalized. My parents refused. At the age of 4, the doctors advised my parents to send me to a rehabilitation program where I would only be able to come home on weekends. They again refused, and I was, instead, placed in a 3-month program where I lived at home on the weekends with my parents and my brother. At the age of 5, I was denied the opportunity to go to a public school because of my disability and personal assistance needs. I was forced to be on home instruction with a teacher coming twice a week for 1 hour one day and 1 1/2 hours the other days.

I grew up in a neighborhood in Brooklyn, New York, where the families were very close. Although I was not attending school with the neighborhood children, I was an integrated member of my neighborhood until high school, participating in a Brownie troop run by one of my neighbors, going to Hebrew school, and spending time with my nondisabled friends and family. At an early age, my nondisabled friends had learned to stand me up with braces and helped me walk if I needed

This chapter was supported in part by a grant (No. H133B0006–91) from the National Institute on Disability and Rehabilitation Research, Office of Special Education and Rehabilitative Services, Department of Education, Washington, D.C. 20202, awarded to the World Institute on Disability. However, the contents do not necessarily represent the policy of that agency, and endorsement by the federal government should not be assumed.

to; together, we easily adapted children's games, so I was never excluded from activities. Even though I was not attending a regular school, my days were very full after 3:00 P.M. when the other children came home.

At age 9, when I finally went to school, I was in a separate class in a regular school. The Health Conservation classes for disabled students were located in the basement. This was the first time I was with other disabled children. I was very comfortable; I never felt that I did not belong with them. We did not eat lunch with the "kids upstairs" or go to recess together. A few of the kids from "upstairs," who were considered to be very good kids, would be allowed to come "downstairs" and help us take our coats off and clean the erasers. The nondisabled children would spend more time with those of us who looked more "normal"— with no speech disability or uncontrollable movements. I remember liking the attention I was getting. It was like having a closet door opened and being welcomed for a short time. I remember feeling conscious of this reaction because a lot of my friends had cerebral palsy with speech disabilities. This is when I became aware of a pecking order. The less disabled a person looks and sounds, the more likely the person is to be minimally "accepted."

I attended school with a lot of kids who were labeled as having mental retardation. Children with profound mental retardation were in institutions, other separate schools, or receiving home instruction. I always felt that the teachers didn't believe most of the students could learn. Because they weren't effective and I was bored, I started teaching some of the kids. At the age of 10 years old, I learned that these children were able to learn. In many cases their families were not pushing the teachers to teach. These events had a very profound effect on me. Many of the children I went to school with never went to high school and were not trained for meaningful jobs. When I see these friends today, I am always saddened by the waste of human potential. I believe too much of the same patterns and practices still exist today.

I, like most of my disabled friends, loved summer camp. At camp, there were people with different disabilities, including some people who were blind and some who were deaf. This was the first time I was with people with so many types of disabilities. I started learning sign language secretively. The speech therapist said I wasn't helping my friends; they needed to learn to lip read. Learning sign language was one of the first times I recall defying authority to do something from a disability perspective.

I went to camps from age 9 to age 18, and these were the only times I was integrated with disabled people. We lived together for weeks; we bonded; we were comfortable together. I feel this was the only time in my life when I was really involved in cross disability and with people of different races. The system had always separated disabled people by labels. We learned to fear our own because of this separation. Coming together at an early age allowed me to see what we had in common. One of the side effects of "mainstreaming" has been the diminution of the integration of people with different kinds of disabilities with each other. If I were going to school today, I would probably not be fortunate enough to meet people with many types of disabilities.

As disabled people, we had social experiences together while we were growing up. We frequently felt like we were on the outside, hearing negative things about other disabled people who were our friends. We didn't understand this prejudice until we were older. The number of people with disabilities different from mine diminished throughout the remaining years of my educational experience.

In order for there to be a strong political movement, it is important for people with all types of disabilities to be respectful of each others' needs. We must be able to share meaningful time together to fester this respect. We really need to look more at that limited moment in time when disabled people are together, not separated from each other. I know other disabled friends, particularly people who had disabilities early on, who also had these experiences. It wasn't just isolated to New York City or to Massachusetts; it occurred all over the country. A string of people exists who went through those programs and who want and are committed to creating a movement that includes people with different disabilities. Many of these people have been involved in cross disability work, and setting up independent living centers and coalitions. Those of us who attended these "special" education programs never saw people as being so different. Lack of exposure causes discrimination. Disabled people's desire to be accepted by nondisabled people has also been a cause of internal discrimination. I believe we must first accept ourselves, and then if nondisabled people don't accept us, so be it.

DEVELOPING RELATIONSHIPS
AND SHARING EXPERIENCES OF DISCRIMINATION

It is difficult when disabled and nondisabled people try to learn how to develop more effective relationships with each other. Nondisabled people have to be able to feel comfortable asking questions such as, "Do you need help?" or "Can I interrupt you?" or "I didn't understand, could you say it again?" Nondisabled people ask these questions of each other. Why are they afraid to ask disabled people? Similar to nondisabled people, disabled individuals will react differently to these questions. For example, I have several friends who have cerebral palsy with speech disabilities. People will ask other people a variety of questions: "Is it alright to say I don't understand them? Can I ask them to repeat what they have said? How often can I ask the person to repeat what he or she said? How does it make the person feel?" Frequently, my friends can be understood when a person listens. On a number of occasions my friends have been asked to give public presentations, but they have also been asked to write the speech so someone else could read it. My friends have been very insulted and become understandably angry because they believe people could understand if they listened. In every instance, my friends have made verbal presentations. These experiences have been both frightening and empowering.

Disabled people usually understand and accept that there are things that we can and cannot do. If I ask a nondisabled person to help me with something, it becomes a bigger issue and a more awkward experience than it does between most disabled people. For me, it feels completely natural to be with other disabled people and to say, "Do you need help?" or "Do you want me to feed you or help you get your jacket off?" In some cases, I'll do whatever seems obvious because I have a close relationship with the person and providing the assistance just feels natural.

I believe it is important for us to learn how to overcome prejudice. I have had two experiences of seeing models to facilitate change that were helpful for me. The first one occurred in 1973 when I was 25 years old and attended an International Red Cross youth camp program for 2 weeks in Norway. The purpose of this experience was to provide disabled and nondisabled young adults with an opportunity to live together in order to share information on how they feel about each other, and what barriers exist, and how they can be overcome. We worked and played together. One of the most exciting parts of this exchange was to learn that disabled people from different continents were experiencing similar problems. It was also wonderful to be in an environment where openness about our feelings was encouraged. We were not told to whitewash our feelings, and we didn't. Friendships still exist from this activity.

I also spent a weekend at Howard University in the late 1960s when they selected a group of people to learn and work together on issues of race discrimination. I was the only disabled person in this group. We read and discussed books written by African-American writers, we drove around the community, and people talked with us about the issues of the riots that had just occurred. For me, it was a very powerful experience because we spent enough time together to begin to think and talk about issues in a different way. To me, this was the same type of experience as the one in Oslo. We built up a level of trust so that people were willing to say things that they might have felt before, but had been off limits to share or discuss. We need to start creating more of these experiences, to bring together thoughtful, creative people who have the potential and the capability to think differently about issues and learn from each other.

MAKING CONNECTIONS

I worked at the Center for Independent Living (CIL) in Berkeley, California from 1975 to 1982. During this time, the organization began to hire people with different types of disabilities. The first time I worked with people with cognitive disabilities at CIL was when two lesbian women, who lived in another county, showed up at our doors at five o'clock. CIL is an office; it did not have a residential program. The people at CIL didn't know what to do because the women said they wanted to stay. The most important concern for me was to determine if they were minors. We decided that because they knew how to locate us, they could be considered competent. A number of the lesbian, disabled women on staff wanted to help them achieve their goal. They wanted an apartment together and to find work other than a sheltered workshop. They needed some personal assistance services to help with time and money management, shopping, and cooking. The county didn't want to provide the assistance because they said it was only for people with physical disabilities. We successfully argued that the women needed this personal assistance and they were eventually given the hours they needed.

I like to talk about this story. We were willing to be very flexible in helping this couple get what they wanted. What we tried to do was have one or two people who would work with them, listen to what they wanted, and do what they wanted to do.

Around this same time at CIL, we had spent many years trying to crack into the developmental disability (DD) system. We knew there was distrust from the professionals and some parents. We thought we would try to develop a working relationship, attend their meetings, and serve on committees. Those of us most committed to this had been in "special" education programs or attended camps with developmentally disabled people. CIL staff would come back and say they didn't want to go to any more meetings because they felt that the DD professionals didn't like them. We couldn't jump over enough hoops. We found we couldn't get through the paperwork and other barriers to integrate developmentally disabled people. One day we heard there was money available that had to be applied for immediately, so we submitted eight grant proposals to do eight projects to integrate developmentally disabled people into our existing services. We didn't even get one project funded after all the meetings. It was a totally demoralizing experience. It was clear that our message, which was that people should have greater choice, was too frightening.

I have similar experiences today in connecting with developmentally disabled people, in trying to get past the barriers the DD system has created. For example, recently I saw some people from a DD program being walked down the block in a group by a staff person. I remember feeling like a wall existed between us even though I always talk with disabled people on the street. The system has created these barriers that separate people from each other.

Today, there is still not enough interaction between the different disability communities. In the DD community, the interaction is still too frequently with providers and family members instead of with developmentally disabled people. The World Institute on Disability received a grant to hold a series of Quality of Life seminars with people with cognitive disabilities. It was a shock to the professionals, I am sure, when we said all the participants and speakers had to be disabled. These seminars confirmed to us that there are really no differences between the hopes and desires of disabled people. Yet, there is still a strong DD system out there that controls the DD population. Today, meeting people with cognitive disabilities, actually being together, is more of a problem than wanting to be together. However, we are continuing to create avenues for meaningful interaction.

CASH SUBSIDIES AND ENTITLEMENTS

As disabled people, we need to develop a system that is more user friendly. We need entitlement programs similar to the ones already in place for disabled veterans. If a person becomes disabled in the military, he or she is provided with a cash benefit on a monthly basis to compensate for the changes that have occurred emotionally and physically as a result of the disability. Those cash subsidies are not means-tested and vary depending on the degree of a person's disability; therefore, the system acknowledges that a disabled person has additional costs. We could look at the Supplemental Security Income (SSI) monthly check becoming the basic monthly grant. A personal assistance allowance and a technology aid allowance, if needed, would go above the basic grant.

I firmly believe that the vast majority of people who should receive cash subsidies would use it responsibly because it is their money. While some abuse always goes on in any system, such limited abuse certainly does not outweigh what I see as the real abuse—the incredible amount of money the system pays to watch over people so that they will not cheat. In the end, people are living in incredible poverty, unable to work because of the real fear of losing their monthly, means-tested check.

An entitlement program could free a lot of the workers from doing ongoing evaluations, determinations, and redeterminations. We could stop spending so much money on making people ineligible who clearly should be receiving services. Some disabled individuals who want to and are capable of working would no longer face the loss of minimal financial support—the SSI check. An entitlement would also allow dis-abled individuals not to think of themselves as people on welfare. Dis-abled people would learn how to incorporate the check into their lives and utilize the money to help cover their needs.

GETTING WHAT YOU WANT AND NEED

I don't like the concept of case management because I don't believe that anyone should be managed. I don't need a manager, but I would like to be able to call someone whom I believe has a broad range of exper-tise. I could talk with the person about what I need, have him or her help me find what is out there, share ideas about what I should be looking for, and help me gain access to programs. If wanted or needed that person could also help to make appointments and make sure things were being done. What is sorely missing in the system is a way to find out what's out there, especially new developments. The system is also failing in providing effective advocacy to ensure people get what they are entitled to.

If a person is not at all capable of managing his or her affairs, then the person needs somebody who can work with him or her to determine what his or her needs are and how to meet these needs most effectively. This system should be available whether or not there's a voucher system or a cash system. A more uniform system that looks at the whole person and their needs when doing evaluations would allow a lot more money to go into the hands of people for the things they really need.

Disabled people, like nondisabled people, don't necessarily know what services or supports they need. For example, I wasn't sure if I was uncomfortable sitting in my wheelchair because I had been sitting this way my whole life. I had nothing to compare it to. When a friend who rides a wheelchair received a new seating system that she said worked well and helped alleviate some pain, I began to look at seating options more seriously. I finally got the department of rehabilitation to agree that it would pay for me to look at these expensive seating systems. I went to the first place, and the workers asked me how I would like to feel when the seating system was finished. I said I didn't have any idea because I only knew the one system I had sat on for more than 30 years. While nondisabled people sit on lots of different chairs, I don't, and the ones I have sat on typically have been uncomfortable. Now that I've been working on seating for 2 years, I know I can feel differently and I have learned to raise my expectations of sitting in a more pain-free and comfortable way. That's an example of not knowing what I need and not knowing about new technology.

People need money to cover ongoing expenses. For example, every 6 months I need to go back to the place where I purchased my seating system to get something else done—I'm sitting a little bit differently, the material in the cushion has worn out, or there are new materials that have developed that would be better. The agency that paid for the original seating system did not understand that these changes are reasonable and need to occur. Services need to be ongoing. New types of equipment frequently prevent future medical problems from occurring. We need to recognize that people should have a right to continue to change their lives and needs. People, in general, are continuing to modify their lives, but disabled individuals frequently are not given the opportunity to do so.

PERSONAL ASSISTANCE

As a person with a more significant disability, I've needed the assistance of others for my entire life to help me perform tasks that nondisabled individuals take for granted. I need assistance with such things as bathing, dressing, toileting, cooking, shopping, and driving. Through the years, my need for personal assistance has grown because my expectations of how I want to function in the world also have grown.

A personal assistant is an extension of my body, and, at my direction, helps me do those things that I am not capable of doing independently. I believe personal assistance services apply to all people, regardless of the type of disability that they have, although some individuals may need assistance with different tasks such as money or time management. These tasks should be considered of no greater or lesser importance than assisting someone with toileting or feeding.

Disabled people view personal assistance as a civil right. An individual with a more significant disability cannot participate as an equal member of society without personal assistance services. There are numerous federal and state laws that prohibit employers from discriminating against qualified disabled people. If the disabled individual cannot get out of bed, dressed, or out of the house because they need personal assistance services, then they can never get to the point of applying for the job. *A disability should not handicap a person.*

One of the challenges of personal assistance services is to encourage disabled people to think about how these services can improve their lives. This is difficult because so few programs exist that enable people to purchase personal assistance services. At the World Institute on Disability, we estimate that there are 10 million individuals who need personal assistance services, but only 20% of them are getting some degree of service, and at least half of the 20% are still having to rely on voluntary services to meet part of their needs. I believe this is one of the next areas we, as disabled individuals and allies, should work on politically.

Paid and Unpaid Assistance

When we, as disabled individuals, believe that we have a right to demand the degree of personal assistance services that we need in order to function in society, we will have overcome a major hurdle in emancipation. Today, people, particularly those with more significant disabilities, are dependent on the good will and charity of individuals to function within society because we do not have the money we need to hire personal attendants. We continually have to fit our needs into the schedules of other people, or, too often, abandon the thought of having our needs met. These needs are not "Cadillac" needs, but needs that nondisabled people typically take for granted.

I use paid and unpaid workers because I don't have enough money to have paid workers when I need them, which is not the most comfortable situation. I don't always want to ask a friend or someone I do not know to help me go the bathroom because it's a very personal task. It's not complicated; I don't need a trained assistant to help me go to the bathroom, but I do need somebody who is willing to assist me and who doesn't feel I am taking them away from something that they would prefer to be doing. Regardless of the nature of the individual's disability, the tasks have to be provided in a manner with which we, as disabled individuals, feel comfortable. I and many other disabled individuals in and outside the United States have come to the conclusion that we want our first option to be having paid workers. Then we can choose if we want to have a friend, a family member, or a stranger volunteer their services. Now, typically, our only option is to choose the unpaid worker, friend, or family member—we see this as a barrier to achieving equality.

Over the next few years, we need to talk about how we would envision our lives if we had adequate personal assistance services. When would we get up in the morning? When would we go to bed? Would we take a nap during the day? How often would we eat? What food would we eat? How often would we visit friends? How often would we go to synagogue? Right now, things have to be so contrived, so measured.

I find it deeply upsetting when nondisabled people talk about disabled individuals as being manipulative when we ask for assistance. If we really want to do something, we have to be able to get other people to assist us. When we don't have the money to pay for assistance, we are forced to think of creative ways to get what we need. We do not consider this manipulation. We consider this to be a sign of intelligence and strong survival skills. The fact that nondisabled individuals will so often use the term *manipulation* is another example of why unpaid assistance is not typically the best way for people to get their assistance. This type of behavior is abusive to the disabled individual.

Family Members and Service Payments

It's very important that we do away with this philosophy that family members should not be paid for the work they are providing. If the disabled individual would like a family member to provide the service, and if the family member wishes to provide that service, then the family member should not be prohibited from receiving payment for that service.

There are a number of reasons why payment is not provided. We live in a sexist society where the work women do in the home is not valued, and most of the family members who are providing unpaid services are women. The government recognizes that the vast majority of people who have personal assistance needs, disabled people of all ages, are already receiving a substantial number of their basic personal assistance services from the family. The government does not want to provide money for the services that are currently being provided for free. Finally, many family members believe that it is wrong to ask for payment for the services they are providing because they believe it is the obligation of the family to provide such services. I don't completely disagree with that belief, but there is a normal range for the individuals involved, a certain amount that people do for each other. It may be 3 hours of phone time or 3 hours of some other kind of help. However, once it gets to 4 or 5 hours, then it is no longer within that normal range. It begins to put a burden on the disabled individual and the family member or friend who is providing the unsubsidized service.

My experience and the experience of many other disabled individuals is that we prefer to be able to pay for our services or to have our services paid for so that there is an employer–employee relationship with the personal assistant. Voluntary services provided by a family member or nonfamily member typically result in the disabled individual not being able to choose the hours of the service, the kinds of services they wish to be provided, or the manner in which the services should be provided.

As disabled individuals, we need to be speaking out more clearly about why we want paid workers, and the conflicts that result for us, our family members, and our friends when we are forced to use unpaid workers. Family members also need to discuss the adverse effects of providing ongoing personal assistance services on their lives and the life of the disabled individual. One should not have to feel guilty about not wanting to provide personal assistance services. There is a healthy separation that usually occurs between family members as they establish their autonomy. Disabled individuals are frequently not allowed to experience this separation because of forced dependency.

It is common for unpaid family members, often called caregivers, to complain about providing services; however, these discussions too frequently put the blame on the disabled person or victimize the disabled person. Instead of paying social workers to convene the "caregivers" to discuss the hardships of their lives, it would be better to allow the disabled person to have a paid personal assistant who would probably not be a family member. The understandable frustration and anger that the "caregivers" feel toward the disabled individual for "tying them down" should be redirected to the government to advocate for payment for services.

Personal Assistance for People of All Ages

Personal assistance services need to be available to people of all ages, including children. A friend, whom I have known for 13 years, has a daughter who has a significant disability, uses an electric wheelchair, and needs the same type of physical assistance that I do. She also needs assistance in money management, time management, and how to make decisions. When her daughter was young, I encouraged my friend to work on getting one of the local agencies to give her money to hire a personal assistant. I thought that a personal assistant would help her daughter learn how to begin making independent decisions and how to help her do things that she couldn't do herself. The family was successful in obtaining some funding and was then able to function more as a family, even though they have not received an adequate number of personal assistance services hours. I believe that my friend's daughter should have been able to receive 24 hours a day of personal assistance services if the family had chosen to do so. At that age, children are functioning independently from a physical perspective and the role of the family, the adults, is not to help the person get dressed, toilet, and perform personal tasks. However, there are very few programs that provide 24-hour assistance. The family hired and trained a personal assistant, which is not an easy task. With the personal assistance hours that the family received, they were then able to devote their time and energy to being a family.

Personal assistance is a service that is being provided for my friend's daughter, and should not be viewed as respite services for the family. Personal assistance service is enabling the daughter to grow up and function in society as a more respected and independent person. If the service is seen as allowing the family to have a break from the daughter, then the daughter is being victimized, being seen negatively.

A disabled individual needs personal assistance services to move about in the community just as they would if they didn't have a disability. Viewed this way, part of the negativity of disability is removed. It's a fact that we need to accept personal assistance as a critical service that disabled individuals need in order to function freely. Failure to have adequate personal assistance services handicaps individuals.

In Sweden, there is a cooperative personal assistance program called the Stockholm Independent Living Group (STIL). A number of years ago, the cooperative was approached by a mother who has a son with Down syndrome; she wanted him to become a member of the cooperative and to benefit from the way the cooperative was providing personal assistance services. The cooperative agreed to accept her and her son into the model, which allows the individuals in the coop to hire and train their own workers. The mother has been helping her son hire workers, and she has been working as the manager. They find the situation more agreeable than having to go through a local home health care agency, and the son is able to function with adequate assistance. He's taking karate classes and participating in many other types of programs. He is much more integrated into the community because of the paid assistance he was able to get, and he feels much more comfortable with the workers he has.

Personal Assistants

We have to be very concerned about programs that require workers to be trained. When training programs exist, the individuals who need the service and their advocates must be significantly involved in the training. Prepackaged training programs are like mass marketing. I believe that there are many problems that result for the disabled individual. Workers tend not to see the people they are working with as individuals capable of exercising decisions. Trained workers tend to believe they know what is best for the disabled person. Also, because these trainings are not designed to meet the needs of an individual, people with cognitive disabilities do not get workers who have learned how to help the individual with particular needs.

When we reach the day when disabled individuals are able to receive adequate funding for the hiring of personal assistants, we will have achieved another significant landmark. In achieving the landmark, we are arguing that workers need to be paid adequate wages with benefits because the individuals performing the services need to value themselves and the work they are performing. If people are inadequately paid and receive inadequate benefits, then they don't value themselves and the work they are doing. Therefore, a personal assistance coalition needs to be developed where we are working with personal assistants to fight for adequate wages and benefits.

On Personal Assistance and Employment

I was talking with a woman who graduated from a training program and is now an employee of a large company. The company never listed personal assistance services as something that they would provide. This person would ask for personal assistance services from a friend on the job. The nondisabled person thought that it went too far and cut into her work and her relationship with this individual. This a common story and I could feel a knot in the pit of my stomach as she related this issue to me because I have also been in situations like that. It would be desirable for companies to recognize this as a reasonable accommodation. Some companies tell their disabled employees to discuss their reasonable accommodations needs and then the company will work with the person to find the best way for them to be provided.

INTEGRATION

One common assumption made by people without disabilities is that the most important thing for disabled people is to spend time with nondisabled people. Some of the most important times in my life were, and continue to be, those spent with other disabled people. I should have a right to choose the people I am comfortable with, who have similar interests, and who understand and share the experiences I encounter as a disabled person. Forced integration doesn't work. I am frequently compelled by articles written by other minority groups who are strong supporters of integration, discussing how integration still has not occurred and how they, too, feel the need to be with their own people, women with women, African Americans with African Americans, and so forth.

Integration is not simply having disabled people in the physical presence of nondisabled individuals. In the disability rights movement, one goal of disabled people is to become integrated members of our communities. Integration must be on terms where we will feel comfortable and equal. Frequently, when we talk among ourselves about integrating with nondisabled people, we often feel like tokens, as if nondisabled people are very uncomfortable being with us. So we may not choose to continually put ourselves into social situations where there is a pretext of integration. For myself, as a wheelchair rider, how can I be integrated when I am not usually able to socialize with my peers because their homes are not accessible? When a nondisabled person says that making their home accessible is an inconvenience, it makes me feel like my friendship is not valued by that individual.

In Berkeley and Oakland, California, there are many disabled people. We have a great opportunity to choose how we live our lives and with whom we spend our time. I don't want my socializing experiences to always feel as if I am working—educating people about what it is like to be disabled. So, while the goal is for all people to be integrated with all people, nondisabled people need to be more thoughtful and involved with talking with disabled people about how we view integration.

A few years ago I was at a meeting with Pat Worth from People First in Canada, and he was talking about when he left the institution and was living in his own apartment. He thought that nondisabled people believed this was a perfect model; yet, he was quite emotional about no longer having easy access to his friends. I was struck by his comments because it seemed to me that he had not had as many choices in choosing his friends as I have had. He was experiencing a great deal of pain because he was in a situation of not being accepted by nondisabled people as much as he would like, as well as not having access to the people who accepted him.

I am very concerned about the continued discussion of the percentages of disabled people and the appropriate statistical balance of disabled and nondisabled people as opposed to a balance based on interests, social aspirations, and professional aspirations. This is not an easy issue to address; although I'm not a separatist, I am also not an integrationists at all costs. At the end of the day, I feel that as disabled people we must feel good about ourselves and be able to choose our friends, and if we choose to spend most of our time outside of work with disabled people, that should not be considered "an inappropriate model." We must have the ability and the opportunity to choose from a broad group the people with whom we truly feel most comfortable, which can change over time, the same way that nondisabled people choose their friends. We need to pay more attention to the emotional scars people are left with when trying to integrate with nondisabled people.

CHANGE AND THE ROLE OF DISABLED
PEOPLE, FAMILY MEMBERS, AND FRIENDS

Change in any society takes time. The past 20 years have seen major advances in legislation for disabled people. I and thousands of disabled people and friends all across the country have fought hard and won unthought of victories with the passage of such legislation as The Americans with Disabilities Act (1990), the Education for All Handicapped Children's Act (now known as the Individuals with Disabilities Education Act) (1975), Section 504 of the Rehabilitation Act (1973), legislation providing for seed funding of independent living centers throughout the country, and other legislation.

These extremely important pieces of legislation are producing changes. Today, if I was 5 years old and my mother took me to my local school, they would not be allowed to dismiss me as a fire hazard, send me home with 2 hours of teacher's visits a week and call it an "education." Today, we have curb cuts on streets throughout the country; buses are becoming accessible; buildings are being constructed with ramps; elevators, wide doorways, accessible bathrooms, and closed captioned television are becoming a reality. These meaningful structural changes are taking care of a very visible and essential piece of our fight for equal participation and access.

Many changes, however, such as entitlement for personal assistance services, still hold a challenge for the future and may change in my lifetime. If disabled people, family members, and friends agree on entitlement across ages, we could more effectively pose arguments. The clearer we can be in explaining why cash subsidies need to be provided on an ongoing basis and why it is not cost effective for these cash subsidies to be given the way they're being given, the more hopeful we can be about change. One of the reasons such changes are not happening is because we are not fighting for them.

The issue of change happening is similar to the issue of daycare for women and children. Many events are occurring within society that are going to make some of these things have to happen, in part because family structures are changing.

THE DEVALUATION OF DISABLED PEOPLE

Last year the census bureau released statistics on the number of disabled people who are employed. Fewer disabled people are working now than in the early 1980s when the unemployment rate for disabled people was at 70%. Forty percent of disabled children are dropping out before graduating from high school, and the number of disabled students attending colleges and universities is decreasing.

Despite legislation, I believe we are not seeing changes in the life quality of disabled people because society as a whole has not made the commitment necessary to truly provide equal opportunities. This lack of commitment, I believe, stems from an unwillingness to acknowledge that disabled people are still perceived as inferior.

One young girl with mild mental retardation had been successfully integrated into kindergarten at a private school. Her parents wanted her to attend an arts magnet public school, in an integrated setting, for which she would need a part-time aide. The school district insisted that she be placed in a special education class. After 12 days of Fair Hearing (a formal appeal process) with three corporate lawyers, the school district lost, although they are currently appealing to the federal district court. The school district is spending hundreds of thousands of dollars to prevent a family from keeping their child in an integrated program.

Such actions have a negative effect on the disabled child's nondisabled peers. The school district's lack of flexibility is, unfortunately, a typical approach to dealing with the integration of disabled people.

Some readers may think that perhaps the school district is right. After all, they've had more experience dealing with "these kinds of children" than her parents have. Wouldn't she benefit from special teachers, experts in helping children like her? The reality is that separate but equal cannot be tolerated in any area, particularly in education. The failure to integrate disabled and nondisabled children at an early age will continue to result in nondisabled adults who fear difference and lack understanding, and disabled adults who fear integration and lack self-esteem.

Another example is the recent change in the way people view suicide for disabled people. A growing number of people with severe physical disabilities have gone before the courts petitioning for assistance in committing suicide, and their supposed wish has been granted. Does society feel no moral obligation to hear the pleas of these people for what they are—cries to live a life a dignity? The records show that these people were asking for services that would enable them to live in the community, not in an institution, hospital, or nursing home. As the government has not provided these services, people fearful of living out their lives in these "hell holes" go to the court for *help*. And what do they get? They get judges who are unable to understand how a person with a severe disability could live a dignified and productive life.

The question to be asked is: If a poor, nondisabled woman of color came to the court and said, "I have been living in poverty my whole life, I see no way out, so please allow me to die with dignity by assisting me in committing suicide," what would the court do? What would society say if these types of requests were granted? Wouldn't we cry out and call this genocide? That's what many of us believe is happening to disabled people today.

THE FEARS OF NONDISABLED PEOPLE

The causes of discrimination against disabled people have some unique twists. Nondisabled people fear disability. They do not want to face the possibility (probability) that at some point they, too, may become disabled. One might hate women, African-Americans, Asians, Latinos, Jews, Catholics, or gays, but there is no fear of waking up some morning and being one of them.

I have had disabled friends tell me some of the thoughts they had about disability when they were nondisabled. For example: I would rather be dead than be in a wheelchair; What a shame that such a beautiful person is disabled; I don't know how I could live my life like that; What a burden that person must be on their family and friends. Imagine how you would feel if someone walked up to you and said, as they did to my friend, "What's a pretty girl like you doing in a wheelchair?" Of course the obvious retort, "What's a good looking boy like you doing walking?" Or the story of a coworker who uses a wheelchair who was approached in high school by a nondisabled student who said, "If I'm ever like you, I hope they shoot me."

The pernicious fear that grips many nondisabled people makes those of us with disabilities feel angry, ashamed, humiliated, unwanted, and, in extreme cases, fearful for our very lives. One way of considering some of these issues is to ask yourself what disability you are most afraid of. Then try to see yourself with that disability. What happens to you? Do you lose control? Do you see your life dramatically changing for the worse? Why? What do you worry about? Do you worry about how your friends will react? About how you will react? What is *your* fear and how do you respond?

THE FUTURE

We all dream of a day when society will have rid itself of the prejudices that have caused millions of people to suffer unnecessarily. We dream of a day when all people can receive a quality education; there are quality jobs for all those who want to work; there are no more homeless people on the streets; health care is provided for all; war is something we read about in the history books as a phenomenon of the barbaric past; preventable deadly diseases such as measles, whooping cough, cholera, AIDS, syphilis, and various sexually transmitted diseases are seen as public health problems of the past; and the deaths of millions of innocent people from famine ceases.

These dreams may seem to be those of a 60s child, out of touch with the reality of a world that has become ever more callous and numb to the crises that surround us. However, I believe that, together, we can meet the challenge of making these dreams our reality.

BIBLIOGRAPHY

Heumann, J. (1990, August). *How women with disabilities can advance into the mainstream of society.* Paper presented at the U.N. Seminar on Disabled Women, Vienna, Austria.

Heumann, J. (1991, May). *The Americans with Disabilities Act: A civil rights victory—A national challenge.* Paper presented to the Employment Law Center, San Francisco, CA.

Individuals with Disabilities Education Act, PL 101–476 (1990).

Rehabilitation Act, Title V, Section 504, PL 93–112 (1973).

III

CASE STUDIES
OF ORGANIZATIONS

12

MADISON MUTUAL HOUSING ASSOCIATION AND COOPERATIVE

"PEOPLE AND HOUSING BUILDING COMMUNITIES"

Julie Ann Racino

The Madison Mutual Housing Association (MHA) and the MHA Cooperative, known for their excellence in the field of housing, have a growing reputation for their inclusive efforts to provide housing to a broad constituency in Madison, Wisconsin, including people of differing abilities (term used by the staff at MHA that includes people with disabilities), ages, income levels, and ethnic backgrounds. They represent the first community, nondisability organizations in the Center on Hu-

This qualitative research site visit took place June 27–29, 1990, and consisted of semi-structured formal and informal interviews, visits to people's homes and cooperative sites, and a review of written materials.

I would like to extend a particular note of appreciation to Judy Olson of the Madison Mutual Housing Association and Cooperative who arranged the visit and opened my eyes to the ties among community, housing, basic human values, and disability issues. Thank you also to the people associated with these organizations, both directly and indirectly, who shared their time, their homes, and their insights. These include Alderperson David Wallner, Randy Wilkins, Darwin Ness, Sandy Dooley, Hollis Gaffney, Judy Wilcox, David Sheperd, Toni Wilson, Lisa Dushack, Anna Paul, and Michael O'Connor. Susan Hobart, on leave at the time of the visit, shared her office for some of the interviews and was present in many of the conversations. Thank you also to Mimi Doyle and Marge Van Calligan of Independent Living, Gail Jacob and Kim Turner of Options in Community Living, and Tracy Miller of Access to Independence. Thank you to Steve Taylor, Bonnie Shoultz, Susan O'Connor, Zana Marie Lutfiyya, Pam Walker, Rachael Smith, and Margaret Hart for their commentary on draft versions of this document, and Rachael Zubal for her continued care of the case studies for this book.

man Policy's national study of organizations supporting people with disabilities.

The Madison Mutual Housing Association and the MHA Cooperative are legally two sister corporations, although in many ways they function as one. As a mutual housing association, the MHA's primary interests are in developing and preserving affordable housing over the long term and in building a body of housing expertise. The Madison Mutual Housing Cooperative manages the housing that is owned by the MHA. The organizations are affiliated through a management agreement; all staff are employees of MHA and members are residents of the MHA housing. The housing is cooperative in nature, controlled by the people who live there, and intended to benefit its members. These two organizations and their relationship with each other are briefly described in this chapter; more detailed information can be obtained from the materials cited in the bibliography at the end of this chapter.

This chapter introduces aspects of housing cooperatives, including how they are organized, the reasons people choose to live in them, and the roles and people—staff, residents, neighbors, investors, and members—associated with the Madison Mutual Housing Association and Cooperative. It specifically examines two cooperative sites designed to integrate people of all abilities, and another cooperative site that includes a group home for older adults.

Everything that the MHA and MHA Cooperative do and stand for is applicable to the lives of people with disabilities because the nature of cooperation and the meaning of living together are central concerns of this categorized group. This chapter examines eight lessons for the disability field that seem particularly relevant as the use of conventional housing options is increasing in this country. While drawing parallels and links with the disability field, this discussion tries to touch on these lessons without changing the basic nature of the organizations by converting their framework from a universal one to the disability-centered focus that dominates the disability field.

The final part of this chapter examines two issues in the future of the Madison Mutual Housing Association and Cooperative, and concludes with a note of hope for their vision of good housing, neighborhoods, and communities; individual and community empowerment; and an inclusive society.

MADISON MUTUAL HOUSING
ASSOCIATION: A COMMUNITY ORGANIZATION

The initial vision of the people who founded the organization was pretty strictly . . . affordable, resident-controlled housing. As time went by, people began to realize how many different groups were touched by this issue. And it became apparent to all of us, it was . . . a complex mission that . . . affected the community-at-large.

Another important part of our mission is revitalizing neighborhoods . . . both in a social and a physical sense. There's a . . . domino effect when you start to improve the physical appearance of property. By doing so, you're more likely to attract residents (who) stay for a long time, invest their time and energy, feel like they have a stake in the community, and . . . try and improve things.

So began my introduction to the Madison Mutual Housing Association, described in their brochure as a unique housing provider that "blends a strong Midwestern spirit of cooperation with the successful model of mutual housing associations that continue to flourish in Europe." Incorporated in 1983 as a nonprofit, tax-exempt organization, the MHA is a membership organization, a licensed real estate corporation, and a property owner that continues to buy, build, renovate, and develop housing cooperatives in Madison, Wisconsin.

In the United States, mutual housing associations take on different organizational structures, but, in general, a mutual housing association is an organization interested in developing and preserving affordable housing stock over the long term. It builds a body of expertise in mutual housing or cooperative development and may provide a range of management services to residents (O'Connor & Racino, 1990).

Born out of discussions at a local bed and breakfast, the Madison MHA has grown into a respected small housing provider with 206 scattered site units in which more than 400 individuals reside. One of the goals of the association is to develop "mainstream"[1] communities, which represent as diverse a group of people as possible—people of different generations, mixed incomes, varying household compositions, racial and ethnic backgrounds, and ability levels. As Judy Olson, the training coordinator, described it:

There are older adults and families with kids living side by side, which is something that has not always been successful, but has been successful with us, single individuals and couples without kids, all types of household compositions and ages. We have made an effort to include (people with) a variety of incomes living side by side. . . We have attempted to bring as racially diverse a group of people into our housing as possible. And long before fair housing laws required this kind of approach, we were doing it.

The housing cooperatives are also inclusive of people with disabilities, with about 10% of the residents being adults with disabilities of varying kinds (as of July 1990).

As a membership organization, the MHA consists of members of the community interested in decent, safe, and affordable cooperative

---

[1]Defined here as representative of the societal population at large.

housing. Through the structure of the mutual housing association, co-operatives are linked to share resources and to have easier access to financial resources. The MHA also helps foster a broader vision of community and neighborhood than individual cooperatives have, including retaining the housing as permanent and affordable.

MADISON MUTUAL HOUSING COOPERATIVE: COOPERATIVE HOUSING

The Madison Mutual Housing Cooperative, organized under Wisconsin Statute 185, is a resident-controlled corporation that manages the housing owned by the MHA. Unlike the MHA, it is not tax exempt and it is comprised and controlled solely by the residents. The Cooperative, whose members also belong to the MHA, has a voice in the development of new housing stock while continuing to focus primarily on housing management. Figure 1 is a visual depiction of the relationship between the MHA and the Cooperative.

All cooperatives are controlled by their members, and are intended to work for their benefit (see O'Connor & Racino, chap. 6, this volume, for a description of housing cooperatives). They are based on the belief that "what we can't do alone, we can do together." According to the Madison Mutual Housing Cooperative's resident handbook and brochures, "housing cooperatives can take many forms—apartments, single family homes, mobile homes, and group homes, to name a few." The features distinguishing a housing cooperative (Furman, 1987) include:

The building and/or land under the building is owned by an organization, not individual members.
The members of the co-op organization are all voting members and own a piece of the co-op.
The board is elected by and from the members and sets co-op policies.
The organization abides by the Cooperative Principles, which are democratic control by membership, open and voluntary membership, limited return on capital investment, continued education, and co-operation among cooperatives.

In a housing cooperative, people do not own their apartment or unit. Each resident owns a membership in the cooperative organization, which then allows them to live in a certain unit. Thus, residents cannot sell their unit or apartment to another person. To obtain affordable cooperative housing, members are expected to work for the co-op.

People choose to live in housing cooperatives for a variety of reasons, including decent, affordable housing; security and stability; a sense of community; ownership; appreciation of diversity as a strength; good neighborhoods; and commitment to the concept of living based on

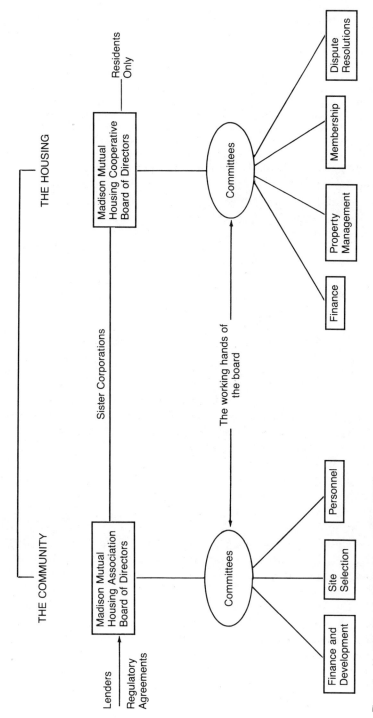

Figure 1. Madison Model. Adapted from Furman (1987).

sharing, cooperation, and participation. David Wallner, an alderperson and housing advocate, described his view of cooperatives and the role they play in Madison, Wisconsin:

> Co-op housing is a very positive model. . . the big issue is empowering people more in their daily lives than standard rental housing provides. It makes people feel more a part of the smaller community and also the larger community. That's real important. People stay there longer, too. . . If you want to create (a) functioning neighborhood, you have people who are there with a sense of commitment.

The Madison Mutual Housing Cooperative's business is to provide housing for its members, either performing or contracting for managerial duties. It oversees the marketing, the screening of residents, the renewal and nonrenewal of members, sets the Co-op's budget and carrying charges (rent), and oversees the collection of those carrying charges. Therefore, all the functions of the management are performed by the members of the Cooperative who are residents in the houses. The Cooperative also pays money to the MHA via a management agreement to take on some tasks such as physical maintenance and resident training.

Organization of the Madison Mutual Housing Cooperative

The Madison Mutual Housing Cooperative consists of smaller cooperative units, scattered throughout eight central neighborhoods of Madison, Wisconsin. The MHA is restricted by its funding to operate in Community Development Block Grant target areas (i.e., neighborhoods where the census indicates that more than 50% of the residents have incomes of less than 80% of the local median income).

The cooperative units can range from single family and two or three flats clustered in groups to larger complexes, such as the 28-unit Reservoir cooperative described below. Residents of the co-op units meet monthly; share the work; share control of the maintenance account; and make joint decisions about membership issues, house rules, and work schedules. The MHA plans to do some "infill" (i.e., buying or building between existing properties that are currently isolated from each other) to help create more of a sense of community among some of the individual sites.

The following is a brief description of three of the larger sites owned by the MHA that will be referred to later in this chapter:

The Reservoir Cooperative   Located adjacent to the MHA offices, the Reservoir cooperative was the first MHA development designed with the specific intent to "integrate people of all abilities." As one staff member explained, "It's a well thought out community." There are 28 units of one, two, or three bedroom apartments, with four barrier-free[2] units. In addition, all first floor units are accessible.[3] The Queen Anne style, four-plex design is built to fit into the appearance and architecture of this older neighborhood. There are two "tot lots" with a clear line of sight from inside the apartments, and vegetable and flower gardens planted and tilled by the cooperative members around some of the units.

The Avenue Cooperative The Avenue cooperative is the MHA's largest and most recent cooperative development; it is located on the site of a 1924 building that previously was the city's "contagious disease" hospital and was previously a research facility of the University of Wisconsin. This 3 million dollar project included an investment by the Wisconsin Power and Light Corporation and support from the distribution of tax credits. The 40-unit site includes six barrier-free units and a total of 36 accessible ones, as well as a universally usable[4] neighborhood park named after James A. Graaskamp, a wheelchair user, chairman of the University of Wisconsin's Real Estate Department, and an early supporter of the MHA's efforts. There is also an accessible community room dedicated to the memory of Liesl M. Blockstein, a Madison community visionary.

The Chandler Cooperative The MHA holds a ground lease for the property on which the housing is built and owns the physical improvements on the land. This cooperative consists of seven single family homes and one licensed group home for eight older adults operated by Independent Living, a nonprofit organization that provides services for older adults. Planned as an intergenerational community, the cooperative includes people of all ages. Although not part of the design of the cooperative, four of the seven single family homes are occupied by people who are Vietnamese, Laotian, or Hmong.

Roles within the Cooperative

The Madison Housing Cooperative has three interlinking levels: the resident or individual cooperative member, the cooperative units, and the Cooperative board and committees. On each level, there are different roles for the members, all of which are necessary for the Cooperative to run smoothly.

---

[2]Barrier-free units are designed in all aspects with accessibility in mind, including roll-in showers, side-by-side refrigerators, cut-away counters, thermostats and fuse boxes at universal height, accessible washers and dryers, among other features.

[3]In this context, refers to accessibility of the apartment to entrance/exit by a person using a wheelchair.

[4]Political terminology widely used by people involved with the "field of physical access." Indicates usability by all people, instead of a common disability language of "accessible to people with disabilities."

Resident's Role   Each resident basically has four major roles (a detailed job description is also given to each resident). These roles include organizing and managing the house, taking care of maintenance for the house, participating in the larger Cooperative, and following both the house rules and those of the larger Cooperative. Each resident signs an occupancy agreement, agreeing to assume these roles and to perform basic obligations such as paying the monthly carrying charges, taking care of his or her own unit, and getting along with the neighbors.

House Roles   Each house has a house treasurer and assistant, a maintenance coordinator, and a house contact person. Michael O'Connor, the first resident of the Reservoir cooperative, described his past responsibilities as house treasurer:

> I was responsible for the books, for making sure that people were paying their common utility bills. . . We all share in those. . . I came up with a system that I thought was fair and worked out.

Each house must have a set of house rules and meet once a month to make joint decisions on sharing the work (e.g., lawn mowing, hallway maintenance) and mutual problem solving (e.g., utility bills, dividing up the house maintenance account).

The decision-making processes vary from cooperative to cooperative, with some, such as the Reservoir, electing to use a modified form of a consensus approach (i.e., a process where all parties agree with a decision), while other sites, such as the Avenue, make decisions by a majority vote. The specific process is decided by the residents and can be changed by them by amending their house rules. Lisa Dushack, the MHA resident coordinator, explained, "It all really depends on the people within. In the smaller units, consensus is generally the way they go because if both units aren't agreeing, they have constant conflict."

Cooperative Board and Committee Roles   The board is legally responsible for the Madison Housing Cooperative and ensures that the needs of the residents are being met. Their roles include: 1) education of residents on the nature of cooperatives; 2) maintaining affordable, decent housing; and 3) maintaining the organization as a viable entity in the community.

The Madison Mutual Housing Cooperative has four major board committees dealing with property management, membership, finances, and dispute resolutions. Recently, the Cooperative was reorganized into 12 geographic districts, partially in an attempt to reorganize the board and to provide better representation and communication throughout the Cooperative. Each district is required to provide representation on the Co-op board. In addition, five board members are selected at-large from the membership.

People Who Shared Their Stories

The people who shared their stories during the visit include residents of the cooperative units, MHA staff, and board members, who may also reside in the cooperative units. Figure 2 provides brief descriptions of each of these people. The people interviewed were broadly representative of the population served by the MHA as well as the larger community supporting the MHA and its residents.

Staff of the Madison Mutual Housing Association (MHA)   The MHA staff consists of 10 full-time employees and several limited-time employees (LTE) who do clerical work. Susan Hobart was the executive director at the time of this visit. She founded the MHA and supervised all employees. While several staff work full- or part-time on Cooperative activities, they are also employed through MHA as part of a management agreement with the Madison Housing Cooperative.

The three staff roles of primary relevance described in this chapter are those of the development director (David Sheperd), the resident coordinator (Lisa Dushack), and the training coordinator (Judy Olson). The development director is responsible for developing financial packages and fund raising. The resident coordinator helps to "organize the residents to get the cooperative units functioning and deals with anything the residents need." The training coordinator conducts training sessions for new residents of the cooperative units; trains residents for special roles, such as house treasurer; trains boards and committees in meeting and facilitation skills; does outreach in the community; and assists with dispute resolution.

The staff turnover of the MHA has been very low; however, there is not a lot of opportunity for upward mobility. Except for the executive director, the positions are "pretty much peer positions" and salaries are based on market studies.

In addition to MHA staff, the organization also relies on other people to assist in housing development and other work, including an architect, an accounting firm, and a law firm.

Residents of the Cooperative   While the cooperative residents are diverse in ages, ethnic backgrounds, and income levels, people with lower incomes continue to be the primary residents, and, like the rest of Madison, the ethnic and racial diversity is somewhat limited. Although a small portion of the people have a disability, this chapter highlights the perspectives of several people living in the cooperative units who either have a disability, are the neighbor of someone with a disability, and/or share a home with a person with a disability (see Figure 2).

The reasons people with disabilities live and participate in the Cooperative are similar to the reasons any person might join and continue

Sandy Dooley, who is 25 years of age, lives in the Avenue cooperative. A member of the cooperative's selection committee, she is also the recipient of a SPARK award for representing the cooperative spirit. Born with spina bifida and paralyzed from the waist down, Sandy obtains support services through Access to Independence.

Lisa Dushack, the resident coordinator, was placed at the MHA as part of her high school program and "liked what they were doing." She has now been at MHA for 7 years, the first 6 as office manager. Lisa was instrumental in hiring an office staff member who had spent 41 years in institutions.

Hollis Gaffney, born on a farm 8 miles west of the Wisconsin Dells, has been a resident of Madison for 19 years and a part of the cooperative since about 1983. Living in one of the older homes rehabilitated by MHA in the Wilmar neighborhood, he obtains supports services through Options in Community Living. Hollis recently started a new job at Hardees and also delivers mail in the cooperative.

Darwin Ness has become a celebrity, having been featured in articles and videotapes for many different reasons, from his story of 50 years in the institution to his life in the community, his zest for recreation including dog sledding in the Yukon, his job at the state office building, and his home and supports. He moved to this cooperative with Randy Wilkins. He obtains support services through Options in Community Living.

Michael O'Connor, the first person to move into the Reservoir cooperative, chairs the parks and recreation committee for Madison's Citizens Commission on Physical Disabilities. Previously house treasurer, Michael has now taken on the job of maintenance coordinator for his unit. He is employed by the city recreation department and obtains support services through Access to Independence.

Judy Olson, described as the "ideal co-oper," has lived in a limited equity co-op for 10 years, a co-op that included two men with disabilities. She has been employed with MHA as the resident coordinator and as the training coordinator. She has a broad range of interests in community issues, including board membership on the Madison Association of Neighborhood Centers.

Anna Paul, part-time maintenance coordinator for MHA, is also the "longest tenured resident" of a "six person unit," which included a woman with a disability and her live-in friend.

David Sheperd came to MHA in July 1983, working as a financial manager and now as the organization's development director. He has a degree in business and learned his real estate experience on the job. On a personal basis, he has been involved in a range of community activities, including peace issues, day care, respite centers, and alternative radio, all as efforts to "try to make the community a better place to live."

David Wallner, through his job as alderperson, represents about 9,000 people in at least five or six neighborhoods in Madison. Involved in neighborhood associations since the mid-70s, he is working toward three major housing goals: (1) keeping the housing stock up; (2) systematic code enforcement to upgrade properties; and (3) getting more families and owner occupants to buy in the district.

Judy Wilcox has a variety of community roles and connections in the area of housing and support, including being past president of the board of Options in Community Living, current resident of the Reservoir cooperative, and a state housing coordinator.

(continued)

Figure 2. Residents, staff, and board members of the MHA who shared their stories.

Figure 2.   (*continued*)

> **Randy Wilkins** shares an accessible apartment with Darwin Ness at the Reservoir cooperative. Randy describes himself as active, like Darwin, and appreciates the social atmosphere, security, and stability that the cooperative provides.
>
> **Toni Wilson,** the new president of the Cooperative board, previously served on the maintenance, selection, and playground committees associated with two of the cooperative properties. She is now involved in implementing a neighborhood watch program and recently attended a neighborhood housing network meeting in Washington. Toni was on welfare the first year she was part of the cooperative, and says she knows what it's like to worry if you'll have a roof over your head.

to live in one. For example, Darwin Ness, who spent most of his life in institutions (see Shoultz, 1989, for more information on Darwin Ness), lives in the Reservoir cooperative with Randy Wilkins, a support worker from Options in Community Living, an organization providing support services to people with developmental disabilities. Randy compared the cooperative to their previous housing situation where neighbors changed every few months:

> For me, the biggest change is, having lived here 2 1/2 years, 75% or more of the people near us are still here. . . We feel more secure. Just sitting outside is a lot more enjoyable and social. Darwin's a real social person, just really likes to interact with people and spend time just gabbing. He can go through the court and know everybody basically. . . so that's important and really nice.

Michael O'Connor, who also lives in the Reservoir cooperative, obtains aide support from Access for Independence, an independent living center. He explains with "co-op enthusiasm" why he enjoys living in the Reservoir cooperative:

> I like the fact you know your neighbors. In a typical apartment complex, you really don't interact with your neighbors. . . I like the idea we are in control. I like the sense of pride. I think we take care of our property because we feel proud of it. . . I like the fact we have input into who we live with. . . I just like the variety of it. I like the fact that it is integrated.

Neighbors, Investors, and Volunteers   Based on principles of cooperation, the Madison Mutual Housing Association, which is responsible for housing development, works together with neighbors, investors, and volunteers. Susan Hobart is acknowledged in the community as being good at public relations and "helping people feel a part of things." David Wallner elaborated, "It's more than public relations. She and her people believe . . . they are part of the bigger picture and they want to be good citizens, good neighbors, those things. It's more than just clichés."

Neighbors   MHA strives to involve people from the neighborhood in the housing development, and, on an ongoing basis, once the housing is in place. From the beginning, they integrate the biggest opponents to site development into the design process. As one staff member said, "That's real key. We try to get the neighborhood, the people who are going to be involved with the housing (who live near the development) to be involved right away."

The staff members of the MHA view relationships with neighbors and neighborhoods as reciprocal. In designing housing, thought is placed into the contributions that the new housing can make to the neighborhoods. For example, in the Avenue co-op, the playground is open because the neighborhood didn't have a playground for the kids playing in a six block area. Integration of cooperative housing into existing neighborhoods is considered of key importance.

Investors   Investors play a critical role because they provide the financial base necessary for the cooperative housing development. To get started, one lender took a few risks for their first mortgage money, and they received block grant money through the Community Development Block Grant. Now that the MHA's reputation has grown, they have an easier time generating development funding. The MHA's most recent development at the Avenue included the use of 1.8 million dollars in tax credits invested by Wisconsin's largest utility company. The MHA seeks to build partnerships between the private investors and the public sector.

Volunteers   Cooperation is also reflected in the volunteer efforts of many individuals, groups, and associations that help to make the vision of affordable housing a reality. For example, Training Coordinator Judy Olson proudly shows the before and after slides of renovations of one their older buildings, noting "the nice wrought iron fence that someone donated to us" and "the architect who donated his time to help us reconstruct the outside to its true historic character." She continues with another slide of a condemned building, saying, "We bought it, and we wouldn't have been able to afford to turn it around without relying on a group called Operation Fresh Start. They take kids who are high school dropouts or at risk of dropping out and give them jobs building houses. Then they turn their lives around. In this case, they turned the building around." A few slides later there is a picture of a volunteer workday cosponsored with the Board of Realtors. Judy continued, "They came out and helped us scrape, rake, and clean up the property, so maybe you're getting a sense of how much we rely on dozens of little and big ways to write down the costs."

LESSONS FOR THE DISABILITY FIELD

Because excellent resource materials on the MHA and Cooperative already exist (see, e.g., Furman, 1987; National Association of Home Builders, NAHB National Resource Center, & ARC-US, 1989), this section highlights lessons for the disability field as it moves toward greater use of conventional housing options. The main areas briefly described are the nature of the organizations, principles underlying the creation of housing options, facing stigma and stereotypes, housing as an empowerment and social issue, meanings of independence, the relationship between housing and support organizations, group homes and cooperatives, and promoting integration through financing.

Value-Based Leadership, Commitment, and Excellence

The Madison Mutual Housing Association and Cooperative are founded on a strong set of clearly articulated values, including a firm commitment that all humanity should be valued and held in dignity, that all people have a right to quality housing, and that people can live and work together cooperatively for the benefit of all. Unlike many disability organizations, this organization has a broader mission with a commitment to the diversity of people who make up neighborhoods and communities in Madison, Wisconsin.

The organization and its founder, Susan Hobart, have received public recognition for their commitment to excellence in their field. They have received an "Orchid Award" from a group called the Capital Community Citizens for beautifying the landscape, an award from the Madison Trust for Historic Preservation for "superior achievement in the rehabilitation of residential property in the city of Madison," and an award from the Business Forum presented to Susan "for her contributions to women and children of Dane County." They are an organization in and of the Madison community.

As with other "good" organizations in our national study,[5] they are constantly improving by learning from their experiences. They have a "together we can find a way attitude" and believe that "we are making a difference." The organization is small and relatively nonhierarchical in nature. The director and her staff are known for making people feel like they are a part of things. Their commitment extends beyond a view of housing to a recognition of its broader social role.

Principles for the Creation of Housing Options

Several key housing principles espoused by the MHA and Co-op are consistent with those recently adopted by the housing subcommittee of The Association for Persons with Severe Handicaps (TASH), including affordable quality housing for all, housing as a right, and integrated housing. In addition, these organizations adhere to Rochdale's Princi-

---

[5]See Racino (1991) for more information on shared characteristics of disability organizations promoting community integration of people with disabilities.

ples of Cooperation described on page 254, this chapter, and principles of individual and community empowerment that will be described in the following sections.

Quality, Affordable Housing for All   Both the MHA and the Cooperative are founded on the belief that quality, affordable housing should be made available to all at a fair price. Because developing affordable housing is a major challenge today, the organization continues to look for new ways to make this possible. The association's approach to low and moderate income housing is based on a vision of housing that "anyone would be proud to live in, whether you're low or high income or in-between." The MHA's government funding places income limits on the occupants of most units, thus limiting the diversity of the residents. However, the MHA has found ways to achieve a "mixed income" housing concept. In the newer MHA developments, some units are priced at "market rates" and subsidize, in part, the other units. This practice helps to promote economic integration and is a tool to use in overcoming "low income stigmatization."

Housing as a Right   Instead of a charity approach to housing, the MHA and Co-op view housing as a right for all people. In order for people who have been traditionally excluded from decent housing to become included, they believe that: 1) people must be given information about options, and 2) people must clearly articulate their need and organize around it. Based on these beliefs, the MHA uses "affirmative marketing" to reach out to groups traditionally excluded, although this has not always been as successful a strategy as they would hope. One group, for example, that is not well represented is the people who have been involved with the mental health system. One staff member explained that these individuals and advocates are just beginning to recognize their right to decent housing.

Integrated Housing   Housing for all also means that the organizations strive to integrate housing in all ways, reflecting the diversity, yet unity, of community. As Lisa Dushack explained, "I think it's really important for people to live together and not have segregated sectors. . . and I think if we are all going to grow in this community, we need to do that." Housing integration, however, is not always easy to achieve in practice. For example, a disproportionate number of people with disabilities live in the Avenue cooperative and people of Asian backgrounds in the Chandler cooperative. The organizations continue to learn from their experiences and do what they can to achieve "mainstream communities" in their housing.

Integration is viewed as benefiting all people as they better understand each other. As one staff member said, "Everybody, not only people with disabilities, but people who come in contact (with neighbors, co-workers), are better off. . . everybody learns; everybody's got different abilitie$ and that's what's key, that's what we found out."

Facing Stereotypes and Stigma

Many of the issues faced by the MHA in their development of housing for people with low incomes appear to mirror those faced by organizations supporting people with disabilities. Three examples of similar issues revolve around neighbors' stereotypes prior to housing development, fitting housing into the neighborhood, and the use of language.

Stereotypes While development is a complex issue, it is striking to hear the similarities in stories told by people associated with the MHA with those told by residential providers. In describing the initial opposition to one housing development, one staff member confided, "It was just people's fears. People have these stereotypes. . . Once people live with each other, they find out (that their experience does not fit their stereotypes)." In this situation, once people moved in, the development "stabilized the neighborhood and increased property values."

Housing that Fits Into the Neighborhood Similar to organizations promoting the integration of people with disabilities, MHA is concerned about how their housing can become indistinguishable from other housing in the neighborhood. As one staff member described, "It fits in with our goal of having housing fit into the neighborhood, so when people drive by they don't point and say, 'That's where poor people live.' It looks like regular housing." Consistent with the concept of normalization, this is one example of how the MHA and Co-op strive for physical integration.

Language People employed by MHA also are conscious of the power of language, and the role all of us play in removing stigma. While they credit the support organizations for teaching them "how to talk," the MHA staff use an "ability, not disability" approach in their daily language. Aware of the political nature of speech, one staff member explained that "instead of saying that's a curb cut for someone in a wheelchair, it's a universally usable curb. Everyone can use it. It removes stigma."

Housing as an Empowerment and Social Issue

MHA is founded upon principles of personal and community empowerment that are promoted in daily practice through resident control of housing, participation, and shared decision making.

Resident Control of Housing Resident control of housing is central to the mission of the organization and to the nature of cooperative living. It is closely tied with many issues discussed in the disability field today—personal empowerment, contribution to society, learning skills, and community empowerment. MHA staff member David Sheperd described how he views this relationship:

> I like to see people control their own housing (be)cause you make your own decisions. . . And it affects everybody when people feel empowered. . . You have a more positive outlook on yourself; therefore, people can be more contributing to society, learn more skills, get better jobs . . . or whatever it takes, because they feel they can take control over their lives. . . The less people who are poor, who are not homeless, who are fed and clothed and sheltered, the better off as a society we all are. So it affects everyone as a whole and individually.

Social Dimensions of Housing   The theme of housing as a social issue permeated the interviews, often tying in with discussions of neighborhoods, families, relationships, and societal issues. Toni Wilson, the Co-op board president, recounted her first meeting in Washington, D.C., as part of the national neighborhood housing network. Speaking with quiet enthusiasm, she said:

> All the people had a goal in common—to have low and moderate income housing. They were concerned about improving the neighborhoods . . . how to get money for housing. . . It was so neat to see all these people coming together as one.

Unlike many issues where the focus is primarily on disability, housing affects everyone in the society and provides a unique forum for bringing together a range of people to solve common social concerns.

Building a Sense of Community Through Shared Decision Making In describing these organizations, one support service provider said, "They gave people choices and control. They build communities, not just housing." Throughout the visit, the people involved with MHA talked about how "we voted," "we had a dedication," and "we decided," thus conveying a sense of ownership and involvement in the work, events, and decisions they described. Although not all cooperative units use consensus, such a process represents a respect for the opinions of each individual. As Randy Wilkins explained, "Any consensus process makes everyone feel like they have a strong voice in things . . . that's important. . . . And having consensus means presumably you're not going to do something that will unduly upset somebody."

One example of a decision that might be minor to some people, but could result in the difference between living in decent housing or not, is the division of bills. Randy conveyed his feelings saying, "That's an important decision, not something to be overlooked because what's a few bucks? A few bucks is a lot to some people." In fact, at another equity co-op,[6] one member, a man who had a traumatic brain injury

---

[6]An equity co-op is a co-op where the interest or value that is invested in the property is over and above any mortgage indebtedness.

from a motorcycle accident, was $30 short in his financial package for rent each month and the other members agreed to pay higher rent to make up the amount. Because of this shared decision, he was able to live and participate in the co-op, something that otherwise would not have been financially feasible for him.

Building Community Through Working Together   Working together, often through committees, is a way for people both to contribute as individuals and participate in shared decision making. For example, Sandy Dooley, who was born with spina bifida, talked about the garden committee that will look at landscaping the Avenue cooperative, and Toni Wilson talked about a playground committee formed between two of the cooperative units. Toni said:

> Six of us and Amy, an intern from the university, helped to plan out the playground. We set up specifics of how we wanted it set up to prevent injuries to children. We had input all along the way. After it was built, the parents would take turns on the playground. Everyone kind of looks after each other's children. You could rely on each other, kind of like one big family. You can go to another member to help you out.

Everyone has an opportunity and is expected to participate in sharing the responsibility and work of the cooperative. People all make different contributions. One staff member explained:

> It's been great because the people who can't help with the physical things are finding other ways. They're chairing committees, helping out with interviews, that type of thing. So it's just getting everyone together and finding out what they can do and promoting that.

In other words, the underlying assumptions are that everyone belongs and has a valuable contribution and role to play. This message is conveyed through sharing day-to-day responsibilities and decision making. This organization gives daily examples, in its committees and other processes, of how people can come together, each with their unique contributions.

Getting Along with Each Other   In many ways, co-ops are an opportunity for people to learn how to get along better with each other—opportunities that are sometimes missed or bypassed in day-to-day lives. As one staff member described:

> People don't come outfitted with all the skills that they need to be in co-ops. And some of the skills that people have sort of culturally missed are some of the most important ones, like being able to talk with people about problems instead of storing up resentments, backbiting, gossiping, and flying into rages.

This lesson is an important one for people in the disability field where there is a tendency to view problems in living together as specific to people with disabilities. As the cooperative experience indicates, people in general have a lot to learn about what it means to share lives with each other.

Getting along together begins with the selection of residents by a committee. The main criteria for selection is being "co-op enthusiastic" and open to participation. Sandy, who is on the Avenue cooperative selection committee, said she asks questions of potential applicants such as, "How would you react if people had a loud party? How would you handle the situation?" When asked what she looked for in response, Sandy smiled and replied, "If they're outgoing and whether they compromise, so they'll take suggestions from other people."

As can be seen from these descriptions, cooperatives offer opportunities for creating new ways of living together. At the same time, cooperatives are not for everyone, and in their own way, can be exclusionary.

Individual Empowerment and Shared Decision Making   Madison Mutual Housing Association and Cooperative provide an excellent example, in philosophy and in practice, of the relationship between individual empowerment and shared decision making. Within the disability field, these two issues often are viewed as being in conflict with each other, with self-determination often equated with "control" or "power over" others, and shared decision making viewed as representing "community," "reciprocity," and "mutuality." Here, the underlying assumption is that both are important and, in fact, mutually increase each other in practice. As Judy Olson said, "We're not talking about the pioneer spirit of Lewis and Clark. It's self-determination within the context of shared decision making." Shared decision making, especially consensus among all members, is built upon a base of individual empowerment.

The Meanings of Independence

Independence is defined in many ways (see Racino, chap. 16, this volume, on the meaning of independence at the Center for Independent Living, California), and several people associated with the MHA and Cooperative shared their ideas about what independence means. Michael O'Connor, with his wry sense of humor, forcefully stated:

> Being independent doesn't only mean being able to get around in the community, being able to work, being able to access the kinds of services in order to live in the community. For me, independence means not needing to rely on the whole social services world.

Lisa Dushack, the resident coordinator, also struggled to share her view on how people with disabilities were on their own even though they had attendants. She added:

> Through the cooperative, we require that everyone participate(s). So they (people with disabilities) are functioning on their own; they aren't

given any special treatment one way or another. They participate a lot of times on committees for interviews. So I guess we really don't see them different in any way, although outside people tend to.

Even though they have a disability, they want to be out and they want to be independent. They are probably capable of more than anybody can imagine. So we're constantly trying to challenge people to see what they can accomplish. We are totally amazed all the time. I think that people just never gave (them) the opportunity to see what they could do.

I guess the best example . . . is within our (MHA) staff. We've got two disabled people, one of whom was in an institution for 41 years. . . And it is amazing what she can accomplish, but she was never given the opportunity. We gave her the opportunity, and it has been wonderful for us and for her. . . You may need to work out a different system or a different way, but generally they can accomplish the same tasks. . . I don't know what we'd do without her.

The Relationship of Housing and Support

Disability organizations are now exploring how adults can be best supported to live in conventional homes. One critical issue is the relationship between housing and support, including the respective roles of housing and support agencies. The following discussions reflect perspectives from the MHA on these emerging issues in the disability field.

Independent Relationship Between Housing and Support   The position of the MHA on the relationship between housing and support was described by Judy Olson:

> We've discussed the issue of housing and support extensively. We decided we cannot be in the position of checking before a person moves in on whether they have adequate supports. Once a person is in the cooperative, if lack of supports affects the housing, then we'll become involved . . . the person has an independent relationship with their support agency.

This separation of roles ensures that people's access to housing is not controlled by disability organizations and separates the landlord's function from that of a service provider and/or support facilitator.

Housing by Housing Organizations   One major decision that disability organizations must make in moving to a housing and support approach is the role they should play in the area of conventional housing. MHA staff and board members shared their views on this issue, concluding that community housing should be the responsibility of housing organizations. The role of disability organizations is to work with a broad-based community organization to ensure that it includes people with disabilities.

To develop housing, David Sheperd, an MHA staff member, and Judy Wilcox, a resident of the Reservoir cooperative, stressed that people really need a strong background in real estate. Funding is very complex and new financial strategies are continually being explored. Typically, disability organizations would not have the time and expertise to do so. In addition, if disability organizations become involved with housing, the result might be "something that looks like a service model instead of a housing model."

Judy Olson often speaks with disability organizations who are interested in developing housing. She reflected about one of her recent discussions:

> They really want to have a co-op for *their* (emphasis added) people who they'd like to bring out of institutions into the community. But they don't know how to expand beyond the clients they are serving to a broader community. And it takes a tremendous effort, and this is not an easy organization to start up.

Judy Olson advised people who are interested in housing inclusive for people with disabilities to work with their local housing organization, to "insert yourself into it, make yourself part of it." She continued:

> It certainly has had a great effect on us to have Options, Access, and Independent Living here in town so close to us, and giving us advice, and advocating for *their* (emphasis added) groups and housing needs within our organization.

If there is not a broad-based housing organization such as the MHA in a community, she recommends that the community needs to develop one.

Roles of Support Organizations   Disability or specialized organizations are available to provide support services for people with disabilities and/or older adults who live in MHA housing. Figure 3 outlines these support organizations.

In relationship to the people in the cooperative, both the Options and Access to Independence support organizations share a philosophy that is similar. They both support people to make their own decisions and are involved in planning for and arranging the support services, including personal care attendants. As one person who lives in the cooperative said about Options, "They are there if you need them." Another resident echoed the same theme saying, "Options . . . helps people, if they need help."

The support staff from Access to Independence and Options play a variety of roles; for example, talking with neighbors and helping people with their cooperative responsibilities, such as changing screens. As Anna Paul, one neighbor of a person with a disability, explained:

> It helped a lot talking with her Options worker. I know they are over-worked, underpaid staff members like everyone else. I was hoping I wasn't going to get that line from them, and I didn't. . . Things seemed to happen and she (a cooperative resident, and Anna Paul's neighbor) knew she could ask them for help with those little projects too.

Although housing is separate from support services, both Options and Access to Independence are involved in a variety of housing-related

Three community organizations that provide support services for people with disabilities and/or people who are older are associated with the Madison Mutual Housing Association.

Access to Independence, an independent living center, is in its second decade of providing opportunities for people with physical disabilities to live independent, active lives in the community in Dane County. As described in their mission statement:

> We believe it is the right of all people with disabilities to have the freedom and opportunity to control their own affairs, and live as they choose within the community. We further believe that this freedom and opportunity will enable people with disabilities to live independently, to pursue educational, career, and other personal goals, and to become active, contributing members of the community.

Community services offered by the center include: 1) helping find personal care attendants; 2) helping locate affordable and accessible housing; 3) assisting with advocacy, both individual and system; 4) offering peer support from others who have gone through similar experiences; 5) teaching independent living skills, such as money management; and 6) working one to one with people to coordinate services.

Options In Community Living is a private, nonprofit organization that "believes that every person has the right to live in a home in the community as an active and accepted member." Options is an excellent example of what has been described in this book as a support organization. Options strives to help people with disabilities and the larger community learn from each other in order to promote mutual understanding, personal satisfaction, and a greater fulfillment of the potential of each individual. (For further information on this agency, the reader is referred to the bibliography at the end of this chapter.)

Independent Living is a nonprofit organization with a 17-year history of "providing services to older adults in their homes . . . to help them retain as much dignity and independence as they are able to." Their current programs include: 1) home chore services; 2) minor home modifications and equipment loan; 3) home sharing; 4) nutrition programs, including home-delivered meals; 5) community advocacy, outreach, and care management; 6) transportation; 7) telephone reassurance and friendly visiting; and 8) home health care. They also now operate the Chandler HOME in a building leased annually from the Madison Mutual Housing Association.

Figure 3. Support organizations.

issues. Access to Independence, like many independent living centers, plays a visible role in the community in the area of housing by providing assistance to developers and associations on housing issues, such as accessibility. The housing coordinator at Access to Independence is involved with the Fair Housing Council, and recently attended an accessible housing workshop sponsored by the Research and Training Center on Accessible Housing.[7] Options views assistance with the location of decent housing as part of their role, and includes this as an important

---

[7]For more information, contact the Research and Training Center for Accessible Housing, North Carolina State University, School of Design, Box 7701, FAS 5-37530, Raleigh, North Carolina 27607-9986.

area in their *Policy on Quality of Life* (Options in Community Living, 1987). These organizations, together with Independent Living, were also involved in planning for the Reservoir cooperative, the first major effort by this housing association to consciously include people with disabilities in natural proportions (i.e., the same proportions as in the population at large) within the cooperatives.

Group Homes and Cooperatives

One of the interesting opportunities during this visit was to discuss what it means to have a group home as part of a cooperative, and whether it is actually possible to do so. As described earlier, the Chandler cooperative has a group home for older adults on site, with the rest of the units being single family homes disproportionately occupied by people of Asian descent.

The Chandler Housing Options for Madison Elders (HOME) opened in the mid- to late 1980s. Independent Living, Madison Mutual Housing, the University of Wisconsin, and the County Commission on Aging came together to explore alternatives for people whom these organizations believed weren't able to reside at home, but did not need nursing home care. According to Independent Living, the residents receive daily supervision, housekeeping services, and medication monitoring from the agency.

Located on land leased by the Cooperative, the group home is operated by Independent Living, which holds a state license for this community-based residential facility (CBRF). The CBRF licensing requires 24-hour supervision and delineates requirements regarding the ability levels of residents who reside in the home. The initial intent by Independent Living was to operate the (group) home on a somewhat cooperative level, where people would be more involved in house chores and making decisions about the home. However, over time the residents have become less involved in the rest of the cooperative, although activities such as yard work continue to be shared. While there are many complex issues involved, the following discussions focus on understanding the dilemmas faced by the MHA and Independent Living while continuing to operate the group home within the cooperative.

Group Homes as Businesses Independent Living staff members view the group home as a "business." As the IL staff member explains:

> It is very difficult to run a business within a cooperative structure. If we (Independent Living) turn over the responsibility of deciding what residents are going to live there, what staff will be hired, and what . . . they are going to do in terms of budgets, and . . . we turn it (over) to the residents to (decide), it really isn't effective.
>
> At times, they (the residents) are not in the best position to make those kinds of decisions or don't choose to make those kinds of deci-

sions, or they are not the best business decisions. They are made on a personal level. There is also the issue of liability.

The MHA also believes the group home is first and foremost a business. However, MHA does not view being a business and part of the cooperative as incompatible because businesses can also be owned and operated on a cooperative basis. Independent Living, in contrast, takes the position that the nature of a business and a cooperative is, at times, in conflict.

Both views of group homes as businesses contrast with developments in the field of disability where efforts are being made to overcome a facility emphasis and place people first. This applies in particular to the area of decisionmaking, where a primary role of a support organization (e.g., Access to Independence, Options) is to facilitate decision making on the part of individuals who are living together.

The Base Membership of the Cooperative   The Chandler cooperative is complex for a variety of reasons, including the fact that four of the seven homes have people who are Vietnamese, Laotian, or Hmong and who do not speak English. The organization, as a result, needs to be aware of cultural issues and backgrounds that are new not only to the Cooperative, but also to Madison, Wisconsin. In addition, because of the disproportionate number of people from one cultural background, integration becomes even more challenging.

At the same time, the group home consists of people who are generally older and from different cultural backgrounds than many of the people living in the single family homes. In addition, some of the people who lived in the group home initially were interested in the cooperative model. However, over time many of these individuals left the Cooperative, and some newer residents may instead have been drawn to the group home because of particular features of its environment. The issues of lack of integration and cooperation across the cooperative tend to be framed by the agencies as being related to the people (e.g., language, frailty), and yet the structure of the group home and the different intents of the two organizations (i.e., MHA and Independent Living) also seem to play a key role.

Residents in the group home are "admitted" by Independent Living through a selection process that includes a nursing assessment, psychosocial assessment, and evaluation of daily living and personal care needs. The organization uses this information to decide the "appropriate level of care" for the person.[8] In contrast, cooperative residents, similar to people supported by Options and Access to Independence, select who will live in the other homes. Older adults at the Chandler HOME used to be involved in the cooperative selection process, but have now with-

---

[8]Additional information added by Independent Living after the site visit.

drawn from that role. As one staff member of Independent Living explained:

> When you select (members) in a co-op . . . a person would come before . . . the selection committee and they would have a chance to say "I think that the person would work well with who we have here." In Chandler HOME, until recently we had one resident who represented all residents (at the co-op selection meeting). They would at least have a chance to meet someone new coming in. . . You get into confidentiality, and it's not that healthy for people to know different things about each other. So, we weren't able to go to the same kind of selection process, plus the people in the other co-op houses do not have a say on who comes to Chandler HOME.

In contrast to the selection for the group home, the Cooperative's approach supports a person's right to have a say about the person or people with whom they will live. This is consistent with emerging practices in the field of disability and offers disability organizations an opportunity to learn from people who have had extensive experience in this type of selection process.

Role of Staff The Chandler HOME has a staffing pattern of four part-time staff (two live-in and two day) and one full-time professional resident manager. The primary responsibilities of these staff members are the care and supervision of the residents and the operation of the household to serve the needs of residents.[9]

Compared to the MHA philosophy that staff are resources for people to solve their own problems, Independent Living staff take on the role of representing the Chandler residents to other members of the cooperative. This is similar to the role of staff in traditional residential services programs, where staff members often intercede and resolve problems for residents. For example, one Independent Living staff member explained:

> The residents asked that I tell the co-op that they no longer wanted kids playing on their porch, which some of the people in the co-op took really hard, and they wondered why we were telling them that, but it was a resident request.

In contrast, the role of the MHA resident coordinator, who works with all the residents in the cooperatives, includes facilitating communication directly between the people involved in a common problem. Similar to the staff of support organizations such as Options and Access to Independence, the MHA staff try to avoid the role of boss, and instead help people to find ways to communicate better with each other. As Lisa Dushack explained:

> I'm here to help them work out the system (of communication), so they can just take that in their everyday lives . . . and not have a per-

---

[9]Additional information added by Independent Living after the site visit.

son come in and work out their problems. . . . I try to be there as a resource.

The role of the MHA staff parallels the emerging roles of staff in the field of disability, with a greater emphasis on facilitation and support.

Promoting Integration Through Financing

This section briefly describes three financial issues faced by the MHA and people with disabilities living in typical homes and places in neighborhoods and communities. These include the federal HUD 202 program, accessibility and home modifications, and strategies for financing. The reader may also refer to the bibliography at the end of this chapter for technical information on financing.

HUD 202 Program   One of the biggest barriers to housing integration for people with disabilities has been the HUD 202 program. The MHA wanted to use this financing for its newest development, the Avenue, to integrate people with disabilities in the housing. However, the development director recounted:

> The 202 program says you can't do it that way. You have to separate . . . the handicapped housing (and) the nonhandicapped housing as they put it. Of course, we got lots of feedback from so-called handicapped people who said, "No, this isn't the way it's going to be done." We tried to convince HUD, but we couldn't do it. It would have been nice financing; it would have been real easy, but we just turned it down.

As Michael O'Connor explained, separate apartment wings or complexes designed for people with physical disabilities were "progressive for their time . . . but that type of housing, or that concept of housing, is out-of-date. . . I don't believe in segregating people."

Accessibility and Modifications   The MHA has worked with architects who have had a 10-year history and commitment to accessibility. As in other places, it took the architects time and experience to learn about barrier-free units and incorporate this learning into their designs. As one staff member said, "It's one of those things you can't learn unless you are really out there practicing." The newer developments include apartments with roll-in showers, side-by-side refrigerators, cut-away counters, thermostats and fuse boxes at universal height, and accessible washers and dryers. Financing, however, continues to be a barrier on some minor architectural items because they may not be reimbursable through government funders. As David Sheperd explained:

> (HUD and other government agencies) are real strict on their cost containment, and that needs to loosen up. Air conditioners—no, you shouldn't have air conditioners. Well, some people need air conditioners, refrigerators with dual doors instead of the freezer up so a person in a wheelchair can reach it. Or amenities for people who are deaf or who are blind.

Strategies for Financing   Financing remains a critical issue facing
the organization, and it has been difficult to continue to develop affordable housing. As David Sheperd said:

> You really can't do affordable housing without subsidy. It is just so hard
> to make the market housing. As federal money has decreased dramat-
> ically and so has the (federal Community Development) Block Grant
> money, we've had to do more creative financing . . . to be able to
> utilize almost all kinds of financing, fund raising, grants, tax credits,
> syndications, everything we can get our hands on.

Through the years, the MHA has tapped a variety of private and
public sources, including Community Development Authority (a city
second mortgage loan program), private loans (based on the Community Reinvestment Act), Community Development Block Grants,
land contracts, low income tax credits, blanket mortgages with the National Cooperative Bank in Washington, and the HUD Section 8 Mod
Rehab Program. In later developments, the MHA has organized so that
"higher income people pay higher rates, which are then used to subsidize the people paying at a lower rate."

When approaching lenders, David believes it's important to arrive
with information such as statistics (e.g., the percentage of housing that
needs to be redone and is deteriorated, the percentage of homeless, the
percentage of people with disabilities in inadequate, substandard housing) and information on what needs to be done and why (e.g., the effect
of land and home costs going up). He also believes that networking is
important; that is, a lender can call a lender in a different city and find
out how a particular finance strategy has worked there.

THE FUTURE

The MHA and Cooperative are recognized within the housing field and
in the disability community as leaders and innovators in cooperative
living in the United States. In the coming years, these organizations face
a number of critical issues about their mission—by-products of their
success. The first is the question of size and scope of these organizations,
often framed in the disability field as a quantity–quality issue. The second is a potential for overidentification with the disability field, which
can undermine their broad-based community mission.

Housing and Neighborhood Revitalization

The MHA is already playing a role in Madison's effort to develop a
Madison-based Neighborhood Housing Service. If formed, this organization would be part of a Neighborhood Reinvestment Corporation and
would work to revitalize neighborhoods through a variety of avenues,
including housing and services development. David Sheperd explained:

The concept of neighborhood revitalization can include fixing up the deteriorating homes . . . getting rid of crime . . . clearing up marketing perceptions . . . bringing in more services—health, support . . . more economic development, more stores, office space . . . whatever it takes to sort of lift up the neighborhood, get the storefronts occupied, and improve the housing, the streets, places for kids to play, maybe a neighborhood center.

While this project is a natural extension of the work of the MHA, at least one person mentioned it might take time and energy away from the basic mission of affordable, resident-controlled housing. As the MHA staff members discussed at their retreat, everyone in the organization is committed to cooperatives: "It was nice to know we all think about that, even though the way we show it or what process we use is different." With the expansion to more units and larger buildings, maintaining the physical quality of the property and promoting social exchange and decisionmaking demand more staff time. The MHA, with its strong commitment to quality, will need to continue to examine plans for expansion in light of the commitment to the cooperatives that already exist.

A Broad-Based Community Organization

An organization such as the MHA, with its inclusive umbrella, often runs the risk of having its mission and nature undermined by its success. Besides the pressure to expand, the organization can also face additional dilemmas. Because responsiveness and inclusion of people with disabilities are not standard practices in conventional housing in our country, the MHA can be viewed as specializing in people with disabilities or in other minority or "devalued" groups. This could foster a view of the organization as a social service agency or a place particularly associated with people with disabilities. This, of course, would tend to undermine the very mission of the organization, which must remain broad based and representative of the community-at-large.

CONCLUSION

The Madison Mutual Housing Association and Cooperative are working today to help build a better community and society through the avenue of resident-controlled, affordable housing. As Toni Wilson, the president of the Co-op board, explained:

I wanted a place (and) an area that was nice, where I didn't have to worry about the children. (In the cooperative) you can count on the people next to you. Everybody's involved. I just think the co-ops are great. They look out for everybody's needs, try to accommodate everyone. It's been a great experience for me.

The lessons the housing association and cooperative share—a vision of a society inclusive of all people; good neighborhoods, housing, and communities; and individual and community empowerment—are becoming increasingly important in the disability field. The Madison Mutual Housing Association and Cooperative offer the opportunity to shift from "disability-colored" glasses to ones used by ordinary citizens, and to view the issues of people with disabilities as those of all people building a society based on individual respect and diversity within the unity of community.

BIBLIOGRAPHY

Furman, M. (1987, September). *The Madison Mutual Housing Cooperative: Resident handbook.* Madison, WI: Madison Mutual Housing Association, 200 North Blount Street, Madison, Wisconsin 53703.

Johnson, T. (1985). *Belonging to the community.* Madison, WI: Options in Community Living.

Johnson, T., & O'Brien, J. (1987). *Carrying Options' story forward: Final report of an assessment of Options in Community Living.* Madison, WI: Options in Community Living.

National Association of Home Builders, NAHB National Research Center, & ARC-US. (1989, May). *Financing housing for people with disabilities.* Washington, DC: Author.

O'Connor, S., & Racino, J.A. (1990). *New directions in housing for people with disabilities: A collection of resource materials.* Syracuse, NY: Center on Human Policy, Syracuse University.

Options in Community Living. (1987). *Options policy on quality of life.* Madison, WI: Author.

Shoultz, B. (Ed.). (1989). *Community living for adults.* Syracuse, NY: Center on Human Policy, Syracuse University.

13

REGENERATING A COMMUNITY

THE STORY OF RESIDENTIAL, INC.

Bonnie Shoultz

New Lexington, a town of about 5,000 people, is the county seat for Perry County, Ohio. New Lex, as the townspeople call it, is in the center of the county. Farmland and the small towns that support the farms make up the northern half of the county. The southern half consists of the foothills to the Appalachian Mountains, which host old coal mining towns that have lost most of their population since the 1920s and 1930s. New Lexington is a bridge between farm, mountain, and mine and the very different cultures that have risen from each. Perry County is an economically depressed area with many problems; about 40% of the county's residents receive some form of public benefits. One resident described it as a "community lost," a place where people have lost hope.

There is another way to view Perry County, however. Most of the people who live there are long-time residents, people who identify with the area. There is a flow of people between the towns in Perry County.

The preparation of this chapter was supported in part by the U.S. Department of Education, Office of Special Education and Rehabilitative Services, National Institute on Disability and Rehabilitation Research, under Contract No. G0085C03503 awarded to the Center on Human Policy, Division of Special Education and Rehabilitation, Syracuse University. The opinions expressed herein do not necessarily reflect the position of the U.S. Department of Education, and no official endorsement should be inferred.

Thanks are given to Julie Racino, Steve Taylor, Doug Biklen, Bob Bogdan, Rannveig Traustadottir, Pam Walker, Joel Yaeger, John Winnenberg, and Sandy Landis for reviewing and suggesting important revisions to this report.

This chapter has previously appeared in Taylor, S.J., Bogdan, R., & Racino, J.A. (Eds.). (1991). *Life in the community: Case studies of organizations supporting people with disabilities.* Baltimore: Paul H. Brookes Publishing Co.

All names used in this chapter are pseudonyms.

People have relatives in many of the neighboring towns, and they see the whole area, not just the town they live in, as their home. In spite of the endemic economic and social hardships, there are people who have created a spirit of "belonging." This spirit is evident in the people affiliated with Residential, Inc., an agency that supports 22 people with developmental disabilities to live in the community. Jonah, the former director of this agency said:

> I like to think of it this way—that in the midst of nearly desperate economic and social conditions, there are people trying to make community life work. People are blossoming, and helping others to do so, and trying to make a difference in their own small ways. We may or may not be making an impact on the larger community, but we are here, living out our vision of what community should be.

To visit Residential, Inc., is not just to visit an agency, but to become part of a community that is embedded in a larger community. The people affiliated with Residential, Inc., include people who have disabilities, people who are paid to provide support to them, and people who are connected to and supporting them through other kinds of relationships—family members, neighbors, co-workers, other town residents, friends, church members, business people, and classmates, all of whom create a sense of "belonging" in the community.

"SHE'D STILL BE MY NEIGHBOR"

Ruby is a woman in her mid-50s who spent much of her life in institutions. In December 1986, she met Evelyn, who was employed as a substitute in the group home, and they became friends. Ruby, who has a severe hearing impairment, had a reputation then as an angry, hostile woman who sometimes hurt the people who worked with her. As a result, many people avoided her, and her case manager (a county employee, not employed by Residential, Inc.,) thought she should be on medication and in behavior modification programs. Evelyn, who is about Ruby's age, had a different perspective. She believed that much of Ruby's anger was due to the fact that so many people in her life had left her and that she no longer trusted those who came into her life to work with her, especially the younger people. Evelyn believed that she could gain Ruby's trust if she could show her that she cared about her and did not plan to leave her. She approached Ruby as a friend, and Ruby responded.

Ruby communicates through writing, body language, and gestures. She uses sign language with people who understand it. Evelyn knows some sign language, but she and Ruby usually communicate with a notepad that Ruby carries at all times. Their conversations are lively and informed, and many other people have learned to communicate with Ruby, partly due to Evelyn's example.

Early in 1987, the agency director asked Evelyn to become Ruby's service planner. This meant that Evelyn would need to make a formal commitment of at least 1 year to Ruby, and that her job would entail learning about Ruby, dreaming with her about her future, and helping her fulfill her dreams. Evelyn gave a lot of thought to this commitment since it was not to be taken lightly. When she agreed, she knew that she had accepted responsibility for much more than paperwork and skill teaching.

One of Ruby's dreams was to have a home of her own. When a small house, next to the home where Evelyn had lived with her family for 32 years, was put up for sale in February 1988, Evelyn thought it might be a good home for Ruby. She knew that having Ruby as her neighbor would involve a new level of commitment, so she pondered the idea until she and her family decided they were comfortable with it. Then she discussed the idea with Ruby and Residential, Inc.

The agency agreed and bought the house for $21,000, a moderate sum for houses in Perry County. The down payment came out of the Residential, Inc., reserve fund. Ruby's monthly rent payments, supplemented by a HUD Section 8 housing subsidy, will pay off the mortgage. However, Ruby will not gain equity in the house. State regulations will not allow her, as a service recipient, to own property; they could seize the home as an available asset to pay for the services she receives. Residential, Inc., however, considers it hers for as long as she wants to live there.

The house was in terrible shape. However, when Evelyn told her neighbors that Ruby would be moving in, one neighbor offered to paint the walls; he spent 3 mornings a week for 6 weeks painting. Others helped with the cleaning, wallpapering, and fixing the cupboards in the kitchen. Ruby and Evelyn found living room furniture at a yard sale, and Residential, Inc., gave Ruby the bedroom furniture she had used and the washer and dryer from the group home. After 3 months of work and planning, everything was ready. Ruby moved in on July 30, 1988, and had a birthday and housewarming party in the house the next day.

After Ruby moved in, she and Evelyn had to work out new routines and come to new understandings about their relationship. Their agreement was that Evelyn would come over at about 7:30 every morning so they could spend the morning together. Ruby works at a sheltered workshop from 2:00 P.M. to 8:00 P.M., so they agreed that Evelyn would visit her after work for a while. When Evelyn is at home, Ruby can contact her in two different ways. There is an intercom system between their houses that is left on all the time for Ruby to use in case of an emergency. If she just wants company or needs something, she goes to Evelyn's house. On weekends, they plan some time together and some time apart. One of Ruby's favorite activities, going to yard sales, is not a particular favorite of Evelyn's. They have come to an agreement that they will go together to a yard sale once a week, usually on Saturday mornings.

Evelyn has also helped Ruby fulfill two other dreams. One is to pursue her interest in art. Ruby paints and does collages, and she enjoys experimenting with other media for artistic expression. One of the rooms in the house is set up as a studio that they are equipping together. Evelyn also wants to get a kiln for firing ceramics in Ruby's basement. She said, "I have a friend who does ceramics, and I figure she would spend a lot of time at Ruby's if she had a kiln. She could show her how to make and fire ceramic pieces, and Ruby would love it."

Another of Ruby's dreams was to reconnect with old friends and family, and to make new friends. With Evelyn's help and support, she has fulfilled this dream. Evelyn explained, "There were so many [staff] who left, and she didn't know why. She thought they had died. We've reestablished contact with a couple of her former staff and also with Ruby's family. She's got a sister in Roseville, which is 15 miles away, and two sisters in the Glouster area. She also has a brother who lives farther away."

Ruby has also become acquainted with some of her new neighbors. Evelyn said, "The people in this neighborhood keep to themselves, but are there if you need them. They were all glad she was moving in instead of a family with young children. She's more the age of the others around here. The man in back of us has a riding mower . . . he mows her lawn and the lawn of the older woman on the other side of him."

Another important person in Ruby's life is Sari, a woman who provides what is called "backup support" for Ruby and Evelyn. Sari was a consultant for Residential, Inc., and is now on the Board of Trustees. She was instrumental in helping the agency make some major changes, and still, although she is no longer on the agency payroll, maintains her commitment to the values held by the people affiliated with the agency. Sari helps Evelyn and Ruby to keep their focus on Ruby's dreams and needs. Although she lives 20 miles away, she spends time with Ruby and Evelyn at home and talks to them on the telephone. She helps with the "thinking through" that must take place when problems arise.

Together, they have resisted some major threats to Ruby's new living situation, especially threats made by state licensure officials who were concerned about Ruby's safety in a house by herself. They insisted that she needed "24-hour supervision." The administrators at Residential, Inc., felt like yielding to the pressure a few times, but Sari helped them frame their responses to the state, which finally agreed that Ruby could continue living in her home. The resolution is that Residential, Inc., will pay for more than 40 hours per week of "service" to Ruby, including Evelyn's time with her. On days when Evelyn cannot be with her, others come in, although Ruby has had a hard time accepting them.

This, too, is an ongoing issue. Most important is that none of these problems was used as a reason for Ruby not to have her own home.

Today, Ruby's reputation is quite different than it used to be. Some of the old struggles still remain, and some people still fear working with her, but more people seem to see her as a capable, enjoyable, artistic, and giving woman. She is valuable to them. Many other people have found their lives enriched because of Ruby—she has reestablished relationships with people who had lost touch, and she has given people the opportunity to explore what "community" means in their lives. She has changed Evelyn's life forever, in a positive direction. As Evelyn said, "I told Residential when she moved in that even if I left the agency she'd still be my neighbor." Evelyn and Ruby are sure of their relationship now. They are neighbors and lasting friends.

WHAT IS RESIDENTIAL, INC.?

One way of defining Residential, Inc., is to say that it is a private, nonprofit agency that provides community living services to 22 people under a purchase-of-service contract with the Ohio Department of Mental Retardation/Developmental Disabilities. None of the people affiliated with this organization, however, would be pleased with this definition. In some ways, it is easier to describe what Residential, Inc., is not. It is not just an agency, although it is incorporated as one. It is not an intentional community, although it can seem like one because it sees its work as including and sharing its vision with the entire community. The people involved see the organization as being part of the community, not insulated from it. It is a group of people who share a common vision of inclusiveness, helping people develop valued roles for themselves, and creating a growing influence on the greater community.

Perhaps Sari's words, written in December 1987 (Landis, 1987) best convey what Residential, Inc., is and what it wants to do:

> Out of all that thinking and talking, writing and listening came our statements about mission and aspirations. They were very simple. We considered the people we had welcomed home [from institutions and elsewhere] "family." This organization of people would stand with, and share life with those we'd welcomed home throughout their lifetimes. We saw our mission as standing with, and assisting our family members as they created their own space, with us, in the "good life" of Perry County. (p. 2)

Sari now calls these efforts "regeneration." She said:

> Regeneration ideas focus on thinking about a particular group or community effort as an opportunity to learn more about itself and recognize the unused or underused resources within the people and the place. Ideas about self-examination, reflection, cooperation, and increasing the capacity and autonomy within individual people, and the organization, became our framework for making decisions and carrying out our work. Our appreciation of our connections with the larger community of people,

associations, and places began to grow within the first year of this new effort within Residential, Inc. Now the focus is more than ever directed toward actively affiliating with individuals and groups that are here in each of our many "communities." (Landis, 1987, p. 2)

A Short History of the Organization

Residential, Inc., was incorporated in September 1976 as a nonprofit organization. Its charter stated that its purpose was "to promote, plan, and operate residential services and facilities for mentally retarded and developmentally disabled citizens in the State of Ohio. . ." Its incorporation was the culmination of a process begun earlier that year by a woman whose son was labeled mentally retarded. She wanted alternatives to the adult foster care homes that were then the only local options for adults who could no longer live with their families, but who wanted to stay in the community.

She formed a board of trustees whose goal was to form an agency that would open group homes. An executive director was hired at the agency's first meeting, and 9 months later the first group residence, a home for eight women, opened in New Lexington. Several of the original board members were still involved in the organization as of late 1990.

One original member, Jonah, became the agency's director in September 1977, and led the organization through the changes to which Sari refers until he resigned his position in early 1988. He became a consultant to the agency, gradually reducing his hours, until November 1989 when he severed any paid relationship and was readmitted to the board. Another original board member, Jeremy, is now the assistant director. People believe this kind of continuity is important to the organization. They don't talk about replacing people, but of changing together and recognizing that people's histories are intertwined through the changes.

In July 1978, a men's residence, originally occupied by eight men, opened. In the next 3 years, the agency started a semi-independent living program in two apartments that were sublet to six men and an independent living program for 15 people. Semi-independent and independent living are funding categories still used by the Ohio Department of Mental Retardation/Developmental Disabilities, and were operated as part of a continuum that encouraged people who were "ready" for more independence to move into new residences that were seen as transitional in nature. Finally, in April 1982, two newly constructed group residences were opened next to each other in New Lexington. These homes, each of which had four residents, were built to be wheelchair accessible and were the last group residences to be purchased or built by the agency. These were the programs the agency operated—and were fairly satisfied with—until 1983.

In 1983, Jonah, then agency director, was asked to do an agency self-evaluation. This led to revolutionary changes in how Residential, Inc., saw its mission as well as how it restructured to provide an organizational climate that could support the new vision to which Sari refers. Sari explained:

> We had an internal evaluation of the organization and spent a few months doing that. An outcome of the evaluation was that people [supported by the agency] were very unhappy and things needed to change a whole lot, and at the same time an RFP [Request For Proposals] came out that was looking for rural communities to help design individualized services for people.

Today, neither Jonah nor Sari want to imply that change cannot happen without a grant. Both feel that what is important is a vision of and commitment to a better way. Therefore, everything one encounters can become an opportunity to bring the vision one step closer to fruition. For example, they redesigned the organization's structure. Jonah described the changes:

> A big part of the change was how we designed the help for people. Before 1983, there were program coordinators who did no or little direct service, but who made most of the decisions about people's lives. We restructured so that there weren't such positions, and (we) funded "service planners" instead. We froze administrators' raises, to emphasize decreasing the discrepancy between pay rates. We instituted a "rule" that each administrator should have a personal relationship with someone. We asked people to be service planners for people, with the understanding that they were agreeing to be committed to it for at least a year.

Jeremy, an original board member and a part-time associate director and part-time service planner described the restructuring:

> We examined what group living was doing to people's lives, and asked the question "Would we want to live there?" Examining that question led us to realize we would not. Some people were already in their own places, but gradually we got the idea everyone should have their own place.

AGENCY PHILOSOPHY: THE "GOOD LIFE"

A major emphasis during and after the restructuring was helping people to form and carry out what Sari calls "important life-defining dreams." The people affiliated with Residential, Inc., believe that most people have a core set of dreams, including:

1. A home of their own (alone or with people with whom they choose to live) and personal well-being
2. Financial security

3. Opportunities for continued education and useful learning
4. Supportive relationships with others
5. A positive status or image in the community

The particulars of each person's dreams are based on and guided by contemplation of each of these characteristics of the good life.

A Home of One's Own, with People One Chooses

Fifteen of the 22 people supported by Residential, Inc., now live in homes of their own (as of October 1989). Ruby's home and three others were purchased with money from Residential's reserve fund—the people who live in them pay rent to Residential, Inc. One of the homes will be owned by Lorraine, a service planner, who borrowed money from Residential, Inc., for the down payment so that James and Ray, two men who lived in the group home until August 1989, could move into the house. Ray's grandfather built the house, Ray's mother was born in it, and Lorraine will eventually own the house for them. Lorraine will also provide a great deal of the support they need to live there. Another man, Ralph, lived with a roommate before he moved into a home that was partially paid for by Residential, Inc. Eventually, Ralph will own the house. Several other people now have homes of their own that they are renting from landlords in the community.

Jenny and Orpha live in one side of a duplex, and their service planner, Linda, lives in the other side with her 2-year-old son, Johnny.

Ben, who lived with Ralph for 7 years, now lives in a triplex that his service planner helped him find. His landlady, who originally refused to let him rent, was prompted by a few of her friends, one of whom was on the Residential board, to give him a chance. Now she and Ben are good friends.

Leon lives by himself in an apartment in the back of a building that also houses the law offices of the board president.

Joshua, an adolescent who once had to live in the state institution because he frequently hurt members of his family, now lives 4 days a week with Jeremy's family and 3 days with his own family.

The people affiliated with Residential, Inc., believe that Residential's role of both the landlord and the support agency puts the people it supports in a vulnerable position; any serious problems they might have with the agency could result in the loss of their home as well as their services. They also believe that it can be difficult for people to have to rely on rental property for homes because they are then subject to the whims of a landlord who may not be concerned with their interests and needs. For that reason, Sari, Jonah, and the others have formed the Perry Housing Association, which will provide opportunities for Perry County residents to own homes of their own. The association membership includes several people with disabilities; it intends to offer its services to a variety of citizens with and without disabilities, especially those who need financial assistance to buy a home, by seeking low- and no-interest loans, and by soliciting funds to assist with down payments.

Moving people into their own homes has meant moving them out of the group homes (reducing their size or closing them). For several reasons, the Ohio Department of Mental Retardation/Developmental Disabilities has been slow to approve such moves. First, it wants the agency to agree to move more people into the group settings because there are still Perry County citizens and other residents of Ohio who should be living in the community. The people affiliated with Residential, Inc., have taken the stand that they must, for now, concentrate on the people to whom they have already made a commitment. They also believe it would be wrong to bring new people into the group homes when they believe they are not a preferred place for people to live. Residential, Inc., offered to support and assist in the development of another residential agency in the county; that agency now exists and offers group home services.

A second problem has been that certain people are classified as "needing" 24-hour supervision that the state believes can only be provided in a group home. Third, the state put money into the men's home, paying more than its value in the Perry County housing market, and paying even more to meet regulations it imposed. Now the state is reluctant to see the home sold for less than it invested. The state approved the moves from the men's home, and all but two of the men have now moved, but the issue of what will be done with the property is not resolved. The women have all moved from the original women's home, and it has been rented to a family that may decide to buy it. Each of these issues requires lengthy discussion, letter writing, and conviction on the part of the agency as a result of the differences in philosophy between Residential people and the state.

Personal Well-Being

Health, safety, nutrition, comfort, and therapeutic assistance are all related to personal well-being. Although these aspects of life are the main focus for many organizations supporting people, Residential, Inc., sees them as necessary, but not sufficient, to enjoy the better aspects of life. The organization ensures that people's needs in these domains are met, and fills out the necessary paperwork to meet the requirements of regulating agencies.

Financial Security

One can identify a number of characteristics that make up financial security. Most of these are typically denied to people who receive state-funded services. Residential, Inc., has worked in three areas to increase people's financial security: 1) ensuring that people have their own money, 2) increasing the amount available for personal use, and 3) ensuring stability in living situations.

The Ohio Department of Mental Retardation/Developmental Disabilities has insisted that Residential, Inc., receive the money for people whose support services cost more than $30 a day (e.g., SSI, Social Security) and spend it as it would be spent in a group residence. To abide by state requirements, Residential, Inc., makes sure everyone receives their own money, keeps receipts and other records of what they have spent, and gives Residential a report every month that can be sent to the state.

One way the organization has worked to increase the amount of money available for each person's personal needs has been to secure HUD Section 8 housing subsidies for people living in rented homes. These subsidies pay a sizeable portion of the rent, leaving much more income for personal use. The use of food stamps, which the agency helps people obtain, has increased personal income. Many people also receive help through HEAP, the Home Energy Assistance Program, which pays a portion of the winter heating bills.

Finally, an important aspect of financial security is stability in one's living situation. Care is taken to help people find homes where the monthly payments will not fluctuate and where they can live with the same people.

Opportunities for Continued Education and Useful Learning

Skills needed for successful living are learned in natural contexts and settings. For example, Ralph's service planner said that Ralph should not be obligated to have "programs" in his own home—he is learning to manage his money, shop for groceries, and keep his house clean without "programs." Ralph and his service planner decide together what he needs to learn and schedule times during the week when Ralph will need to do these things. These times are for both learning and doing the activities. After he has learned a skill, he may do it on his own, with a friend, or in the company of his service planner.

Learning activities go beyond skills of daily living and acceptable behavior. Residential, Inc., encourages people to pursue their interests and talents. One example is Ruby's artistic ability. Other people enjoy traveling, improving their reading skills, going to garage sales, Bible study, and building maintenance. Small towns are full of learning opportunities for people.

Supportive Relationships with Others

The people affiliated with Residential, Inc., believe that family, friends, and acquaintances are an extremely important part of life. Most people have been pulled away and cut off from family, friends, neighbors, and even former service workers they like; to the extent possible, people are encouraged to rekindle these relationships. For example, Leon was reunited with his uncle after losing contact for more than 30 years. After they reestablished their relationship, it became evident that they wanted to spend more time together. Leon's uncle was hired by Residential to do maintenance on their properties together with Leon, who accompanies him on his rounds. Now Leon attends church with his aunt and uncle and has family members with whom he can celebrate birthdays and holidays.

New relationships are also encouraged. With support and encouragement, townspeople have become involved in people's lives. These relationships are often formed through church membership, work, common recreational interests and groups, and other community group membership—they can grow into real friendships and support systems. Most of the "new" relationships seem to be initiated through an introduction. For example, the service planner might introduce the person to his or her neighbors, family members, or friends, and stimulate their interest in the person.

Encouraging informal supports requires sensitivity. If the agency is too visible or too intrusive, the chances of forming a real relationship are diminished. However, if agency employees do not get involved at all, these relationships may never occur. There is a lot of discussion about these issues among the people affiliated with Residential, Inc., and people will try many different strategies to support relationships. They report successes and disappointments, and they learn from each other.

One factor that seems to make a big difference is where someone lives. According to Jonah, "for people who live in their own places, the informal things happen pretty nicely. For the people in the group homes, the system has to kick in and substitute, do things that would happen naturally otherwise."

A Positive Status or Image in the Community

The people affiliated with Residential, Inc., believe that everyone needs to be well-liked, have a good reputation, and achieve important and valued community roles. According to them, the more invisible the agency is in a person's life, the better that person's image is likely to be. Therefore, employees act as support people and friends rather than staff members whose job is to provide supervision and exert control. Publicity about the agency tries, as much as possible, to emphasize the commonalities between people and the right of the people the agency supports to aspire to the "good life," as do other residents of Perry County.

Sari explained that "it took some time, but the people at Residential, Inc., have (been persuaded) that people in the community were prejudiced and could not learn to behave differently toward the people (the agency) supports." This change in beliefs about the community is intertwined with an emphasis on the image, reputation, and roles of individual people; it changes the dynamics of how the agency relates to the community in regard to the people it supports. For the people at Residential, Inc., believing that a person's image is important and can be enhanced means understanding that a disability does not need to be a social handicap. It also means believing that the people involved with the agency can make a difference, not by highly visible (and guilt-provoking) attempts to change attitudes about people with disabilities, but by assisting people to fill valued social roles, exhibiting their own positive regard for the people they support, and quietly assisting other town residents to find positive ways of regarding and relating to someone as an individual.

THE SERVICE PLANNER ROLE

Residential, Inc., would not have been able to move in these directions if it had not restructured and created the service planner position. The service planner does not just plan services; in fact, planning services may be the least important part of the role. Instead, the service planner makes at least a 1-year commitment to one or two people—although many have had much longer relationships—and assumes responsibility for assisting that person to attain and enjoy the "good life" as previously defined. Together, the person and the service planner create what Sari, in her 1987 report (see Landis, 1987), called a "vivid personal dream," a dream filled with details that are meaningful to the person. Then they work together to bring the dream to reality, including all kinds of people to share in the work.

The service planner is responsible for a number of tasks that are traditionally considered the responsibility of direct care workers—filling out forms; completing necessary paperwork; assisting with household chores; taking the person to necessary medical and speech, occupational, or physical therapy appointments; assisting with money management; and other tasks that contribute to personal well-being. One difference between the service planner and a direct service worker is that the service planner's tasks are undertaken for just one or two people; another difference is that the service planner's tasks are interpreted as support, not supervision. That is, the service planner's role in accomplishing these tasks is to work with, rather than establish control over or make decisions for, the person, and to provide guidance, but not to impose his or her judgment or opinions on the person unless safety is threatened. The most important factor is the interpretation the service planner puts on his or her relationship with the person.

The service planner is expected to assume more than the traditional responsibilities. He or she may be involved in helping a person find, move into, or maintain a home of his or her own. Helping a person form a support network or informal support system is seen as a crucial part of the job. The service planner is aware of the person's personal history, and participates in celebrating birthdays, holidays, and major life events. Other aspects of the role include caring about the person's image, working with the person on what he or she wants to learn, and, perhaps, getting out of the way when other relationships become important to the person. As James, the current director of the organization, said, "The service planner is expected to stand with the person and represent his interests as his own."

Because it views administrative support as crucial, Residential, Inc., supports the relationship between the person and the service planner in a variety of ways. According to Jonah, "James and Jeremy end up being the fighters—protecting people's arrangements from the rules and regulations, and the people who enforce them."

One support strategy is to identify a "backup support" person, an individual who supports the relationship and can give the extra motivation, or the extra time that may be needed to make things work for the person with the disability. Jonah said, "We are looking at widening the backup support schemes for people, and trying to honor and support those roles." They are considering identifying backup support people from the larger community and asking them to become involved. They had not done this as of late 1989 because the role, as conceived at that time, required someone with a knowledge of state requirements and politics, and the patience to deal with the red tape. Therefore, they are now reconceptualizing the idea of backup support. If a person has family or friends involved, they can become backup support people, and be effective without having to understand the bureaucracy. In this organization, even the concept of administrative support includes unpaid people, and reaches out into the community rather than only staying internal.

The process of matching a person with a service planner is done with care. Interested individuals are asked to join the organization as substitutes, working where they are needed. As they become familiar with people, relationships may form, and the administrators have the opportunity to see whether the person has the qualities they look for in a service planner. The individuals in this study had been deeply involved in the selection of their service planners. This, of course, helps to get the relationship off to a good start—the people involved begin with a commitment to make it work.

When Residential, Inc., designated this role for people who would traditionally be called "direct care staff," it demonstrated its faith in the capacity of all people, with and without disabilities, in their community and elsewhere, to excel when they are respected, trusted, and supported. Jonah said he had seen people, who in traditional organizations would be thought of as direct care staff, become, when they were selected as service planners, committed, responsible people who made an enormous difference in someone's life. He believes that people will respond if others believe in them.

Jonah and James said, however, that because they have had difficulties in recruiting service planners, they are rethinking the recruitment process. They are beginning to consider all their contacts and connections, not just the people looking for employment who are able to take substitute positions, as potential service planners. The people they are connected to—board members, people who know someone as a friend or neighbor, and so on—may be asked to be someone's service planner, either on a paid or unpaid basis. This might involve redesigning the expectations for the service planner; in some cases, another employee might take care of some of the day-to-day tasks. This employee might also be close to the person, but would not have the service planner's advocacy and planning responsibilities. Nor would he or she be as involved in helping make the person's dreams meaningful or real.

James mentioned several examples of new ways of finding service planners. Leon's new service planner, for example, is the father of Janet, his previous service planner. They had developed a good relationship and when Janet moved, it made sense to ask her father to take on the role, with different responsibilities than she had had. This man is also the neighbor who painted Ruby's walls and is president of the Ohio Township Trustee Association. His connections have benefited many people affiliated with Residential. In another instance, a long-time friend became one person's service planner.

OBSTACLES AND UPCOMING CHANGES

For many years, the people affiliated with Residential, Inc., have faced barriers to what they define as the "good life" for the people supported by the organization. These barriers have loomed larger and changed in nature since the internal evaluation and restructuring that began in 1983. Several of these barriers have already been noted:

The fact that people are not allowed to own their homes if they are service recipients

The requirement that people whose supports cost more than $30 a day cannot receive their own money

The pressure to move someone new into a group home whenever someone leaves

The conflict of interest that occurs when Residential, Inc., is both landlord and support service agency

The need for state approval for people to move from a group home

The problem of what to do with an empty group home, especially if the
state holds a lien on the home

The organization has struggled with these obstacles while the people
involved held fast to their vision of the "good life." In spite of the barriers,
15 people have achieved a part, if not all, of their dreams. Many people
were forced to wait until the approvals could be given and the problems
overcome before they could achieve their goals, and others are still
waiting.

Yet, there are other obstacles, just as onerous, that are still prevent-
ing people from achieving their dreams:

Each person's home has to be licensed as a facility and pass state and
local health and safety codes. They have to be inspected at least
once a year.

People who are living in their own homes, but whose supports cost
more than $30 daily, are required to be classified as group home
residents.

The state only has a few funding categories for adults living in the
community; they are designed around a continuum-of-services
concept that is rigidly interpreted and that ties the level of support a
person needs to a type of housing. These include independent and
semi-independent living, group residence, and ICF/MR categories
of service.

The state payments differ for each person, not necessarily according to
his or her needs; the organization has not been able to pay for
support (outside a group home) for anyone who needs support for
more than about 50 hours per week.

There have been problems finding the right home and support situation
for some individuals. There are two brothers who have been waiting for years while a number of living situations were identified and
explored, but found not to be suitable.

Most of these obstacles are statewide issues. They present barriers
that have deterred other agencies in Ohio from attempting to do what
Residential, Inc., is doing. Although the organization has struggled with
each of these barriers, usually finding a way to make things work for
people, Jonah said:

We haven't been very active in trying to make statewide change. We
really feel like what we're trying to do here . . . only applies where

there are people willing to make long-term commitments to folks. To try wholesale change statewide could be disastrous because people would get out in those individualized situations and be isolated. . .

There's a difference between an organization making a commitment to maintain a person and having people in long-term commitments to each other. I think it takes people in long-term commitments to create an organization. We have a good number of original board members and people that started with the agency. People's history and the organization's history are intertwined.

Jonah's concerns about wholesale change, without the kinds of values the people at Residential, Inc., hold, are legitimate and need to be considered by an organization thinking about moving to the approaches used here.

Dilemmas in Supporting People—A Unique Problem-Solving Style

One situation involved two men who had lived together for 7 years, but were no longer getting along and had begun to fight with each other. One man was injured, and his family members wanted him to move immediately. There were two easy alternatives available for him: the men's group home or an apartment in the local senior citizens' center. Family members felt strongly that these were appropriate alternatives and would solve the problem. The other man was not able to afford the rent payment by himself, so he also had to move. A great deal of pressure was put on Residential, Inc., administrators to accept the easy solution—to move the injured man immediately. James and others agonized over what to do, considering many options. For example:

The injured man could move into his girlfriend's house on a temporary basis. The family, the man, and the girlfriend all agreed.

Before that decision was reached, the other man's service planner offered to stay overnight, without pay, for as long as it took to find both men new homes. His perception was that most of the problems occurred in the late evening and early mornings, and he thought he could defuse them.

Many people spent a great deal of time supporting James and offering suggestions as he struggled with the possibilities and the pressures. Special attention was given to the issues that might compromise their values, even temporarily, and to handling the possible consequences.

They also spent a lot of time trying to sort out what the men involved wanted and could afford, apart from the pressures from family members and others.

Part of their problem-solving approach was to wait and not do anything until a suitable alternative presented itself. Waiting gave more people time to think of natural solutions (e.g., moving into his girlfriend's place for a while). It also gave Dave, the service planner, time to think about staying in their house. Waiting is difficult, especially when it entails resisting pressure for quick solutions, but it seems a crucial component of the approach they use.

When asked whether Jonah saw any dilemmas in supporting people, like the dilemma posed by this situation, where one value—family connections—conflicts with another value, he said, "Well, there are two kinds of dilemmas, the kind you need to learn to love, and the kind you hate to have. That was one that people needed to love." The dilemma came about because the injured man had so many people involved in his life, and because they were willing to engage in conflict with each other, if necessary, on his behalf. Both men are now in their own homes. Ben, the man who was injured, has his own apartment in a triplex, and Ralph has recently moved to his own home, too.

PERRY HOUSING ASSOCIATION
AND OTHER COMMUNITY REGENERATION IDEAS

One of the ways the people affiliated with Residential, Inc., have become a part of the community is through the formation of the Perry Housing Association. Their vision is the regeneration of the community in Perry County, and the association is just one manifestation of that vision.

The Perry Housing Association is still struggling with how it will carry out its mission and is using ideas from a number of sources, including *The Community Land Trusts Handbook* (1982) and a new homeowner's program operated by the state of Ohio. The association has assisted one man, Ralph, to purchase a home, and is pursuing sources of no-interest and low-interest loans to assist other people who cannot get a home through conventional means. The bankers and other leaders in the county have responded favorably to the association's work.

Sari and Jonah are especially interested in the concept of community regeneration. They have purposefully tried to diversify their own incomes so that they will not have to rely on human services work to make a living, and can allow their perspectives to guide their work. Both of them say that being outside the system (e.g., not serving as administrators or consultants) has made them more effective as mentors to the other people affiliated with Residential, Inc. They can still remain involved with the agency, but not be as caught up in the daily pressures and "hassles" that accompany administrative positions. Also, they can more fruitfully pursue their own dream of community if they are outside, working through the organization, but not within it. Jonah said, "It's easier for me to keep analyzing, to keep an idea of our vision, now that I'm out of it. People and agencies need mentors, backup support people, who are outside and can keep them focused on their mission."

Their dream of community extends beyond their work with Residential, Inc., however. Jonah is on the school board in his town, and he works with the County Historical Society on projects that celebrate the county's history. He is a member of the Perry County library board, a member of Consu-Theater, Inc., and the editor of a newspaper he created called *Community Life News*. He is also a co-owner with his mother of the Community Exchange, a gift store on Main Street in the very small, old mining town of Shawnee.

Jonah and Sari are in touch with a number of organizations that discuss and publish materials on community regeneration. The two major influences on their thinking are Community Service, Inc., in Yellow Springs, Ohio, and the Rodale Institute, in Emmaus, Pennsylvania. Both of these organizations have a long history of community work. Another influence is the Highlander Center in Tennessee, an organization that trains people to be community activists. This organization relies a great deal on learning from experience and sharing what is learned.

CONCLUSION

Residential, Inc., is a unique organization that is willing to share its vision, approaches, and problems with the human services world. Its leaders have, over the years, examined and reexamined what the organization is doing, and have committed themselves, by learning from the organization's experiences, to the "good life" for people with disabilities and all the other people the organization reaches in their many "communities." Their vision is shared by new leaders who have continued to develop and refine the approaches that have become "our way of doing things." They are in and of their community; they trust and inspire each other; they are friends.

14

"WE DON'T PUT UP THE ROADBLOCKS WE USED TO"

AGENCY CHANGE
THROUGH THE CITIZENSHIP PROJECT

Pamela Walker

Alternative Living, Inc. (ALI) is a nonprofit agency supporting people with developmental disabilities in Anne Arundel County, Maryland, which includes the small city of Annapolis, and some of the exurban and suburban development south of Baltimore. In the mid-1980s, the agency provided residential support to 79 people with developmental disabilities (125 full-time and part-time staff) to live in small scale settings such as group homes for four or six people or supported apartments for two or three people. These settings were a significant change from the large facilities that many of the people with disabilities had lived in previously.

In addition, the director and assistant director became convinced that further change could be made by the agency, which would even more significantly affect and enhance people's lives. They recognized that even in small residential settings (e.g., three to four people), the supports provided to people are not necessarily individualized in nature. They had heard that other places had already initiated change in an effort to provide more individualized supports—shifting from supporting people in agency-owned group homes and apartments to assisting people to rent and own their own homes with whatever support necessary (Taylor, 1991; Walker & Salon, 1991).

The author wishes to acknowledge the assistance of Carol Beatty, Shelley Halbig, Pamela Butler-Stone, Connie Lyle O'Brien, and John O'Brien in the preparation of this chapter.

All names in this chapter are pseudonyms.

In 1987, in partnership with the Human Services Institute (HSI), a private training and consulting organization in Maryland, and with a 3-year grant from the state developmental disabilities council, ALI launched its "Citizenship Project." This chapter, based on a 3-day visit to ALI in April 1990, begins with a brief overview of the design of the Citizenship Project. The chapter also describes how people's lives and some agency staffing and administrative structures have changed as a result. The last section discusses the lessons and challenges of the agency's efforts at change.

THE CITIZENSHIP PROJECT

The Citizenship Project was designed as a 1-year cooperative effort of ALI and the Human Services Institute, which would begin a process of agency change and lay the foundation for further change through the development of a "strategic plan." The three central objectives of the Citizenship Project were (Alternative Living, Inc., 1988):

1. To empower people to be participating members of the community
2. To demonstrate the effective inversion of Alternative Living, Inc. by changing our role and relationship with those who rely on us
3. To develop the capacity of the community to accept people with disabilities as contributing members of the community (p.3)

The project was also divided into three phases: Phase I—getting to know the people, Phase II—strategic planning process, and Phase III—the strategic plan.

Phase I included three components: 1) get to know 15 people with disabilities, whom the agency staff support, differently through a creative life planning process, using "personal futures planning" (Mount & Zwernik, 1988); 2) plan for their futures with the community and their family and friends; and 3) redirect the agency's resources toward accomplishing these plans.

Phase II focused on gathering information and studying the implications of Phase I for programmatic and organizational change. This involved a meeting of the leadership team (HSI staff, and the director and assistant director of ALI) and program coordinators from ALI (each of whom supervises a number of house counselors and community living assistants) to determine what ALI needed to do in order to see that personal futures planning goals were realized and to identify themes in each of the plans.

Phase III entailed the development and adoption of a strategic plan to guide the organizational transformation of ALI. Figure 1 outlines this strategic plan. The plan laid out a mission statement and a vision, or set of principles, to direct further change, as well as a set of "strategic goals" focused on: 1) individuals with disabilities, 2) internal organization

---

Vision and Guiding Beliefs

ALI has a vision that a person who has the support of family, friends, and ALI, is in control of his or her life, and that the center of the person's life is community. The following belief statements provide the foundation for ALI's mission and the guiding principles for its work. We believe that:

The person

. . . is a citizen worthy of dignity and respect and has a valuable contribution to make to the community.
. . . is competent to make choices both independently and with the help of friends and family.

Relationships

. . . with family can play a vital role in providing support, companionship, and love, and should be actively supported and nurtured.
. . . with friends are formed through a mutual give and take, and give meaning to one's presence in the community.
. . . formed through a support network (which may include family, friends, neighbors, coworkers, and others) will help the person to grow and expand their participation in community life.

The home

. . . is a place that reflects the person's lifestyle, personality, and choices of where and with whom to live.
. . . provides a sense of ownership, security, and control in the person's life.
. . . is the person's base from which to establish a sense of belonging to neighborhood and community.

The community

. . . is the place where one finds dignity and respect through citizenship.
. . . has the capacity to include and welcome all its members.
. . . is the place where individuals, groups, and organizations move beyond self-interest to realize their interdependence and interconnection with one another.

ALI's Mission Statement

Based on these beliefs, ALI's mission is to:

Empower and support persons who rely on ALI to create and maintain a lifestyle of their choice. ALI works with these people to find homes, jobs, friends, and opportunities to participate in everyday community life. ALI is committed to actively build and maintain the networks that will nurture personal growth and dignity as well as sustain and enrich the person's quality of life over time.

Figure 1.   ALI's strategic plan.

issues, and 3) external community issues. These strategic goals are highlighted in Figure 2. The plan was developed with input from the leadership team, as well as ALI program coordinators, house counselors, community living assistants, and office staff, through discussion meetings, questionnaires, and interviews.

Individual Focus

Continue the personal futures planning process to empower individuals to make choices in their lives.

Ensure that the individual's choices with regard to their home and lifestyle are honored.

Direct ALI resources to respond to and honor the choices expressed by individuals.

Those individuals who rely on ALI shall have the opportunity to share in the governance of the agency.

Internal Organization Focus

Revise the individual planning process to be consistent with the personal futures planning process, focusing on individual choices.

Establish a monitoring system that will ensure that ALI's resources and decisions respond to people's choices with regard to home and lifestyle.

Actively respond to staff's concerns about agency and staff role change.

Develop an organizational culture in which:

1. Expectations in terms of authority and accountability are clearly defined and consistently followed.
2. Beliefs and values are internalized and clearly reinforced at each level of the organization.
3. Everyday office norms, such as punctuality, following through on commitments, and honest and open communication contribute to an efficient and well-functioning team.

Establish ongoing orientation and training of staff, board members, and other volunteers that reflect the new mission and belief statements.

Review and revise:

1. By-laws
2. Policies
3. Staff roles, including job descriptions and responsibilities, as well as performance evaluations

Establish a financial planning process to track and allocate available resources to accomplish the mission.

Community External Focus

Reconcile the differences engendered by the transition to a "new" ALI structure with the Developmental Disabilities Administration and other federal, state, and local organizations (pertaining to funding, licensing, regulations).

Advocate on each person's behalf with regard to their choices for work, volunteerism, or daytime opportunities.

1. Advocate for their rights and interests at work or in their day program.
2. Pursue opportunities that reflect people's choices.

Build a partnership with community individuals and organizations to accomplish the mission of ALI, and to contribute to the quality of life in Anne Arundel County.

Figure 2.   ALI's strategic goals.

In 1987, staff from the Human Services Institute facilitated the first 15 planning processes in Phase I. They also provided ongoing training and consultation to agency staff. This included training of what "community" is and strategies for involving people in community places and social networks; training for agency staff in the facilitation of "personal futures planning"; and assistance with the development of strategies for decision making and problem solving. The staff's role was also to help keep the agency "on track" during the course of change by reminding them of their vision within the context of daily, weekly, and monthly decisions.

After completion of the Citizenship Project, HSI phased itself out of ongoing involvement in the agency change process. Over the next year and a half, the agency continued facilitating personal futures planning for 50 additional people (by the time of the visit in April 1990) and worked at implementing the plans set forth for 65 individuals.

WHAT CHANGED FOR PEOPLE

During the personal futures planning, a number of people indicated that they wanted a change in residence. Some people moved to small settings, while others already lived with one or two people, or by themselves, but wanted a change in roommates or a change of location.

Other people did not want to move. Some of these people were in small group homes with groups of people they liked and did not want to move away from, or they were already in apartments with roommates of their choice. In these situations, the agency did two things. First, it worked to change the role of in-home staff to that of a roommate more than a trainer or teacher. Second, it assisted people to make changes in other priority areas of their lives, such as work, relationships, and leisure/community involvement.

Joe and Ed

Joe and Ed both lived in institutions and group homes before moving to their own house. They knew each other prior to living together, and at Joe's personal futures planning meeting he suggested that he would like to live with Ed. In February 1989, they moved into a small house in a quiet, residential neighborhood. Andy, a college student, is paid to be a live-in roommate and to provide a range of support; his brother, Pete, lives in the house and is paid for part-time assistance to Joe and Ed.

Andy has a naturally "social" personality and has used this to help all of them get to know their neighbors. He has a personal sense of ownership and investment in the house and in neighborhood relationships. For instance, when asked about house and yard upkeep, he explained that one of the reasons he attends to this is because of his feeling that "It's my house, too." He and Pete also assist Joe and Ed to maintain other relationships, including helping Joe keep in touch with his mother through cards and phone calls, and helping Ed learn to phone his girlfriend independently. Ed indicated at his planning meeting that he

would like a trip to Disney World, so Andy and Ed made the trip together.

Teresa

Since January 1990, Teresa has shared an apartment with a woman
named Ellen. In the 2 years prior to moving to the apartment, Teresa,
who is labeled severely mentally retarded and has epilepsy, lived in a
variety of other settings. These included: living in a group home for
seven people with disabilities; sharing the home of a staff person and
her children; and sharing an apartment with her best friend, another
woman with disabilities, with staff support. Currently, she rents a two
bedroom apartment with Ellen, who lives there as a roommate and
support provider.

In Teresa's personal future plan, which was developed in March
1988, her "dreams" included a desire for a "smaller living arrangement." At the time of this plan, she was living in the seven-person group
home. The agency, therefore, arranged for her to move in with one of
the agency staff members and her children. However, staff report that
this did not work out because of the conflicting demands on the staff
person's time from Teresa as well as her children. Next, the agency
assisted Teresa to move in with a close friend, with staff support. The two
friends, however, found that they were not well suited for living together. Finally, in January 1990, staff assisted Teresa to rent her own
apartment, and the agency contracted with Ellen to live there as a paid
roommate.

Due to Teresa's lack of experience in various living situations and
the severity of her disability, she represents a person for whom the
agency has had to make "best guesses" about potential living situations.
This has clearly resulted in a lot of movement for her. This planning
process, though, was one of the first that they did when they were all
"new at it." Staff also report that they have now "gotten to know Teresa
better," which will hopefully guard against continued movement.

Shirley

For years, Shirley worked at a sheltered workshop. At a planning meeting, Shirley expressed the desire to be a veterinarian. Staff explained
that they could not "make a commitment that being a vet would happen . . . (but they would try) to find out what she likes about it." As a
result, Shirley has worked in a pet store since the spring of 1989. During
this time, she and the store owner have developed a relationship of
mutual support. Over time, the owner has supported and trained Shirley
to perform a growing number of tasks in the store and has attended
Shirley's meetings at her request. For her part, Shirley makes a valued
contribution to the store, and, as one staff member said, "When she goes
on vacation, her employer hurts."

Cindy

Cindy, who has been labeled moderately mentally retarded, is in her mid-30s and shares an apartment with a friend who has also been labeled as having a developmental disability. Both women previously lived in institutions and group homes. They have been living here for 3 years—since before the Citizenship Project began.

At Cindy's planning meeting in May 1988, she indicated that being with her boyfriend is a top priority. She said she would like to marry him, and have him move in with her and her roommate. She said she wanted to take a vacation with him, which already had been planned. Following this meeting, Cindy and her boyfriend, who is also labeled mentally retarded, went on their vacation to Ocean City, accompanied by a staff member. As a next step, agency staff plan to form a "circle of support" (composed of people selected by Cindy and her boyfriend— staff, family, friends, or other people close to them) around both Cindy and her boyfriend, to assist them in working out plans for the future.

WHAT CHANGED WITHIN ALI

Beginning with implementation of the Citizenship Project, there were three major areas of change for Alternative Living, Inc., which included: 1) new staff positions, 2) changing staff roles, and 3) changing staff attitudes.

New Staff Positions

The new staff positions involved hiring two "community guides," paid for by the developmental disabilities council grant, to help facilitate community connections and relationships. In addition, other people have been hired on a contractual basis to work as community guides. These guides attend personal futures planning meetings and subsequently assist people with a range of needs, including finding jobs, finding volunteer work, and developing and maintaining relationships. The community guides accompany people to various settings, such as job sites; spend time getting to know people in these new settings and assisting the person to meet new people; try to determine what types of support the person needs and who might provide it; and then approach people, if necessary, to determine their willingness and ability to help. The community guides typically spend a few weeks in a setting with the person; after that, they check in to see how things are going and/or to assist with any problem solving.

For example, Henry, one of the community guides, assisted Phil, who is supported by ALI, to get a part-time job working in a local restaurant. His co-workers provide on-the-job training, as well as support when he needs it. For Phil, this is not only a source of work, but also social relationships because he occasionally participates in social gatherings outside of work with his co-workers. Another person assisted by a community guide is Greg, a man in his forties who wanted to "help children, particularly children with disabilities." A community guide introduced Greg to Mike, a young boy who lives in a small group home run by ALI. Mike has severe disabilities and cannot walk, talk, or perform other self-care activities on his own. Greg visits him at least twice a week to talk to him, hold him, and assist him with eating. Mike seems to be content and happy when Greg comes, and Greg values his relationship with Mike perhaps more than any other relationship.

A challenge for the agency has been the high turnover rate of people in the two community guide positions. In the first 2 1/2 years of the project, there were six people in these two positions. According to one staff member, this may have been due to a number of factors; for example, the job can be very demanding, if not overwhelming, to people who think it will be "cushy." Also, the need to find the "right person" for the job may have been part of the reason for the high turnover rate.

Changing Staff Roles

One component of the Citizenship Project was the opportunity to change all staff roles to some extent. One change was to have all staff, not just the community guides, take part in facilitating relationships and community connections. Some staff members have been able to adjust to this new role fairly naturally and easily. For example, Kim is a live-in support staff member for three women with disabilities who live together in a house. During their personal futures planning meetings, all three women chose to stay in this house because they know and like each other, and enjoy living with Kim. Kim has assisted them to form relationships with neighbors and with people in a local church congregation. They offer to bake for a neighbor and to host a church Bible study group in their house. They also participate in neighborhood and church events.

For some staff, particularly some of those who have worked for a long time in more traditional residential services, this change in role has been challenging and difficult. There are three primary reasons for the difficulty: 1) some staff members were used to caregiving and found it hard to change their stance and style to one of support or assistance; 2) some staff members were not convinced of the applicability of the personal futures planning process and its implementation, particularly with respect to someone with severe disabilities; and 3) some staff members have been hesitant about this type of change and assisting people to become more involved in the community because of a "mistrust of the community."

A second change was redefining the role of in-house staff from that of a trainer or teacher to that of a roommate. This does not mean that staff are not involved in any type of teaching or training. It also does not mean that the staff and people with disabilities ultimately have equal control or power within the setting. However, it is an attempt to make the relationship more balanced, giving the person with a disability an increased sense of a shared home and encouraging the staff person to be more like a roommate than a trainer to the person with the disability.

A third change, at the administrative as well as direct-care level, was, as described by the director, the attempt to "turn the power structure upside down—giving power to people with disabilities." This was envisioned within the context of the Citizenship Project to occur through an agency role of listening to people (within the personal futures planning process); assisting them to make decisions about dreams, needs, and desires for their future; and then assisting them to make some of these a reality.

Since the beginning of the Citizenship Project, the agency staff have assisted people to make decisions about things they would like, and assisted them to attain some of these things. However, agency administrators recognize that the actual inversion of the power structure "has not happened very well," and that they still retain significant power and control over people's lives. For example, they still determine which decisions or desires will be responded to, in what ways, and in what time frame. Some of the constraints to the actual inversion of power include the agency's position within a bureaucratic human services system and the staff members' dilemmas over safety issues versus personal choice.

Changing Staff Attitudes

Agency change included the staff's attempt to change their views of people with disabilities and the community. Participation in the personal futures planning process, and being part of some of the change process, has influenced many staff members to change their perspectives about people with disabilities and, in turn, to change the way they treat them. As one staff member explained, "We view people differently; we don't put up the roadblocks we used to." Several staff members echoed this sentiment.

Effort has also been spent trying to work through difficulties they have relinquishing some of their power and control over people with disabilities. Time is spent at staff meetings allowing them to express their feelings about this.

Finally, many staff have begun to change their attitudes about the community, seeing it as a potentially supportive and nurturing place rather than a hostile one. This change has come as they have witnessed specific examples of support given to people in various community settings. They have let go of some of their overprotectiveness, while at the same time maintaining a concern for safety and well-being of the people they support.

LESSONS AND CHALLENGES FOR THE FUTURE

Throughout the course of their efforts at change, ALI staff members have learned a great deal about personal and agency change from successful experiences as well as challenging experiences. Several areas they have learned about, and challenges they face, are described in the following sections.

Personal Futures Planning

The agency used personal futures planning with individuals as a significant component of agency change. It was an attempt to change the way they provided support, and change the hierarchy of power and control by listening to people with disabilities first, giving them power and control, and basing supports on people's requests and desires.

The initial personal futures planning processes resulted in some significant change for people whom the agency supports in terms of living arrangements, work, and other areas of their lives (Mount, 1989). In the meantime, staff and people who were not involved in these initial planning processes noticed some positive changes and requested the same. For example, staff report that people began asking, "When's my meeting?" Based on the initial successful experiences and the enthusiasm generated by them, the agency initiated 50 additional personal futures planning processes in the following year and a half. This resulted in a situation where they accumulated an increasing, and eventually overwhelming, number of personal futures plans while the staff time, energy, and resources to commit to them was simultaneously decreasing. Such a situation has the risks of "institutionalizing" a tool such as personal futures planning so that it becomes routine, and the possibility for significant change resulting from it is diminished.

In terms of the planning itself, agency staff realized that it was not an end result in itself, but a tool. As the director said, "We need to keep going back to the plans and changing and revising the directions we are going with people." They also learned that there is not an ideal number of people for a planning process, and that there can be advantages, depending on the person and circumstances, to having both small and large groups.

The agency learned about the importance of also including the person with a disability when following up with the plan. For instance, as one staff member explained, "At first, it was . . . here's what we can do for you; later, it was more like . . . what things can you do to contribute to working toward this?"

Also, in follow-up, the agency found that it was those people who were most vocal themselves, or who had a vocal person committed to them, who tended to have the most changes as a result of their personal futures planning process. This was not due to a problem inherent in personal futures planning, but rather to conducting a large number of personal futures planning processes over a short period of time with inadequate resources to respond to them. In light of this, a challenge to the agency for the future is to ensure that a small group of committed people are involved in each personal futures planning process.

Planning with people who have severe disabilities has also been a challenge to the agency. Admittedly, they have "stumbled" more in trying to determine what types of living arrangements, roommates, jobs, and other community involvements will be best suited to the person's likes and needs. Staff members also have concerns about life changes, safety, and well-being of people who have severe disabilities and may be more vulnerable. They already have experience assisting some people with significant impairments to live in their own homes and/or work at regular jobs. They can build on the lessons they have learned from this experience to assist others.

Related to this, a challenge to the agency is to assist all staff members to have positive experiences with personal futures planning. This can help the staff, particularly those who have worked in traditional human services with people having severe disabilities, to see how these people can be assisted to make choices, live in their own homes, work, and participate in other aspects of neighborhood and community life.

Agency Change

Whether an agency uses personal futures planning and/or other tools and means for organizational change, there are some lessons that can be learned from ALI's experience about agency change. First is to be cautious about letting the enthusiasm of the initial changes lead to too much change too soon. It is important that agencies proceed slowly, taking the time to learn from changes and experiences. The determination of how much to change, and when, is critical (Lyle & O'Brien, 1991). Second, at the same time that the agency was attempting to make significant changes, the larger system in which it is embedded remained the same. For instance, many people's "homes" are still licensed and highly regulated, and it is still difficult to assist people who receive Medicaid funding and/or who have high levels of needs to live in their own homes and apartments. While staff members don't put up the "roadblocks" they used to, other "roadblocks" are still in place.

The agency learned that it was important, but also difficult, to get all staff members involved in and excited about the changes. This was particularly true for some of the part-time and overnight staff, as well as some staff members with backgrounds in traditional human services approaches. Many strategies have been utilized to try to generate and increase enthusiasm, including sharing stories at staff meetings, sharing stories in an agency newsletter, and giving staff members the opportunity to raise and discuss concerns, problems, and strategies. These, however, have not succeeded in generating unanimous enthusiasm.

During the course of any type of agency change, new roles, demands, and pressures are placed on staff; they will need time and positive experiences to adjust to the changes. They may also need new and different types of support from agency administrators (Lyle & O'Brien, 1991). One factor that made the process of change difficult for some staff members at ALI was the large number of personal futures plans. These resulted in some staff members feeling overwhelmed by new tasks and commitments, and they saw that some of the plans were not resulting in significant change for people. Based on this, a continuing challenge to the agency is to determine how to support staff members in new and different ways, and how to involve staff members in ways that give them the opportunity to experience significant and meaningful personal change for people they support.

Assisting People with Life Changes

In the process of personal futures planning, the agency learned that not everyone wanted to move. However, they recognized that: 1) this did not mean the person might not want to move some day; 2) there were other changes that could occur in the person's life that could also have a significant impact (jobs, relationships); and 3) some people might not want any changes where they are living (or working) because they have had little experience with change and/or are not aware of other possibilities.

ALI already has assisted numerous people to make some changes in their lives, particularly in the areas of housing and jobs. A challenge to the agency is to stand with these people for the long term, recognizing that people's lives are complex and that situations that may seem to be going well after a few months may "fall apart" within the next few months (Lyle & O'Brien, 1991). Agency staff and administrators recognize that the changes that have been made are just a beginning, and that significant challenges lie ahead in the continuous support of people. There are a few aspects of this, in particular, that will need attention. First, agency staff, particularly the community guides, have been quite successful, at least in the short term, in finding community members who are willing to support people within work places and other community settings. However, the challenge will be to ensure that these supports continue to be provided for the long term. Also, some people with disabilities may need ongoing support by a paid worker for a long period of time (several months or even years). The agency must make sure that it has the capacity to support people with such needs, and ensure that they also receive equal opportunities for community involvement and participation. Second, the agency has some very competent, capable people as live-in, paid roommates. It must continually seek ways to recognize and support their work. This will help minimize staff turnover and at the same time contribute to increased stability in people's lives.

Work

Prior to Citizenship Project, ALI did not typically involve itself in work issues. Most people who lived in the residential settings went to sheltered workshops. However, in planning with people the agency discovered that getting a job was a high priority for a number of people. Therefore, the agency became involved in assisting people to find work.

If, however, a paying job cannot readily be found, agency staff members try to help the person find volunteer work or an activity that is meaningful to them. Some people have clearly expressed a desire to "help others." For a few people, however, this has resulted in their participation (albeit as a "helper") in highly segregated settings. Such settings are not the most desirable for people who are already devalued in society. It is positive that the agency has responded to people's need to "help others" and make contributions to their communities. A challenge for the agency is to continue assisting people to find ways of doing so, but in integrated, valued settings.

Support for Children

Although the agency has made efforts to make settings more homelike, children who are served by the agency have remained in the small group homes to a greater extent than adults. This is largely due to the issue of guardianship, and the inability of the agency just to go out and recruit families for these children to live with. However, the issue of children in these types of settings is a challenge for the agency to face in the future. One option includes deciding not to operate group settings for children and, instead, offering in-home supports or assistance in finding another family for a child.

CONCLUSION

This chapter describes an agency that, before initiating a process of change, was providing supports with which many people and professionals would have been very satisfied. However, for the director and assistant director of this agency, that was not good enough. Although the residential settings were small, they realized that people still were not being listened to very well, did not have much choice about where and with whom they lived, and were still being "fit into" the service system. Within the context of this realization, they had the courage to change and try a new way.

This path of change has not been an easy one to take—bringing with it new difficulties and challenges for which there are no guidebooks. In the process of change, they have learned a lot about the people they support and a lot about themselves. The greatest lessons of their experience have to do with the complexities of people's lives and personal change, and the complexities of organizations and organizational change. Overall, the experiences, lessons, and challenges of the agency in the process of change are invaluable resources for other agencies that may be considering making changes in the way they support people and in their organizational structure.

BIBLIOGRAPHY

Alternative Living, Inc. (1988). *Strategic plan, 1988-1989.* Annapolis, MD: Alternative Living, Inc.

Lyle, C., & O'Brien, J. (1991, August 1). [Personal correspondence].

Mount, B. (1989, September). *New dreams, new lives, new directions for Alternative Living, Inc.: A report on the initial outcomes, findings and implications of the Citizenship Project.* West Hartford, CT: Graphic Futures, Inc. for Human Services Institute and Alternative Living, Inc.

Mount, B., & Zwernik, K. (1988). *It's never too early, it's never too late: A booklet about personal futures planning.* St. Paul, MN: Metropolitan Council.

Taylor, S.J. (1991). Toward individualized community living. In S.J. Taylor, R. Bogdan, & J.A. Racino (Eds.), *Life in the community: Case studies of organizations supporting people with disabilities* (pp. 105–111). Baltimore: Paul H. Brookes Publishing Co.

Walker, P., & Salon, R. (1991). Integrating philosophy and practice. In S.J. Taylor, R. Bogdan, & J.A. Racino (Eds.), *Life in the community: Case studies of organizations supporting people with disabilities* (pp. 139–151). Baltimore: Paul H. Brookes Publishing Co.

15

"I'M NOT INDIAN ANYMORE"

THE CHALLENGE OF PROVIDING CULTURALLY SENSITIVE SERVICES TO AMERICAN INDIANS

Susan O'Connor

PAUL'S DRUGSTORE

I met Anna, Della, and Reena in September 1989, during a 4-day site visit to Southern Hills Developmental Services (SHDS), an agency providing services to people with disabilities in the small South Dakota community of Hot Springs. After talking with each of these women during the first few days of my visit, I was delighted to be asked to join them on a sunny fall day to have coffee at "the drugstore." We all piled into my rental car for the short journey that would have been a quick walk for the three women on any other day, but first Della wanted to show me where she lived and worked.

Being from a small community in the midwest and growing up in the late 1950s and 1960s, I was reminiscing about that romanticized

I would like to extend a special thanks to all of the people of the Southern Hills Developmental Services for their warmth and welcome on my visit, especially Becky Schweitzer, JoAn Dean, Karan Goesch, Paul Hemiller, Carol Fast Horse, Duane Leighton, Ron Bagola, Terry Steele, and Vera Sawalla who spent time sharing their work and stories with me. A very special thanks goes to Freida Wounded, Ida Warrior, and Dorothy Cutgrass Donnell for inviting me into their homes and sharing their experiences with me. And finally, to Lilah Pengra and Janet Moran for the time and compassion that goes into their work. They all made me want to return!

It is important to identify myself within the context of this chapter. I am a European-American; I visited the Pine Ridge Reservation and SHDS for only a brief time. I do not presume to know or be able to clearly depict the richness and depth of the Lakota culture and all that surrounds the people's daily lives. It is only through further dialogue, listening, and mutual respect that we can begin to listen to each other. I personally was grateful for what I learned.

feeling of small town hospitality that I sometimes believe I grew up with. The worries of the city were far away and a sense of familiarity was already with me after these few short days. I followed my new friends into territory that I realized they knew quite well.

As we entered Paul's drugstore, I was struck by the emptiness of the shelves. It was as though the drugstore was only a facade for the important part of the store, the soda fountain in the back. A woman appeared wearing bright pink lipstick that matched her polyester smock; her beehive hairdo and pointed glasses completed a classic, stereotypical image of small town America that I had stored away. She followed us to the back. Della knew exactly where she was going and what she wanted. "Hi, Diane," she said with a wave, but little eye contact. Both Reena and Anna repeated the greeting and were immediately responded to by name. To avoid feeling out of place, I did the same as we all snickered. We passed a half full rack of greeting cards and made our way to the soda fountain, where the women had things to discuss and coffee to order. From a corner, just a few feet away, came a yell of "Hi, Della." All three women turned to respond with a greeting and a wave. A woman stood behind the J.C. Penney ordering counter with catalogues strewn about. She quickly walked over to Della, whispered something to her, and they giggled as she returned to her spot.

Diane seemed to know what each of the women wanted before they ordered. Yet, on this day, they added a doughnut to the order because I had offered to pay. Della got up and moved to one of the three kitchen-like tables used by patrons. The conversation, in which Diane was an active participant, revolved around how much weight the women had lost. Anna reminded them that she had won the trophy several weeks in a row for losing the most weight. All were impressed. The familiar word TOPS (Take Off Pounds Sensibly), one of the first major weight loss programs, came up several times. They talked about weighing in, and as the conversation continued and the coffee cups emptied, several other women passed through to order coffee or to make a purchase. It was as though they needed to see who was there and offer a quick "hi."

After we finished, the three women seemed to be in a hurry to get on with their respective evening activities. They all exchanged goodbyes, and Della waved and said, "I'll see you tomorrow."

This was a very ordinary Friday afternoon activity for women living in a small town. The difference, however, was that Della, Anna, and Reena are American Indian[1] women, and the other women are not.

---

[1]The word Indian is used throughout this chapter because it is what the people I talked with choose to be called.

Anna and Reena lived most of their lives on the Pine Ridge Indian reservation located about 50 miles away from Hot Springs. Della and her sister, who was described by agency workers as severely disabled, had been taken off the reservation when they were very small and placed in one of South Dakota's state institutions. Della went mainly "to keep her sister company." All three of these women are labeled by the social service system as having a disability and are living in Hot Springs receiving services from SHDS. At Paul's drugstore none of this seemed to matter; everyone appeared comfortable in this situation. Yet, behind this warmth and inclusiveness lies a deep history not always filled with such acceptance for the individuals and the agency that encourages them to be part of this community. This is a story about such an agency and the people it serves. It looks at how one small agency strives to meet the needs of all the people they serve, especially the Indians who make up half of the people using their services. It also touches on the lives of people in a rural community and the services to these people from a small agency trying to maintain its autonomy at a time when bigger is presumed to be better.

In order to better understand the meaning of services to Indians, it is important to look not only at programs, but also at the cultural background of the people using the services of this agency. Therefore, the first discussion will be about the Pine Ridge Indian Reservation and the Lakota culture, including some of their traditions. This will be followed by a description of the Hot Springs community and Southern Hills Developmental Services, and the challenges they face in providing culturally sensitive services.

During my visit, I interviewed and spent time with the agency director and staff as well as people receiving services. I attended an evening in-service and visited the vocational and residential services. I also accompanied them on several of the social activities within the community that are part of their daily lives. One day was spent with Janet,[2] an Indian staff person at SHDS, and Anna and Reena on the Pine Ridge Indian Reservation. Because this chapter focuses on an agency run mainly by non-Indians, many of the perceptions of the Indian culture are described through their understanding of that culture. These understandings come from talking to Indians on the reservation and at SHDS, as well as living in a community where both Indians and non-Indians live. Also unique to this agency is the fact that it's director, Lilah Pengra, holds a Ph.D. in anthropology. These factors guide how the agency staff struggle to provide culturally sensitive services.

---

[2]With the exception of Janet Moran and Lilah Pengra, all other names are pseudonyms.

THE LAKOTA OF PINE RIDGE

> They made us many promises, more than I can remember, but they never kept but one; they promised to take our land and they took it. (Red Cloud, Chief of the Oglala Sioux, 1870)

Driving through the Black Hills in South Dakota, heading south toward the community of Hot Springs, there is little that reminds one of Chief Red Cloud's words. The countryside is extraordinary in its richness and beauty, but one must imagine the early west and what happened to Chief Red Cloud and his people. Today, much of what remains for the Sioux is in the form of reservations. For the tourist, souvenirs suggest memories of cowboys and Indians. The great Mt. Rushmore, with the heads of presidents, offers the visitor the illusion that the history of the West began when the great white men were carved into the mountainside 50 years ago.

The promises that were broken when the land was taken from the Sioux, as they were from many Indian tribes across this country, have had an overriding effect on their lives today. Although this chapter is not written directly about the loss of that land, the story of Indians being supported at SHDS cannot be understood without knowing the context of their culture and the oppression they have faced.

Pine Ridge

The Pine Ridge Indian Reservation, located in the rolling hills and prairie land in the southwestern corner of South Dakota, is home to approximately 22,000 Lakota Sioux Indians. In this state of 700,000 people, Indians comprise 75,000 of that number. The per capita income on the reservation is $4,600, only one third of South Dakota's average, and the lowest in the country. Unemployment on the reservation is more than 80%. Only 2,000 people are employed in an 11,000 person work force, mainly in government or tribal jobs.

In the past, the reservation had several places where people could buy groceries, especially produce. It also had a cannery and a moccasin factory that has now moved to Rapid City. There are several grocery stores on the reservation, but many people drive to communities just off the reservation, which are called border communities, to buy their items at more reasonable prices. Most jobs now require people to leave the reservation and this presents the problem of transportation. There are many small towns on the reservation and a lot of miles between them. Often, even for doctors' appointments, people must hire someone to transport them, which could cost as much as $20 round trip.

Most people live in small government-built homes in scattered housing projects. In many cases, a large number of family and extended family members live in one household. Housing availability is an issue, especially in the more rural areas around the reservation.

Many of the reservation's residents fall in a world between European-American and Lakota traditions as they have interacted with communities outside the reservation in order to survive monetarily. Yet, this land remains the spiritual center for many of the Lakota people and is said to be the place where the soul of the nation endures.

Lakota Culture

The term Lakota refers to the tribal name as well as the language spoken by the Lakota Sioux. Historically, the Sioux moved from North Carolina to Minnesota, and then to the plains. By the late 1860s, through a treaty with the U.S. government, they had already been confined to territory in South Dakota that at the time covered nearly half of the present day state. That amount of land decreased to the size of today's reservations as a result of "agreements" in 1876 and 1889 with the U.S. government as well as the discovery of gold in the Black Hills, making the land more valuable to the government and non-Indian people. There are two reservations where Lakota Sioux live today, one called Pine Ridge where most of the Indians discussed in this chapter are from, and the other called Rosebud.

During the early attempts at assimilating Indians into mainstream culture, both the federal government and the church constructed schools and worked to instill western values within the Indian culture. According to Grobsmith (1981), many children were taken from their homes and placed in boarding schools where they were forced to learn English and to give up many traditional ways and practices. They were whipped if they spoke Lakota to each other, and were often sent to work as domestics in non-Indian households during the summer. In spite of such attempts, the language and the culture of the Lakota survived, but not without some acculturation of values and beliefs from non-Indian culture.

Lakota Traditions, Values, and Beliefs

The spirituality of the Lakota people is something very sacred to them, and has an impact on many areas of their lives, including social interaction, feelings of identity, and disability. Although all Lakota people do not practice any or all of these ceremonial traditions, they remain an important part of the culture. There were many ceremonial traditions that were highly discouraged and were illegal until the 1950s. Sun dance, for example, a ceremonial ritual, was illegal from the 1880s to the 1950s; yet, it survived and began to thrive again in the 1950s.

Sun Dance   The sun dance is the most sacred of Lakota rituals. It is used today to unite the Lakota people in a ritual of self-awareness, political consciousness, and common identity (Grobsmith, 1981).

Yuwipi   Another ceremony that was illegal for 40 years, but survived because it went underground, is the yuwipi ceremony. This ceremony focuses on curing and healing and is also important for resolving conflicts in a person's identity; for example, someone who lost something or someone considered to have a problem with drinking. Yuwipi is seen as a healing of the community as well as the individual, so there is strong community support; yet, the focus remains on one person.

The Sweat Lodge   The sweat lodge is considered one of the oldest rituals in Lakota culture. It is a ceremony or purification rite that is performed regularly. It is sometimes a preparatory cleansing for another ritual such as sun dance, or sometimes it is a rite unto itself. The purpose of the sweats is not just a physical cleansing, but a spiritual purification for men and women.

Today, many of the ceremonies thrive; this includes both religious and cultural ceremonial functions such as pow-wows. These are practiced along with Christianity, which was absorbed and practiced by the Lakota. Some of the Indians participate in several religious and cultural practices; therefore, they might belong to the Catholic and Episcopalian churches, but still take part in the sweat lodge and sun dance.

Equally as important as traditions are the strong values of the Lakota culture. They are often described as sharing, family oriented, respectful, and aware of their individuality. The expectation with sharing is that when you need something you can ask for it or when you have something others may need, they can ask for part of it. Family is also highly valued in this culture. This includes being part of a family as well as honoring its members, which can mean staying together in the face of outsiders. Respect is also an important value. For example, using limited direct eye contact and simply respecting the presence of others without needing to engage in extensive verbal exchange are behaviors common to many Indian people and are misunderstood by many non-Indians. Finally, individuality, another value in the Lakota culture, is one way that people express their distinct characters. Understanding these values is important in trying to understand the culture of the Lakota people.

On the reservation, there remain political separations that affect how the Indians interact with each other as well as how they interact with people outside of the reservation. Some of the separations are related to the beliefs about differences between Indians who are considered to be full bloods and those who are mixed bloods.[3] Some people believe that the higher percentage of full blood a person is, the more Indian he or she is. When asked what it means to be Indian, one staff person replied, "Well, it's blood!"

---

[3]Although inferring that a person's race depends on blood can be viewed as racist (Three Rivers, A., 1990), the words full blood and half blood and full breed and half breed were used interchangeably by both the Indian and non-Indian staff with whom I talked.

Understanding the Lakota culture, if only to the limited degree presented here, is integral to understanding the Indians served at SHDS and becoming aware of the differences that may surface as these two cultures meet. Having some knowledge about the community they are coming to is also important.

THE BORDER COMMUNITY OF HOT SPRINGS

A windy road going south through the Black Hills leads to the small community of Hot Springs located about 60 miles south of Rapid City. Hot Springs, a town of approximately 5,000 people, is a border community to the Pine Ridge Indian Reservation.

Many of the community people are in some way, usually through employment, connected to either the state Veterans Home or the federal Veterans Administration Medical Center. There are two Department of Housing and Urban Development (HUD) high-rise buildings serving the community whose population comprises at least 50% older adults. As a result of this large percentage, they are not viewed as a devalued group by community standards.

A border community carries many negative connotations as well as stereotypical attitudes because of increased opportunities for the Indian and non-Indian cultures to meet. As exemplified in the story that opened this chapter, there are many relationships that have developed by people getting to know each other through activities, such as combining the pow-wow and the rodeos. Often those Indians and non-Indians traveling each circuit have shared interests.

There are also a number of prejudices that have developed about the Indian population, one of which concerns the consumption of alcohol. Alcohol is sold in the border communities and not on the reservation. People who want to buy or consume alcohol must drive to border communities; therefore, alcohol-related violations and accidents on the highway between Pine Ridge and Hot Springs continue to increase, as they would given any group in a similar situation. According to Lilah Pengra, the director of SHDS and a member of the community, there is a tendency for negative stereotypes.

> Often a prejudice in the community confuses poverty and the things associated with poverty such as alcoholism . . . with being Indian . . . people don't understand that being drunk is not part of the Indian culture . . . it becomes magnified when it's Indian.

Another area that lends itself to negative stereotyping within the Hot Springs community is the eligibility of Indians for surplus commodities. Sometimes commodities are sold for cash by the Indians to people in town or ranchers in the area who are enthusiastic buyers. These interactions can be viewed two ways. One is that the Indians are taking advantage of the system. The other, which takes into consideration the lack of jobs and the history of poverty that exists on the reservation, is that they are reversing a bad situation. Two of the major commodities given to the Indian people are powdered milk and cheese. Many of the Lakota people have a lactose deficiency, which makes these products useless; therefore, they trade them for items that they need.

SOUTHERN HILLS DEVELOPMENTAL SERVICES

Southern Hills Developmental Services is one of 17 Adjustment Training Centers (ATCs) in South Dakota providing community services to adults with disabilities. Each ATC is a private, nonprofit organization offering both residential and day services. ATCs are governed by regulations from the department of human services and are highly reliant on funding from the division of developmental disabilities (Racino, O'Connor, Shoultz, Taylor, & Walker, 1989). Each of the ATCs vary in size from those serving as many as 200 people to others, such as SHDS, serving 22 people with only enough funding for 14 people. SHDS has a total of 17 staff, 6 Indian, one of whom is a member of the board of directors, and 11 non-Indian. High staff turnover is an issue at the agency as they must compete with the two Veterans' facilities whose wages can start as high as $7.20 an hour.

Looking beyond the traditional ways of providing services is what makes SHDS different. The vision that the agency has created over the past year is one that all of the people served can live in places of their own, or with a roommate, and work in the community. There is also a vision of inclusion and a push to look at the individual and his or her specific needs. Much of this vision was created and is driven by the director, Lilah Pengra, who has contributed a sensitivity and awareness to the issues concerning the Indian population. Although she believes that there should be an array of services on the reservation, she also feels an obligation to deal with the situation that presently exists. She explained: "What I'm trying to do is to get staff to understand you can teach someone to cope with this environment, to live successfully in Hot Springs, but you don't have to teach them not to be Indian to do that."

Lilah is very adamant about making the distinction that culture is not exclusive to Indians, that we all have cultures that have an impact on our lives. However, she said, "It is just most striking here; we're dealing with a group (of people) who have been blatantly stripped of power for many years."

The importance of cultural backgrounds is an awareness that is part of the agency's philosophy for all of the people whom they serve. Lilah explained:

It's a very individual thing. You can't just say this client is Indian; therefore, we are going to put him on a savings program, and this person is not so we're going to put him on this program. Of course not, there is individuality there . . . if you teach everyone exactly alike, you think you're not discriminating, but yet you are because everyone has different needs and different values.

A major focus during 1990 was on Indians being served by the agency and how their needs were or were not being addressed.

Services Provided by the Agency

SHDS supports people in a number of ways. The agency has one traditional group home with a 50-year mortgage through Farmers Home Administration (FmHA). Lilah, however, does not think that having this mortgage will hinder them in moving people into places of their own. This home offers beds to 14 people. The residents eat together in a dining room crowded with tables. Staff in the group home provide support and try to facilitate connections with people in the community. For the most part people are free to come and go within the community.

There are also eight people in community training services, which is support offered for a certain number of hours per week to assist residents with shopping, cooking, money management, or other supports that they may need. Funding comes through the Home- and Community-Based Services (HCBS) waiver through which the agency receives $38 a day per person.

Six of these individuals live in subsidized senior citizen high-rise apartment buildings at two locations in town. They are not allowed to have roommates in these apartments because of rules by the Hot Springs housing authority. They pay $95–$112 per month; general housing stock would cost $185 in Hot Springs. The biggest problem in helping people move into the community is the difference in the amount of money they must pay for rent if subsidized housing is not available.

The agency has tried to create flexibility in the provision of services. Lilah explained, and several staff members reiterated, "We're trying to develop alternatives with the system we have, you know "A" versus "B" and nothing in between."

SHDS provides a variety of work situations as well. Although many of the people who live in the house attend the ATC day program (what many would call a sheltered workshop), there have been community alternatives developed during the past year by Pat, the vocational coordinator, and two full-time people, both Indian. From fall 1988 to fall 1989, people started working at a factory in town or joined a work crew at Archies, a local restaurant and bar that closed because of a fire. The contact with Archies was made because someone who used to work at the bar began to work for SHDS. The importance of connections and people who know people in the community plays a large part in job acquisition. Pat is trying to work with local businesses such as Pizza Hut to develop jobs. One problem with acquiring jobs at local businesses is that they are often family owned and tend to hire family members first.

ISSUES OF CULTURE AND SERVICES

Services on the Reservation

In order to understand how staff at SHDS think about providing services to Indians, it is important to provide a context related to services on the reservation and the culture as SHDS staff understand it. This has a great deal of impact on how they approach provision of services.

Indians have typically received services through the Indian Health Services, Bureau of Indian Affairs, and the state social service system in South Dakota. The point of entry usually comes through the Indian Health Service, a branch of the public health service providing health and medical services on the reservation, including a well-baby clinic, emergency and surgery services, maternity care, and all hospitalization needs. It also attends to environmental health care issues in public places such as schools. The service deals with every kind of disability, yet, people with developmental disabilities are a low priority because issues such as mental health and alcoholism receive the most attention, at least in terms of dollars spent. Bonnie, the case manager at SHDS, said, "When people are referred to services off the reservation, it is often because families feel they have tried everything and now must try the white way." There are also public health nurses who make home visits to families on the reservation. Janet talked about her mother's experience as a visiting nurse on the reservation:

> She used to go in and they would check babies' feet and hands for signs of fetal alcoholism. There was one mother who knew something was wrong with the baby, so whenever my mother would come, she would hide the baby and say it wasn't there or that her grandmother had it. Mom could usually hear the baby cry. They hide them because they are afraid you're going to take them away.

The lack of trust in services makes many people leery of seeking them out. As Janet said, "The culture would tend to take care so people would tend not to enter the system."

"Maybe Parents Would Keep Them Home if They Had Some Help"

SHDS is invested in trying to provide culturally-sensitive services to Indians who are forced to move away from their communities because the services they need are only available off the reservation. Often, such services are not sensitive to their cultural needs. Indians may have, according to Lilah, "difficulties when they move to cities because of cultural conflicts. This often leads them back to the reservation where, in many cases, they are absorbed back into their families and are often written off to the system." Janet reiterated, "For a lot of Indians, those who are mentally retarded, maybe parents would keep them at home . . . if they had some help."

Providing services off the reservation has become a major challenge to SHDS. Lilah reiterated that their major commitment would be to serve the Indians on the reservation. She explained:

> I think for many individuals it would be better to stay in their own community with their family. . . We really should have an agency on the "res"; there used to be but it closed because of health standards. . . There were . . . different values on how things should be done. If the standards are culturally biased and are applied, then you close the place instead of finding other ways to do it.

One example related to the lack of services on the "res" involves an Indian man living on the reservation who was on the SHDS waiting list. His main "work" on the reservation was his daily visit to the post office where he greeted everyone who came in to do business. He was described as "having nothing to do" in the referral, but Lilah said:

> He could be trained to be a mailman. He knows everybody and they all know him and like him and talk with him . . . why should we take him out of that? He lives with his sister. The main problem is the inconsistency in taking his medications. He is the kind of person where if we had an outreach on Pine Ridge it would be perfect. Don't take him out of his community just so he gets his meds everyday.

If a child is taken off the reservation it is usually because all other possibilities have been exhausted and the family can no longer provide the necessary support. Sometimes it is the result of the death of a significant caregiver. The actual separation from the reservation means more than just physical removal from the land, especially for those families who are full bloods. This distinction of blood, described earlier in this chapter, has an impact on how staff at SHDS understand the needs of people being referred to the agency. The family name can also tell them about the family and aid in their understanding of the person's background. Lilah explained:

> Indians could identify which communities were mixed and which are more traditional. If the person is from one community, I only have to see a name and know it's a more traditional family, or from another community I'll know they are much more white-oriented and have a lot more experience with white teachers and ministers. They speak English. They understand the rules of both.

These insights help Lilah and the staff identify what it will mean for the person and family to adjust to a new environment.

For example, when I asked if people being served by the "res" who were now earning money were more valued because of these earnings, one Indian staff member responded, "It could be looked at positively by half breeds but not by full bloods. To them they have lost a family member to white society. It is a failure." Looking at each individual then becomes a priority in service provision. An example of this individualized support can be seen in John, a young Indian man in his 20s who had been referred to SHDS.

"We Had to Build Trust": John's Story

John is a 24-year-old man caught between two worlds. His label of "dually diagnosed" seems in some strange way to describe the two worlds he has had to straddle by being part of the human services system and moving off the reservation. John has little connection with his father, and for a number of years he lived with his foster mother on the reservation until she could no longer support him. His natural mother died at his birth.

Before coming to SHDS, John had lived in six agencies, including psychiatric institutions throughout the state. In these institutions, he was told that he had such severe behavior problems that nobody would keep him. He was known to "walk into a place and disrupt everything." When he was referred to SHDS, a long list of "behaviors" and problems came with him.

When John first came to SHDS he wouldn't do anything. Pat explained:

> He felt restricted. He had to take on white man's community, but we didn't want him to feel he had to become a white man. We wanted to let him know that he could go back to Pine Ridge, that we weren't going to keep him from his friends. He wouldn't even talk; he needed to adjust to us. He got here, rebelled, and didn't want to do anything. We gave him a lot of leeway, time, and space. Basically, we just gave him support and that worked. We also had to build trust.

On several occasions John went back to the reservation, only to return when his stepmother said she couldn't keep him. John had a strong desire for physical labor and to work outdoors; he rejected many of the indoor jobs found for him. Finally, he got a job breaking up old concrete for a cement crew. Now he has expressed an interest in working on a ranch, a prevalent job in the area. As Pat said, "It would be a great job for him because he likes (the) outdoors."

The agency has also tried to support John by listening to his needs and respecting his culture. John believes that he possesses spirits; he is often pursuing ways to rid himself of them, and he has expressed a desire to go to a medicine man. Pat explained, "We found a medicine man that he can go to because that's what he wants." SHDS will support John when and if he chooses to see a medicine man.

Often, during referrals, there is little consideration given to where family members live or how the job market is in a particular area. Hot Springs has been good for John not only because of its proximity to the reservation, but also because he has an uncle living in one of the nearby veterans' homes whom he can visit when he chooses. Staff at SHDS are open to arranging visits to the reservation at John's request. Although all of the things John struggles with are not solely related to cultural differences, at SHDS he is listened to and respected rather than being written off as a behavioral problem as he had been in the past.

CHALLENGES OF PROVIDING CULTURALLY SENSITIVE SERVICES

Support at SHDS is viewed in many ways and occurs on many levels. An awareness of the needs of people from other cultures has been challenging to this agency, but it has also helped them to grow.

One challenge is their desire to hire bilingual staff. At the time of my visit, there were three bi-lingual staff members and three members who are Indian and only speak English. Lilah discussed some of the concerns of her non-Indian staff regarding people speaking Lakota within the agency, including that the non-Indian staff think they are being talked about when they hear Lakota. She said, "I told them, 'Yeah, but maybe our clients think that when you're speaking English.' I use every opportunity . . . to bring cultural awareness without beating them over the head and saying this is cultural awareness."

There have been a number of opportunities created within the agency to at least begin to respond to the language needs of the Indians being served. The agency now pays for a teacher of the Lakota language, and staff can attend classes on their own time. Within 6 months, class enrollment rose from one staff member to six. Although the staff will not become bilingual, they will at least understand some of the people who speak only a few words of Lakota. This effort by the staff demonstrates a receptiveness to the Lakota language and provides another way to communicate with the Indians.

There are people served at SHDS who may only speak in one-word sentences in English, but use four-word sentences in Lakota. Bonnie described how the degree of oral language used by non-Indians is greater than that used by Indians so that assessments "do little to measure abilities." The agency is looking at more non-traditional ways to learn about the people they serve as well as trying to view the person's actions as indicators of their abilities. Bonnie explained:

> We have to take into account the person. One individual had a propensity for . . . taking candy in the house. That would be looked at as being very negative, but this person took the time and effort to: a) figure out where the candy box was, and b) determine when staff was or was not located near the kitchen, find the key, use it, relock the box, and return the key to its place. Verbally that wouldn't score high, but it took a lot of thought to do so.

The issues of privacy and comfort with silence are also important. Although the dominant culture (typically defined by European-American, middle-class norms and values) in this country has a tendency to want to fill silence, this is not required by most Indians. There is a need for company, meaning that someone is simply there, but not necessarily speaking. The issue of silence is also important to understand the needs of a family when they bring a child to SHDS. Bonnie explained:

> With a Native American family I introduce myself then I make a generic remark. . . Then I will remain silent and wait for their response. If I get overly assertive I usually don't elicit any responses and it becomes a negative situation. We don't do a lot of social history taking. Usually this is a grief process because they are losing a family member, so I don't want to ask too many questions.

This awareness and sensitivity is important to Indian families, as it should be to all families, especially when they are letting go of a child. It is equally as important for contacts with the agency and the child in the future. Although this may never be a place where a family feels completely at ease, there is an attempt to make the family trust and feel welcome at any time versus feeling that their child is no longer a part of their world and culture. Many of these lessons can be applied to all families.

"I'm Not Indian Anymore": The Story of Anna Brave Heart

The changes that occur individually for Indians leaving the reservation to receive services, and the respect the agency tries to show for each person, is exemplified in Anna's story, beginning with her move to Hot Springs.

Anna is a warm and friendly 26-year-old woman who has lived in the SHDS group home since 1988. Her round face and smile seem to welcome nearly everyone she meets. Her blue polyester pants and colorful flowered shirt fit the stereotypical image of the dress of a small town older woman in the midwest. Anna is well known in Hot Springs; few can avoid her engaging "hi's," whether it be a wave as they drive down the street or a chat as they sip on their coffee in one of the local cafés.

Since moving to Hot Springs, and into the group home at SHDS, Anna has become very active in the community. She has joined an aerobics class and goes to TOPS exercise group two times a week where she has won trophies for her weight loss on several occasions. Anna speaks both Lakota and English, and she is involved in the Lakota chapel, the Catholic church, and a Bible class made up of Indians and non-Indians. Anna also works on a job crew at the workshop and often, on weekends, she visits her boyfriend who lives in a nearby high-rise. She lives a very active life, and as Janet said, "She doesn't like being alone. She likes people."

Before moving to Hot Springs, Anna lived on the reservation with her family in one large room. She worked closely with her grandmother to take care of the other members in the household; they struggled financially. After her grandmother's death, which is still difficult for Anna, she was moved into the nursing home on the reservation by the department of social services. Anna lived there for a short time, but she was moved because state law had an age requirement and Anna was too young to continue living there. The only alternative was to move off the reservation, so she was moved to Hot Springs and into the group home. Since moving, Anna has had almost no involvement with her family even though the agency has tried to keep such connections as open as possible. However, she has returned to the "res" several times for visits.

After moving to Hot Springs, Anna struggled with the changes that she encountered living outside the reservation. One of her first requests was to tell the staff that she didn't want to babysit: "I had enough of taking care of kids." Yet, there were many other things that would unfold as time went on, aspects of her life that were different as she and the staff discovered what it meant to Anna to be Indian. Anna would return to the reservation and people would tell her that she was different. Lilah pursued what being different meant to her at that time and she responded: "I don't know, I don't know, well, I'm not Indian anymore." When asked what makes her Indian, she replied, "wearing dresses." It is common in the dominant culture for women to wear pants instead of dresses. Anna wore sweatpants to her exercise programs and aerobics classes, and at her cleaning job she saw other women wearing pants and started to alternate them with dresses. Yet, to her, this represented not being Indian as she had worn dresses all her life. Some days, according to staff, Anna puts her "other clothes" on; dealing with that transition is important to her. Another activity that Anna found different was getting her hair cut. "We didn't even think of it," said one staff person. "She identifies that with being different than home."

Anna also discovered that her opportunities to speak Lakota were very limited. Although she speaks English very well, keeping and using her native language was important. The staff found a friend in the community who also speaks Lakota with whom Anna could spend time. They have since developed a friendship. They meet weekly for coffee, a piece of pie, or to attend church together.

The SHDS staff were confronted with conflict as some of them referred to one of Anna's habits as "theft." Lilah explained that Anna took things as a result of the poverty that her family lived in. She described the situation:

> Having adapted to living on the streets for a long time, she likes to accumulate things. She must feel secure enough, and when she's ready to let go, she will, and if it takes 20 years that's fine. You can't expect her overnight, to change, for all she knows the next meal may not appear. Why should she believe we are telling her the truth. She's making plans for when it's going to be like it was.

Now, Anna seems happy with her new environment. She chose to stay in the group home for a while, and said that she doesn't want to live alone for now.

"I Get a Little Lonely Sometimes": Reena's Story

Reena, like Anna, had lived with her family on the Pine Ridge reservation for most of her life. She is a small woman, less than 5 feet tall, with a square build. Her straight brown hair hangs to her shoulders, and she has a soft spoken manner and a giggle in her voice. Reena's slow moving pace and good natured smile make people like her immediately.

Reena was referred to SHDS by the Indian Health Service after her mother died and there was some speculation of abuse. As she talks about growing up, she conveys a strong sense that she was a major contributor to the work that went on at home. Upon moving to Hot Springs, Reena lived in the group home for about 6 months. She quickly insisted that she move out on her own. Now, she lives in one of the two subsidized high-rises about two blocks from the group home, where she is a frequent visitor. If she has a problem, she knows she can rely on the people there to help her out. Reena also receives community living training, which means that a staff person spends 20 hours a week with her to support her with shopping or other needs she may have. Although she may feel lonely at times, she still wants to live alone: "I get a little lonely sometimes. I don't want a roommate though; I want to live by myself. I like that, I really do. I got my refrigerator and my radio and my TV." She also proudly shows visitors her sequin work and the shawl she uses for pow-wow dances.

One of the issues that the staff had to work out with Reena was to encourage her to make her own choices, while at the same time trying to offer her some skills so that she wouldn't be taken advantage of in the community. Both culturally and personally, Reena is someone who will often give people things; sharing is part of her nature. Since moving on her own she has had frequent visits by one of the men who works at the veteran's home up the hill from her. On a number of occasions he has asked Reena for money and/or food, which she has often given him. The staff thought she was being taken advantage of, and began advising

Reena on how to become more assertive, a valued skill in the mainstream culture. They tried to teach Reena that she could say "no" to him if she wanted. Reena described using this new skill: "I say go to work and make your own money!"

Yet, learning to be "assertive" has presented Reena with conflicts and has been hard for her. Practicing this new skill alienated Reena from her own culture on a visit home. On one visit, a male cousin who was underage asked that she buy alcohol for him and she refused. After the incident, Reena felt somewhat ostracized. She was ignored and not spoken to for several days. Consequently, she doesn't want to stay very long with her family; yet, the agency has worked to help Reena contribute with food and gifts for the children when she does return home so that sharing occurs. However, if not viewed within the larger cultural context, what is empowering in one situation, and maybe necessary, may be alienating in another environment.

Another issue that often comes up in service system living is diet. After a check-up, Reena was found to have high cholesterol and was placed on a low cholesterol diet. Previously, part of her daily diet was traditional Indian frybread, which she made every day from scratch. However, frybread is high in cholesterol, as it is made with lard, and it was recommended that she not eat it. Instead, the staff helped her choose other types of oils to fry it in. This may seem trivial, but unless people are aware of the differences and the importance of details in a culture, this aspect of Reena's culture could have easily been ignored.

COMMUNITY CONNECTIONS

Within a small community, especially, there is a strong need for personal connections and being well-acquainted with neighbors. The agency sees community integration as more than a presence and uses every opportunity and every connection as a possible way to introduce the community to the people in the agency, as well as the agency to the community. Bonnie summed up her feelings about SHDS and what they were learning: "One of the things I appreciate from a small agency is that we all make mistakes and we share that with the clients, that we are all learning and growing. This is a neat agency for that."

Their relationship with the Indian community is also very important. Lilah talks about how she has been told on several occasions to go to Indian Health Services for financial help. She commented, "I intend to." Indian Health Services and the tribal council[4] are potential re-

---

[4]The tribal council is the main governing body of the tribe and consists of a president, vice president, and representatives from all of the communities on the reservation. The function of the council is to administer programs and services to members of the tribe, and to develop and conserve tribal property and resources.

sources, but it is important that they see how SHDS is benefiting their people.

CONCLUSION

It was difficult to focus on this agency in any one way. The agency's awareness of cultural differences has created a great deal of sensitivity toward all the people they serve. This chapter could also have been a story of community integration in small town America because the strengths of SHDS also lay within this realm. The stories here present a variety of ways in which an agency has attempted to be sensitive and respectful to Indians and their culture. These insights, sensitivities, and ways of treating people are reflected in the fact that many of the people involved in this agency come from another culture and challenge those around them to pause and think before forcing the same kind of service on everyone. There is a sense of mutuality that exists, making it clear that the staff are not the only teachers. The staff are continually presented with lessons from people outside of their own world: a different language, different customs and traditions, and an insight into the history of oppression that makes up the lives of many of the people they serve. If services must take place off the reservation, the Indians who are served must be listened to, respected, and be part of creating those services. They must not have to totally give up pride in their heritage and their histories to receive support.

Knowing people for who they are and really listening to them is something that is very difficult for us all, and especially for agencies who must follow guidelines and regulations that depersonalize and categorize culture, class, gender, or disability. SHDS has tried to support Indians living within the Hot Springs community; yet, they do not have the answer to a happy life. The Indians have been placed outside of their homes and their culture into communities that have many stereotypes about their disability and their heritage. The larger, more looming issues of powerlessness, poverty, and oppression that American Indians face in this country must continue to be brought to the surface for real change to occur. In the meantime, there are pockets of people and agencies who are challenging themselves, their beliefs, and their values. These are people often tucked away where the scope of their work may appear limited, but where changes occur daily between people. They are people who make relationships, respect, and listening priorities.

Everyone has a history, whether it is a history from living as an American Indian, an African-American, a European-American, or any of the other numerous ethnic groups that inhabit this country. Although there are many factors such as ethnicity, race, social class, and gender that make each of our experiences different, people must begin to recognize and strive, as the people of SHDS are doing, to challenge their assumptions, their prejudices, and themselves, and work *with* people rather than against them. We must begin to acknowledge and learn from the rich histories and the oppression that has made up so many of our lives.

BIBLIOGRAPHY

Grobsmith, E.S. (1981). *Lakota of the Rosebud: A contemporary ethnography.* New York: Holt, Rinehart and Winston.

Racino, J.A., O'Connor, S., Shoultz, B., Taylor S.J., & Walker, P. (1989). *Moving into the 1990s: A policy analysis of community living for adults with developmental disabilities in South Dakota.* Syracuse, NY: Center on Human Policy, Syracuse University.

Three Rivers, A. (1990). *Cultural etiquette. A guide for the well-intentioned.* Indian Valley, VA: Market Wimmin, Box 28, Indian Valley, VA 24105.

16

CENTER FOR INDEPENDENT LIVING

DISABLED PEOPLE TAKE THE LEAD FOR FULL COMMUNITY LIVES

Julie Ann Racino

The Center for Independent Living (CIL), the "first organization of its type in the world," is a visible symbol of the independent living movement, the international civil rights movement of disabled people.[1] Since 1972, when a coalition of severely disabled people founded the Center, CIL has become a mecca for the disabled. It is "now recognized worldwide as the inspiration and archetype for more than 300 independent living centers" (Center for Independent Living, 1989).

Following the civil right's and women's movements, disabled people took the lead to create conditions where they would be free to live their own lives and participate fully in the community. Called the independent living movement, it brought people with all kinds of disabilities

This chapter is based on a qualitative research site visit conducted October 19–20, 1989, with a subsequent visit on December 7, 1989. The author wishes to thank Judy Heumann, board member; Michael Winters, Executive Director of CIL for facilitating this visit; and Gerald Baptiste, Associate Director, for his time, insights, and arrangements during the hectic days following the earthquake. Thanks also to Adina Frieden, David Lewis, Phil Chavez, Sandra Stone, Marcia Ortiz, and others for sharing their insights and time during the visit; to Chris and Joel Sarch for the hospitality they extended during and subsequent to the earthquake; to Bonnie Shoultz, Susan O'Connor, Pam Walker, Rannveig Traustadottir, Sally Johnston, Judy Heumann, and Steve Taylor for their comments on draft versions of this chapter; and to Rachael Zubal for her assistance in the preparation of this chapter.

[1]The author uses the political terminology of disabled people, which is preferred language by people associated with this organization instead of people-first language, such as people with disabilities. Use of the word disabled in this chapter stems from a form of disability pride—"disabled and proud."

together to work for supportive services, and the federal, state, and local governmental changes necessary for full community participation. Emerging from the Physically Disabled Students' Program at the University of California-Berkeley, CIL was designed and operated by disabled people, with the goal of integrating disabled people into the community-at-large.

CIL and the people associated with it have played a powerful role in the history of disability legislation in this country. The associate director described their role in working with other groups around Section 504 of the 1973 Rehabilitation Act:

> A group of people from CIL (together with a coalition from the Bay area) took over the federal building in San Francisco. . . . Well, everybody was saying, those disabled people, they'll be here for a couple of hours and then have to go back to the hospital. . . . Little did they know that those disabled people were from Berkeley.
>
> They ended up staying . . . (more than) 23 days. It was getting such hot publicity that people started coming out in droves in support. The Black Panthers were coming down bringing food everyday . . . all types of churches (were involved); everybody was coming in. The mayor realized they were serious. (Part of) the group . . . decided to trek to Washington to tell the story as it unfolded. They did a candlelight vigil. With the publicity, they finally set out (the regulations for the) law.

CIL has also played a major role in change in California, for example, in the area of accessible transportation, which is still a critical issue across the nation. As Gerald Baptiste, the associate director, said:

> We have pretty accessible transportation. Again, one group of disabled people decided to go to (the) San Francisco . . . transit terminal where the buses come over. . . . This was peak hour when everybody was trying to get off work and get back (home). A group of disabled people went over and laid down in front of the buses. So they (the transit authorities) realized we had better get to the negotiating table with these people. So that's how we were able to get accessible buses in this area.

The current mission of CIL, as adopted by the board of directors in 1987, is "to create and maintain independence for disabled people through providing services, advocating for the rights of disabled individuals, and nurturing a system of support in the community." Since its inception, CIL has maintained a focus on both supportive services and advocacy, although the balance has changed during the years. Throughout its first 16 years, CIL provided direct services to more than 140,000 people, built 500 residential ramps free of charge for wheelchair users, helped 1,000 people secure jobs, and assisted more than 600 students to complete the independent living skills training program (Center for Independent Living, 1989).

Starting with a grant for $15,000, CIL reached its financial zenith in 1978 with a budget of $3.2 million and 200 employees. Partially resulting from cutbacks in funding for social efforts, as of October 1989, CIL had 51 employees and a $1.8 million budget.

HOW IS THE CENTER ORGANIZED?

CIL is a membership organization with more than 500 members who elect the governing board. The board consists of approximately 15 people, with more than 51% mandated to be disabled people, although more than 70% of the board currently represents this primary constituency. The organization's key management positions are held by disabled people who have a long-term commitment to CIL. The executive direc-

---

Housing   Supports people to locate and secure accessible, affordable housing with an increased emphasis in recent years on people who are homeless. Also, builds ramps and facilitates home modifications.

Attendant Referral   Recruits, interviews, checks references, prepares and updates a list of attendants, helps mediate and resolve any problems that arise with attendants, helps with attendant management and training, and helps people to figure out the best way to use their attendant service hours.

Independent Living Skills Training   Holds classes and works with individuals to learn specific independent living skills, such as money management and socialization.

Youth Services   Hosts workshops on topics selected by disabled teens, provides peer support opportunities, matches disabled teens with adult mentors, helps teens locate jobs, and assists youth to use other CIL services.

Peer Counseling Services   Support and active listening between two people who have similar disability backgrounds. Also, a service type funded by the California Department of Rehabilitation.

Job Development   Helps job seekers with goal identification, interview skills, résumé writing, job search techniques, and actual referral and follow-up. Also, conducts disability awareness workshops with employers and affirmative action officers within companies.

Benefits Counseling   Helps people to receive all of the benefits that they are entitled to, and helps people who have trouble with these benefits.

Blind Services   Provides peer counseling, reader referrals, talking book certification, and skills training to "blind and low vision clients."

Deaf Services   Makes all CIL services accessible to deaf and hearing impaired individuals and referrals.

Independent Living Skills Training (Mental Disabilities)   Program specifically designed for people with mental disabilities; it was previously based on a classroom model and then changed to one-to-one training in independent living skills.

Figure 1.   Services provided by the Center for Independent Living.

Passage of the Americans with Disabilities Act   This was "on the top of the list across the country." One staff member explained, "ADA is exciting. People who think that ADA will be devastating to their business will see that they're wrong. The 1990s will open up a lot of new changes."

Personal Assistance Services   Personal care could be included in a national health insurance plan, but other critical issues such as pay scales for workers also must be addressed.

Employment   This will continue as "a very important issue for people with disabilities . . . in the 1990s and into the 21st century. Two thirds of the disabled capable of working are unemployed. One third of those employed are on the low end of the pay scale. Benefits are a work disincentive. They lose their medical and Medicare, and companies will not provide the type of insurance they need."

Health Insurance   "We need a national health plan that would include people with disabilities. A number of insurance companies will not include you if you have an existing health problem. Insurance companies say if you go to work, you're not disabled."

Telephone Relay System for Deaf   Only a few states such as California have it, but it's needed nationwide.

Figure 2.   Systemic advocacy issues (1989).

tor, Michael Winters, has held his position for 7 years, and the associate director, Gerald Baptiste, has been with the organization for more than 11 years.

Currently, the Center is organized based on a departmental model, with the service areas mentioned in Figure 1 under four "unit coordinators" in the areas of housing, employment, peer support, and advocacy (which includes benefits counseling and client assistance).

CIL continues to be actively involved in both individual advocacy and systemic advocacy, although many of the staff members report 80%–99% of their time is now spent on the supportive services listed in Figure 1. Critical systemic advocacy issues, as expressed by staff members, are included in Figure 2, and are shared here because of their continuing importance in the disability field.

WHO ARE THE STAFF MEMBERS AT CIL?[2]

Some of the key CIL staff members hold a deep personal commitment to what the organization has stood for in the lives of disabled people in Berkeley, the United States, and around the world, partially because their personal experiences with disability and the agency have touched their own lives. The following are a few stories about their lives in relationship to the Center for Independent Living.

---

[2]All names used in this chapter are actual names except for those marked by an asterisk (*), which are pseudonyms.

Katie Clemons*

I've been working at CIL about 9 months this particular round (as coordinator of attendant referral). In 1974, I was living in Oakland and working full-time on politics. I ended up having my wheelchair broken all the time. In those days, things are better now, if you had wheelchair problems . . . you'd be down for a month. Finally, some guy at this place that I bought it . . . said call CIL. . . . They came, got me, wheeled me in, jacked up the chair, and fixed it like in an hour. I was so impressed.

Anyway, it was a very small staff . . . they had a little Volkswagen van that was the only transportation in those days . . . they had advocacy . . . attendant referral. I had always worked with my friends who had been involved in the same things I was in, and they had taken care of me. Then (I met) all these people with attendants. And it's like, "I want attendants." So, first I started volunteering, and then I wanted a job so I could get attendant money.

I went to the director, who was Ed Roberts at the time, and said, "Could I work for you?" In those days it was very loose, and he said, "What would you like to do?" I said, "The only thing I've ever done is politics." He said, "Great, you can work with Sam*." Mostly, up until the time I moved to Mexico in 1981, I worked in what was called the community affairs department. . . . We did transportation organizing . . . health and welfare benefit organizing . . . (and) we went to city, regional, state, (and) federal hearings and gave testimony.

During those early years, Katie was part of the coalition that participated in the sit-in for the Rehabilitation Act of 1973. She explained, "It has transformed a lot of our lives, a very personal experience that was the most important thing many of us have done or may ever do in our lives."

Gerald Baptiste

I lost my sight at 29. . . I went to sleep one night and woke up (unable to see) one morning. I thought I was just tired because I was working 16-hour days. I was at a job at the county and . . . waiting tables and taking legal accounting and doing jam sessions. . . I found out (the loss of vision) was hereditary; 9 out of 10 times it doesn't come back. I continued to work, and after 15 years . . . I had two discs (from my back) removed. Six months to a year after the operation, I decided to put in (file a disability claim) for my back, not my eyes.

While I was recuperating I (decided to) give up 6 months to the movement. I started in blind services 11 years ago. . . I had not totally accepted my disability. I would take the glasses off even though it hurt (my eyes). I didn't want to explain. . . Not only did I come to like what I was doing, but I liked what the Center was doing. . . I got the nerve to take (the glasses) off because I realized that this is . . . part of me. And the person who has the problem is the person over there wondering. . . I don't have a problem. I know what it is.

Some of the "old guard," such as Judy Heumann and Ed Roberts, have moved on from CIL and are now involved in disability work internationally through the World Institute on Disability (WID). Some of the newer people may not have been part of the same struggles, and may have been drawn to the movement partially as a result of its success in reaching and influencing the mainstream rehabilitation community. Marcia Ortiz, who is a job coordinator at CIL, is an example of a person whose training and roots partially stem from her experiences in rehabilitation services.

Marcia Ortiz

> I was teaching in a developmental model . . . I thought this is not real; this is not going to help their lives. . . . I went through this seminar with Marc Gold. That really changed my outlook and the way I saw myself, saw what I need(ed) to be doing to help . . . the people I was working with potentially have a quality of life that was comparable to my own. . . . I started looking around the community in terms of what resources they had available and how else they could use those resources. . . . I saw the people I was working with in a totally new light. And I really enjoyed seeing them in a new way because it . . . rejuvenated my energy and my focus and it made me have more ideas and hope.

Today, CIL is a combination of the "new" and the "old," and this history and the dilemmas it reflects will be touched on briefly in discussing how the organization has changed with the times.

WHAT ARE INDEPENDENCE AND INDEPENDENT LIVING?

Independence and independent living are defined in many different ways. The people at the Center for Independent Living shared the following meanings to express the foundation of CIL's efforts to promote full community participation. To the people at CIL, independence and independent living mean:

Different things to different people.
You know what you need and if you can't do it all yourself, you know that you have to get some help and you can get it.
Learning how to do what you need to survive.
Empowerment . . . to make decisions for themselves and to have the types of policies that allow it.
Being able to live as well as you can as well as you are able to.
It varies with every individual . . . mainly the freedom to make your own decisions about things.
All disabled people have the right to live the kinds of lives they want . . . the rights to participate in community and politics . . . rights like anyone else.

Independent living is based on the recognition of a choice of life-styles and the removal of barriers that impede such choices. As one staff member explained, "Some people will never be able to live totally on their own. A lot of people don't want to live totally by themselves. It's their choice." Another person said, "You might need an attendant or you might need a therapist; in some ways, we all have some barrier to living as independently as we would want to. But just the ability to make your own decisions and your own choices . . . that's what living independently is." And as David Lewis, CIL community relations coordinator, concluded:

> For people who have experienced independent living, I don't think they would ever have anyone take control of their life again. . . . We have a right for equality, a right to participate in any part of society that anyone else does. I hate to be treated special, the back of the bus syndrome. It still happens.

THE BERKELEY COMMUNITY: AN ACCEPTING PLACE

Berkeley is a community of about 80,000 to 90,000 year-round residents. Partially because of its reputation as an accepting community, more than 15% of the population has a disability of one kind or another. Several people at CIL believe the nature of the Berkeley community was instrumental in starting the independent living movement. David Lewis talked about the community he has chosen to call home:

> This is a very open, accepting community. I don't know if the idea of independent living would have taken off the same way in another place. The Bay Area is a very special community. In other areas, people fend more for themselves. With the earthquake, there was little looting. It sums up the whole Bay Area. People are into community and living. If you live here 2 or 3 years, you understand. They really deal with people on face value. People are open. They deal with you on a one-to-one basis, not as disabled, gay, or black. I've been here 10 years. Every time I leave I feel different. I don't feel that I stand out here. . . . Little kids are exposed to people from all over the world. The exposure is there. You can't avoid disabled people.

At the same time, the Center for Independent Living has also achieved community accessibility and acceptance of people with disabilities in the city of Berkeley. The Berkeley community and the center mutually influence each other. As Katie explained:

> I think Berkeley is the most disabled-friendly community in the United States. There's no question about it. They have a disabled commission and open up all issues. It's very, very accessible . . . that has a great deal to do with the fact that CIL was very community oriented in terms of advocacy on the (city) codes for . . . restaurants and that kind of stuff.

Looking at Berkeley today, one sees a city that has responded to include its disabled citizens and to ensure that their daily needs are part of the city's daily business. The following is one example shared by a staff member that other communities may want to investigate:

> One thing that is really, really invaluable, the city of Berkeley has—emergency attendant services. They also have emergency wheelchair repair and emergency transportation if you break down or something. . . . I think they have emergency interpreters, too. It's called, "Last Call Emergency Services." It is funded by the city, and it is absolutely a Godsend because there are times when an attendant doesn't show up. (In) Berkeley, you just call this number and they have attendants on call, who are on beepers. The city pays them $10 for a call and the client pays them $7. It can mean the difference between getting out of bed or getting your catheter changed, or whatever, but I think it's just tremendous.

Berkeley still has its own problems, but it's become a place where the government and disabled people have started to join together to develop a quality community life.

LESSONS FOR THE FIELD OF DEVELOPMENTAL DISABILITY

The Center for Independent Living was selected for study because many "good" practices identified in the Center on Human Policy's national study of developmental disability service organizations appear similar to those in the independent living movement. In particular, the visit was structured to explore the meaning of independent living for people with developmental disabilities as perceived by people involved with the independent living center.

This section highlights six major areas of concern to people interested in the field of developmental disabilities, presents the views of members of CIL, and draws some implications in relationship to people with developmental disabilities. The areas addressed include: choices and decision making, peer support, working with attendants, disability awareness, advocacy and services, and transition and independent living.

Choices and Decision Making

Choices and decision making are critical areas in the developmental disability field, often complicated by the attitudinal issue of the perceived inability of people to express choices, legal issues surrounding competency, and ethical issues related to safeguarding. Although staff members at CIL seldom have experiences with the complex forms of these issues, the organization maintains a strong stance about choices and decision making that is often lacking in the parent-, provider-, and professional-dominated discussions in the field of developmental disabilities. Views of CIL staff members made prominent in this section include the importance of individual preferences, learning from mistakes, the lack of opportunities for disabled people to make choices, and decision making.

Individual Preferences   One important value underpinning this organization is its strong recognition that each individual is unique. They understand that personal preferences extend to the smallest aspect of a routine, and that people generally prefer to do things their own way and not have their choices imposed by others. Katie explained:

> The thing that we, all of us, feel strongly about is that . . . you have 20 people with 20 different ways of doing things. Everybody has their own way they like to be helped out of their shirt, or put on the toilet, or whatever, and they don't want someone coming in with preconceived notions.

While a respect for individual preferences creates a strong foundation for decision making, it does not address the nature of any relationship when two or more people wish to do things their own ways. It does, however, stress the role of the disabled person as employer and the primary decision maker. As in all relationships, however, there is a process of negotiation and exchange that cannot be neatly boxed and labeled within the roles of employer and employee (see Adler, chap. 10, this volume).

This strong belief in individual preferences is also reflected in the strategies for day-to-day living discussed in support groups and in individual peer counseling sessions. One of the main roles of the staff is to present options, so people can use the information to make decisions that suit them. As Lisa Simmons,* who works in "blind services," described:

> It's funny because each system works for a different person, and my system of organizing things might not work for you and vice versa. . . . We really try to get the individual to see what works for them. . . I feel it is my responsibility to give people the options, then it is up to them to decide how to do it.

Although Lisa will share her experiences about what has been helpful in her own life and the lives of other people, she recognizes that many solutions are possible for any given problem. She continued by giving specific examples of strategies a person with a visual impairment might use to organize a wardrobe:

> There are actual little plates that you can attach to your clothes. It's very cumbersome so that's really not recommended. Then there's tying knots, and that can also be very difficult, tying (a) different number of knots for each color. . . . Another way to do it is by color. Put one side of the closet with purple, one side with blue, and in the middle maybe the neutrals. And some other people organize by outfit. I don't nor-

mally wear the same blouse and skirt together all the time, so it would be difficult to organize by outfit. One person I know bought only one color.

In addition to presenting options and sharing personal experiences, staff members can also help disabled people gain confidence in themselves and their capacity to make choices. This is viewed as a critical role that CIL plays because the tendency on the part of people and agencies is to try to take care of disabled people. In doing so, a person's own strength, self-esteem, and sense of security can be undermined. As one staff member explained about CIL:

> I grew up with a mother (who) was disabled and (had) been part of the disabled community here for some time. Coming into CIL is putting out information and putting out choices and leaving it up to them rather than doing it for them. When dealing with disabled people, people want to take care of them. It can undermine people's confidence and sense of security. . . . We supply transportation, telephones . . . (we) don't undermine them.

From CIL's viewpoint, supporting people's choices is intimately tied to a respect for each individual, an individual's respect for herself or himself, and the person's right to a life of dignity.

Learning from Mistakes   One of the ways that human beings learn is by making their own mistakes, observing what occurs, and deciding what it means in their lives. Even though parents often wish their children would accept the wisdom of their experiences, the scenario of learning from and through one's own efforts repeats itself generation after generation. It is often considered to be part of the process of growing up and moving toward adulthood.

Disabled children, however, often do not have these opportunities because their lives may be regimented and controlled by many people with good intentions who feel they know what is best for them. Sandra Stone, who works with disabled youth, compared this experience with that of being a parent:

> The thing we have to remember is . . . they're going to make mistakes. And sometimes watching kids make mistakes is really hard. Having had my own you've got to cringe and let them do it . . . that's how they're going to learn . . . and pick up the pieces. So I think that kids with disabilities don't get that chance because their lives are so organized and supervised, and everybody knows what they need. And they don't get a chance to kind (of) make choices.

Sandra described a relationship based on hard work and caring, of being there with people through the mistakes and throughout their lives. As Sandra explained, she would intervene if she could prevent a situation that was totally destructive; however, she starts from the base that we all make mistakes, whether we are disabled or nondisabled. In contrast, when disabled people make even minor mistakes, service providers and others may curtail their future opportunities for choices. Being told that they are not ready when they make a common, human mistake, the world of the disabled person becomes more restricted. Also, through the loss of external support and caring, their own confidence and willingness to take risks may be undermined.

Lack of Opportunities To Make Choices   Disabled people, even as adults, may have few opportunities to make choices. For example, people who have lived in institutions can reach adulthood without having had any opportunities to make even simple, day-to-day choices that most people take for granted. Phil Chavez, who has been involved for 14 years with the independent living movement, explained:

> (In) a lot of institutions, you don't get a choice (of) what you eat (or) what you wear. . . (Even with) basic things like food and clothing, you have no choice. You wear what they give you and you eat what they put in front of you. . . . The people . . . that come from institutions . . . have been the most difficult people to work with in terms of teaching independence because what teaching independence is all about is . . . freedom to make your own choices. . . . That concept of making your own choices is really alien to them and not something they ever understood.

Sometimes a disability label may lead to the curtailing of opportunities for choice. As another CIL member explained, developmentally disabled[3] people who are "mainstreamed in group homes" still may be restricted in making even simple daily decisions. This appears to be based partially on a view of the people as lacking the capacity to make choices and also on the tendency of providers to take on the decision . . . making role for these individuals. This staff member recounted:

> Particularly the developmentally disabled don't get a chance to make choices. People don't even make simple choices about what they're going to wear . . . someone just comes along and pulls the clothes out of the closet. So if you can't even make those kinds of choices, how are you going to make other choices in life?

The following are two stories from one of the CIL staff members about some expectations of providers that she found to be unusual. The stories center around the issues of diet and relationships, two common areas of contention between disabled people and providers. In each of these stories, the position of the providers appeared to be that their actions were taken on behalf of or in the best interest of the disabled

---

[3]Common terminology used during this visit; however, the meaning appeared to vary with different staff members.

person. The CIL staff member, however, saw these events in another light:

> Susan was an older woman, and she was just very warm. . . . So we hit it off right away. . . . She used to come to school with these strange (carrot) sandwiches . . . and really weird dietary kinds of things. . . . We used to make hamburgers, and she used to bring lunch. Her care provider was some kind of strict . . . vegetarian. . . . Susan wanted this hamburger, and her care provider would not let her have the hamburger. And the care provider was saying . . . she will get real excited when she gets home, and it's not good for her mucous membranes . . . and these health kinds of things.
>
> This is real weird, too. Sam couldn't go home and visit his mother because the careprovider said when he went home he came back really upset. Therefore, she (the care provider) said he wasn't going to visit his mother.

While many providers feel that they must make such judgments about health and relationships for disabled people, this staff member found it incomprehensible that it was within someone's right to do so. How could a provider assume the right to disrupt a relationship in this way or to control an adult from making a decision about what they would eat? These were not even matters of life and death, but of everyday preferences.

Decision Making As Adina Frieden of CIL's independent living skills program explained, "When anyone is living their life and being an adult, we set goals unconsciously all the time. People with disabilities are not often challenged enough, given enough chances to make decisions." Part of the work of CIL is to offer disabled people new opportunities that will challenge them to grow and develop.

People have many different ways of making decisions. Part of the process of helping people to become independent is to determine with them the ways they already use to make decisions. For example, as described in a goal-planning book for disabled youth (Summer, 1984), prepared under CIL auspices, people can approach decisions and choices in some of the following ways:

Let the environment decide.
Let other people make the decision.
Act without reflection.
Postpone thought and action.
Decide against someone or something.
Go along with the crowd.
Base decisions on what feels right.
Do what pleases others or makes them happy.
Weigh the facts.
Become overwhelmed and indecisive.

Summer (1984) advises that once a person determines the ways she or he makes decisions, the next step is to "take control of your life." According to Summer, this is accomplished by "weighing the facts," which is an approach also supported by service agencies involved in the lives of disabled people.

Whenever agencies and workers become involved with disabled people, the tendency is to help disabled people decide in the right way by the right process. The right way usually means the acceptance of the "mainstream" values of the dominant culture, often to a standard not achieved by most members of the society. In Western societies, the right process tends to be based on valuing a rational approach. Although CIL recognizes the diversity in decision-making approaches and lifestyle values, they accept this rational, fact-weighing approach as the best decision-making process for disabled people to aspire to.

Peer Support

Peer support, as a concept, tends to be poorly understood in the field of developmental disability, in part because of the strong discrimination and stereotypes that people with these labels face. Because developmentally disabled people are often viewed as "not like us" by other people, the language of "peer" has been used to enforce segregation and exclude these individuals from activities with nondisabled people of the same age. One CIL staff member explained that this lack of valuing of developmentally disabled people is pervasive and extends to the disability community. She continued:

> I see (people with) developmental disabilities being . . . on the bottom rung (of a ladder) . . . because they don't have anyone to advocate for them, and they don't really advocate for themselves much. I really think it's a bad thing.

This is starting to change as self-advocacy groups continue to proliferate across the country and a national self-advocacy organization of people with developmental disabilities is being formed. However, on a day-to-day basis and in political life, developmentally disabled people are not part of the mainstream of the disability community.

Peer support—support and exchange by people with similar disabilities—can take many forms, including peer support groups, classes, and individual peer counseling sessions. The concept is similar to that shared by most self-help groups, such as women's movement groups, Alcoholics Anonymous, and fathers' rights. In some ways, the self-advocacy movement of people with developmental disabilities has similar self-help roots, although it has become more politicized on the national scene.

One new staff member explained the benefit of peer support:

When I first got here, I applied for SSI. . . . I was becoming increasingly frustrated. It should be a prerequisite to work with clients to go through this. It's monstrous. On top of everything else, you end up feeling bad. Here you get treated as a human being. You get treated with respect. . . . Other people don't understand or they don't care. In that respect, we do a lot.

Peer counseling is one method or strategy of peer support. As described in Figure 1, peer counseling is now a fundable category under the California Department of Rehabilitation, and is defined as "basically support and active listening between two people with similar (disability) backgrounds." As one staff member explained, "The difference between peer counseling and strict counseling is that there's a lot more sharing and personal exchange."

CIL was involved in earlier research studies on peer counseling and what it might mean in the lives of people with disabilities. One person who worked as a peer counselor 14 years ago said, "CIL proved that peer counseling was a really viable option and that it was cost-effective for people to live independently."

As outside organizations have incorporated new practices promoted by the independent living movement, the methods for peer support have changed, going full circle from individual to group and finally back to working with individuals. Phil Chavez talked about his observations through the years:

> Hospitals and rehabilitation centers in general have improved to the point that we're seeing a lot fewer . . . strictly spinal cord injury clients. . . . They've come around to our way of thinking. . . . They realize you just don't work with the physical body, . . . you have to deal with all the psychosocial issues of the disabled. . . . In a sense, we've come full circle back (to) where we are working (again) with individuals who slip through the cracks.

Support groups, whether formal or as a part of other activities, give people an opportunity to talk about issues they might otherwise not have a chance to discuss. Peer support gives people a chance to find out that they are not alone, and to benefit from the experiences of people who have faced or are facing similar issues. Sandra Stone talked about one of the camping trips with children in the youth group, she said:

> People need to talk about their fears of abandonment; (they) need to check out how they are accommodating to their disability. . . . (They talk about) girlfriends, boyfriends, having children, feeling (their) parents don't think they are perfect (as children), sexuality, (and) equipment. . . . If you have lemons, make lemonade; if a wheelchair, pop wheelies. . . I'm quiet, just let them say their stuff. We like each other as people. . . I'm legally blind. I know what it's like to be disabled. I was mainstreamed with no peer support, either sink or swim.

Peer support also provides opportunities for friendships and a chance to talk about issues that other people, including parents, might be concerned about. Disabled adolescents, like their nondisabled peers, are forming their own views of the world and need opportunities to discuss their emerging issues with peers away from the eyes of parents or other adults. Sandra continued:

> The peer stuff is very important. . . . Our program is good to meet people, make friendships. In support groups, people can talk about families and the struggles people are going through in their daily lives. . . . Some of the families would be aghast at what we would say.

Assisting people to make friendships and support connections outside the disability community, however, does not seem to be part of what CIL sees as a primary role.

Working with Attendants

People with developmental disabilities are now being supported in some parts of the United States to hire, supervise, and manage their own attendants—workers who can provide assistance with a range of daily living and personal assistance needs. Katie explained about the change in people whom they have supported through the years, "It's really a testament to the movement because some people coming to us for attendants . . . clearly would have been in nursing homes 10 years ago."

Based on discussions with staff members, developmentally disabled people involved with CIL appear to have mild disabilities and live with families, in institutions, or in group homes. Most participate in the independent living skills training program. One staff member talked about the future role of the independent living center with developmentally disabled people: "In the (19)90s, maybe we'll be working with more developmentally disabled people now that they live in group homes. If they start to mainstream, we'll need to provide support services."

Working with attendants is a new area of interest for most agencies in the field of developmental disabilities. This independent living center, together with others in the United States and Canada, has a long history of involvement in attendant services and is knowledgeable about the strengths, problems, and issues in the design of such a system. A few of these areas are discussed here, as described by Katie, who also has an extensive history in the use of a personal attendant system.

Recruiting, Interviewing, and Problem Solving   The recruiting, interviewing, and reference-checking of attendants is done by the attendant referral department at CIL, together with the huge outreach that is necessary for recruitment. The department also takes the job orders, works with people to some extent on attendant management, and problem solves issues between attendants and the people they work for.

During their most recent outreach project, CIL placed notices on all of the community college bulletin boards and contacted employment offices. They received the most response from a radio advertisement on a soul station.

Katie described why it was important to have disabled people involved in the interviewing process for personal care attendants:

> When . . . somebody . . . comes out of a home health class and . . . refer(s) to people as patients, . . . we can say, they are people just like me. (They) need to be gotten out of bed in the morning, but then they go about their regular day. Patient applies (only) when you are in the hospital.

Each attendant is required to sign a code of ethics that they have read. This includes a statement that they can't abandon a client or breach confidentiality. Problems do, at times, occur, including attendants "ripping off" people, and people who continually ask attendants to work overtime or who frequently change the schedule. CIL does what it can to help resolve these issues, but it has limited resources to do so on an extensive basis.

Training of Personal Attendants   As described earlier, each person has his or her unique ways of doing things, and each attendant must be trained to work cooperatively with each individual. Because of the importance of this individual orientation, Katie said, "There's a very strong bias in terms of people being able to train their own attendants." At the same time, Katie explained that a training program might also be useful, if certain conditions were met, including the attendant being paid to go to it. In describing the content of such a training and orientation program, she suggested:

> I think a lot of the stuff they would need to learn is (that) each person is an individual and you need to work cooperatively with the person. And if you think you're coming in to take over their lives, you're not. . . . And here are some different types of transfers (i.e., ways of lifting and moving a person), but just be willing to learn whatever it is your particular person wants to teach you.

Wages, Benefits, and Turnover   Similar to support staff in the field of developmental disabilities, attendants tend to be poorly paid workers who may not even have the basic benefits that workers in other fields take for granted. The turnover in these positions is high; it is hard for people to live on what they earn as an attendant. Katie explained:

> The county only pays $4.25 (per hour), and that's horrible . . . because the cost of living is so high out here. . . . A lot of our attendants have recently been the kind of people who really wanted to keep doing it,

but it is very hard because they have no benefits. I think that's what makes people move on, and that's what makes the turnover so high.

Partially because of the low wages and lack of benefits, disabled people will compromise what they need in order to come up with a schedule that is reasonable for the worker. While compromise is an important part of any relationship, these are often compromises born of necessity and based on a starting point of inequality. As one staff member explained:

> We'll talk with them about what is the best way to divide up the hours. . . . It's a delicate balance . . . even being able to find somebody at that rate. (If) they need . . . somebody for 2 or 3 hours in the morning and an hour at night . . . we might just say 2 hours in the morning and 2 at night. Some people just really compromise what they need in order to get an attendant.

Modes of Personal Assistance   Personal assistance can be set up in a variety of different ways. When the generic personal attendant system is made available to people with developmental disabilities, agencies typically are responsible for hiring, firing, managing the workers. In contrast, the preferred form or mode by many people involved in the independent living movement tends to be called the "independent provider mode" in California (see also individualized funding in Canada, in Adler, chap. 10, this volume). Katie explained why this mode, where people find and hire their own attendants, has been viewed as critical:

> Where the welfare department hires the person . . . the attendant does get benefits, but the clients get a lot less service because the county spends the money on the benefits. . . . The people do not get a choice of workers. Now, for some people, that's not a problem . . . (they are) glad to have a guaranteed person coming out.
>   Traditionally, in this state . . . people we represent . . . have been opposed to anything resembling home health where you do not get to choose your own attendant and train, and so on. . . . Perhaps we have had a more hard line stance in holding the line against home health agencies getting into the picture at all because we feel strongly that they're making money off this situation and there's not enough to go around anyway. Up until the recent past, we haven't had that many clients who weren't capable of training their own attendants.

Even when people are capable of managing their attendants, they may prefer that an organization perform some of the management functions for them. Other people may not be able to do the management, but would prefer a relative or friend to perform these functions instead of an agency. Increasingly, it is becoming important for personal assistance to be set up so different ways are possible, not based on disability, but on preference. This could include direct management by the disabled person or someone selected by them, management by an agency, or shared functions between an agency and the person and/or their representative.

Disability Awareness

People who were involved in the work for the implementation of Section 504 of the Rehabilitation Act in the 1970s, vividly recall the massive disability awareness efforts of the time, particularly with employers and schools. These efforts often included trainings or programs that helped employers and students learn about the experiences of disabled people and confront their own stereotypes and myths. These efforts are continued today at CIL. As one staff member described these efforts:

> (Disability awareness) is basically providing training for people who are not familiar with working or being with disabled people. . . . It could be going down to the Oakland Coliseum, . . . to a kindergarten or first grade class. . . . I went to county nursing homes and taught their staff. . . . They have some of the same stereotypes and misconceptions that a first grader or kindergartner would have.

Through youth programs, CIL continues to touch the lives of nondisabled students at a time when their views of the world and people are still being shaped. The programs are oriented toward students becoming aware of and accepting differences between people, while also conveying a message of similarity among all people. As one staff member explained: "Disability awareness (helps) . . . (nondisabled) youth . . . to be more receptive of the kids with differences; . . . it's good for them to be more aware of differences in our society, and, I think, more tolerant of people." With the increased emphasis on "mainstreaming," staff members at CIL believe it is imperative that disability awareness and sensitivity training be conducted where disabled students will be mainstreamed. As David Lewis elaborated:

> Mainstreaming works . . . (but) it's not easy on the people being mainstreamed. They need to make a commitment. It's difficult at times to be that person. My secretary said it's hard to be the only person (at work) who is not white. It's hard to be the only anything, but you have to do it.

As these staff members explained, little attention has been given to the hidden leaders of the mainstreaming movement—the individual students, who through personal courage made it possible for the next generation, hope to have an easier experience. Through student leadership, visible changes have occurred, both at school and at work. As one staff member said, "The longer the ILC has been in existence, the more and more people have been mainstreamed. We are starting to reap the benefits of 504 . . . lots of highly trained people ready to work."

Advocacy and Services

One of the most critical issues facing this organization is the tension between its two major functions of advocacy and services. Mentioned in the agency's recently developed 5-year plan, this tension between advocacy and services was also on the minds of the people at CIL at the time of this visit.

The associate and executive director of CIL are actively involved in national advocacy issues, particularly through their leading roles in the national organization of the independent living centers (NCIL). However, on the systemic advocacy level, most staff members believe that "advocacy is much diminished," partially because the movement "was in its heyday in the seventies and eighties."

Many of the staff members believe that "advocacy is done most often within a service context." By this, people mean that they will fight, when necessary, to have the individual obtain the benefits or services that they need. This is partially possible because laws are now in place for people to file individual lawsuits.

CIL is also placing a greater emphasis on having "staff think about teaching persons to advocate for themselves." Staff members are proud that CIL has an advocacy perspective, holding the perspective that "when it's necessary, we will go down to the county board of supervisors, and we will get on coalitions, whatever it takes."

What is viewed as most critical, however, is service to clients. As the associate director explained, "The field is so sophisticated now, (funders are) looking more to see that we'll deliver . . . quality services. . . We have some (independent living) agencies who only did advocacy (and) couldn't leverage money with foundations. . . We must maintain both services and advocacy." Another staff member described this tension:

> The organization's gone through a lot of changes . . . but it had to do services. People who donate money don't like to hear the word advocacy. It is hard because it is a fine line. You have to tone down your act. This organization has been involved in the disabled movement . . . had to be advocates. This organization is very influential in all major legislation in this country. It's always been an advocate and a service coordinator.

The nature of the organization's systemic advocacy has changed with the times and now more emphasis is placed on negotiation as the process for achieving change. Previously, more visible activism would have been the primary strategy. A CIL staff member explained:

> In the old days, we would have been carrying out wild actions, but it would have been necessary because it was not an accepted and understood thing—that discrimination against the disabled was a really bad thing, that it was a minority group.

We've changed the way we advocate. We don't need to go to the streets the way we used to. Now we sit down and convince people. The role of advocacy has changed, and we need to do things in different ways. Our reputation from the 1970s helps; people know if we believe in something, we're not going to give up.

Transition and Independent Living

Developmentally disabled people are involved with CIL primarily through an independent living skills training program, located in a house on the same street as the main center. Phil and Adina explained, "We aren't like the rest of CIL, (we're) more programmatic" and "we're the only structured program."

One of the major issues faced by the organization today is to create a vision and decide how to support people who have not been involved with the independent living centers. In some ways, this tension is being played out around transition programs and their place in an independent living center. The two major positions on this issue are discussed below with information about what the current impasse seems to suggest.

The Experiences of Staff at CIL   The staff members who are most involved with developmentally disabled people on a service basis are deeply concerned that independent living will not become a reality unless these individuals obtain greater support than they currently have. These staff members have concluded that the solution would be to create a transitional program for individuals viewed as needing more services than other CIL clients. Phil explained his views:

> I thought it would be great to have a transitional program for people who can't make the leap from family to their own place. Unfortunately, some folks . . . are opposed to any residential component. They think HUD (Department of Housing and Urban Development) buildings are institutions.

Adina added, "It's important to have a transitional program so people don't need to leap over a chasm. For people who are mentally retarded, it is almost impossible to do it. The old guard won't have anything to do with transitional programs."

The "old guard" is deeply committed to a vision of people living fully in the community, and they seem to be concerned about what it would mean to establish residential programs for any group of disabled people. This view gets labeled as philosophy because the transition of what it means on a day-to-day basis has not occurred, leaving developmentally disabled people without the support to live in their own place.

What We Have Learned and What the Impasse May Represent   People at CIL are just becoming familiar with information on the creation and efforts toward a new vision of life in the community for people with multiple (mental and physical) disabilities. This vision, being transformed into reality in parts of the United States (see Part I, this volume), supports the right of all people to live in their own homes with the availability of supports.

With this information, the question can be transformed from "Do we need a transitional program?" to "How can we support people to lead the same range of lifestyles as anyone else?" This reformulation would support the vision of the "old guard" as well as the discussion about what role CIL can and should play in supporting this vision on a day-to-day basis. This discussion offers the opportunity to re-examine the role of the independent living center in a society that has been changed by its efforts so that "mainstreaming" now applies in ways that even "the old guard" might not have imagined.

Ted,* who participates in the independent living skills program said:

> I hope it works out to my benefit. . . . I just like to see myself better in a lot of things and try to make myself a lot better. . . . I'll know if it works, if it feels good inside. . . . People treat me the same way they do everybody else. I want it that way.

Ted and people considered more severely disabled have a right to a home with the personal assistance and supports they need. People at CIL, in alliance with others, should settle for nothing less.

CONCLUSION

The Center for Independent Living at Berkeley, a part of one of the most important social movements of the past decades, stands today as the bearer of the great responsibility that comes with the honor. As Gerald Baptiste astutely explained, "Organizations must grow with the times."

However, as the climate in this country has resulted in decimated funding for social efforts, this organization has increasingly relied on financing that it believes restricts its efforts to advocate in the manner to which it has become accustomed. While the organization may say the times demand new methods for change, the picture of disabled people crawling up the steps of the Capitol in Washington, D.C., for passage of the Americans with Disabilities Act (ADA) touched the hearts of many people nationwide in a way negotiation will not and cannot.

The movement has reached a new stage, one where a more inclusive vision of full community life must include a broader base of people. Because of its efforts, CIL has led the way. In the future, it can continue such a leadership role by reaffirming its place in the movement, by creating new stories of the 1990s that inspire the best in people, by distinguishing the service roles of an independent living center, and by developing a stronger, broader community base for the work and challenges still ahead.

BIBLIOGRAPHY

Center for Independent Living. (1989, June). *History of CIL.* Oakland: Author.
Independent Life (A Quarterly Publication of the Center for Independent Living), 2539 Telegraph Ave., Berkeley, CA. 94704.
Rehabilitation Act of 1973 (PL 93–112).
Summer, C. (1984, September). *Counseling disabled young people and their families: Guidelines for service-providers in independent living programs.* Berkeley, CA: Model Approaches to Life Transition for the Disabled (MALTD), Center for Independent Living.

17

CONCLUSION

Julie Ann Racino, Susan O'Connor, and Pamela Walker

In the Introduction to this volume, key features of the support/em-powerment "paradigm" or framework are outlined and compared to those for rehabilitation and independent living. These features include: how the problem is defined, the locus of the problem, the social roles people play, the solutions to the problem, who controls or holds power, and desired outcomes. In this Conclusion, aspects of these three major frameworks are briefly highlighted (see Racino, Taylor, Walker, & O'Connor, chap. 1, Table 3) as well as the management framework that is highly influential in the disability field.

Part I of this book introduces the concepts of support and choice in the context of housing and community living. The framework for Part I is constructed from a view of support and choice that basically represents an agency perspective on responsiveness, being person-centered, and personal decision making. In Part II, the personal perspectives of those who experience disability in daily life are shared in the form of essays. Part III is a research-based presentation of the perspectives of people involved with organizations that have important lessons to share with the disability field. This conclusion draws more heavily on indepth participant observation research studies that examine "support" and "choice" from the perspectives of people with disabilities and their families.

The research on support and choice was developed in conjunction with the Center on Human Policy's qualitative research team: Bob Bogdan, Ellen Fisher, Zana Marie Lutfiyya, Susan O'Connor, Julie Ann Racino, Pat Rogan, Bonnie Shoultz, Michelle Sures, Steve Taylor, Rannveig Traustadottir, and Pam Walker. The Center's qualitative research includes studies of the lives of individuals with disabilities and families, organizational studies, studies of community places, generic social service settings, employment sites, and policy research of states.

FRAMEWORKS AND PERSPECTIVES

There are many different ways of understanding and viewing the world and our own relationship to it and to other people who share it with us. Each of us is influenced by a variety of factors that shape our own personal views, including our cultural background, ethnicity, personal experiences, and lifestyle preferences. However, within any society, there are also assumptions about "how things are" and "how they work;" sometimes these are society-wide beliefs, and other times they are primarily centered within a segment of society or within a profession or field. The following are a few sketches of frameworks that are critical to recognize as we begin to listen to the perspectives of individuals with disabilities and families and begin to create a climate for mutual and supportive dialogue.

The Rehabilitation Framework

The rehabilitation framework can simply be described as representing how most disability professionals (particularly those in rehabilitation, special education, psychology, and, increasingly, social work) are trained to view the world, people with disabilities, and their own role in relationship to people's lives. The rehabilitation framework or a similar version of it guides work in most human services fields for adults living in the community. This occurs across disability groups, whether developmental disabilities, mental health, head injury, physical disability, or aging, although some of these are still more highly influenced by a traditional medical model. While in many ways a vast improvement over the medical framework, it still retains many of its central features on issues regarding decision making and the roles of professionals. The rehabilitation framework is one of the major guides for professional and paraprofessional training, applied and basic research, social policy, and practice in the field.

While there are many distinctions across disciplines and fields, these tend to be minor compared with the professional tendency to frame issues from the expert viewpoint (i.e., the professional knows best). Many of these professions may include in their training and framework the importance of changes in attitudinal, political, economic, social, cultural, and administrative issues within society. However, the primary thrust of many of these disability professions is to examine what can be done to assist individuals or families, therefore focusing on private, personal troubles instead of social change. Professionals have also been taught to view success (typically as defined by professionals) in terms of the effects of their interventions, whether for improving relationships or community connections, various aspects of behavior, or communication or life functioning.

New "innovations" (e.g., supportive living) tend to be interpreted and implemented within the predominant frameworks because it controls both the definition of the problem and "acceptable" or "reasonable" solutions. Part I of this book, for example, is framed to some extent from this perspective because the focus is still primarily on how agencies, professionals, and paraprofessionals can modify their work to be more responsive and person-centered. The framework takes for granted that professionals will remain central to these decisions, which is true partially because professionals still hold the power to "allow" people with disabilities to decide.

The Independent Living Framework

The independent living framework represents an effort by people with disabilities to change the guiding framework of rehabilitation and other areas such as special education to better reflect their wishes and perspectives. At its inception, it primarily emphasized the aspects of personal control of their own lives and moved attention away from the definition of "them" (people with disabilities) as the problem to the issues in society that create conditions that exclude people from participation and contribution. Although it influences the way in which rehabilitation is practiced, the framework itself is not well known or accepted outside of a narrow disability circle.

The independent living framework represents a "people first" perspective on self-determination of one's own lifestyle and presents people with disabilities as a minority group that has been discriminated against in society. It seeks to make changes in society by focusing on the "abilities not the disabilities" of people with disabilities, including their ability to organize as a political force to effect the conditions of their lives.

Because of the nature of this movement, including the lack of a clear role for people without disabilities, people with mental retardation have not been well represented, instead coalescing through groups that are often supported by disability paraprofessionals. The independent living movement has now become somewhat synonymous with the country's independent living centers, which have accepted some of the features of the rehabilitation paradigm in relating to people with mental retardation.

The Management Framework

In addition to the rehabilitation framework described earlier, the disability field is also dominated by a particular management framework that influences how problems are understood and how solutions are approached. The dominant management view comes from a perspective of organizations and relationships that reflect a Weberian model based on rationality, causality, and sequence (e.g., Warriner, 1984). At the management levels in human services, this framework controls the way in which decisions such as funding, quality assurance, and planning are addressed. It is the basis underlying the replication of service mechanisms that have been promoted throughout the United States and in other countries, such as Great Britain.

In contrast, sociological views of organizations tend to be based on a view that agencies are social systems each having a history of their own. This book's chapters on agencies and systems draw on these perspectives, suggesting a somewhat different approach to understanding and solving agency issues and problems. They are consistent extensions of work being done in areas such as corporate management and company excellence in response to the nature of today's rapidly changing environment.

The Support/Empowerment Framework

The support/empowerment framework is an attempt to reframe the major theoretical and practical guides in the field of mental retardation to reflect an alliance among people with disabilities, professionals, friends and family, and those who would participate in such alliances, if given the opportunity to do so. While retaining the independent living movement's features of personal control, the support/empowerment paradigm also has as its vision an inclusive society where power is shared among people in a way that does not exist today. Such a society would attend to "minority" interests, viewing this in the best interest of all, not simply that of the particular group.

This support/empowerment framework presents one way of pulling together a variety of diverse efforts of people working in different directions. It draws for its central features on:

Community and regeneration efforts (Lehman, 1988; O'Connell, 1988)
The self-determination movement (Perske, 1989; Worth, 1989)
The power of social roles and of labelling (Bogdan & Taylor, 1982; Wolfensberger, 1983)
Sociopolitical efforts across minority groups (Heumann, 1986; Zola, 1987)
The role of policy (Lakin et al., 1989; Turnbull, Garlow, & Barber, 1991) and agency change experiences (Gardner, Chapman, Donaldson, & Jacobson, 1988; O'Brien, 1987)
Personal relationships and friendships (Lutfiyya, 1991; Strully & Strully, 1985; Tyne, 1988)
Community support in education (Biklen, Ferguson, & Ford, 1989; Stainback, Stainback, & Forest, 1989)
Community support in recreation (Hutchison & Lord, 1979)
Community support in employment (Nisbet & Callahan, 1987; Wehman, Hill, Wood, & Parent, 1987)

Social acceptance (Bogdan & Taylor, 1987; Taylor & Bogdan, 1989)
Social and community change (Driedger, 1989; Groce, 1985)

It recognizes the importance of all of these diverse contributions to the lives of people with disabilities, and the necessity of approaching complex issues from a variety of vantage points.

Some professions, notably sociology and anthropology, approach the world from a framework that validates a variety of different perspectives and lifestyles. Because of this, these types of fields offer the possibility to highlight the perspectives of those who tend to be undervalued or devalued in society, and whose views are often hidden from the general public and from the professions. These perspectives provide a very different, and infinitely more complex, view of human life, sometimes in stark contrast to those of the dominant or accepted viewpoint. However, this type of work is often not viewed as practically usable by the professions that deal with human beings on a day-to-day basis, partially because the sociologists and anthropologists who are not from an applied research branch may be reluctant to draw social action implications from their findings.

With a support/empowerment framework, the perspectives of individuals with disabilities and their families are given greater weight than currently is prevalent in the "system" and the "field." Using this framework results in a need to reframe most disability issues, raising new questions about assumptions that are taken for granted. Because of the extensive ramifications implied by this framework some people have referred to this kind of change as revolutionary. Table 1 includes some examples of the implications of the support/empowerment framework for research, training, theory, policy, and practice.

LEARNING FROM THE LIVES OF INDIVIDUALS AND FAMILIES

The support empowerment framework is based on a view of the world that raises the perspectives of individuals and families up from their current unequal power position.

Yet, little is known about how people with disabilities perceive and relate to the world, although the literature in this area is starting to increase. As the authors of this book accompany individuals with disabilities and families in their daily lives, they are learning about their experiences with agencies and others who enter into their lives. This volume ends with some contrasting perspectives on what support and choice mean from a different vantage point.

A wide discrepancy exists between what families, individuals, and professionals view as support.   Individuals with disabilities and family members feel supported when they are listened to and understood from their perspective. This does not mean that other perspectives are not

Table 1.   Future directions indicated by a support/empowerment framework

Selected Examples

Research studies on housing and homes

Meaning of home, including differences based on gender, culture, ethnic, and age variations

Perspectives of generic agencies, such as housing organizations, and community places on issues of inclusion or integration

Personal experiences of living in integrated housing and different neighborhoods from perspectives of individuals with disabilities and their neighbors

Research studies on "support"

Effect of cash subsidies on household and family life and exploration of financing from an individual perspective

How alliances are formed and perceived by the people involved, including critical factors in "partnerships"

Roles of workers and their relationships with people with disabilities, conducted from perspectives of all parties

Training

Need for an identity group for people whose role is related to community life for people with disabilities

Need for training in support approaches and implications, including ways to better understand the perspectives of individuals with disabilities and families

Theory

Need for new concepts to guide us in the future that are community based and only secondarily disability based

Need for new theory on the relationship of individuals to communities, agencies, systems, and society grounded in a more egalitarian and less protectionist and conformist base

Practice and Policy

Need for support with local agency change efforts and systems change, including leadership training at all levels

Need to change to a more formative versus summative evaluation approach to encourage learning in times of rapid change

Need for reflective and thoughtful policy analyses that encourage broad discussion and public debate

---

helpful or even welcomed, but that a feeling of support is connected with a confirmation that the situation as people experience it is valid.

Sometimes what people may want from an agency is very different than what they get. For example, a person may want help with purchasing goods for their child, and, instead, receive instruction on being a "good" parent. Workers can become so preoccupied with doing their jobs that they neglect the purpose for which these services were created. There is a big difference between supporting a family and running a family support service, and between supporting a person to live in their own home and operating a supportive living program.

Being with and caring about people may be more important than what one does. Professionals view support more in terms of concrete actions that result in successful outcomes often defined on their terms. While individuals and families also want good things to occur and problems resolved, they often realize the complexity of their life issues and the limitations of making a complex situation better. Being with and caring about people as they try to deal with what occurs in their lives and letting them know that they can count on someone else during times of crises may be some of the more important roles that workers can play.

The little things count, and the little things are not so little. Sometimes the most important things in life are confused with the little things that occur. The remembrance of a birthday, a note on Mother's Day, a question about a son or daughter, an acknowledgment by a doctor of the humanity and uniqueness of one's child can all be things that sustain people on a day-to-day basis. These are the "little things" that add up, either slowly wearing away one's strength and confidence or instilling courage and hope for another day. People often underestimate the role these "little things" can play.

Support occurs in all settings, whether recreation, work, home, or community. Whether looking at support in the sense of concrete services and actions or personal experiences, it is a critical dimension across all life domains from recreation and leisure, to work, to domestic and community activities and places. The most evident aspects of support do not seem to vary based on this aspect of the nature of the setting. The methods of "providing support" seem to vary dependent on the philosophy and orientation of the agency, not on the needs and desires of the people.

Many human services are neutral or harmful to people with disabilities and families. Contrary to what many people would like to believe, the studies of the authors of this volume concur with McKnight's analysis (n.d.) that people with disabilities are often hurt as well as helped by services. People with disabilities are often enveloped in a cocoon of services that disrupts their personal connections and limits their opportunities for both relationships and contributions. Connection with some "supportive" services may actually be an unwanted entry into out-of-home placement, and may be a way of socializing people into accepting a professional frame of reference as the "right" way to view a situation.

Individual workers can and do transcend boundaries and develop mutual and supportive relationships with people with disabilities. One of the hopeful signs is that workers can and do transcend their strict role boundaries, and, sometimes at personal cost, develop relationships with people with disabilities, move toward alliances to address the negative effects of systems, and offer the personal support that systems do not. One way to think about the role of workers and organizations is as opportunities, in a segregated society, for these alliances to take place.

Workers have both implicit and explicit roles that affect their relationships with people with disabilities and families.   Workers may negotiate their explicit roles with individuals with disabilities and families. This may include changes in tasks performed, increased direction by people with disabilities and families, and more flexible schedules. Implicit roles, however, may not change because they reflect values that underlie the relationship and are not necessarily recognized by the parties involved. A meeting that takes place to discuss how a team should relate to a family or individual is one example of an implicit role that is taken for granted; yet, it implies numerous control dimensions.

Human services workers view "the system" differently from individuals with disabilities and families.   The formal organization of the service systems, as constructed in charts, policies, and procedures, and presented by policymakers and workers, is very different when constructed from the viewpoints of families and individuals with disabilities. Individuals with disabilities and families construct their view of how the systems work based on how these systems can be actively used to meet their own purposes. They are not simply passive recipients of the system. Systems that workers distinguish, such as generic and disability agencies, are not constructed or differentiated in the same way by individuals with disabilities and families. This has critical implications for understanding "integration into generic agencies."

Workers are socialized into making what families and individuals with disabilities perceive to be unwarranted judgments.   Workers are placed in a position to make judgments about the lives of people with disabilities and families, often without adequate information and without the people's consent for intrusion into those areas. They are socialized into viewing their opinions and viewpoints as right, and their judgment as final. Part of the socialization of individuals with disabilities and families is to accept this framework or otherwise be designated as unworthy of assistance; a "bad" family or client; or as difficult, aggressive, or dysfunctional.

Personal relationships are the source of concrete assistance for individuals with disabilities and families, as well as a source of emotional support.   People in relationships do a certain amount for each other that is considered a "normal" part of their relationships. This is also true for people with disabilities. Sometimes the "doing" goes beyond what others consider fair to give; this may be called stress. When people see no way out, they may seek others outside their network to help solve the situation for or with them. What is typical for people to "do" for each other in a relationship varies from one relationship to another.

Home is one of the bases for the development and formation of relationships.   Friendships can be fostered by exchanges and visits in one's home, sharing meals, becoming familiar with the personal touches in a home that reflect who people are, learning about who visits and calls at home, seeing how the house is structured for activities and lifestyle, and simply sharing one's personal space with another.

Unequal power relationships between agencies and individuals with disabilities influence the nature and perceptions of alliances.   Families and people with disabilities are socialized into being grateful for whatever assistance they can get. When people with disabilities and families come together with workers, they bring their past experiences as the starting base for the new relationship. Given the power inequality that exists, assumptions by individual workers that they are relating to people "as equals" serves to perpetuate this power inequality.

Individual people weave together "informal supports" and relationships with services, although service structures may interfere.   People do "interweave" formal services and "informal supports" on an ongoing basis in their lives. The way in which they do so is sometimes considered private and not something they wish to share, especially with someone with whom they have not yet developed trust. People who are experienced with services try to determine the rules of a system (i.e., learning what the system thinks is good) and assess the trustworthiness of workers to see which information to divulge about their personal lives. People may be justifiably concerned about how this information may be used in the future in opposition to their personal wishes.

Agency accountability and personal choice are, at times, in conflict with each other.   People may be willing to take certain risks in order to live their life the way they would like. Sometimes, the alternative is to forgo activities of living that are personally meaningful to the individual. However, when these personal decisions are viewed from the perspective of an agency, group interests can and do take precedence over these personal decisions. Agencies need to be concerned to some extent about public perceptions and group needs; what may be a good decision for an agency is not necessarily in the best interests of the person.

Human services workers usually hold the power of definition in their roles with families and individuals with disabilities.   Social control includes the power to define what is considered "good" whether it is behavior, relationships, or actions, and it includes the power to exert this definition over others. When agencies and their workers are involved in the relationship of "formal services" and "informal supports," they may widen the area over which they have control and dominance, and thus exert even more influence in people's lives.

When people with disabilities come in contact with professionals, they may find the agenda of the workers and agencies expanded into other areas of their lives without their consent. If they are labeled as "neglectful," "incompetent," or "bad," they may also face more blatant forms of social control that can include court actions or direct interference with individual and family relationships. The individual or family may no longer have the choice to remove themselves from the service system that they sought out for "help."

CONCLUSION

The current movement toward offering individuals and families more choices and moving to more of a "support" approach basically maintains the power structure as it exists while increasing the market options available to people. Professionals have been in the position of deciding what is in the best interests of people with disabilities and families. Ultimately, discussions are needed by all people involved about who will control fiscal resources, define what the "problem" is, and determine what potential solutions will be regarding how people with disabilities and others will live together.

In order to develop and form alliances to move forward, we must first come to better understand each other's perspectives. This will mean a need to reflect, listen, and seek increased safe dialogue for all people whose lives are affected. The support/empowerment framework implies the need for many changes in individuals, communities, agencies, systems, and society, and the belief that such changes are possible, if we work together.

We are embarking on a new journey, and we can either take the short path in the same way we have before with little change, or we can start on an unknown path that promises a better future life for all of us. We can tread a path that aims to make life better only for people with disabilities, or we can choose the road where we will walk with people with disabilities and others as we seek to create a better world where everyone belongs and is valued.

> Deep down we must have real affection for each other, a clear realization or recognition of our shared human status. . . It is helpful to have a variety of approaches on the basis of a deep feeling of the basic sameness of humanity. We can then make joint effort to solve the problems of the whole of humankind. (Dalai Lama Tenzin Gyatso, 1984, p. 60)

BIBLIOGRAPHY

Biklen, D., Ferguson, D., & Ford, A. (Eds.). (1989). *Schooling and disability: Eighty-eighth yearbook of the National Society for the Study of Education, Part II.* Chicago: University of Chicago Press.

Bogdan, R., & Taylor, S.J. (1982). *Inside out: The social meaning of mental retardation.* Toronto: University of Toronto Press.

Bogdan, R., & Taylor, S.J. (1987). Toward a sociology of acceptance: The other side of the study of deviance. *Social Policy, 18*(2), 34–39.

Driedger, D. (1989). *The last civil rights movement: Disabled People's International.* New York: St. Martin's Press.

Gardner, J.F., Chapman, M.S., Donaldson, G., & Jacobson, S.G. (1988). *Toward supported employment: A process guide for planned change.* Baltimore: Paul H. Brookes Publishing Co.

Groce, N. (1985). *Everyone here spoke sign language: Hereditary deafness in Martha's Vineyard.* Cambridge, MA: Harvard University Press.

Gyatso, T. (Dalai Lama). (1984). Compassion in global politics. In T. Gyatso, *Kindness, clarity, and insight* [Address to the Los Angeles World Affairs Council]. Ithaca, NY: Snow Lion Publications.

Heumann, J. (1986). The independent living movement for the elderly. In C. Estes, J. Heumann, & C. Mahoney (Eds.), *Toward a unified agenda: Proceedings of a national conference on aging and disability.* San Francisco: Institute on Health and Aging.

Hutchison, P., & Lord, J. (1979). *Recreation integration: Issues and alternatives in leisure services and community involvement.* Ottawa: Leisurability Publications, Inc.

Lakin, K.C., Jaskulski, T.M., Hill, B.K., Bruininks, R.H., Menke, J.M., White, C.C., & Wright, E.A. (1989, May). *Medicaid services for persons with mental retardation and related conditions* (Project Report No. 27). Minneapolis: Center for Residential and Community Services, Institute on Community Integration, University of Minnesota.

Lehman, K. (1988). Beyond Oz: The path to regeneration, *Social Policy, 18*(4), 56–58.

Lutfiyya, Z.M. (1991). "A feeling of being connected": Friendships between people with and without learning difficulties. *Disability, Handicap & Society, 6*(3), 233–245.

McKnight, J.L. (n.d.). *Do no harm: A policymaker's guide to evaluating human services and their alternatives.* Evanston, IL: Northwestern University.

Nisbet, J., & Callahan, M. (1987). Achieving success in integrated workplaces: Critical elements in assisting persons with severe disabilities. In S.J. Taylor, D. Biklen, & J. Knoll (Eds.), *Community integration for people with severe disabilities* (pp. 184–201). New York: Teacher's College Press.

O'Brien, J. (1987). Embracing ignorance, error and fallibility: Competencies for leadership of effective services. In S.J. Taylor, D. Biklen, & J. Knoll (Eds.), *Community integration for people with severe disabilities* (pp. 85–108). New York: Teacher's College Press.

O'Connell, M. (1988). *The gift of hospitality: Opening the doors of community life for people with disabilities.* Evanston, IL: Northwestern University.

Perske, R. (Ed.). (1989). *Self-determination.* Minneapolis: Institute on Community Integration, University of Minnesota.

Stainback, S., Stainback, W., & Forest, M. (Eds.). (1989). *Educating all students in the mainstream of regular education.* Baltimore: Paul H. Brookes Publishing Co.

Strully, J., & Strully, C. (1985). Friendship and our children. *Journal of The Association for Persons with Severe Handicaps, 10*(4), 224–227.

Taylor, S.J., & Bogdan, R. (1989). On accepting relationships between people with mental retardation and non-disabled people: Towards an understanding of acceptance. *Disability, Handicap, & Society, 4*(1), 21–36.

Turnbull, H.R., Garlow, J., & Barber, P. (1991). A policy analysis of family support for families with members with disabilities. *The University of Kansas Law Review, 39*(3).

Tyne, A. (Ed.). (1988). *Ties and connections: An ordinary community life for people with learning difficulties.* London: King's Fund Centre.

Warriner, C. (1984). *Organizations and their environments.* Greenwich, CT: JAI Press.

Wehman, P., Hill, J.W., Wood, W., & Parent, W. (1987). A report on competitive employment histories of persons labeled severely mentally retarded. *Journal of The Association for Persons with Severe Handicaps, 12*(1), 11–17.

Wolfensberger, W. (1983). Social role valorization: A proposed new term for the principle of normalization. *Mental Retardation, 21*(6), 234–239.

Worth, P. (1989). You've got a friend. In The G. Allan Roeher Institute, *The pursuit of leisure* (pp. 73–78). Downsview, Ontario: The G. Allan Roeher Institute.

Zola, I.K. (1987). The politicization of the self-help movement. *Social Policy, 18*(2), 32–33.

APPENDIX A

HOUSING AND SUPPORT ORGANIZATIONS

HOUSING

Community and Housing

Enterprise Foundation
505 American City Building
Columbia, Maryland 21044
410-964-1230

Habitat for Humanity
Habitat and Church Streets
Americus, Georgia 31709
912-924-6935
(There are also regional offices
throughout the United States)

Institute for Community Economics
151 Montague City Road
Greenfield, Massachusetts 01301
413-774-7956

Local Initiative Support Corporation
666 Third Avenue
New York, New York 10017
212-949-8580

McAuley Institute
1320 Fenwick Lane, Suite 600
Silver Spring, Maryland 20910
301-588-8110

National Low Income Housing
   Coalition (NLIHC)
1012 14th Street, N.W., #1500
Washington, DC 20005
202-662-1530

Women's Institute for Housing and
   Economic Development
179 South Street
Boston, Massachusetts 02111
617-423-2296

Housing Accessibility and Design

Research and Training Center on
   Accessible Housing
North Carolina State University
School of Design
Box 7701
Raleigh, North Carolina 27607-9986
919-515-3082 (voice or TDD)

Housing Associations and Cooperatives

The Cooperative Initiatives Project
Page Associates
236 Gulf Road
Belchertown, Massachusetts 01007
413-253-3118
203-523-0890

The National Association of Housing
   Cooperatives
1614 King Street
Alexandria, Virginia 22314
703-549-5201

Perry Housing Association
Box 78
Shawnee, Ohio 43782
614-347-4193 (Beth Ferguson,
   President)

Prairie Housing Cooperative
102-113 Market Avenue
Winnipeg, Manitoba R3B 0P5
CANADA
204-943-3392

The Reservoir Cooperative
Madison Mutual Housing
    Association
200 North Blount Street
Madison, Wisconsin 53703
608-255-6642

Housing Financing

Creative Management Associates
P.O. Box 5488
Portsmouth, New Hampshire 03801
603-436-6308

National Association of Protection
    and Advocacy Systems, Inc.
    (NAPAS)
900 Second Street, N.E.
Suite 211
Washington, DC 20002
202-408-9514

Housing Subsidies

State of Connecticut
Department of Mental Retardation
Housing Subsidy Program
90 Pitkin Street
East Hartford, Connecticut 06108
203-725-3842

Housing Trust Funds

Co-op Fund of New England
108 Kenyon Street
Hartford, Connecticut 06105
203-523-4305

Housing Trust Fund Project
570 Shepard Street
San Pedro, California 90731
213-883-4249

University Resources-Housing and Support

Center for Community Change
    Through Housing and Support
University of Vermont
John Dewey Hall
Burlington, Vermont 05405
802-656-0000

Institute on Disability
Morrill Hall, 3rd Floor
University of New Hampshire
Durham, New Hampshire
    03824-3595
603-862-4320

Research and Training Center on
    Community Integration
Syracuse University
Center on Human Policy
200 Huntington Hall, 2nd Floor
Syracuse, New York 13244-2340
315-443-3851

Research and Training Center on
    Residential Services and
    Community Living
University of Minnesota
Institute on Community Integration
University Affiliated Programs
212 Pattee Hall, 150 Pillsbury Drive,
    S.E.
Minneapolis, Minnesota 55455
612-624-6328

SUPPORT

Assistive Technology

RESNA
1101 Connecticut Avenue, N.W.
Suite 700
Washington, DC 20036
202-857-1199

University of Illinois-Chicago
Institute for the Study of
  Developmental Disabilities
1640 Roosevelt Road
Chicago, Illinois 60608
312-413-1647

Community Organizations

Appalachian Ohio Public Interest
  Group
36 South Congress Street
Athens, Ohio 45701
614-593-7490

Highlander Center
1959 Highlander Way
New Market, Tennessee 37820
615-933-3443 or 615-933-3445

Consultant Organizations-Support

Human Services Institute (HSI)
Ridgely Building-Suite 140
5575 Sterrett Place
Columbia, Maryland 21044-2605
410-740-0123

Responsive Systems Associates
58 Willowick Drive
Lithonia, Georgia 30038
404-987-9785

Local Support Organizations

Centennial Developmental Services,
  Inc.
Residential Supports
3819 St. Vrain
Evans, Colorado 80620
303-339-5360

Developmental Services of Strafford
  Co., Inc.
1 Forum Court, 113 Crosby Road
Dover, New Hampshire 03820
603-749-4015

Options in Community Living
22 North Second Street
Madison, Wisconsin 53704
608-249-1585

Residential, Inc.
Box 101
Lexington, Ohio 43764
614-342-4158

Medicaid Financing of Support Services

National Association of State Mental
  Retardation Program Directors, Inc.
113 Oronoco Street
Alexandria, Virginia 22314
703-683-4202
(also for state contact information on
  supportive living)

Personal Assistance

National Council on Independent
  Living
Troy Resource Center for
  Independent Living
4th and Broadway
Troy, New York 12180
518-274-1979

Research and Training Center on
  Independent Living at The Institute
  for Rehabilitation and Research
  (TIRR)
3400 Bissonnet, Suite 101
Houston, Texas 77005
713-666-6244

World Institute on Disability
Research and Training Center on
  Public Policy in Independent
  Living
510 16th Street, Suite 100
Oakland, California 94612
415-763-4100

APPENDIX B

SUGGESTED READINGS

The bibliographic entries included in this section are among the resources available on community living for adults with developmental and other disabilities. A more extensive annotated listing of readings is included in: Shoultz, B. (Ed.). (1990). *Annotated bibliography on community integration* (Revised). Syracuse, NY: Center on Human Policy.

Choices, Decision Making, and Empowerment

Biklen, D. (1990). Communication unbound: Autism and praxis. *Harvard Educational Review, 60*(3), 291–314.

Deegan, P. (1992). The independent living movement and people with psychiatric disabilities: Taking back control of our own lives. *Psychosocial Rehabilitation Journal, 15*(3), 3–19.

Flynn, M., & Ward, L. (1991). "We can change the future" — Self and citizen advocacy. In S. Segal, & V. Varma (Eds.), *The future for people with learning difficulties* (pp. 129–148). London: David Fulton.

Guess, D., Benson, H., & Siegel-Causey, E. (1985). Concepts and issues related to choice-making and autonomy among persons with severe disabilities. *Journal of The Association for Persons with Severe Handicaps, 10*(2), 79–86.

Lord, J., & McKillop-Farlow, D. (1990, Fall). A study of personal empowerment: Implications for health promotion. *Health Promotion, 2–8.*

People First of Washington. (1990). *A handbook for people thinking about moving.* Tacoma, WA: Author.

Ridgway, P. (Ed.). (1988). *Coming home: Ex-patients view housing options and needs. Proceedings of a national housing forum.* Burlington, VT: Center for Community Change Through Housing and Support, University of Vermont.

Williams, P., & Shoultz, B. (1984). *We can speak for ourselves: Self-advocacy for mentally handicapped people.* Cambridge, MA: Brookline Books.

Williams, R.K. (1991). Choices, communication, and control: A call for expanding them in the lives of people with severe disabilities. In L.H. Meyer, C.A. Peck, & L. Brown (Eds.), *Critical issues in the lives of people with severe disabilities* (pp. 543–544). Baltimore: Paul H. Brookes Publishing Co.

Worth, P. (1989). You've got a friend. In The G. Allan Roeher Institute, *The pursuit of leisure* (pp. 73–78). Downsview, Ontario: The G. Allan Roeher Institute.

Commitment and Leadership

O'Brien, J. (1987). Embracing ignorance, error, and fallibility: Competencies for leadership of effective services. In S.J. Taylor, D. Biklen, & J. Knoll (Eds.), *Community integration for people with severe disabilities* (pp. 85–108). New York: Teachers College Press.

Provencal, G. (1987). Culturing commitment. In S.J. Taylor, D. Biklen, & J. Knoll (Eds.), *Community integration for people with severe disabilities* (pp. 67–84). New York: Teachers College Press.

Financing

Community Information Exchange. (1987). *Vital resources: An annotated bibliography in community economic development.* Washington, DC: Author.

Funding of places, not people, creates poverty. (1990). *Australia and New Zealand Journal of Developmental Disabilities, 16*(3), 285–286.

Hemp, R., Youngwerth, C., Haasen, K., & Braddock, D. (1991, June). *Financing assistive technology: An annotated bibliography.* Chicago: Assistive Technology Financing Project, The University of Illinois at Chicago University Affiliated Program.

Housing Technical Assistance Project. (1989). *Volume I: The development process; Volume II: The financing mechanisms.* Washington, DC, and Upper Marlboro, MD: Housing Technical Assistance Project, Association for Retarded Citizens-USA and National Association of Home Builders National Research Center.

Morris, M.W., & Golinker, L.A. (1991). *Assistive technology: A funding workbook.* Washington, DC: RESNA Technical Assistance Project in association with RESNA Press.

Smith, G.A. (1990, November). *Supported living: New directions in services to people with developmental disabilities.* Alexandria, VA: National Association of State Mental Retardation Program Directors.

Smith, G.A. (1991, January). *Community Supported Living Arrangements: A guide to Section 1930 of the Social Security Act.* Alexandria, VA: National Association of State Mental Retardation Program Directors, Inc.

Smith, G.A., & Aderman, S. (1987, July). *Paying for services.* Alexandria, VA: National Association of State Mental Retardation Program Directors.

Tarmon, V. (1989). *Client to consumer: An assessment of individualized funding projects in the United States.* Toronto: Service Planning Council of Metro Toronto.

Housing

Carling, P.J. (1989). Access to housing: Cornerstone to the American dream. *Journal of Rehabilitation, 55*(3), 6–8.

Carling, P.J., Randolph, F.L., Blanch, A.K., & Ridgway, P. (1988). A review of the research on housing and community integration for people with psychiatric disabilities. *NARIC Quarterly, 1*(3), 1, 6–18.

Housing Technical Assistance Project. (1989). *Working with non-profit developers of affordable housing to provide integrating housing options for people with disabilities.* Washington, DC, and Upper Marlboro, MD: Housing Technical Assistance Project, Association for Retarded Citizens-USA and National Association of Home Builders National Research Center.

Kappel, B., & Wetherow, D. (1986). People caring about people: The Prairie Housing Cooperative. *Entourage, 1*(4), 37–42.

Laux, B., & Moran-Laux, C. (n.d.). *"Your place or Mine?": A handbook for home ownership.* Portsmouth, NH: Creative Management Associates.

O'Connor, S., & Racino, J.A. (1990). *New directions in housing for people with severe disabilities: A collection of resource materials.* Syracuse, NY: Center on Human Policy, Syracuse University.

Randolph, F., Laux, R., & Carling, P. (1987). *In search of housing: Creative approaches to financing integrated housing.* Burlington, VT: Center for Community Change Through Housing and Support, University of Vermont.

Schwartz, D.C., Ferlauto, R.C., & Hoffman, D.N. (1988). *New housing policy for America: Recapturing the American dream.* Philadelphia: Temple University Press.

Individual and Family Planning

Baumgart, D., Brown, L., Pumpian, I., Nisbet, J., Ford, A., Sweet, M., Messina, R., & Schroeder, J. (1982). Principle of partial participation and individualized adaptations in education programs for severely handicapped students. *Journal of The Association for Persons with Severe Handicaps, 7*(2), 17–27.

Brost, M.M., & Johnson, T.Z. (1982). *Getting to know you: One approach to service assessment and planning for individuals with disabilities.* Madison, WI: DHSS-DCS.

McGowan, K. (1987). *Functional life planning for persons with complex needs.* Peachtree City, GA: KMG Seminars.

Mount, B., & Zwernik, K. (1988). *It's never too early, it's never too late: A booklet about personal futures planning.* St. Paul, MN: Metropolitan Council, DD Case Management Project.

O'Brien, J. (1987). A guide to life-style planning: Using *The activities catalog* to integrate services and natural support systems. In B. Wilcox & G.T. Bellamy. A comprehensive guide to *The activities catalog: An alternative curriculum for youth and adults with severe disabilities* (pp. 175–189). Baltimore: Paul H. Brookes Publishing Co.

Vandercook, T., York, J., & Forest, M. (1989). The McGill Action Planning System (MAPS): A strategy for building the vision. *Journal of The Association for Persons with Severe Handicaps, 4*(2), 205–215.

Multicultural Issues

Asbury, C.A., Walker, S., Maholmes, V., Rackley, R., & White, S. (n.d.). *Disability prevalence and demographic association among race/ethnic minority populations in the United States: Implications for the 21st century.* Washington, DC: Howard University, Research and Training Center for Access to Rehabilitation and Economic Opportunity.

Banks, J.A., & McGee, C.A. (1989). *Multicultural education: Issues and perspectives.* Boston: Allyn and Bacon.

Baxter, C., Poonia, K., Ward, L., & Nadirshaw, Z. (1990). *Double discrimination: Issues and services for people with learning difficulties from black and ethnic minority communities.* London: King Edward's Hospital Fund.

Cross, T.L., Bazron, B.J., Dennis, K.W., & Isaacs, M.R. (1989). *Toward a culturally competent system of care.* Washington, DC: CASSP Technical Assistance Center.

Harry, B. (1992). *Cultural diversity, families, and the special education system: Communication and empowerment.* New York: Teachers College Press.

Joe, J.R., & Miller, D. (1987). *American Indian cultural perspectives on disability* (Monograph Series No. 3). Tucson, AZ: Native American Research and Training Center, University of Arizona.

Kalyanpur, M., & Rao, S. (1991). Empowering low-income black families of handicapped children. *American Journal of Orthopsychiatry, 61*(4), 523–532.

New Roles for Support Staff

Biklen, D. (1988). The myth of clinical judgment. *Journal of Social Issues, 44*(1), 127–140.

Lutfiyya, Z.M. (1991). "A feeling of being connected": Friendships between people with and without learning difficulties. *Disability, Handicap and Society, 6*(3), 233–245.

McKnight, J. (1978). Professionalized service and disabling help. In J. McKnight, *Disabling professions* (pp. 69–91). London: Marion Bayars, Inc.

Minnesota Developmental Disabilities Planning Council. (1990). *Friends: A manual for connecting persons with disabilities and community members.* St. Paul, MN: Author.

Mount, B., Beeman, P., & Ducharme, G. (1988). *What are we learning about bridge-building?* Manchester, CT: Communitas, Inc.

O'Brien, J., & Lyle O'Brien, C. (Eds.).(1992). *Remembering the soul of our work: Stories by the staff of Options in Community Living, Madison, Wisconsin.* Madison, WI: Options in Community Living.

Racino, J.A. (1990). Preparing personnel to work in community support services. In A.P. Kaiser & C.M. McWhorter (Eds.), *Preparing personnel to work with persons with severe disabilities* (pp. 203–226). Baltimore: Paul H. Brookes Publishing Co.

Ward, L. (1988). Developing opportunities for an ordinary community life. In D. Towell (Ed.), *An ordinary life in practice: Developing comprehensive community-based services for people with learning disabilities* (pp. 68–79). London: King Edwards Hospital Fund.

Personal Assistance Services

Centre for Research and Education in Human Services. (1990). *Self-directed attendant services: Toward a consumer oriented policy and perspective on personal support services.* Kitchener, Ontario: Author.

Litvak, S., Zukas, H., & Heumann, J.E. (1987). *Attending to America: Personal assistance for independent living.* Berkeley, CA: World Institute on Disability.

Nosek, M.A. (1990). *Personal assistance services for persons with mental disabilities.* Houston: Baylor College of Medicine, prepared for the National Council on Disability.

Nosek, M.A., Potter, C.G., Quan, H., & Zhu, Y. (1988). *Personal assistance services for people with disabilities: An annotated bibliography.* Houston: Independent Living Research Utilization, Research and Training Center on Independent Living at TIRR.

Racino, J.A. (1991, September). *Thoughts and reflections on personal assistance services: Issues of concern to people with mental retardation.* Paper presented at International Symposium on Personal Assistance Services, Berkeley, CA (reprinted in *Disability Studies Quarterly, 12*(1), 81–86, Winter 1992).

Research and Training Center on Public Policy in Independent Living, InfoUse, & Western Consortium for Public Health. (1991, September). *Personal assistance services: A guide to policy and action.* Oakland, CA: World Institute on Disability.

Ulicny, G.R., Adler, A.B., Kennedy, S.E., & Jones, M.L. (1987). *A step-by-step guide to training and managing personal attendants. Volume 1: Consumer guide.* Lawrence, KS: Research and Training Center on Independent Living.

Principles in Community Living

Bradley, V., & Knoll, J. (1990). *Shifting paradigms in services to people with developmental disabilities.* Cambridge, MA: Human Services Research Institute.

Dowson, S. (1991). *Moving to the dance or service culture and community care.* London: Values into Action.

Ferguson, P., Hibbard, M., Leinen, J., & Schaff, S. (1990). Supported community life: Disability policy and the renewal of mediating structures. *Journal of Disability Policy Studies, 1*(1), 10–35.

Governor's Planning Council on Developmental Disabilities. (1987). *A new way of thinking.* St. Paul, MN: Author.

Nirje, B. (1985). The basis and logic of the normalization principle. *Australia and New Zealand Journal of Developmental Disabilities, 11*(8), 65–68.

Racino, J.A. (1992). Living in the community: Independence, support and transition. In F.R. Rusch, L. DeStefano, J. Chadsey-Rusch, L.A. Phelps, & E. Szymanski (Eds.), *Transition from school to adult life: Models, linkages, and policy* (pp. 131–148). Sycamore, IL: Sycamore Publishing Co.

Smull, M.W. (1989). *Crisis in the community.* Alexandria, VA: National Association of State Mental Retardation Program Directors.

Taylor, S.J. (1988). Caught in the continuum: A critical analysis of the principle of the least restrictive environment. *Journal of The Association for Persons with Severe Handicaps, 13*(1), 45–53.

Taylor, S.J., Biklen, D., & Knoll, J. (Eds.). (1987). *Community integration for people with severe disabilities.* New York: Teachers College Press.

Turnbull III, H.R. (1988). Ideological, political, and legal principles in the community-living movement. In M.P. Janicki, M.W. Krauss, & M.M. Seltzer (Eds.), *Community residences for persons with developmental disabilities: Here to stay* (pp. 15–24). Baltimore: Paul H. Brookes Publishing Co.

Wolfensberger, W. (1972). *The principle of normalization in human services.* Downsview, Ontario: National Institute on Mental Retardation.

Wolfensberger. W. (1991). *A brief introduction to social role valorization as a high-order concept for structuring human services.* Syracuse, NY: Training Institute for Human Service Planning, Leadership and Change Agentry, Syracuse University.

Quality

Bradley, V.J., & Bersani, H.A. (Eds.). (1990). *Quality assurance for individuals with developmental disabilities: It's everybody's business.* Baltimore: Paul H. Brookes Publishing Co.

Bradley, V.J., Ashbaugh, J.W., Harder, W.P., Stoddard, S., Shea, S., Allard, M.A., Mulkern, V., Spence, R.A., & Absalom, D. (1984). *Assessing and enhancing the quality of services: A guide for the human service field.* Cambridge, MA: Human Services Research Institute.

O'Brien, J., O'Brien, C.L., & Schwartz, D.B. (Eds.). (1990). *What can we count on to make and keep people safe? Perspectives on creating effective safeguards for people with developmental disabilities.* Lithonia, GA: Responsive System Associates.

Options in Community Living. (1987). *Options policy on quality of life.* Madison, WI: Author.

Schalock, R. (Ed.). (1990). *Quality of life: Perspectives and issues.* Washington, DC: American Association on Mental Retardation.

Vivona, V., & Kaplan, D. (1990, March). *People with developmental disabilities speak out on quality of life: A statewide agenda for enhancing the quality of life of people with disabilities.* Oakland, CA: World Institute on Disability.

Relationship of "Informal" and "Formal Supports"

Bulmer, M. (1987). Interweaving formal and informal care. In M. Bulmer, *The social basis of community care* (pp. 172–209). Winchester, MA: Allen & Unwin, Inc.

Hagner, D. (1989). *The social integration of supported employees: A qualitative study.* Syracuse, NY: Center on Human Policy, Syracuse University.

O'Brien, J., & Lyle O'Brien, C. (1992). Members of each other: Perspectives on social support for people with severe disabilities. In J.A. Nisbet (Ed.), *Natural supports in school, at work, and in the community for people with severe disabilities* (pp. 17–63). Baltimore: Paul H. Brookes Publishing Co.

Pearpoint, J. (1990). *From behind the piano: The building of Judith Snow's circle of friends.* Toronto, Ontario, Canada: Inclusion Press.

Traustadottir, R. (1991). *Supports for community living: A case study.* Syracuse, NY: Center on Human Policy, Syracuse University.

Wiseman, J. (1979). *Stations of the lost: Treatment of skid row alcoholics.* Chicago: University of Chicago Press.

Relationships

Forest, M. (1989). *It's about relationships.* Toronto: Frontier College Press.

King's Fund Centre. (1988). *Ties and connections.* London: Author.

Lutfiyya, Z.M. (1990). *Affectionate bonds: What we can learn by listening to friends.* Syracuse, NY: Center on Human Policy, Syracuse University.

Mount, B., Beeman, P., & Ducharme, G. (1988). *What are we learning about circles of support? A collection of tools, ideas, and reflections on building and facilitating circles of support.* Manchester, CT: Communitas, Inc.

O'Connell, M. (1988). *The gift of hospitality: Opening the doors of community life to people with disabilities.* Evanston, IL: The Community Life Project.

Perske, R. (1988). *Circle of friends.* Nashville, TN: Abingdon Press.

Taylor, S.J., & Bogdan, R. (1989). On accepting relationships between people with mental retardation and nondisabled people: Towards an understanding of acceptance. *Disability, Handicap & Society, 4*(1), 21–36.

Service Coordination and Brokerage

Beardshaw, V., & Towell, D. (1990). *Assessment and case management: Implications for the implementation of "caring people."* London: King's Fund Institute.

The G. Allan Roeher Institute. (1991). *The power to choose: An examination of service brokerage and individualized funding as implemented by the Community Services Society.* Downsview, Ontario: Author.

Lippert, T. (1987). *The case management team: Building community connections.* St. Paul, MN: Developmental Disabilities Program of the Metropolitan Council.

Salisbury, S., Dickey, J., & Crawford, C. (1987). *Individual empowerment and social service accountability.* Downsview, Ontario: The G. Allan Roeher Institute.

Wolfensberger, W. (1990, August). Service brokerage sanity & insanity. *The Safeguards Letter, 16,* 2–5.

Societal and Community Change

Driedger, D. (1989). *The last civil rights movements: Disabled People's International.* New York: St. Martin's Press, Inc.

Groce, N.E. (1985). *Everyone here spoke sign language: Hereditary deafness on Martha's Vineyard.* Cambridge, MA: Harvard University Press.

Lehman, K. (1988). Beyond Oz: The path to regeneration. *Social Policy, 18*(4), 56–58.

Lord, J. (1985). *Creating responsive communities: Reflections on a process of social change.* Toronto, Ontario, Canada: OAMR.

McKnight, J.L. (1987). Regenerating community. *Social Policy, 18*(3), 54–58.

Support Organizations

Johnson, T.Z. (1985). *Belonging to the community.* Madison, WI: Options in Community Living.

Johnson, T., & O'Brien, J. (1987). *Carrying Options' story forward: Final report of an assessment of Options in Community Living.* Madison, WI: Options in Community Living.

Klein, J. (1992). Get me the hell out of here: Supporting people with disabilities to live in their own homes. In J.A. Nisbet (Ed.), *Natural supports in school, at work, and in the community for people with severe disabilities* (pp. 277–339). Baltimore: Paul H. Brookes Publishing Co.

Mount, B., & Caruso, G. (1989, September). *New dreams, new lives, new directions for Alternative Living, Inc.: A report on the initial outcomes, findings, and implications of the Citizenship Project.* Annapolis, MD: Alternative Living, Inc.

O'Brien, J., & Lyle O'Brien, C. (1991). *More than just a new address: Images of organization for supported living agencies.* Lithonia, GA: Responsive Systems Associates.

Racino, J.A. (1991). Organizations in community living: Supporting people with disabilities. *Journal of Mental Health Administration, 18*(1), 51–59.

Shoultz, B. (Ed.). (1989). *Community living for adults.* Syracuse, NY: Center on Human Policy, Syracuse University.

Taylor, S.J., Bogdan, R., & Racino, J.A. (Eds.). (1991). *Life in the community: Case studies of organizations supporting people with disabilities.* Baltimore: Paul H. Brookes Publishing Co.

Taylor, S.J., Racino, J.A., Knoll, J.A., & Lutfiyya, Z. (1987). *The nonrestrictive environment: On community integration for people with the most severe disabilities.* Syracuse, NY: Human Policy Press.

Systems Change

Canadian Association for Community Living. (1987). *Community living 2000: A time of change, a time of challenge*. Downsview, Ontario: Author.

Housing & Intellectual Disability Project. (1988, February). *The need for coordination between the Ministry of Housing (MOH) and Community Services Victoria-Office of Intellectual Disability Services (CSV-OIDS)*. Collingwood, Victoria, Australia: Author.

McWhorter, A. (1986). *Mandate for quality. Volume III: Changing the system*. Philadelphia, and Cambridge, MA: Temple University and Human Services Research Institute.

The National Development Team (NDT). (1990). *National Development Team site visit series*. London: Author.

O'Brien, J., & Lyle, C. (1986). *Strengthening the system: Improving Louisiana's community residential services for people with developmental disabilities*. Decatur, GA: Responsive Systems Associates.

Racino, J.A., O'Connor, S., Shoultz, B., Taylor, S.J., & Walker, P. (1989). *Moving into the 1990s: A policy analysis of community living for adults with developmental disabilities in South Dakota*. Syracuse, NY: Center on Human Policy, Syracuse University.

Rothman, D.J., & Rothman, S.M. (1984). *The Willowbrook wars: A decade of struggle for social justice*. New York: Harper & Row.

Taylor, S.J., Racino, J.A., & Rothenberg, K. (1988). *A policy analysis of private community living arrangements in Connecticut*. Syracuse, NY: Center on Human Policy, Syracuse University.

Towell, D. (Ed.). (1988). *Enabling community integration: The role of public authorities in promoting an ordinary life for people with learning difficulties in 1990s*. London: King Edward's Hospital Fund for London.

Values-Based Training

O'Brien, J., & Lyle, C. (1987). *Framework for accomplishment: A workshop for people developing better services*. Decatur, GA: Responsive Systems Associates.

Wolfensberger, W., & Glenn, L. (1975). *Program analysis of service systems: PASSING 3*. Toronto, Ontario, Canada: National Institute on Mental Retardation.

Wolfensberger, W., & Thomas, S. (1983). *PASSING: Program analysis of service systems' implementation of normalization goals* (2nd ed.). Toronto, Ontario, Canada: National Institute on Mental Retardation.

Women with Disabilities

Fine, M., & Asch, A. (Eds.). (1988). *Women with disabilities: Essays in psychology, culture and politics*. Philadelphia: Temple University Press.

Matthews, G.F. (1983). *Voices from the shadow: Women with disabilities speak out*. Toronto, Ontario, Canada: The Women's Educational Press.

Traustadottir, R. (1990). *Women with disabilities: Issues, resources, connections*. Syracuse, NY: Center on Human Policy, Syracuse University.

Women and Disability Awareness Project. (1989). *Building community: A manual exploring issues of women and disability*. New York: Educational Equity Concepts.

INDEX

DATE DUE

JUN 17 96 F			
AUG 25 '99 X			
AUG 5 1999			